Tropic of Hopes

UNIVERSITY PRESS OF FLORIDA

Florida A&M University, Tallahassee
Florida Atlantic University, Boca Raton
Florida Gulf Coast University, Ft. Myers
Florida International University, Miami
Florida State University, Tallahassee
New College of Florida, Sarasota
University of Central Florida, Orlando
University of Florida, Gainesville
University of North Florida, Jacksonville
University of South Florida, Tampa
University of West Florida, Pensacola

Tropic of Hopes

California, Florida, and the Selling of American Paradise, 1869–1929

HENRY KNIGHT

UNIVERSITY PRESS OF FLORIDA

Gainesville/Tallahassee/Tampa/Boca Raton
Pensacola/Orlando/Miami/Jacksonville/Ft. Myers/Sarasota

LIBRARY OF CONGRESS CATALOGING-IN-PUBLICATION DATA
Knight, Henry, 1982–
Tropic of hopes : California, Florida, and the selling of American paradise, 1869–1929 /
Henry Knight.
p. cm.
Includes bibliographical references and index.
Summary: An examination of how land barons, railroad kingpins, and journalists, among
others, "sold" Americans on the idea of Florida and California as a paradise within reach.
ISBN 978-0-8130-4481-1 (alk. paper)
1. Florida—Economic conditions. 2. California—Economic conditions. 3. Florida—
Population—History. 4. California—Population—History. 5. Florida—Social
conditions. 6. California—Social conditions. I. Title.
HC107.F6K58 2013
330.9759—DC23   2013015086

UNIVERSITY PRESS OF FLORIDA
15 Northwest 15th Street
Gainesville, FL 32611-2079
http://www.upf.com

For Rachel

Contents

Figures

Tables

Acknowledgments

I am grateful to many people and institutions that have, in different ways, helped make this book a reality. First of all, the UK's Arts and Humanities Research Council gave me funding to undertake a one-year MPhil in 2006. Without that financial support or the subsequent three-year grant to complete a DPhil the research for this book would never have gotten off the ground.

At the University of Sussex, I could not have asked for better supervisors and mentors than Dr. Clive Webb and Dr. Sue Currell, who together guided and constantly pushed me to consider new questions. Clive and Sue are experts in different fields in American studies and history and were an ideal team, helping me navigate interdisciplinary waters and recognizing the value of a comparative approach to studying California and Florida. Most important, they shared my enthusiasm for the project and always made themselves available to talk about its progress.

From the study's inception with my discovery as an undergraduate at the University of California, San Diego, of the colorful and exotic landscapes of California citrus labels, the body of archival research behind this book evolved considerably and the output benefited from the work of a number of scholars. On the research side, Dr. James Cusick, curator of the P. K. Yonge Library of Florida History at the George A. Smathers Libraries, University of Florida, went above and beyond the call of duty to ensure that I had a very productive research stay in Gainesville. The archivists at the California State Library and at the special collections departments at the University of California, Los Angeles; the University of California, San Diego; and the Bancroft Library at the University of California, Berkeley, were also universally helpful and friendly. Thanks are due to all the institutions that have provided permission to reprint images held in their archives.

On the output side, Dr. Richard Follett (University of Sussex) and Dr. Margaret Walsh (University of Nottingham) provided a valuable interrogation at an early stage of this book, as did Dr. Robert Cook (University of Sussex) and Dr. David Nye (University of Southern Denmark) further down the line. Richard and Robert form part of a strong faculty of Americanists at Sussex, along with Dr. Jarod Roll, who enabled me to present a small part of this project at the Marcus Cunliffe Centre for the Study of the American South. My fellow postgraduates Kate Nowicki, Roger Johnson, Zoe Hyman, Nadja Janssen, and Matt Glazebrook critiqued earlier chapters in a supportive workshop. Other elements of the work received useful feedback at conferences of the British Association of American Studies and Historians of the Twentieth Century United States. Finally, I am immensely grateful to the two readers assigned by the University Press of Florida, whose insightful reviews and suggestions were extremely helpful.

The University Press of Florida, especially director Meredith Babb, has been supportive of this work since they first received the proposal. Since then Meredith has walked me through the process of completing a book. Similarly, copy editor Kate Babbitt has dedicated a great deal of time and ink to improving the manuscript. Any errors remaining are entirely my own.

However inadequately, I would also like to acknowledge the support of my mother, Lidia, and my father, Alan. They read passages of this work, but far more important, they taught me more than anyone else about the value of research and writing—and a few other things besides.

Lastly, my fiancée Rachel has probably heard more about things tropical than she ever imagined or wanted. She has been with me every step on this journey, and I am eternally grateful for her support, her patience, and her faith in me. This book is dedicated to her.

Introduction

In 1882, a journalist in the *Los Angeles Times* wrote, "There is no portion of the United States which presents so interesting a study as that known as the semi-tropical States." Southern California and the U.S. South were soon to be linked by railroad, and the writer explained that "semi-tropic California" and "the semi-tropic States fringing the Gulf of Mexico" both had a "diversity of climate, of products, of people and of customs, which is unknown to any other portion of the habitable globe." The two regions of "semi-tropic North America" were both profoundly similar and distinctly different: "In many respects they could not be more different if an ocean separated, instead of two great oceans inclosing them. Again, in many other respects, their similarities are so great as to strike one with the likeness." One particular comparison stood out. Across semi-tropic North America, the journalist wrote, "Florida more than any other of these resembles Southern California."[1]

Taking up the comparative theme articulated by the *Times* writer, this book traces how, in the decades after the U.S. Civil War, promoters of California and Florida created new images of those states that emphasized their tropical qualities. California and Florida were not the only American states to be viewed this way: Texas and Louisiana were also often described as tropical regions by boosters and writers.[2] However, California and Florida were the states about which the words "tropical" and "semi-tropical" were used most often in promotions and descriptions. While it lacked a fixed scientific or geographical definition, the term "semi-tropical" was applied to lands, climate, products (especially citrus), and peoples that shared qualities with—even though they remained outside of—the tropics. ("Sub-tropical" was similarly defined as bordering the tropics). Such references proliferated in the titles of pamphlets promoting immigration, horticultural periodicals, and the marketing publications of land companies and in countless magazine articles, state guides, and exhibitions. In 1890, thousands of visitors to the National Farmers' Alliance Convention in Ocala, Florida, attended the town's promotional "Semi-Tropical Exposition," while the Panama-California Exposition, which was held in San Diego in 1915, prompted the publication of *Semi-Tropic California*, a book that aimed to confirm "that here on the eastern shores of the Pacific Ocean is today the garden spot of the world."[3] At events and in publications, tropical ideas were used to sell the two states to settlers, tourists, and investors, recasting California and Florida from unwanted backwaters to renewing "tropics" that offered a range of hopes for incoming Americans.

The book covers the period from 1869 to 1929, when both southern California and peninsular Florida were fundamentally transformed through promotion and development. In 1869, when the first transnational railroad was completed, easterners dismissed remote and underpopulated southern California as part of the Great American Desert and many northern Californians saw that region of the state as the "cow counties" because of the vast cattle ranches that had covered the region since the days of the Spanish empire.[4] Mining had also left a legacy of lawlessness that negatively influenced eastern perceptions of the state. As one migrant to San Francisco wrote, the state was often "looked upon as a place lawless in the extreme, without any security for life or property— without any civilized institutions; . . . *in fact, it is believed to be a place as much to be shunned and avoided as the deserts of Africa*, and about as soon to be thought of with any view to settlement and a future home."[5] That same year, Florida suffered also; northerners perceived it as a former Confederate state that had just been readmitted to the Union. The peninsula was also viewed as a swampy "wasteland." As travel writer George Canning Hill wrote in 1888, "Of Florida the people of . . . the North really knew nothing until long after the close of the war of the sections. To the most of us it was as a forbidden land," associated "in the common imagination" with the Everglades, the bloody Seminole wars, and "ever moist lowlands . . . heavy with the poisons of malaria."[6] In 1869, California and Florida, the southwestern and southeastern corners of the nation, appeared foreign, even "forbidden" zones to northeasterners.

In the following decades, however, the two states underwent major transformations, eventually becoming leading destinations for American tourists, settlers, and investors. By the 1920s, southern California and south Florida were drawing many thousands of visitors each year and were experiencing real estate booms. This book explains how the selling of California and Florida as semi-tropical lands fostered these transformations as national tropes about imperiled notions of American society, identity, and republicanism were projected onto the two states. In their efforts to convert "foreign" environmental deterrents into enticements for white U.S. residents, including those who were alienated by the industrializing changes of the Gilded Age, state boosters disseminated images of California and Florida as homelands that were simultaneously tropical and republican. In both states, promoters evoked optimistic and exclusionary ideas of American renewal that clustered around two themes: health-restoring leisure and rewarding labor. In this process, boosters marginalized ethnic and racial minorities in both states; they sold California and Florida as special lands that could nurture the formation of reinvigorated Anglo-American societies.

Promoters of California and Florida were invariably white—or "Anglo," as they sometimes called themselves—people who wanted to associate themselves with "Anglo-Saxons" rather than with the southern and eastern Europeans who entered the United States in vast numbers in the late nineteenth century.[7] Whites owned and controlled the major booster organizations in both states and wrote, edited, and published the promotional literature. The material in this book thus describes the motivations and ideals of white Americans. While ethnic and racial minorities were often the subjects of boosterist material, they were neither the authors nor the intended readers. Consequently, their presence was constantly manipulated in these texts and images, and their voices were silenced. During this period, Mexican, Chinese, and other ethnic minorities in California and African Americans and Native Americans in Florida constructed communities that struggled against the sociopolitical, economic, and cultural obstacles that white elites imposed on them.[8]

Nonwhite peoples did not docilely accept the "colonialist" attitudes of white promoters who advocated Anglo-American expansion into new, quasi-tropical domains. However, that resistance is not my chief concern.[9] Rather, this book focuses on boosterist representations of California and Florida—a literature that was defined by exclusionary notions of race and civilization. Indeed, the historical value of such promotional imagery lies, in part, in this exclusion, since it shows how racist stereotypes and social inequalities were made consumable and even enjoyable. Such texts presented racial hierarchies as "natural" developments in the new and prosperous communities forming in semi-tropical America.

The connection between economic change and the decline of republican ideals is a theme of the book. These ideals had been central to conceptions of national identity and expansion since the American Revolution. For the revolutionary generation, "the sacrifice of individual interests to the greater good of the whole formed the essence of republicanism and comprehended for Americans the idealistic goal of their Revolution."[10] After the industrialization and urbanization of the nineteenth century, however, those republican ideals appeared for many Americans to be increasingly at odds with social realities. In both California and Florida, boosters evoked and adapted republican notions of virtuous, independent life in order to promote their states. Striving to attract wealth and settlement, they consistently harked back to the classical ideals of a more harmonious society founded on republican principles. Yet increasingly they did so as a means of furthering, not sacrificing, individual interests, particularly the interests of corporations, invoking republican rhetoric in order to realize the self-interested economic goals of corporate bodies that were powerful in both states by the early twentieth century. The promotional imagery of semi-tropical America thus serves also as a case study in how the agents of corporate capitalism co-opted, and arguably corrupted, traditional republican ideology to promote their own ends.

Boosterism has been expertly studied by historians who have focused on single states. This book, however, offers the first detailed comparative analysis of the promotional imageries of both California and Florida.[11] One of the strengths of comparative history is its ability to shed fresh light on a subject by juxtaposing it with another: in this case, by studying the selling of California, we can better understand the selling of Florida, and vice versa.[12] While historians have (often justifiably) described California and Florida as exceptional, these geographically distant states were also connected through similarities in terms of climate, tourism, and agriculture.[13] Moreover, both were imagined and sold through tropical lenses, which brought California and Florida into a unique relationship that involved both partnership and rivalry. While tropical imagery was by no means the only discourse that state boosters used—northern California and the panhandle of Florida were less often referred to in these terms—it became pervasive in the promotion of southern California and peninsular Florida and helped propel the rapid settlement of those two areas at the turn of the century. Perhaps the best justification of a comparative approach, however, is that this was the view taken by thousands of Americans at the time, such as the midwestern founders of the Pasadena colony who chose southern California over Florida. California and Florida are nowadays often associated as the homes of Disney theme parks, but they were also closely linked in a much earlier period. After the Civil War, their promoters actively engaged with each other—both as rivals and as advocates of states that had similar challenges and goals. These similarities produced a relationship that helped the two states craft their own identities. As one journalist observed of the two states in 1883, "Each claims to [be] the 'Italy of America,' the winter sanitarium of the country, and the true semi-tropical paradise."[14]

I study California and Florida in terms of the ideals, plans, and publications of Americans who promoted the states. The focus is on the literary and visual representations that were touted in order to sell the states, although works of fiction also contributed to popular notions about California and Florida. As Stephanie Foote has argued, "regional fictions" had a distinct appeal in nineteenth-century America; to an audience dominated by affluent white women, such literature presented people and places that had seemingly "'escaped' the dubious improvements of a stronger and more integrated urban economy." In the process, regional fiction contributed to growing internal tourism.[15] On the West Coast, Helen Hunt Jackson's 1884 novel *Ramona* altered Anglo visions of southern California's past, while Frank Norris's *The Octopus* (1901) articulated anti-railroad sentiment in the West. While Florida lacked such influential novels, Harriet Beecher Stowe's travel pieces on the state were hugely popular. Fiction aided the booster canon of pamphlets, guides, and articles that functioned more directly as advertisements that explicitly described the benefits of settlement, tourism, and investment.

By boosters, I refer to a group of journalists, businessmen, and developers who wrote about California or Florida with promotional motivations. Biographical information is available for some but not all of these individuals, since many of the texts were anonymous. Booster pamphlets and articles frequently echoed one another, articulating widely held "corporate" beliefs that were deployed to sell land, attract tourists, or raise a city's profile. For the sake of concision, therefore, I use terms such as "California boosters" and "Florida promoters." This does not mean that all of them agreed on all issues but rather that they had mainstream opinions that produced a chorus effect in the literature. I have collated an extensive range of archival texts and ephemera—including land, immigration, and tourist pamphlets; travel guides; regional and horticultural magazines and newspapers; and advertisements—through which California and Florida were packaged and sold.

These sources were invariably biased, selling hopes and ideals in the service of vested interests. They were all, in a broad sense, advertisements. Some were literally so—for example, pamphlets published by land companies—whereas magazine articles and travel books were more oblique, their advertising functions lurking within journalistic descriptions of places and peoples. The key methodological issues are nonetheless consistent. Although promoters frequently stressed the veracity of their work, the descriptions were often sanitized, focusing on "positive" aspects of the states while diminishing or removing awkward or undesirable realities.[16] Historian C. Vann Woodward thus warned that "the historian, like the purchaser, should observe the most ancient rule of the market place, *caveat emptor*" when analyzing the promotional literature of the New South.[17] As with advertisements (and other written sources), the reception of the material is hard to gauge. Where available I have tried to include publication figures or commentaries, but these are not clear-cut evidence of the impact of boosterism. Advertisers can run ineffectual campaigns, and promotional pieces did not necessarily influence their intended audiences. As the Los Angeles Chamber of Commerce noted of its own activities, "It is to be admitted . . . that a large part of the work has been in the nature of advertising the country, of which direct and tangible results cannot always be shown."[18]

If "tangible results" are tricky, however, it is possible to chart aspects of internal growth in both states and show how promoters regularly cultivated specific images of those places as a means of bringing in visitors and settlers.[19] The imagery and themes promoters deemed persuasive are suggestive of mainstream ideals relating to a more desirable life and society in California and Florida. As Roland Marchand has written about product advertisements, these sources "actually surpass most other recorded communications as a basis for *plausible inference* about popular attitudes and values."[20] At the same time, the boosterist constructions were not abstract images divorced from real life. On the contrary, they were the voices of active organizations involved in building infrastructure, tourism, agriculture, and urban growth. Boosterism was a key part of a broader process of social and cultural change in California and Florida. Charles Postel has noted how "the term *booster* often carries the pejorative connotation of the shrewd speculator," yet it can also be "used . . . to connote the culture and practice of promotion as an essential part of the late nineteenth-century world of settlement and development."[21] For California and Florida—states far removed from the nation's major cities—boosters played an essential role in the psychological conversion of fearsome wilderness into lush homeland, of waste places into American gardens. They were an influential group who represented railroads, chambers of commerce, state agencies, hotels, real estate companies, and local periodicals. Promoters such as Charles Shinn and Charles F. Lummis in California and James Wood Davidson and Ethan V. Blackman in Florida epitomized affluent white groups who were inspired not only by economic incentives but also by hopes of improving and defining their emerging societies. They envisaged and fostered industrial, social, and cultural "progress" while educating far-away Americans about the natural and social conditions of their states. More than just salesmen, these boosters saw themselves as, and they indeed were, promoters of economic growth and social formation.[22]

Railroad companies exemplified the blending of economic and social motives in booster practices. On the West Coast, the Southern Pacific Railroad had become a promotional powerhouse by the 1880s.[23] Thanks to federal grants, the railroad obtained a vast amount of public land in California (ten million acres in 1882, according to one estimate), for which it sought settlers.[24] The Southern Pacific was expressly dedicated to selling land to settlers on small-scale farms, especially colonies, as a model for creating prosperous republican communities that would produce food that would be shipped on the railroad's cars and would provide publicity for California. As one railroad agent put it in 1882, "We advance civilization, and accelerate progress, when we fasten men, by ownership, to the land they cultivate."[25] In Florida, extensive railroad construction in the 1880s and 1890s accompanied major promotional efforts of transportation companies to sell land to settlers.[26] The railroad empires of Henry Plant and Henry Flagler owned hotel and tourism agencies as well as land and agricultural interests, and the boosterist literature they funded and published united ideas of leisure and labor in peninsular Florida.

California and Florida were also "sold" at dozens of fairs and expositions across the nation (for which the railroad companies were key contributors), in tourist and immigration guides, and in regional magazines. Of the latter, the *Californian* (1880–82) was followed in 1894 by *Land of Sunshine*, which was edited by Charles F. Lummis and was funded by the Los Angeles Chamber of Commerce, and *Sunset*, which was launched in 1898 by the Southern Pacific Company. Magazines were similarly important in the promotion of Florida, including *Semi-Tropical*—a Reconstruction-era periodical edited by a former state governor, Harrison Reed—and, from 1899, the *Florida East Coast Homeseeker*, which represented Flagler's sizeable railroad and land interests. A careful trawl through these magazines provides a fuller picture of how California and Florida were imagined and sold.

At the same time, the selling of California and Florida requires a much broader geographical analysis that includes the Northeast and Midwest, where the majority of promotional texts were distributed.[27] These were the most populous and wealthiest parts of America, and they were also the regions from which many of the promoters originated. Examples include Lummis, who was from Massachusetts, and Davidson, who had lived most of his life in New York before settling in South Florida. "What is the character of the population of Southern California?" asked the Los Angeles Chamber of Commerce in 1891. "It is mostly eastern, representing true American enterprise, stability and refinement."[28] While Florida did receive some arrivals from neighboring southern states, its promoters focused their efforts on the Northeast and Midwest, targeting the "vigorous and thoroughgoing Northern and Western men who constitute the bulk of the immigration to Florida."[29] Moreover, promoters from those regions who migrated to California and Florida infused their works with an autobiographical faith in the benefits of travel and resettlement. Without exception, they looked back to what they had left behind and made pointed comparisons. The two states were thus contrasted with the "older" parts of America as boosters articulated hopes and expectations that California and Florida could progress without succumbing to the undesired consequences of industrialization that were evident in the colder, more populous regions of the nation. Their desire to set these states apart is what encouraged them to the word "tropical" to describe California and Florida.

The two states were not so similar, of course, in reputation or reality. California had several important advantages over Florida. California was historically a free state and was associated with a legacy of opportunity bequeathed by the Gold Rush. It was dry and arid but capable of remarkable agricultural productivity, given irrigation, capital, and skill. In contrast, as a former slave state that was on the losing side in the Civil War, Florida had experienced the pain of defeat and lingering sectional tensions between North and South. It was also damp and widely considered to be a more intimidating environment for permanent residence than California (although, in reality, California also had a serious malaria problem). Because of this, Florida offered cheaper land.[30] A journalist in the *Daily Alta California* echoed common opinion when he declared, "Both climates are recommended for the health, but that of California has an advantage in being healthful the year round, while in Florida the dreaded malaria rules in summer."[31] Climate apart, California benefited from the historic American faith in the West as a source of republican rebirth, whereas Florida suffered from connotations of the South as a land of backwardness and decay. Although Florida attracted many Georgians and other southerners who were untainted by such beliefs, the state's promoters targeted northerners and midwesterners who undoubtedly were influenced by these ingrained stereotypes.

The differences between California and Florida did not prohibit comparison, however. As a journalist in the *Los Angeles Times* observed, "In what is known as the Southwestern States, meaning thereby the Gulf States, one finds one portion of Semi-Tropic America; the other and far lovelier part is Southern California."[32] Many West Coast boosters proclaimed that southern California offered the benefits of a quasi-tropical climate without the oppressive heat and disease associated with the southern states. Indeed, this distinction was crucial to southern California's semi-tropical imagery. New Orleans, for example, had long been regarded as semi-tropical, but because of yellow fever and cholera epidemics in the 1850s that were widely reported in the North, the city carried disturbing connotations of infection and death. Such threats were still alive during the booster era; the last yellow fever epidemic in the United States took place in 1905.[33] Southern California was promoted as a superior tropic; its dry, desert climate eliminated the water-borne diseases of the Gulf States. Numerous California boosters recognized that Florida mostly closely resembled their own state.[34] But precisely because of this "resemblance," Florida was the southern state Californians denigrated most frequently. The booster arrows flew back the other way, of course, although Florida boosters increasingly found value in looking to southern California for inspiration, partly to overcome sectional prejudices. Boosters thus characterized Florida as "semi-tropical" rather than "southern."

The only scholar who has discussed the vision of California as "semi-tropical," however, has marginalized it. In *Inventing the Dream*, Kevin Starr acknowledges "the semi-tropical comparison" evoked by promoters yet argues that the state's "inventors" settled instead on a "more civilized" Mediterranean vision of a new Italy or Spain; the semi-tropical image "eventually collapsed under scientific scrutiny, but more than this—from its first appearance it did not sit well with the American imagination," as it "allowed nature a wild, defiant luxuriance which could never be subdued by industry" and suggested a fearful "sun that would sap the Northern European sources of the American will, turning industrious immigrants into loafers."[35] Other California historians have echoed this argument, dismissing the semi-tropical representations as "counterproductive."[36] They believe, in short, that the boosters got it wrong.

This conclusion fails to account for how and why leading promoters in both California and Florida consistently sold their states in tropical terms. Indeed, such promotion was so successful and "productive" in California that Florida boosters assiduously emulated the semi-tropical concept. For over fifty years, semi-tropical imagery appeared in countless publications in California and Florida. It was not "extreme" but *mainstream*, a term noted writers such as Charles Dudley Warner and Harriet Beecher Stowe and irrigation promoter William Ellsworth Smythe used because they considered it to be the best description of southern California and Florida. Furthermore, the Mediterranean distinction Starr made is somewhat misleading, since what Americans considered to be the "semi-tropics" included the Mediterranean.[37] In the lexicon of the times, Spain, Italy, and Greece were "semi-tropical countries," just as Charles Nordhoff's California was both "semi-tropical" and "the Italy of this continent."[38] As the

Los Angeles Times explained, "Oranges . . . are grown all over the semi-tropical world," a zone that included "Spain, Italy, Northern Africa, China, Southern California, Florida, and Palestine."[39] While these countries did not share identical latitudes, they were understood to exist in a quasi-tropical zone because of their climates and natural products. Mediterranean comparisons were, in that sense, a subset of a global semi-tropical notion—a calculated link with the "civilized" semi-tropical regions of Europe.

Yet California and Florida were also seen as fundamentally different from Old World semi-tropics in terms of their social conditions, a reflection of the ambivalent, if not derogatory, opinions many Anglo-Americans had about Italy and Spain. According to their boosters, California and Florida lacked the supposedly decrepit contemporaneous sociopolitical conditions of the Mediterranean nations, which, as one article put it, made Italy home to "a race of paupers." In contrast, Florida was "the home of the independent American citizen."[40] California and Florida were seen as "new" rather than "old": tropics of hope rather than decay. Even though they had been populated by Native Americans, African Americans, Spaniards, and/or Mexicans for decades and even centuries, they were now a tabula rasa ready for Anglo-American settlement and progress. The states were sold as unprecedented opportunities for northerners and midwesterners to tame fertile nature by means of their superior energy and enterprise, while that nature in turn would help Anglo-Americans learn to enjoy leisure and life. Infused with these ideas, tropical imagery was not "an extreme" that failed as "a controlling metaphor"; rather, it was a concept that filled the dreams and imaginations of white Americans for over half a century.[41] Instead of dismissing it, we should recognize and try to explain its appeal.

This book argues that the selling of California and Florida as tropics of hope successfully combined two dominant discourses in American expansion.[42] The first, republican ideology, envisaged the formation of homogeneous communities defined by middling wealth, self-directed labor, and "a society of equal and virtuous citizens"—an independent entity that avoided the Old World curses of concentrated wealth, class division, and unremitting poverty.[43] As David E. Nye has written, white Americans from the Revolution onward narrated continental expansion as a republican process made possible by technologies that included the axe, the mill, the canal, the railroad, and the irrigation ditch.[44] These "foundation narratives," as Nye terms them, ascribed meaning, justification, and impetus to the westward settlement of Americans. Technologies became the means by which settlers crafted a "second creation" of the landscape and experienced republican rebirth.[45] Foundation narratives, of course, incorporated the exclusionary assumptions of Manifest Destiny, championing white settlement. These narratives often deleted aspects of racial conquest altogether, in part because these stories had to be "progressive and optimistic. . . . They gripped the imagination and convinced people to leap into the unknown."[46] The end result of expansion was to be social homogeneity and equality—at least in terms of a more meritocratic society than the one left behind. The belief was that enterprising settlers could become independent through land ownership. Through these foundation narratives, remote and intimidating environments were "Americanized" into virtuous republican homelands.

The second discourse—colonialism—contrasted with republican ideology by stressing development based on hierarchy and inequality. As Paul Spickard writes, "European American expansion across the North American continent . . . had a colonial quality to it—it was the homeland of other peoples, and the United States took it by force and made subjects of the former owners—and racial hierarchy was made in that enterprise."[47] Whereas republican expansionism focused on the homogeneity of a broadly independent white citizenry and often obscured nonwhite peoples who did not fit into this mold (and who were left, as Nye shows, to construct their own "counter-narratives"), colonialism demanded unequal coexistence and explicit forms of domination within new societies—for example, between landowners and workers—and justified these as necessities of development.

Race and environment formed a critical nexus. Colonialist writings highlighted how race and environment were intertwined, together defining the capabilities of peoples and their societies. I have termed such ideas *formation narratives*. They are the discursive alternative to foundation narratives—which described humans shaping nature—because they attribute the formation of national and individual characteristics to the physical environments in which those traits emerged—including, up to a point, racial traits. Thus, white Europeans and Americans were said to have evolved into a superior, energetic race partly because they had always inhabited colder lands that challenged their inhabitants, whereas nonwhite peoples were said to be backward and listless partly due to the heat and fecundity of the tropics. Pseudo-scientific doctrines reinforced this logic. Lamarckian ideas of evolutionary inheritance, which posited that species inherited the acquired traits of their ancestors, were widely accepted in the United States and Europe and made environmental factors appear fundamental to human development. As a colonialist writer on India put it, "A country may be said to make its inhabitants in that their faculties and dispositions are largely influenced by its physical and climatic conditions."[48] The movement of a race into a new climate and environment—such as the kind of expansion promoters of semi-tropic California and Florida envisaged—had the potential to play havoc with the idea of a causal connection between race and environment. Thus, colonial writers often applied a crucial caveat. The writer on India, for example, rapidly qualified his statement by stressing "that race has a great resisting power" and persisting "qualities."[49] This notion suggested that while environment could improve or corrupt an individual, his or her racial characteristics and capabilities were essentially hardwired and immutable. Such faith infused the formation narratives that were created to sell California and Florida as quasi-tropical environments that would benefit whites and white society.

For our purposes, the significant preexisting formation narratives in the United States in this period related to whites' conceptions of their own rapidly industrializing society, on the one hand, and of foreign tropics, on the other. So-cioeconomic convulsions in late-nineteenth-century America deeply troubled its citizens. In the words of Robert Wiebe, the period was characterized by the transformation from an antebellum "society of island communities" to an urban, industrial nation.[50] Fears of debilitating overcivilization grew among middle-class urban Americans who felt divorced from healthful nature.[51] Although much of the Midwest remained agricultural, farmers there were increasingly de-pendent on capital and suffered worse than many city dwellers during the bank-ing collapses of 1873 and 1893, which brought severe nationwide depressions and widespread unemployment and labor unrest.[52] While beleaguered farmers across the South and West joined the Populist movement, urban Americans in the North lamented the influx of supposedly "unassimilating" immigrants from southern and eastern Europe. After the 1890 census announced the closure of the frontier, there was no longer an "open" West to sustain visions of a route to landed independence.[53] Indeed, for Frederick Jackson Turner, who declared its closure "the end of the first chapter in American history," the frontier had formed the basis of the nation's greatest formation narrative: Americans were exceptional because their character and society had been forged in the New World encounter of "civilized" humanity with a "savage" continent.[54] What kind of Americans would be formed without that struggle?

All of these factors combined to amplify fears about the future of America and its citizens, and boosters of California and Florida exploited those fears. As remote and distinctive states, California and Florida suited new formation narratives for white Americans that were constructed around ideas of labor and leisure in fertile surroundings. According to promoters, the two states were especially prolific regions that made prosperous small farming possible and, therefore, offered republican alternatives to both the urban industrial North and the agricultural hardships of the Midwest. Land promoters in California and Florida tapped into America's ideology of an egalitarian society of self-directed citizens as they envisaged a mating of American "enterprise" (a term that encompassed human, technological, and financial capacities) with quasi-tropical nature—the offspring of which would be progressive agricultural communities of independent settlers.[55] Technology, in particular railroads and land reclamation, was a key factor in boosterist efforts to narrate white domestication of new semi-tropical domains.

The environmental exoticism of California and Florida, however, led inevitably onto the second formation narrative, which related to Anglo conceptions of foreign tropics. These were deeply ambivalent: they envisioned rare natural fertility alongside poverty and sickness.[56] A global discourse that intertwined race, environment, and empire cast the tropics as places less fit for white settlement and progressive society. To an extent, this belief justified European imperialism as a prerequisite for tropical development.[57] But the same belief also made the imagined geography of the tropics frightening for whites, since they were associated with alien environments and backward societies. Charles Dudley Warner wrote in 1896 in a southern California promotional magazine that "it has become an accepted deduction that the Anglo-Saxon will dwindle and become inefficient in the tropics. His intellectual faculties may not be atrophied, but there will be no physical energy behind them to make them effective."[58] These views were so pervasive in the United States that they influenced national policy. As Eric T. Love has shown, racial and environmental anxieties acted as a "formidable obstacle" to attempts of the United States to colonize tropical nations.[59] White Americans (including prominent statesmen such as Charles Sumner and Carl Schurz) objected to annexing "hot" lands on the grounds that they were home to "undesirable" nonwhite populations incapable of self-government; they believed that Anglos could never thrive in such environments.[60] Tropical regions, then, would always be home to nonwhite races—with "neither language, nor traditions, nor habits, nor political institutions, nor morals in common with us," as Schurz declared. According to those who held such views, the absorption of such peoples threatened the republic's future.[61]

The promoters of semi-tropical Florida and California thus carved out an enticing middle zone between the overly industrial North and actual tropics. Semi-tropical imagery was thus applied to two states that formed part of the continental United States and officially shared in its language and political institutions (less so, perhaps, its traditions and habits) since 1821 (Florida) and 1848 (California). This language encompassed a range of attractive ideas relating to the tropics while jettisoning some of the more terrifying possibilities. The appeal of tropical imagery to many boosters was that it enabled them to

have their cake and eat it too: they could appeal to Anglo expansionist attitudes about fertile regions yet do so without the risks, strife, or moral dilem-
mas that were inextricable from overseas imperialism. Above all, while both
California and Florida offered rare natural benefits, they were conceived of as
fundamentally different from foreign tropics in terms of both race and society. In both states, boosterist visions reflected—and were reinforced by—government policies such as official exclusion of potential Chinese immigrants in
California and the disenfranchisement and segregation of African Americans
in Florida. The promotional imagery skillfully located American republicanism
and rebirth alongside racial dominance and subordination of nonwhites. These
tropic-like lands were expressly under the control of incoming white American settlers, tourists, and developers who could pursue restorative leisure and
democratic prosperity there. Thus, while foreign tropics continued to appear
to be anathema to republicanism in racial and environmental terms, California
and Florida were packaged and sold as fertile frontiers: a tropic of hopes where
Anglo-Americans could prosper and multiply.

The book combines a chronological and thematic approach to the study of
the selling of semi-tropical California and Florida. The first chapter provides
historical context for later developments in boosterist imagery. It looks at the
antebellum period and the early connections between the two states, then focuses on the decade after the Civil War. The chapter considers how four influential travel guides—two about California and two about Florida—articulated
the states' tropical qualities, in many ways setting the tone for later boosters.

Chapters 2 and 3 cover the promotion of semi-tropical California and Florida during the late nineteenth century. The twin emphases on leisure (Chapter
2) and labor (Chapter 3) reflect the versatile nature of booster literature. Canny
promoters identified southern California and peninsular Florida as lands that
provided for two somewhat contradictory qualities: healthful, exotic leisure
and rewarding agricultural labor, both of which became fundamental to the
burgeoning economies of the two states. The visions of leisure and labor similarly invoked concepts of American renewal and were contradictory only if
we ignore the different audiences that were being targeted—often in the same
texts. The leisure appeal of a tropical land was directed toward affluent tourists
who would patronize railroads and hotels and invest in the region. Promoters
stressed the leisure benefits of their "tropics" in hotel pamphlets, magazines, and
health guides. The economic and social incentives of semi-tropical agriculture,
meanwhile, were described for prospective settlers from a range of economic
backgrounds who would settle, raise and ship crops, and contribute to steady
material growth. Semi-tropical agriculture dominated both horticultural peri-

odicals and the publications of immigration and land companies. If California and Florida were conceived of by some as tourist paradises, their land boosters were keen to stress that these were *American* paradises: that is, environments for productive American activity, not for idle loafing. As J. W. Brewster, an Illinois man who had settled in Santa Barbara, California, wrote to the *Chicago Daily Tribune* in 1875, "Spare these sunny shores the incursions of immigrants allured from comfortable homes by accounts of Paradisaical perfections that will exempt them from laborious struggle."[62] Together, leisure and labor formed the core of a boosterist literature that presented ideas of both racial hierarchy and republican homogeneity in the U.S.'s semi-tropical states.

Chapters 4 and 5 chart the promotional imagery of the states in the Progressive Era through the related themes of land reclamation and cities. As the states became more populous and better known, boosters increasingly looked to new environments, including unreclaimed "waste" spaces and fast-growing cities. As Chapter 4 shows, the interior regions of California's Imperial Valley and Florida's Everglades became focal points for promotional efforts in which tropical metaphors again came to the fore: for tourists, deserts and swamps were sold as pure wilderness experiences, while for potential farmers and householders, developers depicted them as the only remaining semi-tropical lands open to the American of modest means. But as agribusiness increasingly dominated in southern California and south Florida, increasing land values and farming cooperatives contributed to a widening gap between landowners and field workers. Land companies and conservationists in both states nonetheless depicted irrigation and drainage as vital forces in a healthy, internal expansion that would produce independent American citizenries. As the success of irrigation in southern California became a symbol for boosters of "swampy" south Florida, promoters in each state proclaimed the republican conquest of tropical wilds.

Chapter 5 looks at the promotion of the unofficial capital cities of semi-tropical America: Los Angeles and Miami. As agriculture became more capital intensive, urban environments acquired greater prominence in the promotional imagery. Many settlers who went to southern California and Florida in the early twentieth century were older, wealthier, and desirous of a comfortable, suburban lifestyle—a desire that boosters fostered through visions of alternative cities that contrasted with the ugly industrial metropolises of the Northeast and Midwest. In chambers of commerce pamphlets, magazines, and guides, Los Angeles and later Miami were sold as tropical cities where American urban life could be thoroughly improved. Los Angeles served as a model for Miami; both cities were boosted as idyllic, verdant cityscapes. Mexicans in Los Angeles and

African Americans in Miami were not wholly excised from these images, but they were limited to subordinate roles as manual workers and servants; white urban planners strove for racial segregation in both cities. The promotion of Los Angeles and Miami evolved easily from earlier boosterist visions, and by the 1920s, the cities represented urban epitomes of the ideal of semi-tropical homelands for Anglo-Americans.

The book reaches four main conclusions. First, contrary to what scholars have argued, semi-tropical imagery that veered between exotic fantasies and familiar narratives of American settlement was central to the promotion and transformation of southern California and peninsular Florida. Second, the semi-tropical visions were not identical in California and Florida, since California had advantages over Florida that caused the latter to look to the West Coast for inspiration. Third, in both states the tropical comparisons depended on attitudes drawn from both republican ideology and colonialism that were embedded in nineteenth-century U.S. society. Promoters seized upon and skewed traditional republican ideology in order to bolster self-interested programs of capitalist development and racial hierarchy that contributed to stratified social realities. Fourth, the two states benefited from a rivalry that ultimately legitimized them as hotter lands that were being domesticated by and for white Americans. As a California newspaper observed in 1887, "We can suffer nothing by comparison with Florida; we must gain much. Such competition as does exist only stimulates the spirit of travel and inquiry, and we are therefore to congratulate [ourselves] that our heritage is made more prominent by comparison with that of our Florida friends."[63] Competition was not destructive but beneficial; it was a driving force for the two states that were reimagined as America's tropic of hopes.

"Our" Tropical Lands

Reinventions of California and Florida after the Civil War

Before the U.S. Civil War, both California and Florida were conceived of as far-off and exotic lands that had little in common with the North or Midwest. In the 1870s, the previously negative trait of tropicality that both states shared became the impetus for the reinvention and marketing of California and Florida as the "two summer-lands of our country."[1] This vision, however, was crafted from the contrasting reputations and social realities of the two states. Semitropical America did not appear identical in the new versions of California and Florida.

This chapter focuses on four prominent books written in the mid-1870s that played a catalytic role in how the two states were reconceived and sold as American "tropics." By the late nineteenth century, travel guidebooks had become big business in the United States and had become popular with middle-class readers. Guidebooks were also often directly promotional, sponsored by railroads and land companies that appreciated their influence in attracting visitors and settlers. Anne Hyde has written of how travel guides invariably struck a balance between observing things "new, curious, and wonderful" and others that were reassuringly "American."[2] In the cases of southern California and Florida, however, the sheer exoticism of the environments meant that the early guidebooks often mimicked the writings of white Americans about foreign tropical lands; the latter commodified the tropics as primitive but desirable areas awaiting Euro-American possession and cast the indigenous peoples as idle and unthinking.[3] In the semi-tropical states, guidebooks characterized Native Americans, Mexicans, and Chinese in California and Native Americans and African Americans in Florida in similar ways as they sought to recast these two states for white Americans. They also addressed growing anxieties about the increasingly urban, industrial character of society in the "older" states by promising that the special natures of California and Florida offered viable alternatives. The authors of the guidebooks I focus on here—Charles Nordhoff and Benjamin Truman in California and Harriet Beecher Stowe and Edward King in Florida—envisaged hopeful futures in which Anglo-Americans could realize personal and social benefits in semi-tropical climes.

For an antebellum American, California and Florida would probably have seemed an unlikely pair of states to consider together. Major factors differentiated them: western versus southern; mountainous versus flat; desert versus swamp; free versus slave. In broad brushstrokes, California was emblematic of the "wild and woolly" far West: a "rip-snorting mining camp" of a state, offering chances for wealth and freedom that, to the chagrin of observers, often swelled over into lawlessness.[4] Florida, meanwhile, was a sleepy backwater—part of yet peripheral to the slaveholding South, unwanted despite the three brutal wars of removal the U.S. military had conducted against the Seminole Indians.[5] One fundamental difference between the two states reflected divergent relationships with that most vital of American concepts: freedom. California was admitted as a free state in 1850 (after intense national debates over how the new state would break the fragile balance of free and slave states), whereas in Florida, slavery had been legal since it was formalized as a territory of the United States in 1821 and then achieved statehood in 1845. Any comparative study of California and Florida in the postbellum period must acknowledge these different origins: Florida was affected by slavery, the Civil War, and Reconstruction, while California was removed from that damaging history. As a West Coast journalist wrote in 1883, "Florida has suffered from disadvantages, such as the Civil War, to which California has been a stranger, and has never received any such impetus as the gold discovery gave this State."[6]

The comparison, then, is a somewhat imbalanced one. State population statistics from 1840 to 1870 tell only a fraction of the story but are nonetheless also revealing. In 1850, the two states had similar-sized populations, but twenty years later, California's population was three times larger than that of Florida. This increase was deeply indebted to the Gold Rush but also reflected the fact that California was considerably larger than Florida (155,900 square miles versus 54,861). Although Florida exceeded California in terms of population per square mile in both 1850 and 1860, in the two decades after 1850, California's

Table 1.1. Total population and population per square mile, California and Florida, 1840–70

Year	California		Florida	
	Total Population	Population/ sq. mile	Total Population	Population/ sq. mile
1840	n/a*	n/a	54,477	0.99
1850	92,597	0.59	87,445	1.59
1860	379,994	2.44	140,424	2.56
1870	560,247	3.59	187,748	3.42

Note: * Data unknown; California part of Mexico.
Source: Carter et al., Historical Statistics of the United States: Millennial Edition, 1:192, 213.

population rose by an average of three persons per square mile, whereas Florida's rose by less than two (Table 1.1).

California was aided by the free labor ideology of the antebellum North. In the free states, popular ideals about the right of individuals to pursue economic and social independence through their own labor constituted an ideology that crystallized into a political force during the crisis over the potential expansion of slavery westward.[7] "In the free labor outlook," Eric Foner has written, "the objective of social mobility was not great wealth, but the middle-class goal of economic independence. For Republicans, 'free labor' meant labor with economic choices, with the opportunity to quit the wage-earning class. A man who remained . . . dependent on wages for his livelihood appeared almost as un-free as the southern slave."[8] The entrenched presence of slavery in the South dissuaded potential migrants from the North, who saw a two-tiered society that degraded labor and offered little scope for upward mobility. As T. B. Forbush of the New England Emigrant Aid Company stated of Florida, "While slavery cursed the land, few northern men could be induced to settle there."[9] Florida's growth was hindered by the Civil War and Reconstruction, and sectional legacies continued to make the southern state a problematic prospect for many Americans well into the last years of the nineteenth century. In contrast, California developed a glow of democratic, albeit speculative, opportunity through its associations with westward expansion and the Gold Rush. Many perceived it as a land where republican ideals of free labor could be realized.

Despite these differences, antebellum California and Florida shared certain things that informed later promotional visions of them. Both were former

Spanish colonies that became part of the United States following bursts of expansionist energy; both contained topography that was considered intimidating; and, for most Americans, both were climatically distinctive and geographically remote. Indeed, at the heart of all these similarities was the idea of remoteness, of being "lands apart" from a core United States (meaning here the Northeast and Midwest). When Charles Nordhoff declared in 1872 that southern California "is a region almost unknown," he did not mean that Americans had never heard of it but that they had almost no direct experience of it. It was so far outside the sphere of Anglo-American traditions and history as to be foreign—which, of course, until 1848, it had been.[10] J. S. Adams, Florida's first commissioner of immigration after the Civil War, explained that Florida "is still a *terra incognita*, to a great extent. Her capacities are comparatively untested and unknown."[11]

Florida and California were most obviously remote in spatial terms. While Jacksonville in northern Florida was a not-inconsiderable 835 miles from New York City, California's main city, San Francisco, was over 2,500 miles away, across an expanse that was dreaded for the barriers it presented, including the so-called Great American Desert, the Rocky Mountains, and the Sierra Nevada range, which had notoriously claimed the lives of the Donner party in 1846.[12] California and Florida were also termini, the ends of the domain of the United States. They led on to the Pacific Ocean and the Caribbean Sea, two bodies of water that, unlike the Atlantic Ocean, offered no links to familial (or national) heritage for the majority of white Americans. Theirs was a remoteness, then, in terms of bordering the "other," the unknown. National expansionists had cited access to these bodies of water as justifications for claiming both Florida and California, but those appeals were matched by queries about the worth of the territories.[13] In 1819, when the Senate debated the purchase of Florida from Spain, Virginia's John Randolph exclaimed, "What is Florida? A land of swamps, everglades, filled with frogs, tadpoles, snakes, terrapins, alligators, mosquitoes, gallinippers, and ague and fever! Why, sir, a man would not emigrate to that country, even from purgatory!"[14] During the Mexican-American War, Massachusetts senator Daniel Webster—troubled by the potential expansion of slavery—opposed the acquisition of California into the Union largely on the grounds of its remoteness and inaccessibility.

The sense of remoteness was manifest in other traits: ancestral, topographical, and climatic. Florida and California were former Spanish missionary colonies that were inextricably separate from—foreign to—America's celebrated origins. During the Revolution, Florida had been a Loyalist stronghold, but in 1781 England had lost it to Spain. Subsequently, Florida's unsettling presence as a foreign haven for runaway slaves spurred General Andrew Jackson's raids and the purchase of the territory. The Seminole Indians, an amalgamation of tribes that had entered Florida from neighboring lands and numbered perhaps 5,000 in 1815, resisted the efforts of the U.S. government to remove them to the West. Because they had intermarried with runaway slaves, the Seminoles assumed a frightening reputation in the minds of whites. As Michael Paul Rogin has written, Florida "contained a tribe of mixed Indians and Negroes which, in the whites' cultural nightmare, joined liberal black physical passion to Indian violence. The tropical Florida landscape seemed physically to embody" these worst fears of unbounded savagery and racial mixture.[15] Military conquest and removal of the majority of the Black and Indian Seminoles was achieved only after a series of wars from the 1820s to the 1850s that made Florida a jungle battleground in the American imagination. As a later promoter recalled, "For many years Florida was looked upon as unfit for human habitation . . . as a vast expanse of swamp and poor lands, the real home of alligators, snakes, deadly insects, and the Seminole Indian." Tellingly, in this promoter's mind, the latter did not quite qualify as human inhabitants.[16]

California appeared foreign in its own way. Ownership of the territory passed from Spain to Mexico in 1821, and by the time of the Mexican-American War, California had a population of some 15,000 Spanish-speaking people of Mexican and Spanish heritage. After the annexation of California was confirmed with the Treaty of Guadalupe Hidalgo in 1848, these Californios and Mexicans became an internally colonized people who were economically and socially disenfranchised through legislation such as the California Land Act of 1851 and extralegal violence perpetrated by Anglo settlers.[17] Imperialistic rhetoric supported a political process of power displacement. Incoming whites disdained California's Hispanic inhabitants as improvident—in the words of one visitor, they were "an imbecile, pusillanimous, race of men, and unfit to control the destinies of that beautiful country."[18] Even more derogatory attitudes were expressed about California's Native American population, who were decimated even as they gave scant armed resistance, their numbers falling from 100,000 in 1850 to between thirty and fifty thousand by 1870.[19] Southern California was denigrated as a land without water or worth that was often dismissed in the East as a "forbidding expanse of arid desert."[20] As with Florida, the strangeness of the environment suggested its unsuitability for agriculture. While both a swamp and a desert could be tropical, neither represented an attractive proposition.

Finally, Florida and California were remote from the northern states because of their hotter climates. Prevalent notions about the interconnectedness of environment and the character of peoples made this a significant difference.

Indeed, while it became a major selling point of both states, climate initially presented a problem for promoters who had to convince potential settlers that sun and heat did not presage enervation and degeneracy, a sapping of individual virtue that would be fatal to civilized progress. The rhetoric of U.S. expansion had been predicated on "the ancient conviction that the temperate zone was the one proper field on which to raise an empire of Anglo-Saxon peoples," people whose industrious traits had evolved in colder climates where agriculture required hard work. In contrast, warmer southern climes contributed to the failings of republics in Latin America and the supposed laziness of "tropical races."[21] Environmental influences thus merged with biological and racial factors to distinguish between a white "temperate" zone and a Latin-African "tropical" one, and this distinction fed into U.S. policymaking. In 1867, Congress authorized the annexation of Alaska—which offered a cold climate that, as Harvard biologist Louis Agassiz wrote, would allow for "settlement by our race"—but rejected William Henry Seward's attempts to obtain the Caribbean island of St. Thomas. Henry Adams observed that the policy of the U.S. government regarding expansion could be reduced to one pithy statement: "No annexation in the tropics."[22] Precisely where California and Florida fit in this discourse was unclear, since their "southern" climes, Spanish pasts, multiracial populations, and closeness to Central and South America blurred the fundamental fact of U.S. statehood. But if the environmental aspects of their remoteness were largely immovable, other factors were not. In the late 1860s, technological developments in California and political developments in Florida brought the two states "closer" to the rest of the United States, initiating their reinvention as desirable semi-tropical states.

The Wild and Woolly West: California

California's remoteness was diminished when the transnational railroad was completed in 1869. While Florida had suffered defeat in the Civil War, California profited. The conflict enabled Congress to finally pass the Pacific Railroad bill, which had long been held back by southern objections. Before the railroad was completed, a land journey from the East took several months and often lives, while sea voyages around Cape Horn or via Panama could be longer and deadlier.[23] After the Central and Union Pacific railroads met at Promontory Peak, Utah, they created the new reality (for those who could afford it), of travel from New York to the Pacific Coast in seven days in the comfort of a Pullman carriage.[24] Furthermore, the companies behind the Central Pacific and Southern Pacific Railroads had obtained large tracts of federally granted lands in

California and the West that they sought to sell to easterners and midwestern-ers. Along with the California Immigrant Union (CIU), a newly formed private promotional group, the railroads began issuing pamphlets designed to attract home-seekers and visitors.[25]

The immediate effects of the transnational railroad on California were a far cry from the optimistic forecasts, however. The scheme's promoters had prom-ised a tide of migrants and prosperity for the West, but instead the new link ushered in a glut of goods from eastern cities, while the Suez Canal siphoned off much of the anticipated trade between Europe and the Far East. The initial effect of the railroad in California was in fact a financial depression.[26] This was the reason for the formation of the CIU, a group of San Francisco business-men under the presidency of Caspar T. Hopkins, who lamented California's "shrunken and shrivelled" condition.[27] Recalling Thomas Paine's famous Revo-lution-era tract, Hopkins and the CIU published a pamphlet entitled "Common Sense Applied to the Immigrant Question" in which they discussed the core issues that related to California's "political economy" and future civilization.[28]

Hopkins felt that the state's mining origins were central to its socioeconomic malaise. The mining craze spawned by the discovery of gold in 1848, his pam-phlet explained, had thoroughly skewed development, producing an errant so-ciety in which "restlessness" was endemic. California was a poster child for the rootless communities of the "wild and woolly" West—a bonanza frontier from which people left as often as they arrived. Writing that "mining for the precious metals was never heretofore the principal business of the Anglo-Saxon race, nor of any race claiming a higher rank than semi-civilization," Hopkins asserted that mining had undermined California's social development.[29]

The state's mining associations were not always viewed so negatively. As Carey McWilliams has observed, it was primarily to the Gold Rush that Cali-fornia owed its dramatic growth and eminent sense of exceptionalism.[30] The discovery of gold near Sutter's Mill and subsequent influx of prospectors linked California with the promise of wealth and opportunity. Population swelled: within twelve months, the figure had soared from 26,000, excluding Indians, to (briefly) 115,000.[31] Of these, possibly four-fifths were white Americans, mostly men, nearly half of whom engaged in mining. By the early 1850s, most of the ore had been panned out of California's streams and mining had become a capital-intensive industry that was not profitable for the average prospector.[32] Never-theless, the impact of the Gold Rush was profound. The state obtained a large influx of migrants, a bustling port in San Francisco, and a plausible reputation as a modern-day El Dorado. Over the course of the 1850s, California's increase in population was over five times greater than that of Florida.

However, the Gold Rush also imprinted onto California the stamp of frontier life, and this created a sizeable problem for later promoters seeking migrants. In the 1850s, high levels of violence plagued San Francisco, where criminal gangs made up of former prospectors clashed with a citizens' Committee of Vigilance in a period of urban lawlessness that eastern newspapers condemned. San Francisco, one writer explained, "had become synonymous for all that was most shameless in profligacy" and "for all that was wanton and brutal in ruffianism," a city where life and property were "at the mercy of the lawless."[33] Although the violence subsided and the Committee of Vigilance disbanded, other effects of the Gold Rush persisted. According to the CIU, "the hap-hazard life of the miner gave character to all branches of business," and in the process, "the cheap land that might have grown through tillage into a fortune [was] forsaken for a squatter's chance on city lots," as the "patient plodding of honest industry [was] trampled . . . in the mad rush for chances in the lotteries of universal speculation."[34] The healthy progress and capital accumulation of a predominantly agricultural population had been impossible amid such an "eccentric beginning."[35] Populist fiction accounts such as Bret Harte's articles in the *Overland Monthly* that glorified "the Western miner as an unkempt, bearded, red-shirted rowdy" only sustained troubling links between California and the rough society of a mining frontier.[36] As a later migrant from Pennsylvania to San Diego recalled, tales of violence "firmly convinced [easterners] that California was a wild, far-off country, where a man could fill countless tooth-picks with gold dust; but where he was likely at any turn to be shot full of innumerable arrows—all poisoned, and where, after his murder, his beard would continue to grow."[37]

The other major issue for California's promoters was its Chinese population. While mining had produced a volatile society of speculators, the railroads had introduced what the CIU viewed as a disturbing racial element into the state. In the process of building their line, the Central Pacific had imported thousands of Chinese workers, many of whom stayed on as laborers and servants. Coinciding with the depression of the 1870s, their presence sparked an intense anti-"coolie" movement by whites who saw the Chinese as a threat to their livelihoods and their young society.[38] Hopkins linked this fear to the need to attract white immigrants to California. Although he conceded that the Chinese in "moderate" numbers had "proved a serviceable makeshift" in terms of railroad construction and cheap labor, he warned that they jeopardized California's future.[39] Their "pecuniary" value to the development of the state was far outweighed by the damage they wrought as a heathen, unassimilating population that was incapable of republican citizenship. Hopkins argued that continued Chinese immigration (which was legitimized by the Burlingame-Seward Treaty of 1868) would, if unsurpassed by an influx of whites, create a desperately dangerous situation in which free and democratic institutions would be in the hands of what he considered to be unfit peoples. He pointed to the "Spanish American provinces on this continent" for examples of precisely this dreaded outcome: "Those countries, after years of colonial existence, all threw off the Spanish yoke. What did they gain by it? Though they *copied* from the United States the forms of a polity possessing no life to them, *because they were incapable of originating anything of the kind themselves,* they have none of them been able to preserve their liberties, in anything like an American sense, nor to keep the peace among themselves for ten years in succession."[40]

Republicanism, then, succeeded or failed in relation to human and racial capabilities. "*A people naturally loving liberty can alone be expected to maintain it,*" Hopkins wrote, just as "*a people incapable of desiring liberty for its own sake, or whose history for ages proves that its natural condition is that of submission to despotism, political, social, mental and religious* . . . can never be expected to comprehend [the] *spirit*" of free government.[41] Whether or not whites were the dominant immigrant group in California would thus dictate whether or not it would be a republican society. Although California was a former Spanish province like those to its south, it was also different—"free"—because of an incipient Anglo-American population imbued with the "spirit" of republicanism. The growing presence of alien races, however, meant that the state was at risk from the phenomenon that had afflicted Latin America. So was the U.S. South. Pointing to the Reconstruction amendments, Hopkins observed that millions of "yet uneducated blacks . . . vote to-day throughout the whole South," a race the "masses" of whom "may safely be presumed incapable" of comprehending "that system of ideas constituting the American Government." The prospect of a similar eventuality in California—through the importation "by the hundred thousand" of Chinese peoples who would become the "permanent [and voting] majority"—portended disaster since neither "Chinese [n]or Negro . . . have ever been known to aspire to anything like the Anglo-Saxon idea of liberty or progress." Both races lacked "the doctrine of development [that] is the true American thought." "Caucasian" immigrants from the East Coast and Europe were thus desperately needed, not only to create a more stable society—founded upon agriculture, commerce, and manufacturing rather than mining—but also to preserve in California the republican "spirit" of the United States.[42]

The transnational railroad brought these issues into sharper focus because it reoriented California's relationship with the rest of the country. "Hitherto isolated," Hopkins wrote, "we are led for the first time in our existence . . . to look beyond the present moment, to study the past and contemplate the future" in order to derive from the rest of the world "our own destiny."[43] Despite its initial negative effects, the railroad presented a crucial opportunity. Social improvement was achievable if promoters could attract a population "that shall come here for the sake of the advantages our State offers, independent of mining, . . . prepared to engage *permanently* in agriculture and manufactures."[44] The challenge lay in convincing such persons of California's worth, including the benefits it could offer to Anglo-American civilization.

Tropical California in Travel Guides

In 1872, Collis P. Huntington of the Southern Pacific Railroad commissioned journalist Charles Nordhoff to tour California and produce a new, enticing description of the state. The railroad wanted to overturn, as Nordhoff put it, the fact that "California is to most Eastern people still a land of big beets and pumpkins, of rough miners, of pistols, bowie-knives, abundant fruit, queer wines, high prices—full of discomforts, and abounding in dangers to the peaceful traveller."[45] The title of the book Nordhoff wrote, *California for Health, Pleasure, and Residence*, articulated the various goals of his sponsors: to attract both affluent invalids and pleasure-seekers who would buy train tickets, visit hotels, and perhaps return as residents and industrious settlers of various classes who would buy land—raising its value—and produce specialty crops to be shipped by the railroads.[46] Serialized in *Harpers* magazine and New York's *Tribune* and *Evening Post*, the book became a best seller and was revised several times. "In this little book of travel and suggestion the author expresses what others have thought, and will awaken in many minds sentiments and ideas which were ready to be awakened," rang the high praise of the *New York Times* reviewer. "Such books are, without question, among the most effectual promoters of emigration."[47] Nordhoff's writings on California became so renowned that later promoters claimed that they "have been read in almost every intelligent household in the United States." The founders of a town in California's Ojai Valley even named their town after him.[48]

Tropicality shaped Nordhoff's vision of the Pacific state. Like Hopkins, he made critical comparisons with Central and South America, but he injected a powerful new term into the picture: tropical. A passage from the book's preface (which is worth quoting at length) recast California as the location of a uniquely rich natural resource that was for the first time undergoing "northern American" development:

When a northern American visits a tropical country, be it Cuba, Mexico, Brazil, or Central America, he is delighted with the bright skies, the mild climate, the wonderful productiveness of the soil, and the novel customs of the inhabitants; but he is repelled by an enervating atmosphere, by the dread of malarious [*sic*] diseases, by the semi-barbarous habits of the people, and often by a lawless state of society. Moreover, he must leave his own country, and is without the comfort and security he enjoys at home. *California is our own; and it is the first tropical land which our race has thoroughly mastered and made itself at home in.* There, and there only, on this planet, the traveller and resident may enjoy the delights of the tropics, without their penalties; a mild climate, not enervating, but healthful and health-restoring; a wonderfully and variously productive soil, without tropical malaria; the grandest scenery, with perfect security and comfort in travelling arrangements; strange customs, but neither lawlessness nor semi-barbarism.[49]

As the reference to tropical "penalties" attested, Nordhoff's appropriation of the word was something of a calculated gamble; it forced him to confront, and then dismiss, a range of fears related to enervating air, degeneracy, disease, and "semi-barbarous habits." Why did Nordhoff evoke such a risky comparison, especially since California is considerably north of the Tropic of Cancer?

The italicized line provides the key: "California is our own; and it is the first tropical land which our race has thoroughly mastered and made itself at home in." In a sense, the sentence epitomized the thesis of the guidebook: it married California's exotic natural characteristics to the stabilizing forces of U.S. control. Nordhoff's reference to "our race" made it clear that his intended audience was white Americans, for whom California was the "first" land of its type to become a potential "home." If this implied that further tropical lands might eventually be mastered as well, it also reinforced popular conceptions of the tropics as currently unfit for white settlement. California, therefore, appeared to be unique: a tropical land that was nonetheless "healthful" and "secure" for Anglo-Americans.

Nordhoff's background suggested a latent fascination with tropical lands that influenced this vision of California. After coming to the United States from Prussia as a boy and being orphaned, he served an apprenticeship in a printing house. This experience turned him away from the confinements of the office even as it introduced him to the lure of distant locales: "The perusal of books of travel had always given me great pleasure, and in them I had frequently read glowing accounts of the invigorating and restoring powers of sea air and tropical climes."[50] At fifteen he obtained a berth on a U.S. naval ship about to embark on a voyage to Southeast Asia, the Hawaiian Islands, and California, which was then in the midst of the Mexican-American War. Like another seafaring visitor to the state, Richard Henry Dana (who commented "in the hands of an enterprising people, what a country this might be"), Nordhoff saw Mexican California as a place of unrealized natural potential.[51] It was, he remembered, "a most unproductive or rather nothing-producing country—a great fertile waste in which everything would grow but nothing was . . . except, indeed, beef."[52]

When he returned in 1871, Nordhoff had become a prominent U.S. journalist with a penchant for travel pieces.[53] He was arguably most famous, though, for an article in the *North American Review* attacking urban corruption in a New York City controlled by the Tweed Ring.[54] Nordhoff lamented both the "misgovernment" of eastern cities, predominantly by Irish immigrants, and a widening gap between "the very rich and the very poor; of idle, luxurious, over-cultivated, [and] poor, ignorant, and vicious people, together with a great mass of hard-working, poorly accommodated, struggling, honest men and women, living from hand to mouth." He opined that "great cities are, so far, the curse and puzzle of our civilization."[55] The remedy he proposed was a restructuring of voting practices in a way that would prevent the influence of demagogues and return "wise" leaders to power—a policy, incidentally, that conservatives troubled by the biracial state governments in the Reconstruction South also advocated. Nordhoff took with him to California concerns about the divisive influences of urban modernity upon "honest" citizens, and they contributed to his vision of California as a tropic of republican hopes.

New railroad expansion within the state underpinned this vision. By 1871, a Southern Pacific line snaked southward through the state's interior valleys, including the vast San Joaquin, into southern California—a region pejoratively referred to as the "cow counties" by many northern Californians because of the cattle *ranchos* owned by people of Spanish-Mexican origins. The railroad lines, which Nordhoff enthusiastically detailed, impelled an expansion of promotional efforts for parts of California besides San Francisco and northern California. Although Nordhoff praised San Francisco and the Sacramento Valley, it was southern California that most intrigued him: "By reason of its fine healthful climate, its rich soil, and its remarkably varied products, [it] deserves the attention of farmers looking for pleasant homes and cheap and fertile lands, combined with a climate the best, probably, in the United States."[56] A tropical metaphor was plausible for southern California because of its warmer climate, its suitability for so-called "semi-tropical fruits," and its stronger ties to Mexico and Mexicans.[57] The region was also becoming home to the first small colonies of U.S. settlers who were using irrigation on arid fields. Through such efforts, southern California could become "the real garden of the State."[58]

Emphasizing the redemptive potential of this "garden" for Americans by comparing it with "old" cities in the East, Nordhoff provided both push and pull factors for easterners.[59] The guidebook featured a scathing appraisal of eastern cities such as New York as stifling, overcrowded, and overrun by a "semi-barbarous foreign population" (especially the Irish) who were disturbingly in-fluential in politics and society.[60] By contrast, California promised a fecund nature and a mild climate—and, importantly, no "enervating" effects—while the state's "foreign" peoples posed no threat to Anglo authority. Nordhoff re-ported that California's Indians were "a useful class"; he found that near San Bernardino, "it was thought a great advantage for a man to 'have' an Indian."[61] In addition, according to Nordhoff, the formerly wealthy Californios were in terminal decline, a "natural" consequence of their improvidence. "They had none of the energy and ingenuity of civilized life. They merely lived; they planted no trees; they ploughed few fields; and a soil which is the richest in the world, and a climate in which the orange, the vine, the almond, and olive flourish, served them merely for pasture."[62] Nordhoff's guidebook thus fostered a colonialist view of southern California that appeased Anglo anxieties about its remote-ness. "To the settler from the far-off East," Nordhoff wrote, "it is an important advantage that California has, in a remarkable degree, a well-settled, orderly, and law-abiding population. Three races—the Indians, the old Spaniards, and we 'Americans'—live there harmoniously together."[63] Harmoniously but within a reassuringly defined hierarchy: "Being white, and of the superior race," Ameri-cans "have the privilege of entering any Indian's house."[64] Readers were assured that in California, Anglos had social and racial predominance, especially since the state's ethnic and racial "others" demonstrated the slow traits of tropical peoples. The white settler was innately more energetic, Nordhoff claimed, al-though he issued a warning: "Let him only keep his Eastern habits of industry, and beware of the curse of California—idleness and unthrift—to which no doubt the mild climate predisposes men."[65]

Notably absent from Nordhoff's statement about California's "three races" were the Chinese, whose presence unsettled him, perhaps because they had largely been introduced into the state by his corporate employers. He was am-bivalent about a people who were "alien from our manners, habits, [and] cus-toms" but also "patient, respectful, extremely quick to learn, faithful to their instructions, and make no fuss." The Chinese had "endurance for any labor or climate" and might even "make . . . persistent toil once more fashionable among us [whites]." He advised tourists to explore San Francisco's Chinatown (although he warned of pervasive gambling and opium dens). In spite of their positive values, however, Nordhoff believed that the Chinese were inassimilable—a "disordering and disorganizing [presence within] our own society." Concluding that "without Christianity, free government is impossible," Nordhoff echoed Hopkins's fear that the Chinese were a threat to republican California.[66]

The writer therefore looked beyond San Francisco, where many Chinese had settled, and focused his attention on southern California, a region that promised new formation narratives for U.S. settlers. Nordhoff used an approach that he evidently felt would appeal to easterners—as it surely appealed to him. Mining was a past chapter in state history, irrelevant given the fertile land that only awaited industrious cultivation. The Old World "curses" of crowding and dependence on wages that afflicted the East could be exchanged for the new and healthful conditions of southern California. Nordhoff observed a colony of German American migrants in Anaheim who had together purchased small tracts of land and begun cultivating vines and fruit trees. "The men are masters of their own lives; they have achieved independence, and what to an average New York mechanic would seem the ideal of a fortunate existence." He reported that the Southern Pacific railroad was making "three millions of acres open to settlement" in the San Joaquin Valley alone and claimed that the "Anaheim experiment" could be "successfully repeated in a hundred places in this State."[67] Colonies of white Americans were thus "mastering" tropical California in a process that would produce better Americans who were freed from the constraints of industrial society.

This idea of citizens benefiting from California's distinctive environment was reaffirmed by the journalist Benjamin Truman in another book commissioned by the Southern Pacific Railroad. A former Union correspondent during the Civil War and a former advisor to President Andrew Johnson who had moved to California in 1866, Truman became owner of the *Los Angeles Star* and fell in love with southern California. Claiming that many "Eastern people know nothing of this Paradise of the Occident," Truman's first booster work, *Semi-Tropical California* (1874), sought to combat this ignorance and asserted the tropical aspects Nordhoff had emphasized—with one alteration.[68] Truman stressed that the region was "entitled to the appellation of 'Semi-Tropical California,'" by which he meant portions of Monterey, San Luis Obispo, Santa Barbara, Ventura, San Bernardino, and San Diego Counties, with a particular focus on Los Angeles County and the nearby San Gabriel Valley.[69] By adding the prefix "semi," Truman qualified Nordhoff's tropical comparison, and his term thereafter appeared with far greater frequency as a descriptive term in the literature that promoted southern California. For boosters such as Truman, "semi-tropical" meant a sanitized version of the tropics that was stripped of the "penalties" and unprogressive qualities of more southern climes and was perfectly conducive to Anglo-American progress.

Truman had worked as a journalist for the *New York Times*, the Philadelphia *Press*, the Washington *Chronicle*, and the San Francisco *Bulletin*, and his background gave authority to his guidebook, whose stated object was to "bring permanently into notice the county of Los Angeles [and] Semi-tropical California." He described himself as "a writer of acknowledged reliability," and a claim of "nothing but facts" preceded his depiction of southern California as a place where "with a small capital, industry and economy, forty, twenty, ten acres of land, will in time yield an income greater than can be derived from an equal space in any other locality." The region's remoteness meant that it was untouched by the social problems of the Northeast and that social mobility was eminently attainable. "Look this way, ye seekers after homes and happiness!" Truman proselytized, "ye honest sons of toil, and ye *pauvres miserables* who are dragging out a horrible life in the purlieus of large eastern cities! Semi-tropical California welcomes you all."[70]

Anglo-American ascendancy was clear in Truman's treatment of California's Mexican population. The latter were associated with a premodern past, a "romantic glamour" that still "overhangs the region."[71] Truman both romanticized and marginalized Mexicans: Los Angeles "and its vicinity thronged with memories of a by-gone age, and a population of foreign habits and birth [that] presents a number of interesting features for examination not to be found elsewhere, and well worthy of careful inspection."[72] But the state had been redeemed from native sloth by the arrival of the "Anglo-Saxon pioneer": "I first visited Los Angeles in 1867. Crooked, ungraded, unpaved streets; low, lean, rickety, adobe houses . . . and here and there an indolent native, hugging the inside of a blanket, or burying his head in a gigantic watermelon, were the, then, most notable features of this quondam Mexican town. But a wonderful change has come over the spirit of its dream, and Los Angeles is at present—at least to a great extent—an American city."[73] The image of a Mexican "native" gorging on a huge fruit was emblematic of the twin offspring of tropicality: bounty and lethargy. In contrast, the modern Los Angeles of improved roads and buildings was efficient and "American," offering the fruit without the indolence. Truman praised the "impetus given [to] commerce and agriculture . . . by the American and European element" in California.[74] The state's legacies of conquest thus were translated into a romantic backdrop against which the progressive contributions of Anglo-Americans could be highlighted.

Semi-tropical California offered opportunities for better health as well as wealth. Like Nordhoff, Truman emphasized the benefits of the climate for eastern invalids, who usually went to Florida, Cuba, or southern Europe in search of restoration. Southern California was preferable to all of these, since Florida and Cuba, like Italian resorts, were "covered with a rank, rich growth of tropical vegetation, saturated always with moisture, and undergoing a constant and rapid decomposition."[75] He cited fellow promoter William McPherson, who contrasted the benign atmosphere of California with that of Florida, where the popular resort of St. Augustine was "too warm in summer, and too damp throughout the year," a malarial "combination of heat and moisture" that could "conspire against health and life."[76] Truman thus evoked some of the negative attributes of tropicality—dampness and decay—to denigrate Florida even as he cited the semi-tropical benefits of California. His stance anticipated West Coast notions of semi-tropical America, in which California was said to have "warmth without moisture" and "a semi-tropical sun without the enervating heats which are born of quick evaporation in a fungus and rank vegetation."[77] As Truman's guidebook declared, "Los Angeles County (the heart of Semi-tropical California) has no equal in the world."[78]

The Sleepy and Swampy South: Florida

In the 1860s, Florida was perceived as a remote state not only because of its environment but also because of its political history: the state had seceded to join the Confederacy in 1861 and had fought against the Union in the Civil War. With the exception of the Battle of Olustee in 1864, the war was fought outside Florida, but the Union army campaigned extensively in the northern part of the state in an attempt to capture Tallahassee and restore Florida to the Union so Abraham Lincoln could gain the state's Electoral College votes. In addition to the turmoil left by Union occupation, railroad projects that had been initiated in the 1850s died, and after the war the state had only sparse transportation facilities with which to attract settlers or investors.[79] Moreover, Florida suffered the wounds of the defeated South, including an end to its economic foundation: slavery.[80] For slaveholding whites, the Civil War meant a vast decline in wealth. Emancipation contributed to a decline in average farm values in Florida from $2,502 in 1860 to $777 in 1870.[81] A desperate need to bring in new settlers and fresh wealth gripped the state. As George Pozzetta wrote, "In no other period of Florida's past . . . have residents of the state attempted to entice settlers southward with a greater sense of urgency and need than in the decades following the Civil War."[82]

The end of the state's political exile aided this cause. In 1868, Florida was readmitted to the Union under the Reconstruction plan of Congress. One year later the state's Republican government created the position of commissioner of lands and immigration. The first appointee, J. S. Adams, was "entrusted [with] the oversight and promotion of immigration" to Florida.[83] In an early pamphlet, Adams wrote optimistically that "when the inducements of various kinds which Florida holds out to immigration shall be fully known in other sections of the country, it is confidently anticipated that a tide of population from all sections will flow in."[84] But this required confronting and overcoming long-standing objections to the peninsular state. As Adams acknowledged, for potential migrants "some little knowledge of the history of Florida is indispensable to a right understanding and appreciation of her present condition. . . . If Florida has such a desirable climate and such a variety and power of vegetable growth 'why are there not more people there?' is an inevitable question."[85]

In 1870, Florida had the second-smallest population of the states east of the Mississippi, even though it was the second-largest state in that group.[86] The state had been acutely underpopulated even before the Civil War wiped out 15,000 of its white male citizens. In 1860, when the neighboring states of Alabama and Georgia had 964,201 and 1,057,286 people, respectively, Florida's population was 140,424.[87] Various factors contributed to this scant settlement, including slavery, the Seminole Wars, and the natural environment. Legalized slavery in Florida dissuaded potential northern settlers who had been raised on free labor ideals; these migrants instead flooded westward to claim land.[88] John Lee Williams was an exception to this trend. Williams came to Florida in the 1820s for his health, settled in St. Augustine, and helped select Tallahassee as the capital.[89] In his 1837 book *The Territory of Florida*, he stressed the extent to which slavery had cast a pall over his adopted home. The result of the latest Indian war was that rich lands had been abandoned in northern Florida, even though they were available at prices cheaper than in the North or West. These lands should have attracted "northern farmers, mechanics and merchants" as well as southerners.[90] Yet, Williams wrote, "many Europeans, as well as inhabitants of the northern states, object to live in a slave holding country, and we must grant that slavery is an evil."[91]

Yet slavery was not the only obstacle to settlement. The population of the slave states of Georgia and Alabama was much greater than that of Florida. Fears about the environment—including the state's Indian wars and its proximity to the tropics—particularly held back new settlement in Florida. Unlike other southeastern states, where Indian removal had been largely (and brutally) achieved in the 1830s, Florida, as Adams wrote, had been "harassed and plundered by repeated Indian wars from 1816 to 1858."[92] The Seminole Indians, a band that included numerous mixed-race people as the result of unions with runaway slaves, became for whites a terrific symbol of the "savage" wildness of Florida.[93] The narrator of an 1882 novel set in the antebellum period responded to medical advice to relocate to Florida with the lament, "Don't send me down among the Indians and negroes to be scalped and massacred."[94] The Seminoles' guerrilla-type resistance to federal efforts to remove them to the West was overcome only after recurrent wars that lasted until the eve of the Civil War and left perhaps 200 Seminoles in Florida. This small remnant retreated to the Everglades, where its members eked out a survival in island dwellings. Later Anglo promoters would strive, with great success, to absorb the Seminoles into Florida's promotional imagery as tourist attractions and symbols of the state's wilderness. For most of the nineteenth century, however, when the state's environment was still a fearsome unknown, Florida's Native Americans were a major factor in why whites avoided the state.

Another deterrent was the state's swamplike terrain and hot climate—not to mention popular concerns about hurricanes, which boosters countered with dubious declarations that Florida was immune "from those terrific equatorial storms and hurricanes of the tropics."[95] Florida's innumerable lakes and rivers and humid atmosphere suggested to many a hotbed for sickness. Even southern planters were wary of the peninsula and stuck to a thin strip of counties hugging the Georgia border. "I confess I am afraid of these climates so near the tropics," confided a North Carolina planter in 1831 to a nephew bound for Florida, where "the fevers are always formidable."[96] Such testaments reflected an internal contradiction in the idea of Florida: it was perceived as both a destination for invalids seeking a restorative climate and a land of deathly swamps. Williams's view was typically ambiguous: "A southern climate is not necessarily a sickly one. Florida is undoubtedly as healthy as New York," he claimed. Yet while "it is much more congenial to feeble constitutions," it was "perhaps, to the robust . . . too debilitating" because of "situations where stagnant waters and a luxuriant vegetation, usually produce fevers."[97]

For northerners, who expanded the physical lethargy symptomatic of malaria and similar diseases into social traits that were attributed to inhabitants of hotter climes, the southeastern United States and Central and South America were home to "sleepy" populations who demonstrably lacked the energetic qualities of the virtuous citizenry of colder climes. This lethargy dictated labor relations in hot countries. As Thomas Jefferson had written, labor in such environments had to be coerced, since "in a warm climate, no man will labor for himself who can make another labor for him."[98] The expansion of plantation slavery seemed to confirm for northerners that a hot climate provoked the degeneration of individual energy and created something fatal to democracy: a two-tiered society. Because of its location in the southernmost reaches of the United States, Florida was hit hard by these assumptions. In his efforts to overturn the association between climate and slavery, Williams nearly reaffirmed it:"We want industrious and enterprising men and women to come among us . . . to prove that white men, although they may not bear the burning rays of the sun as well as negroes, yet that by order, system and economy, they can accomplish more in one day, than a slave will accomplish in a week."[99] Antebellum Florida thus seemed like a sleepy and swampy slave state that was worth visiting only if one was too weak to survive another northern winter.

These legacies of the antebellum period were compounded by Reconstruction. In the words of Commissioner Adams, postwar Florida was subject to "the political ideas of a triumphant radicalism."[100] After southern whites created Black Codes in 1865 to maintain control over the freedmen, there was a backlash in Congress, which passed new amendments to the Constitution in an attempt to safeguard the civil rights of emancipated African Americans. As a result, black men voted for and took part in Republican governments that came to power in Florida during this period and retained that power until 1876.[101] Reconstruction policies that guaranteed the right of freedmen to vote antagonized North-South tensions. White southerners resented the new importance of African American men as voting citizens and political officers and saw this development as the result of overbearing federal power. White northerners who considered Florida for settlement, in turn, had to consider potential reprisals against them as hated"carpetbaggers." Moreover, racism was strong in the North as well as in the South, and the large presence of emancipated African Americans who were at least de jure social equals under the federal constitutional amendments was an additional cause for concern among northern whites. In 1870, blacks constituted fully 49 percent of Florida's 187,748 citizens.[102] Adams did not ignore these significant "social [and political] conditions" or the fact that there was "much bitterness of feeling" among southerners. However, he argued, and with some justification, that of the southern states Florida was the least troubled by such "bitterness," as it was less populated and less defined by antebellum factors. In many ways, it represented the newest part of the New South: "Florida, though in fact an old State, has all the characteristics of an entirely new-settled State."[103]

Much like Caspar Hopkins in California, then, Adams accepted that certain historical factors had damaged his state's development at the same time that he envisaged a better future made possible by the arrival of enterprising whites. Florida, he posited, was especially capable of improvement because of its rare qualities of soil and climate. These, he felt, would attract settlers from the North and Midwest and would compensate for the state's social inadequacies. "Strong immigration of new men, with new views and new desires" would provide "the means of gratifying the social needs of a progressive society."[104] Encouraging this "strong immigration," however, meant first constructing positive visions of a state that had long disturbed Anglo-Americans because of its tropical and racial characteristics.

Tropical Florida in Travel Guides

Celebrated writers were crucial to the positive new visions of Florida, none more so than Harriet Beecher Stowe and her 1873 guidebook, *Palmetto Leaves*. Published the year after Charles Nordhoff's *California*, Stowe's work was less overtly promotional, since it was not sanctioned by any railroad. But Stowe had a booster's faith in Florida and contributed to state annuals and for a price was willing to pose on her porch for tourists traveling on steamships down the St. Johns River.[105] Moreover, while Nordhoff was a travel reporter describing the West Coast, Stowe was a writer-in-residence in Mandarin, Florida, on the banks of the St. Johns River, where she purchased a farm and an orange grove after the Civil War. She spent the winters of her later years touring northeastern parts of Florida and writing pieces for northern magazines.[106] Many of her articles were responses to the "quantities of letters from persons of small fortunes" Stowe received "asking [for] advice whether they had better move to Florida." In 1873 a collection of these articles was published as *Palmetto Leaves*, which read as a paean to the healthful "outdoorness" of Florida, where, Stowe explained, invalids, tourists, and settlers from the North could enjoy "winter in a semi-tropical region."[107]

Palmetto Leaves has been largely overlooked by scholars, including Stowe's biographers.[108] One provides a single paragraph on the book that nonetheless hints at its broader importance: the collection of sketches became an overnight best seller, spurred a large increase in the number of northerners visiting Florida, and contributed to a doubling in real estate prices around Mandarin.[109] In the context of Stowe's life and works, it is fairly easy to overlook *Palmetto Leaves*. She surely will always be remembered for her 1852 novel, *Uncle Tom's Cabin*, which exposed a mass readership to the brutalities of southern slavery and strengthened the abolitionist cause. But her influence on northern attitudes toward the South did not end with emancipation. Indeed, the author's celebrity amplified the importance of her later works, including *Palmetto Leaves*, an account of Stowe's experiences in a southern state that indicated for her northern readers the progress the South had made in the postwar years.[110] Following *Uncle Tom's Cabin*, after all, the author had been cursed in the antebellum South; the *Southern Literary Messenger* had called *Uncle Tom's Cabin* a "criminal prostitution of the truth."[111] The fact that Stowe lived for half the year in a former Confederate state—and wrote about it in largely, if not entirely, positive terms—ameliorated some of the concerns of northerners about the New South.

Stowe's presence in Florida was used to promote the state to northerners. Pamphlets by Florida land companies in the 1880s declared that "such a noted person as Mrs. Harriet Beecher Stowe, the famous author of Uncle Tom's Cabin, has spent half of her life in this State, and has one of the best orange groves in Florida, yielding her a handsome annual income."[112] But it was her descriptions in *Palmetto Leaves* that were most influential in reshaping northern conceptions of and attracting visitors to the much-maligned state. An 1887 guidebook hailed *Palmetto Leaves* as "the means of causing many [northerners] to establish winter homes in sunny Florida."[113]

As the reference to "winter homes" would suggest, the book was aimed at the wealthy. Stowe's Florida was "peculiarly adapted to the needs of people who can afford two houses, and want a refuge from the drain that winter makes on the health."[114] This approach is evidence that a different class dynamic was at work in Florida. Nordhoff envisioned California as a place where enterprising northerners could make independent fortunes. Stowe's vision was addressed specifically to already affluent northerners. In some passages, Stowe even warned against permanent residence in the state, particularly for Americans ill-suited to hot summers, when malaria was a danger.[115] The guidebook thus contributed to Florida's emergence as a winter resort rather than a destination for year-round living.

Stowe was fascinated with Florida's tropicality, even if she was guarded about some of the "tropical" comparisons appearing in other promotional texts at the time. Dr. Baynard Byrne, for example, a northerner whose letters comparing Florida favorably with Texas formed an 1866 collection, had proclaimed the tropical attractions of Florida for health-seekers and agriculturists.[116] Stowe felt that this was misleading given northeastern Florida's winter appearance, which tended toward a sandy flatness, coarse grass, pine trees, and occasional frosts: "Tourists and travellers generally come with their heads full of certain romantic ideas of waving palms, orange-groves, flowers, and fruit, all bursting forth in tropical abundance; and, in consequence, they go through Florida with disappointment at every step."[117] Nevertheless she filled her guidebook with references to the tropical "romance" of the region. "Spring is a glory anywhere, but, as you approach the tropics, there is a vivid brilliancy, a burning tone, to the coloring, that is peculiar." Florida belonged to the United States, yet it offered escape from it in the form of respite for northerners suffering from cold, consumption, or "nervous excitability."[118] The state was alluringly unrefined, a place where civilized customs were only imported. Stowe wrote that "we should not represent [Florida] as a neat, trim damsel, with starched linen cuffs and collar," but as "a brunette, dark but comely, with gorgeous tissues, a general disarray and dazzle, and with a sort of jolly untidiness, free, easy, and joyous."[119] Florida's environmental foreignness tied it to the tropics, but this was what made it an enticing prospect for Stowe.

Florida's tropical traits also helped make it a desirable postwar destination for African Americans. Indeed, early in the Civil War, numerous northern newspapers had called for the seizure of Florida by the Union so that the state could become a colony for freed slaves.[120] The ambitious plan came to naught, but after the war emancipated African Americans migrated to Florida from Georgia and the Carolinas in search of better opportunities.[121] Ambrose Douglass, a freedman in North Carolina, recalled that "I was 21 when freedom finally came, and that time I didn't take no chances on 'em taking it back again. I lit out for Florida."[122]

The underpopulation of the state and its proximity to the Caribbean suggested a haven for blacks in the United States. An African American reporter from the North wrote in 1872, "Florida is destined to become the Negro's new Jerusalem. Her close proximity to Cuba, Hayti [sic] and Jamaica, makes her the great gateway between the negro tropical belt and the great Temperate Zone of the white race in the United States. . . . Here then the oppressed colored people of Georgia and intelligent and well-to-do colored men of the North must come and pitch their tents."[123] Once in this "new Jerusalem," however, African Americans faced the concerted efforts of whites to reclaim social, political, and economic domination during the flux of Reconstruction.[124] Because Florida had more available land and a higher percentage of black landowners than other southern states, Ku Klux Klan violence was directed against economically independent freedmen.[125]

Promoters of Florida—whites who were often complicit in the push for white supremacy in the state—appropriated the potentially subversive idea of Florida as a tropical "gateway." In 1876, a correspondent for the Atlanta Constitution reported that en route to St. Augustine, (where "the elegant residence of Mrs. Harriet Beecher Stowe was viewed from a distance with much delight"), "palmetto and plants [grew] in a profusion and thickness unequalled anywhere else in America. The scenery is entirely tropical, and a constant novelty and surprise to most of our party. . . . Indeed this land would almost realize the poet's dream of paradise."[126] After the Civil War, the process of claiming Florida's tropical benefits for whites focused on health tourism more than on agriculture. For Stowe, Florida's attractions were best enjoyed as a winter visitor, since "no white man" could be expected to work there all summer. The settler from the North sometimes needed "an attack of malarial fever or two to teach him that he cannot labor the day through under a tropical sun as he can in the mountains of New Hampshire." The Florida frontier thus appeared markedly different from the celebrated frontiers of the West (and even southern California) that were associated with independent white settlers who were carving livelihoods from the wilderness. This frontier was tropicalized: it grew with a "tropical rapidity," and visitors had to beware of the "fiercest extremes of tropical temperature."[127] Common sense dictated that whites could not labor persistently and profitably under such foreign conditions.

This posed a serious question about the progress of Florida under a free labor regime. As Stowe wrote, "Who shall do the work for us? . . . in this new State, where there are marshes to be drained, forests to be cut down, palmetto-plains to be grubbed up, and all under the torrid heats of a tropical sun."[128] In answering this question, *Palmetto Leaves* concluded with a lengthy discussion of the prospects for African Americans in a free labor system in Florida. A fierce opponent of slavery, Stowe saw emancipation as an unremitting good, but the specific meaning of free labor was another matter. As historians have shown, competing notions of what free labor meant invoked different approaches to reconstructing the South. The definition itself was in flux: many white northerners and freedmen defined freedom as the ability to reap the fruits of their own labor, which could best be accomplished by owning land.[129] In this republican view, African Americans had the thrift and enterprise to succeed as independent laborers. But when Radical Republicans in Congress proposed that small parcels of land be provided for the freedmen, they met fierce opposition from white southerners and conservative northerners on ideological and material grounds. These opponents believed that as former slaves with inferior capabilities, African Americans were fundamentally unfit for the independence of land ownership and needed to be taught how to work.[130]

Stowe's *Palmetto Leaves* fell close to the latter view. African Americans, she wrote, were "the natural laborer[s] of tropical regions"—but "natural" to Stowe meant that they were good manual workers, not that they could be enterprising farmers who were capable of producing crops on their own land.[131] In this colonialist approach, white expansion into Florida depended, to some degree, on the willingness of African Americans to perform grunt labor under Anglo direction. Happily for a white employer such as Stowe, "the black laborers whom we leave in the field pursue their toil, if any thing, more actively, more cheerfully, than during the cooler months. The sun awakes all their vigor and all their boundless jollity."[132] Indeed, for Stowe, African Americans in Florida were a kind of ideal agricultural proletariat: contented, well-disciplined, and suited to tropical conditions. A white captain who had surveyed Florida's "swamps and lagoons" with an entirely African American crew had taught Stowe that "the negro constitution enabled them to undergo with less suffering and danger the severe exposure and toils of the enterprise," while the "good nature which belonged to the race made their toils seem to sit lighter upon them than upon a given number of white men." Wealthy northerners considering Florida for leisure or investment could take note of the fact that the captain "valued [his crew] for their docility, and perfect subjection to discipline." Indeed, African Americans were superior to the "lower classes at the North" because they were "more obedient, better natured, more joyous, and easily satisfied."[133]

Stowe thus described Florida's development in colonialist rather than republican terms. Indeed, her core question—"Who shall do the work for us?"—was essentially a betrayal of the free labor ideology. Since "us" presumably meant whites, the terminology assigned otherness to those would work for incoming Anglo-Americans. Similar to Nordhoff's use of "we 'Americans,'" Stowe's language fixed identities and roles along racial lines. Tellingly, despite her antislavery crusading, she exhibited a strong tendency to compare African Americans in Florida to animals. Cudjo, who she encountered at Mandarin's wharf, was "misshapen, and almost deformed . . . black as night itself; and but for a glittering, intellectual eye, he might have been taken for a big baboon,—the missing link of Darwin."[134] Simon, laboring under a scorching sun, had "a boiling spring of animal content . . . ever welling up within," while, at Fernandina, Stowe witnessed a "low, squat giant of a fellow, with the limbs and muscles of a great dray-horse."[135] In Stowe's mind, these freedmen functioned as thoughtless workhorses who needed to be overseen by paternalistic whites who were the true agents of civilizing change. Stowe's depiction of African Americans as contented field workers who aided the Anglo-led development of Florida reached a northern public already impatient with the length and expense of Reconstruction.[136] The famous abolitionist author's characterization of African Americans resonated with the suspicions of white northerners that the Radical Reconstruction goals of racial equality were misguided, if not downright "unnatural"—not least in a tropical land where nature surely dictated different roles for the two races.

Edward King's *The Southern States of America* (1875) was another significant travel guide by a northern author who imagined Florida in tropical terms. A native of Massachusetts, King was a well-known writer who was employed by *Scribner's* magazine to produce a series of articles on the postwar South, where he traveled in 1873 and 1874. With the financial backing of *Scribner's Magazine*, King repeatedly chartered private trains to the South and then wrote about his travels. Featuring illustrations by an accompanying artist, J. Champney, King's book generated international interest: the *Examiner* of London reviewed it as "a work of such genuine value that it might have successfully appealed to the public without the recommendations of any illustrations whatever."[137] A skillful and experienced writer who had covered the Franco-Prussian War and the Paris Commune, King combined eloquent descriptions of climate, scenery, and architecture with conservative appraisals of Reconstruction, politics, and race in the South. Above all, *The Southern States of America* was imbued with boosterist rhetoric. King proclaimed that "there are so many superior inducements offered by the peninsula [of Florida] to those in search of new abiding-places."[138]

Following Stowe's example, King saw "subtropical" Florida as a place that was foreign to but was being reshaped by white northerners. In Jacksonville, he found, "the North has swept on in such a resistless current that, so far as its artificial features are concerned, the city has grown up according to the New England pattern, though foliage, climate, sun—all these are the antipodes of those of the North!"[139] King connected Florida's natural remoteness to the "advent of ambitious Northerners" who, since the end of the war, had headed south in search of health, orange farms, or the "phantom Pleasure." Like Stowe, King expressed fears about the state's wilderness in the summer. Settlers were warned of the "danger of malarial disease" and "the black swamp canal" that "sends up a fetid odor of decay." He described the months of December to April as free of malaria, however, and cast Florida as "our new winter paradise," linking the peninsula's climate with that of "Hawaii [and] Southern Italy," two places that wealthy Anglo-Americans would have considered as vacation destinations rather than places for settlement.[140] In Stowe's and King's guidebooks, Florida's potential was more limited than that of California: it was a seasonal retreat that promised "the most delicate and delightful tropical scenery" for "overworked and careworn" northerners.[141] These authors presented leisure, not labor, as the state's defining attraction.

Like Stowe, King saw African Americans as picturesque human emblems of exotic Florida.[142] Observing a Jacksonville square, King described "the lazy, ne'er-do-well, negro boys" who had the "unconscious pose and careless grace of Neapolitan beggars." Occasionally "among the dusky race" he saw "a face beautiful as was ever that of [an] olive-brown maid in Messina." King found some condensed essence of the South in this "lazy" scene that combined poverty and leisure, race and sensuality. "This is the South, slumberous, voluptuous, round and graceful," he wrote. "Mere existence is pleasure; exertion is a bore."[143] He characterized African Americans as fixtures in this romanticized South, "unconscious" and "ragged," banjo players and deck hands. The sketches that accompanied the book showed distinctly apelike servants attending to whites, a series of representations that reflected and reinforced northern acquiescence with southern assertions that the freedmen were primitive and unthinking.[144] These depictions far outweighed King's solitary admission that "the balance of power in the State is at present held by the blacks, led by a few white men." He soon qualified this statement with the prescient statement that "the Conservative element is rapidly gaining strength, and it is noted as somewhat remarkable that Northerners who settle [in Florida] gradually find themselves leaning to Conservatism," since it offered political "protect[ion]" from "ignorance and vice."[145] As King foretold, the days of Reconstruction in Florida were numbered. They ended with the victory of the Democratic Party in the state's 1876 gubernatorial election. The "redemption" of home rule signaled the departure of federal troops from Florida and the imposition of a state government predicated on white supremacy.[146]

Although it hinted at this impending reversal of Reconstruction, King's bestselling guidebook spent little time on sociopolitical unrest, opting instead for the more compelling vision of Florida's commercial future, which included a railroad that would one day run the length of the peninsula and take Americans to within hours of Cuba. He mediated anxieties about the suitability of the environment for white settlers with expectations that the state would be harnessed eventually, one way or another, given the rare healthful and productive benefits it promised. Although winter tourism was prominent in the guidebook, agriculture, too, made an appearance. "The fitness of Florida for the growth of tropical and semi-tropical fruits is astonishing," King wrote, anticipating what would soon become a dominant theme in promotional literature. To be sure, King warned, "the labor question in Florida, as elsewhere in the Southern States, is perplexing and startling," and he questioned the ability of "Northern and Western" settlers to adapt to the southern reaches of "the vast sub-tropical peninsula." Migrants who were "native to the South," he felt, would probably have to work the future sugar plantations of South Florida. Whether these natives would be black or white he did not specify, although Stowe had already made clear who were considered "the natural laborers of the South." Here, after all, was a U.S. state that was fundamentally different from the rest because of its tropical qualities. This distinctiveness would become crucial to its promotion and growth. King offered a hint of what was to come: "We have within our boundaries a tropic land, rich and strange, which will one day be inhabited by thousands of fruit-growers," he wrote, "and where beautiful towns, and perhaps cities, will yet spring up."[147]

In the decade after the Civil War, guidebooks for California and Florida engaged with long-held, disdainful notions of the states as remote and constructed new images of them as America's own tropical lands. Following technological and political developments that decreased the states' remoteness, influential writers-cum-boosters such as Charles Nordhoff in California and Harriet Beecher Stowe in Florida envisaged fertile locales that because of their exotic pasts, climates, and inhabitants presented attractive expanses for incoming whites. These early formulations of tropical California and Florida emphasized the unique traits of lands that belonged to the United States.

California had many advantages over Florida at this time, perhaps alluded to in Nordhoff's declaration that the state "was the *first* tropical land which our race has thoroughly mastered."[148] He would surely have accepted that Florida was equally as "tropical" as California—if not more so—but not that Anglo-Americans had "thoroughly mastered" it. At the time he was writing, Florida was struggling to overcome the physical and psychological damage that slavery and civil war had perpetrated. California's promoters faced other hindrances, including notions of a violent mining frontier and a growing Chinese population. By focusing on southern California, however, guidebook writers such as Nordhoff and Truman shifted attention to the region's undeveloped potentialities. Their efforts helped reinvent California, setting the tone for new visions of the Golden State. As William Henry Bishop wrote of California in 1882, "A very large part of the State outside of the mining and lumbering districts displays some of those tropical characteristics in which its charm to the Eastern imagination consists."[149]

Similar claims about "tropical characteristics" were made by guidebook writers in postwar Florida. But the southern state's appeal was circumscribed in comparison with California's, geared toward invalids and winter visitors rather than industrious settlers. Florida's associations with slavery, Indian wars, and malarial swamps added troubling elements to the mix, fueling northern concerns about its livability. Even Harriet Beecher Stowe, who liked Florida enough to live there half the year, found it difficult to foresee white settlers carving out independent lives in its muggy environment. African Americans thus assumed a crucial position in her vision of state development. At a time when blacks voted and took part in Florida's Reconstruction governments, however, Stowe and King represented African Americans as manual workers who had wells of "animal content" but showed little sign of the intellectual and enterprising capabilities republican citizenship demanded. In the waning years of Reconstruction, Stowe and King articulated colonialist visions of tropical expansion in which affluent northerners came to and developed Florida, employing African Americans who lacked the innate capabilities to thrive as truly independent citizens. Tellingly, Stowe saw benefits in the 1876 "redemption" that would produce greater northern investment in Florida. In 1877, when the *New York Tribune* reported the murders of African Americans by whites in northern Florida, Stowe responded by defending the state's white population as a "remarkably quiet, peaceable, and honest set of people."[150]

Although different in important ways, California and Florida were both represented in largely—if never exclusively—positive terms as "our" tropical lands by U.S. guidebook writers in the 1870s. They hoped for an alternative to the industrializing future of the Northeast and Midwest. This ideal would characterize the promotion of California and Florida for decades. In "tropical," however, they also invoked a term that had the potential to disturb Anglo-Americans with its racial and social implications. Promoters of California and Florida often had negative views of foreign tropics. In the following decades, then, boosters crafted the concept of "semi-tropical" lands, a term that distinguished the two U.S. states from "backward" overseas tropics. For settlers, promoters focused on opportunities for republican independence and agrarian prosperity in their semi-tropical lands, thereby narrating "American" rather than "tropical" forms of society and progress. As the next chapter shows, promoters also strove to attract winter visitors by disseminating visions of quasi-tropical climates, landscapes, and "primitive" racial others, all within America's borders.

2

A Climate for Health and Wealth

The Lure of Tropical Leisure on American Soil

In the late nineteenth century, California and Florida were sold as tropical destinations for American health-seekers and pleasure tourists. Railroad and hotel
companies, periodicals, travel writers, and tour agencies deployed visions of
recuperative leisure that demonstrated a fascination with the "primitivism" of
the environments, incorporating American beliefs that tropical regions existed
at simpler or "earlier" stages of social development than the urban industrial society of the North.[1] In America's semi-tropical states, promoters asserted, white
tourists could reap the benefits of healthful contact with premodern nature and
cultures without abandoning the comforts of progressive modernity. "It was a
novel sensation to sit under your own flag, inside your own nation, and drink
lemonade made from fruit grown on the place, eat bananas and oranges and
figs . . . all from the same patch," wrote a New Yorker in southern California
in 1880.[2] Descriptions of similar experiences were replicated in countless depictions of Florida, which also afforded pleasures akin to traveling abroad but
within the sphere of republican civilization. In 1885, a Chicago-based Florida
land company declared that "the Golden Peninsula's popularity as the foremost
health resort is ever increasing, and in no portion of the great Republic are there
to be found phases of development and progress more wonderful and interesting than those that are growing in this semi-tropical clime."[3]

This chapter traces the selling of California and Florida as leisure-filled
tropical escapes for "over-civilized" tourists, especially from the Northeast,
where many feared that rapid industrialization and urbanization were dam-

aging citizens. Tourist-oriented boosterism, unlike promotion designed to attract permanent settlers, was geared toward an affluent and exclusive fraction of society who could afford winter travel. In the Gilded Age, vacationing anywhere—but particularly to places as distant from most Americans as California or Florida—was financially prohibitive; it required free time and funds for travel, accommodations, and activities. Transportation was expensive: in 1883, when middle-class professions such as lawyers and doctors earned approximately $1,200 a year and the average city clerk less than $1,000, a first-class railroad ticket from New York to California cost $115 and a third-class ticket half that.[4] Tickets to Florida were cheaper—$31 from New York (by ocean steamer or rail) and $22 from Cincinnati—but sufficiently high for state immigration promoters to organize a convention at Jacksonville in 1887 calling for "a concession of rates so as to enable people to come to this State" who were not wealthy tourists.[5]

Exclusivity did not diminish the significance of the promotional imagery aimed at winter visitors, however. While it is impossible to quantify the number of tourists who visited the two states in these years—as one Florida survey acknowledged, "There is no positive way to assemble all facts regarding the arrival and departure of tourists"—the promotional literature enticed countless Americans to and shaped their views of southern California and peninsular Florida. Moreover, tourist guides and hotel pamphlets illustrated the attitudes of Anglo elites who influenced local development as tourism grew into a core industry in both states.[6] These boosterist texts conceptualized new identities for California and Florida as places that offered tropical renewal for white Americans.

Promoters knew that there were many reasons to attract tourists. Tourists brought wealth, raised publicity, and returned as settlers. "This wealthy tourist travel is worth catering to, not alone for the money which it brings into a place, but also for its indirect benefits," a Los Angeles journalist wrote in 1891; pleasure tourists could "make up their minds to remain, or induce their friends to do so," while "others may be led to invest capital and all of them, who are pleased, are good walking advertisements of the place."[7] This was a double-edged sword, of course. Disappointed visitors occasionally denigrated California and Florida because of bad weather, financial annoyances, or other irritations. In 1886, New Yorker Margaret Etheridge Maynard complained of her winter visit to St. Augustine, Florida: "I expected to revel in delicious figs, dates, bananas, Japan plums . . . and all the other things those romancers that write the Florida circulars pretend you are going to have in a 'semi-tropical climate,'" but instead she encountered rain, poor fruit, and pervasive real estate speculation.[8] "Land sharks" who targeted gullible visitors were a problem in both states. As an 1886

California guidebook admitted, "There are land-swindles in California, as there are in Florida."[9] However, visitors who benefited from their experience supported the publicity effort. Dr. A. A. Ward, an Ohioan who came to San Diego County in the 1880s, wrote to the San Diego Chamber of Commerce, "It has benefited my wife's health. . . . I believe if anyone in the first or congestive stage of consumption would come here they would get well, or at least . . . make no further progress for the worse."[10] Invalids and tourists also returned to become residents. The Santa Fe Railroad's Passenger Department reported that "in this way the country has been built up, health and pleasure seekers of one year becoming the settlers of the next."[11]

California and Florida also helped soothe national concerns about the experience of leisure, contributing to a broader shift to consumerist conceptions of U.S. citizenship. In Gilded Age America, vacationing was both desired—as a counterbalance to what many perceived to be an excessively busy, materialistic society—and feared since it ran counter to traditional values of thrift and industry demanded by both Protestantism and republicanism.[12] Boosters of southern California and Florida emphasized the positive consequences of outdoor leisure as a healthful pursuit that improved the citizens of an increasingly industrial and urban United States: the nation's industrial output had increased by 75 percent in the decade after Appomattox.[13] Faced with the shift to industrialization in their society, upper- and middle-class urban Americans worried not only about the influx of immigrants from southern and eastern Europe and the associated threat of working-class unrest but also about the effect on their own physical and mental well-being.[14] While the emergence of the eugenics movement and new organizations dedicated to the restriction of immigration testified to growing concerns about the supposed decline of an Anglo-American race, urban obsessions with "neurasthenia"—a kind of chronic nervousness that had a bewildering array of physical and psychological symptoms—are evidence of a distinct unease with the stultifying effects of modern life.[15] George M. Beard's 1881 treatise *American Nervousness* described neurasthenia in pseudo-scientific language as an affliction caused by "modern civilization," that was "especially frequent and severe in the Northern and Eastern portions of the United States—as "nervousness develops very rapidly in our climate"—and that weakened in particular male "brain-workers" and educated women, both vital elements of U.S. society.[16] The fear that America's overcivilization presaged its fall into "degeneracy" had deep roots in republican ideology, especially the idea that wanton republics (most famously, Rome) would collapse under their own enfeebling pursuit of luxury. But anxiety about the changes in the United States resonated with middle-class Americans familiar with Herbert Spencer's works on social evolution, which argued that organisms were improved or diminished by use or disuse and that environmental inheritances shaped human development.[17] "Nervous exhaustion" was an apparent consequence of America's industrial progress, and Beard frantically warned, "All our civilization hangs by a thread."[18]

As affluent Americans searched for remedies for overcivilization, leisure tourism emerged as a phenomenon with important connotations. Winter vacationing was not new: for decades, wealthy Americans had traveled to southern European and Caribbean resorts. After the Civil War, however, expanded railroad coverage and the growth of an American leisure class precipitated a significant growth in internal tourism.[19] The desire for improved health was often inextricable from a longing for a more primitive environment than the urban North, and race was a crucial identifier of such an environment. Racial primitivism, including the notion of the "noble savage," pervaded the cultural beliefs of middle-class whites, who at once denigrated and envied the "savage" peoples who supposedly lived outside the materialism and restless pace of modern existence.[20] For Beard, "The savage and the child laugh or cry when they feel like it" and therefore lived free from nervous diseases.[21] Tellingly, among the numerous remedies for nervousness that proliferated in the 1880s, many encouraged Anglo-Americans to cultivate relaxation by learning from "Oriental people, the inhabitants of the tropics, and the colored peoples generally."[22]

Because of widespread beliefs in the connection between environment and racial mores, the tropics were a natural setting for American fantasies of restorative leisure. Interest in the tropics had also been fostered by Frederick Edwin Church's popular paintings. Church, who had painted *Niagara* (1857), the icon of the Hudson River School, was a leading landscape artist when he produced a series of paintings on location in Latin America, including *Twilight in the Wilderness* (1860) and *Rainy Season in the Tropics* (1866). Some 12,000 people saw Church's *Heart of the Andes* (1859) in a gallery in New York City and the *New York Times* hailed a painting "in which all the luxuriance of tropical life, and all the varied beauty of organic lines and colors, are displayed in most brilliant effect."[23] These paintings, as one art historian writes, represented a "Colonial Sublime, suggesting that the North American viewer owned the South American view as his back garden."[24] They introduced thousands of Americans to exotic, verdant, and scarcely peopled tropical landscapes. Yet although Church's popularity indicated a growing public appetite for visions of the tropics, the absence of humanity or society in these paintings hinted at the disdain with which whites viewed tropical peoples. As a southern writer commented in 1866, many Americans believed "that tropical and semi-tropical populations are often idle, sensual, effete and miserable."[25] Although the tropics appeared to be an antipode to the crowded, developed North, there was also a curious connection between the two environments: both industrial city and primitive tropic produced a similarly negative effect on inhabitants. The overcivilized American confronted some of the same problems as persons from tropical locales: idleness, effeminacy, degeneracy. Neither location offered hopeful formation narratives for a generation of "nervous" Americans.

Semi-tropical environments within the nation's borders, however, were another matter. According to tourism boosters, California and Florida offered a promising median zone between the two extremes. Healthfulness was a major factor here. Promoters tapped into contemporary medical theories that advised sufferers of nervousness or consumption to travel to such climes for the winter.[26] A health guide to Florida stated that "a large number of persons in the United States are suffering from diseases, the majority of which may be greatly relieved by a change of climate."[27] Numerous texts contrasted the curative effects of California or Florida's climate with the damaging coldness of the North, including statistics of "Deaths from Consumption" (reproduced from census data) that showed their states to be havens for sufferers of the disease.[28] Although the medical benefits of a change of climate were exaggerated (if not illusory), promoters nevertheless persuaded "invalids" to make trips south and west. The arrivals of these visitors drove hotel construction and land investment in California and Florida, opening the way for a broader tourism pursued by pleasure-seekers.

Although the leisure imagery of the two states was connected by the concept of healing climates, the themes of boosterism for the two states were different. Promoters of southern California created a "Spanish fantasy past" that romanticized the pre-U.S. period as a fiesta of easy living and Latin contentment.[29] In 1890, booster-journalist Charles H. Shinn reported an Anglo fascination with the "land of the Padre, the Indian neophyte, the leather-clad Spanish soldier, and the jovial old Spanish ranchero." Incoming tourists imagined "the true lotus land where no one ever had a care, and where it seemed as if it were always afternoon."[30] In Florida, wilderness dominated booster imagery. Although the Civil War site of Fort Pickens in Pensacola harbor became a popular site for tourists, promoters of peninsular Florida largely eschewed the region's human-created past and instead sold tourists on its verdant nature, including river and hunting excursions that opened up the "healthful influences of nature" far "removed from the contentions of a busy life," as a New Yorker visiting Florida for health reasons wrote.[31] Boosters depicted ethnic and racial minorities in the two states in similar ways: as "picturesque" natives for the curious gaze of

Anglo-Americans. Southern California and Florida were also both envisaged as sites where white women could become healthier and more fertile and white sportsmen, released from effete urbanity, could reclaim their masculinity. The two states were presented as tropical destinations that supported traditional notions of race and gender.

Tourism boosters thus affixed notions of tropical leisure to Anglo-American ideals of social progress and economic development. They located pleasure and relaxation as natural characteristics of the modern civilizations that were emerging in the two states, setting California and Florida apart from the destructive effects of modern urban America. The 1885 *Florida Annual* declared, "Thousands of souls are yet to find in South Florida the one place in North America where they can realize their ideal of a semi-tropical home, where a life of easy comfort can be enjoyed under laws and political institutions adapted to American genius."[32] Boosters presented California and Florida as places where wealth could be invested, as exotic lands that were sources of capitalist growth—that vital characteristic that, as much as "laws and political institutions," distinguished "American genius" from tropical societies. As a travel writer stated in an 1885 *Los Angeles Times* piece on the two states, "Despite sundry disadvantages . . . Florida will yet be one of the twin garden spots of the New World, and excepting the El Dorado of the Pacific, the brightest, sunniest clime in all this broad land—a veritable paradise to the tourist and the invalid, where health will come on healing wings, and wealth will follow in its train. Then all hail! to the two great sanitariums of the globe—Florida and California!"[33]

Semi-Tropical California for Health and Pleasure

The promotion of semi-tropical California to tourists incorporated two major strands: a fascination with the healthfulness of the climate "for imparting vim and energy to a tired and fatigued system" and a romanticized mythology of the region.[34] As Kevin Starr writes, "Two key symbols of identification for [the] emerging region were the sun and the Spanish past."[35] Each fed into new formation narratives for Anglo-Americans who could improve in an exotic setting that served as a therapeutic alternative to the rapidly industrializing East. Although California had been a U.S. state since 1850, it seemed decidedly foreign to most visitors. The California Excursion Association reported how "by many travellers this country is likened unto Palestine," and references to Italy, Spain, and Mexico were also commonplace.[36] The land, one visitor observed, featured "the sun, the genial air, and the fruits, flowers, and semitropical suggestions of a perpetual summer."[37] Tourism boosters encouraged "orientalized" visions of southern California as somewhere that was in the process of evolving from a romantic foreign backwater to a progressive Anglo-American civilization. Boosters translated the ongoing displacement of Spanish-Mexican culture and peoples into a "picturesque" tourist experience, even though the region's rapid development meshed awkwardly with longings for a premodern escape. A fascination with what was being displaced thus fueled tourist growth, and boosters displayed a kind of "imperialist nostalgia": the desire to possess and promote what they helped destroy.[38]

Railroad construction made the tourism phenomenon possible by bringing southern California within the reach of affluent easterners. Seven years after the transnational railroad was finished in 1869, the Southern Pacific Railroad completed a line from San Francisco to Los Angeles. Direct tracks between southern California and the East soon followed—in 1881, the Southern Pacific connected with the Texas and Pacific at El Paso; a new, independent Southern Pacific line to New Orleans was finished two years later; and in 1885 the Santa Fe Railroad was completed, breaking the Southern Pacific's monopoly, reducing fares, and contributing to a brief real estate boom in Los Angeles County. In 1870, there was not a single mile of railroad in southern California; twenty years later, the region boasted over 2,000 miles.[39] As an American railroad agent wrote in 1896, the railroads "have shortened the distance to southern California thousands of miles and made it possible for tourists and investors to visit your semi-tropic land with every chance of their becoming converts to your health-giving sunshine and beautiful surroundings."[40] The railroads were leading boosters; they published thousands of pamphlets, funded magazines, and formed passenger departments that hailed the health and pleasure benefits of "semi-tropical" California. In a typical description, L. H. Nutting of the Southern Pacific informed tourists that the state was "originally part of Mexico [and] has inherited [Mexico's] good name for healthfulness of climate." It was a region where "hues of the ocean and sky rival the tropics, and the profusion of vegetable life and loveliness also suggest a far-southern clime." But Nutting reassured readers that, in California, "every man lives under his own vine and fig-tree, and breathes the free air of America."[41]

Although the geographical boundaries of the region were not always fixed, semi-tropical California became synonymous with southern California. For William Henry Bishop in 1882, southern California was everywhere south of San Francisco; for other promoters then and later, it was the counties south of Tehachapi Pass.[42] In either case, intrastate contrasts emerged in the tourism literature of California. Southern California, for example, did not include the Yosemite Valley, which became a famous destination for tourists that was representative of the rugged West of spectacular views and hunting thrills.[43] In southern California, by contrast, climate and health effects were paramount and the region was more representative of lands beyond the U.S.'s southern border. As one West Coast promoter explained, "Semi-Tropical California" consisted of counties whose "climate—or, more properly speaking, climates— are milder and show less variation between winter and summer."[44] Localized booster organizations heightened the internal divisions. Defining southern California as "from the northern part of Santa Barbara County to the Mexican line" (about 30 percent of the state), the Southern California Bureau of Information declared, "The climate of California is good; that of Southern California is better."[45]

The emergence of semi-tropical California as a promotional phenomenon contributed to deep cultural, economic, and political tensions between the state's up-and-coming southern counties and its older northern ones.[46] In Northern California, long the powerhouse of the state, boosters reacted jealously to the growth of southern California and showed a reluctance to reapportion political representation. For their part, some southern California promoters called for a split in the state. "So unlike are the California of the North and the California of the South that already two distinct people are growing up," wrote Los Angeles promoter and climatologist Joseph P. Widney, who pushed for southern California to become independent in 1888.[47] Widney's political position was a minority one, to be sure. Large booster organizations such as the Southern Pacific Railroad spanned the entire state—its headquarters were in San Francisco and it had extensive holdings across southern California—and saw the development of the southern counties as a benefit for all of California. Nonetheless, as Widney observed, a distinct "California of the South" was developing in which semi-tropicality was becoming a defining feature.

Tropical references increasingly permeated the selling of southern California to tourists.[48] A freak summer hail storm in Pasadena in 1884 was reported as "a novel experience for a semi-tropical paradise in June."[49] Mary Vail, whose 1888 pamphlet was intended as an antidote to the more fanciful claims of real estate dealers, stated that "California, and southern California in particular, lies in a semi-tropic clime."[50] An 1888 guide to Santa Barbara promised visitors an enchanting stay by "Semi-Tropic Seas," while a representative collection of "souvenir views" described a lush park with palm trees as "a typical Southern California semi-tropic scene."[51] Palm trees were not, in fact, native to the region; they had been introduced by horticulturists who delighted in the exotic ambience they provided. Countless souvenir photographs featured palm-lined streets, and guides reported the admiration of tourists for the luxuriant vegeta-

Figure 2.1. A typical example of the visual promotion of Los Angeles, a city that benefited from a strong good roads movement that turned it and its environs into an "automobilist's paradise." *Source*: *California Souvenir Views: A Collection of 64 Views of California and Arizona* (Los Angeles: B. R., 1902). Courtesy of Department of Special Collections, Charles E. Young Research Library, UCLA.

tion of southern Californian parks and boulevards (Fig. 2.1). Visitors imbibed this imagery. "The land," writer and lecturer Kate Sanborn reported of southern California in 1893, "is not a tropical one, but a semi-tropical."[52]

The curative attributes of California's winter climate, meanwhile, supported formation narratives of an American tropic of hope for ailing visitors. Its "health-giving, invigorating, and ever-enjoyable climate," declared an 1888 pamphlet, made California a place "where hope is extended to all sufferers" of weariness or disease in the East.[53] Individual examples of recovery were presented as proof. In 1880, for example, one magazine reported that a Cincinnati grain merchant who spent the winter in southern California for health reasons was "much improved," adding that "he has spent the past four years in Florida" (apparently with no such recuperation).[54] Collectively such cases constituted a "health rush" of "nervous" and "pulmonary exiles" from the East to southern California.[55]

As with Florida, California's quasi-tropical climate was cast as a remedy for the psychological and physical maladies associated with the frigid industrial Northeast. As Massachusetts-born writer Helen Hunt Jackson explained in an 1883 magazine article, "Climate is to a country what temperament is to a man—

Fate."[56] Arguing that climate, like temperament, determined the "point of view of a man's mental and spiritual vision," Jackson asserted that a change of climate potentially allowed for a more hopeful outlook on life for neurasthenic Americans. Southern California was particularly alluring because its semi-tropical climate suggested the contented freedom of the tropics without undermining the progressive traits of natives of colder climes. For Jackson, "The tropics are tropic because the sun shines down too straight: vegetation leaps into luxuriance under the nearly vertical ray; but human activities languish; intellect is supine; only the passions, human nature's rank weed growths, thrive."[57] Her view was typical of Anglo-American conceptions of tropical backwardness, a belief that also accounted for the fascination of many whites with the tropics as places released from the constraints of civilization. Civilization had developed in "the temperate zone, [where] the sun strikes the earth too much aslant. Human activities develop; intellect is keen; the balance of passion and reason is normally adjusted; but vegetation is slow and restricted. As compared with the productiveness of the tropics, the best that the temperate zone can do is scanty." In this view, even though northerners had superior rational capabilities, they were divorced from a kind of latent productivity that only the tropics provided. In certain locales, however, the stark divisions vanished: "There are a few spots on the globe where the conditions of the country override these laws, and do away with these lines of discrimination in favors. Florida, Italy, the south of France and of Spain, a few islands, and South California, complete the list. These places are doubly dowered. They have the wealths [sic] of the two zones, without the drawbacks of either."[58] Like the Mediterranean countries but "new"—and therefore untainted by Old World problems of overcivilization or entrenched political corruption—the environments of the United States' semi-tropics could provide personal and social reinvigoration.

The California Excursion Association, a leading promoter of tourism in the region, used semi-tropical imagery as a metaphor for the state's regenerative qualities. Founded and managed by Warner Bros. in the 1880s, the association, a tour operator based in Los Angeles, disseminated detailed pamphlets about southern California throughout the East and Midwest.[59] The company recognized the role these texts played in attracting tourists: as C. A. Warner explained in a booster meeting held August 14, 1888, at the San Diego Chamber of Commerce, the covers of their guidebooks were crucial since "a person who picks up such a book is inclined to read it, if the outside catches his eyes.... He sees the words, 'Southern California,' and wants to know something more about this subject."[60] Significantly, the association's 1887 guide was entitled *Southern California: A Semi-Tropic Paradise* (Fig. 2.2).

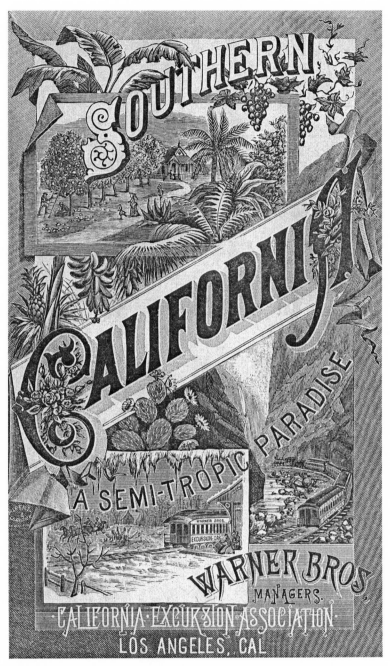

Figure 2.2. Many promotional images emphasized California's semi-tropical bounty. *Source*: Warner Bros., *Southern California: A Semi-Tropic Paradise* (Los Angeles: Times-Mirror Co., 1887). Courtesy of the California Historical Society, San Francisco, California.

The cover depicted a landscape bursting with cacti, fruit, and palm trees, traversed by the civilizing symbol of the excursion train in the foreground and inhabited by a family with a cottage set in a citrus grove. California's semi-tropical nature, such images asserted, could be enjoyed with the foundations of modern technology and domestic comfort in place. Inside, the pamphlet gave ample reasons for those easterners who were "stimulate[d] . . . to overwork, mental and physical," and "suffering from nervous prostration" to visit the West Coast.[61] American readers were informed that they were weakened by an excess of "electricity"—a consequence of cold climates and mechanical technologies—but that relief could be found in an extended stay in southern California, a region that was "almost non-electrical." This lack of electricity led some new-comers to think they were becoming "lazy" when in fact they were experiencing the "healing power of nature." Advertisers stressed the "wonderful coolness of our almost tropical position," which made "health resort[s]" such as the Hotel Arcadia in Santa Monica a year-round delight. Elsewhere the guidebook high-lighted the "resources and commercial prosperity of our Semi-Tropic Land," and it encouraged wealthy tourists to invest in the booming region.[62]

Indeed, the idea of investing in land and houses was increasingly prominent in promotional literature. "Nowhere within the Union can wealth make a home surrounded with beauty and tropical growth so speedily as in Southern Cali-fornia," the *Los Angeles Mirror* stated.[63] Theodore Van Dyke's 1886 guidebook connected tourism to profitable opportunities created by increasing land prices. Van Dyke was already a renowned promoter, having written two popular trea-tises on hunting and fishing in California, but his 1886 work highlighted the climate's influence on health and pleasure and the economic benefits it prom-ised.[64] "We have yet to read any book wherein a more careful and thorough resume is presented of the climate of Southern California, a question so vital to invalids," wrote a *New York Times* reviewer.[65] "The number of people here who were once invalids, but who now appear as well as any one, is very great," Van Dyke wrote, before turning his attention to the phenomenon of higher land values. "Their prices may be based upon a false foundation—to wit, climate, scenery, and general comfort. Nevertheless, people pay them."[66] Van Dyke at-tributed this willingness to pay higher prices for land to southern California's recent emergence as a leisure destination, which had created such an increase in the "demand [for land] . . . that the shrewdest and wealthiest businessmen-men familiar with Florida and all the pleasure resorts of America—consider it a certain basis of calculation." Evidence for this could be found in the bold new plans to build a hotel at the cost of over $300,000 on Coronado Beach, which would, in time, "make the rarest watering-place in the world," bordered by the

Pacific and "a thousand gardens [of] tropic fruits."[67] As health and pleasure tourists flooded into the region, many coastal hotels were built to cater to the more affluent, including the Arlington in Santa Barbara (1876), the Southern Pacific–owned Del Monte in Monterey (1880), and, south of San Diego, the Coronado (1889), the largest and one of the most luxurious hotels in the world of the time. By 1900, more than 100 tourist hotels were in operation in south-ern California, symbols of the region's emergence from northern California's shadow into a place where sun-kissed leisure defined the landscape.[68]

Promoters of tourism in southern California juxtaposed these modern at-tractions with visions of a romanticized and vanishing regional history. For example, Van Dyke wrote of "the old Spanish ranch-house glimmering afar through the hazy sunshine in which the silent land lay always sleeping."[69] As boosters asserted the benefits of California's semi-tropical climate, they simul-taneously constructed what historians refer to as a "Spanish fantasy past" that presented a history of paternalistic friars, romantic fiestas, heroic vaqueros, crumbling missions, contented Native American workers, and a leisure-filled Latin existence.[70] This fantasy version of the past was a curious shift in the region's self-image.[71] In earlier decades, Anglo-Americans had disdained Cali-fornia's pre-American past, but in the 1880s and 1890s they romanticized the Spanish-Franciscan period, creating a pervasive motif in southern California that influenced boosterism, art, literature, theatre, architecture, clothing design, and songs. This new version of the past spawned tourism events such as La Fiesta de Los Angeles and the Mission Play, a three-hour-long pageant about California's mission heritage. "There has been a sudden development of interest in the Spanish days of the southwest and the Pacific coast," remarked Charles Shinn in 1890. "Literature begins to recognize the lasting and unique elements of romance in the long-trampled native Californian, whom the *gringo* squatter called a 'greaser,' and robbed or shot."[72]

Indeed, literature was crucial to this shift, since a work of fiction—Helen Hunt Jackson's 1884 novel *Ramona*—catalyzed the Spanish fantasy past into a promotional theme. The book was originally written to expose the maltreat-ment of Native Americans in the state—in Jackson's mind, a kind of *Uncle Tom's Cabin* for California's mission Indians. The plot told of a tragic love affair in Spanish-era California between Ramona and Alessandro, an Indian, who loses his land to and then is murdered by white squatters. However, the book's greatest effect was that it generated interest in a romanticized version of Span-ish California that effectively sanitized the brutalities of racial conquest and enticed thousands of eastern tourists to the region.[73] The book sold 7,000 cop-ies within three months of publication and went on to become a national best seller.[74] Within a few years, promoters were hailing *Ramona* for having struck "deep into the vein of gold-bearing quartz" that became the Spanish fantasy past.[75] Easterners were drawn by Jackson's descriptions of the "delicious, languid, semi-tropic summer [that] came hovering over the valley," and *Ramona* was the inspiration for countless pleasure tours in southern California. Visitors could tour Ramona's "real" home, the ruined missions, and old Spanish neighborhoods in search of this "languid" Latin past.[76] The railroads were more than happy to provide excursions. A reporter explained in 1898, "There are very few spots where the old-time Spanish ranchero, with its princely hospitality, its extraordinary generosity and its delightful manana [sic] customs, yet remains at all intact, and these few spots are in several old Spanish settlements along the line of the Santa Fe Railroad from Santa Ana to Oceanside."[77] Residents absorbed the imagery too: although the public library in Los Angeles owned 100 copies of *Ramona*, there was a waiting list for the novel in which, the city librarian recalled, the "characters are pure fiction . . . but the scenes are photographically true."[78]

The Spanish fantasy past tapped into the desire of Anglo-Americans for preindustrial modes of leisure. In an 1899 guidebook published by the Santa Fe Railroad, Charles Keeler captured the ideal of idle Latin pleasure: "They were the days of dark caballeros with gay costumes and jangling spurs . . . of tinkling guitars that marked the rhythm for merry dancers, and of free, open-handed hospitality."[79] Implicitly such imagery softened the harsh realities of American displacement of Mexican communities.[80] The tourist boom of the 1870s and 1880s further changed the social status of Mexicans in southern California, where "the Mexican population fell from majority to minority status."[81] The expanding tourism trade created a need for a "service-worker labor force" to build and maintain hotels and urban improvements, and Spanish-surnamed persons who were squeezed out of better occupations and off the land increasingly filled menial positions.[82] Although ostensibly giving voice to California's Spanish-Mexican heritage, the Spanish fantasy past took the focus away from the modern reality that Mexican American residents of the state were being pushed off the land and into menial wage labor.[83]

Mexican communities in California became part of Anglo tourist itineraries. Boosters converted impoverished ethnic barrios into picturesque landmarks befitting a quasi-tropical destination. Describing the Los Angeles barrio of "Spanish Town," a magazine writer bade the reader: "Come, let us go through Sonora."[84] The barrio "revived" in American visitors a "recollection of Mexico . . . but of a very shabby and provincial Mexico": mescal and tequila were easily available (signs of the amoral tendencies of the locals), while the quarter had the scenic "vestiges of an arcade system of the kind known in some form to travellers in most tropical or semi-tropical countries." American tourists could wander the Mexican quarter safe in the knowledge that this was American soil and the natives were unthreatening remnants of a conquered society: a people "which has gone to the wall" and were "for the most part engaged in the coarser kind of work," "improvident, and apparently contented with their lot." Promoters presented Mexican poverty through the lens of "historic" Latin contentment, affirming the interlinked hierarchies of race and class in California. "Only here and there . . . a Spanish name . . . rises into prominence in the state of which they were once owners."[85]

Tourism boosters offered spatial and temporal journeys into Spanish California that promised escape from the stresses of industrial America. Guides reported the "picturesque scenes of Mission, Mexican and Indian life . . . with their manners and customs utterly foreign to anything else found in the United States."[86] Another travel book explained, "To see Capistrano, or San Luis Rey, or Santa Ines, is almost like visiting a foreign land . . . oriental in character."[87] As tourists entered premodern surroundings, they could experience an environment typified by leisure and pleasure rather than American graft and work. This positive portrayal did not extend to positive appraisals of Mexicans in the region, however. Even Jackson wrote that Mexicans in California had lived unproductively, "with no thought or purpose for a future more defined than 'Some other time; not to-day.'"[88] This explained why the "restless" and "insatiable . . . Yankee[s]" were California's "conquerors"; part of the "inexorable logic" by which "the country steadily [fulfilled]" its "destiny." Yet the colonialist rhetoric of conquest mixed nostalgia with envy about how these "old" Californians had lived. There was a "charm" in Spanish California: "Simply out of sunshine, [the Californios] had distilled . . . an Orientalism as fine in its way as that made in the East by generations of prophets, crusaders, and poets." Seeking new formation narratives, Anglo-Americans in southern California hoped to imbibe this foreign charm and shed their nervous conditions. Perhaps, Jackson wrote, "as the [Spanish] generations move on, the atmosphere of life in the sunny empire they lost will . . . revert more and more to their type," leading ultimately to a "toning down" of the "tireless Yankee beat" and a happier United States in which "money and work will not be the highest values."[89] A different kind of ambivalence characterized the ways boosters encouraged tourists to visit California's Chinatowns. Advising every tourist to visit Chinatown both in the daytime and at night, J. P. Widney added that "the Chinaman . . . is dishonest, generally insolent, and, after making . . . the family dinner, spends his nights gambling in the dirty hovels of Chinatown."[90]

Nevertheless, as an 1896 booster magazine noted, "'Chinatown' is the Mecca of tourists."[91]

Somewhat paradoxically, tourism promoters directed these fantasies of escape from America's material obsessions toward regional economic growth. La Fiesta de Los Angeles, a lucrative Spanish-themed weeklong festival that the Los Angeles Chamber of Commerce had begun in 1894, was inspired by both the Mardi Gras tradition of New Orleans and the desire of Anglo-Americans in Los Angeles to adopt Latin-style leisure.[92] "The Saxon is too little a man of holidays," one writer explained. "Environment has had most to do with this."[93] The lure of exotic California for tourists had a growing cash value. As promoter Charles F. Lummis wrote, "Of those who come merely to *see* California, a vast proportion are attracted by our Romance," to the extent that "the Missions are, next to our climate and its consequences, the best capital Southern California has."[94] A profound contradiction thus ran through the images presented to tourists. In the jargon of the period, "civilization" was, at its heart, an economic concept; the term was used to mean a society driven by commerce.[95] Promoters invariably shared the view that capitalist growth was synonymous with civilizing progress. The concept of overcivilization, however, included profound fears that America had become excessively materialistic and lost touch with nature and joys more basic than money-making. The reason the Spanish fantasy past was so popular was partly because it suggested a happier society unspoiled by capitalist ambition. This posed problems for boosters. For Harry Ellington Brook, the Californios' was "an easy-going and picturesque existence [in which] money . . . was scarcely needed" or valued.[96] The arrival of Anglo-Americans had ended this "easy-going order of things"—which, Brook quickly stressed, was "of course a change for the better. It was the coming of what we call 'civilization.'"[97] Yet boosters also liked to consider a potential curtailing of American excesses in semi-tropical California. Casting the region as the meeting point of the "two bloods [who] share the Western Continent," the "old Campo Santo" and the "Anglo-Teuton," J. P. Widney wondered if the "kindly spirit of that type of [Spanish] civilization which is now rapidly passing away" might yet improve Anglo-Americans, since it "had in it nothing of the rush and the drive, the restless energy" of California's conquerors.[98] Half-articulated in such passages lurked an unspoken unease that, by selling southern California, Americans risked diluting its very appeal as a semi-tropical retreat from industrial development.

Such contradictions notwithstanding, promoters hailed the tourist pleasures of a pre-capitalist Spanish California as they built and sold hotels and towns across the region. Development reached a crescendo when competition among railroads and the influx of winter visitors sparked a three-year real estate boom centered in Los Angeles County that began in 1886.[99] The value of city lots increased almost daily. The speculative frenzy collapsed under absurdly inflated prices, briefly damaging southern California's growing national reputation. As Charles Turrill of the San Diego Chamber of Commerce wrote, "During the winter season of the year . . . the number of visitors to Southern California is greater than at any other time. Without any fixed occupation except the pursuit of pleasure, it is natural that these should frequently be induced by the flaring advertisements and by all the machinery of the real estate gambler, to speculate in lots. And . . . it is only the unlucky who squeal. Such has been the case in Southern California."[100] The boom-and-bust experience exposed the contradictions in the promotional imagery. Surveying the height of the boom, Charles Dudley Warner wrote the following verdict: "If the present expectations of transferring half-frozen Eastern and Northern people there by the railway companies and land-owners are half realized, Southern California, in its whole extent, will soon present the appearance of a mass-meeting, each individual fighting for a lot and for his perpendicular section of climate."[101] While booster groups would have appreciated acknowledgement of their role in attracting "half-frozen Eastern and Northern people," the prophecy of a southern California swarming with people would have riled those who depicted an idyllic destination free from the exasperating problems of modern materialism. "For the invalid or tired one of the world," as one representative statement went, "there are [in southern California] soft tones, divine odors and restful breezes to lull him into forgetfulness of the rush and hurry and stress and toil he has left behind."[102] Some astute observers recognized that rapid development put this promotional narrative at risk. Tourists desired pristine nature and Latin heritage, Grace Ellery Channing observed in 1890, yet opportunities to find these resources were diminishing. "For, year by year, as the ranches go, as the 'Greaser' and the Indian go, as all the semi-tropical Spanish Bohemianism is driven farther back, the picturesque-loving tourist takes refuge more and more in 'tramping' it through the by-ways of California."[103]

For southern California's tourism promoters, the nostalgia had its limits. Despite the negative press that followed the bust, the region rebounded quickly. "There is perhaps no section of the country which is attracting more attention from the tourist than Southern California," stated a passenger agent for the Alton Railroad Company in Chicago in 1894.[104] By the turn of the century, it was estimated that over 20,000 tourists came annually for the winter to Los Angeles alone.[105] The boom also confirmed the desire of Americans to benefit from semi-tropical California financially as well as in terms of health and pleasure. The lesson for the Southern California Bureau of Information was obvious: "This southern California climate has a specific money value . . . a definite commercial value above and beyond its desirability as a means of imparting renewed life and vigor to the sick and dependent."[106] Both the effects of the climate and the "driving back" of the region's "Spanish Bohemianism" were cited as evidence of a positive racial transformation: a shift from Latin to Anglo dominance. "White Americans seldom, if ever, contract consumption here," a medical doctor informed the Chicago Tribune in 1892. "It not infrequently carries off the native Mexican and Indian races, but I cannot recall a single case of a white person contracting the disease in Southern California."[107] The Spanish fantasy past, meanwhile, served as a springboard for American rejuvenation in new pleasure resorts. As Charles Keeler wrote, "The power of the missions is gone, the people to whom they ministered are largely dead and scattered, and the buildings are rapidly crumbling into dust. . . . They hold the poet and painter in their spell, but for the pleasure-seeker there are brighter scenes and happier hours awaiting in the modern centers of life, where the past is forgotten and where the days are too short to crowd in all the diversions which are at hand."[108]

For boosters, this life of outdoor pleasures meant Americans who were healthier than the "nervously exhausted" men and women of the East. A magazine article on the "California Woman" declared, "First and best of all, California offers woman Nature's greatest gift, good health." In fact, the article claimed that it was common "to hear tourists and visitors comment favorably upon the physiques of the California women," who were "much taller than the average women of the Middle and Atlantic Coast States," "more robust," and "rosier, healthier, and prettier." Highlighting the connection between environment and human evolution, the writer added that this improved condition was "largely a result of our delightful out-of-door weather."[109] Famous tourists reinforced southern California's emergence as a place where Anglo-Americans could recover their health. In 1895, Elizabeth Bacon Custer, the widow of Gen. George Custer, recounted in a California magazine her railroad journey across "the long strip of American desert," which made her group long to be "rewarded . . . after coming out of that hopeless country, with every evidence of tropical luxuriance."[110] They were not disappointed, finding Southern California to be as exotic as Italy but far superior in social terms. While it was difficult in Italy to "escape from the sight of beggars, from squalor and poverty," American tourists in southern California could "see all that nature can do" and enjoy the "old missions [that] . . . add immensely to the picturesqueness of the land" but "at the same time [be] in the midst of our own countrymen, the most delightful people in the world, and made more so by the sunshine that mellows and enriches nature." The near-

Figure 2.3. California magazines attracted tourists to the West Coast with images of outdoor leisure and healthful living in "winterless" semi-tropical California. *Source: Land of Sunshine* 3, no. 2 (July 1895): 57. Courtesy of Mandeville Special Collections Library, University of California, San Diego, California.

tropical setting made physical and psychological renewal possible. "There is nothing like the effect that life in the open air has upon the disposition as well as the health," Custer wrote. The article included an image of a white couple relaxing amid the leafy vegetation of a California garden (Fig. 2.3).

Such pictures of healthy white Americans at home in tropical surroundings infused the formation narratives of southern California. Consider the cover of *The Land of Sunshine*, a pamphlet published by the Southern California Bureau of Information that was disseminated at the 1893 World's Fair in Chicago. The image showed in the foreground a flowering garden and a classically dressed woman (reminiscent of the image of Columbia that had graced earlier paintings that celebrated westward expansion). An embodiment of youth and health-fulness, she held a bough of oranges against her loins, implying a connection between the fruitfulness of California and the fruitfulness of the state's human inhabitants (Figure 2.4).

Behind her spread a serene landscape of tall palms, orchards, and a Fran-ciscan mission—all symbols of the region's tourist appeal. But the land was marked also by clear signs of American technological enterprise: a steamship

Figure 2.4. In this promotional image, California's version of Lady Liberty casts her gaze over a semi-tropical landscape that offers both romantic and modern pursuits, including missions, citrus groves, and steam-powered technology. *Source:* Harry Ellington Brook, *The Land of Sunshine: Southern California* (Los Angeles: Southern California Bureau of Information, 1893). Courtesy of the California History Room, California State Library, Sacramento, California.

and steam engine navigated the semi-tropical land that thus thrived with "energetic" progress. Indeed, the approving gaze of the woman fell in the direction of the steam-powered innovations of industrial technology, affirming them as benign but not dominant features of this "land of sunshine." Sufficiently domesticated by modern technology, southern California represented for Anglo-Americans a unique opening: a tropic destination, as the Chicago fairgoers were told, that was home to "none of the depressing heat or the insect pests" of rival Florida. Instead, it offered a "bracing . . . climate that makes the sick well and the strong more vigorous."[111] Health was thus married to wealth in California, where leisure had become a serious business. "I think over all the lovely features of that semi-tropical land," Custer wrote, "[and] they all beckon to me to return."[112]

Semi-Tropical Florida for Health and Pleasure

As winter tourism became a bigger phenomenon in the United States, southern California promoters grew wary of the postwar recovery of the Gulf South. Boosters presented both California and Florida as sites of restorative climates and nature and invalids in the colder North responded, a trend noted by the self-named "Exile" in an 1882 letter to the *Florida Dispatch*. The author had traveled for health reasons to Santa Barbara from Pennsylvania, where he had owned a farm neighboring that of the recipients of his correspondence, the Ashmead brothers, who had since moved to Jacksonville, Florida, and become publishers of the *Dispatch*. Like numerous boosters, including the *Los Angeles Times*, which reprinted his letter, Exile saw a strong connection between their new homes: "Florida and California are the twin sisters of Uncle Sam, separated, to be sure, by a long distance, but having many points of similarity," among them a historical foreignness, a healthful climate, and unique opportunities for development.[113] "First, they have both been obtained from the Spanish, the relics of whose civilization, language and customs still remain as a fringe to the social life of the inheritors. Then, too, both claim an unexceptionable climate; but are sparsely settled, both are rich in undeveloped possibilities, and both are washed by the ocean." The differences, the writer claimed, were "probably more emphatic" than the similarities—topographically, for example, "sloppy" Florida was much flatter and wetter, while mountainous California's rainy season came in the winter, not in the summer—and thus personal preferences were inevitable: "The arid parched look of nature [in southern California] from June to November is at first gruesome; but I must believe that our drier country and our lack of rank vegetation are advantages not possessed by

Florida." Nonetheless he concluded that a special union existed between California and Florida: both states competed for and received the seasonal influxes of "exile[d]" Americans, especially "the over-worked busy men and the nervously prostrated women of the colder North."[114]

Although small numbers of invalids had traveled to Florida before the Civil War, the state emerged as an American "sanitarium" in the decades after the war.[115] The state's claims of healthfulness were aided by a report by the surgeon-general of the United States Army that stated that "as respects health[,] the climate of Florida stands pre-eminent."[116] The report, which was quoted extensively in promotional texts, indicated that cases of malaria contracted in Florida were mild compared to elsewhere in the country, refuting notions about the dangers of the state's swamplike conditions (in winter, at least).[117] Most health-seekers came to the northeastern part of the state, staying in the seaboard towns of Jacksonville and St. Augustine, from where they visited freshwater spas such as Silver Springs and took steamboat trips along the St. Johns and Ocklawaha Rivers.[118] Tourists came by steamboat and train into Jacksonville, which served as the state's entrepôt until railroads penetrated the peninsula in the 1880s. Prior to then, the Civil War, limited state finances, and complex litigation issues meant that Florida's scant railroad mileage hardly increased at all from 1860 to 1880 (402 to only 518 miles).[119] In the 1880s, however, magnates Henry Plant and Henry Flagler, who received generous land grants from the state's Redeemer governments, constructed railroad networks and lavish hotels down the Gulf and Atlantic coasts, opening the peninsula to extensive winter tourism. In 1888, New Englander George Canning Hill proclaimed that "the rest of the country has found its Persian gardens" in Florida's new resorts that were being built down "a peninsula [that] projected . . . into the neighborhood of the tropics."[120]

As had happened in southern California, tourism to Florida evolved from a phenomenon built around a warm, restorative climate into a growth industry infused with ideas of tropical leisure. Promoters focused on two tropes: the recuperative qualities of climate and the peninsula's "wildness of tropical vegetation," which suggested gendered benefits for visitors that included an opportunity for men to develop masculine virtues and associations of female fertility with tropical bounty.[121] No Spanish fantasy past was constructed to sell Florida, with the notable exceptions of local promotion of St. Augustine (the capital of Spanish Florida) and recurrent references to conquistador Ponce de Leon's legendary quest for the fountain of youth.[122] Daniel G. Brinton's 1869 guidebook commented that the "ancient fame [of the fountain of youth] still clings to the peninsula," where "the tide of wanderers in search of the healing and rejuvenating waters still sets thitherward."[123] Whereas California boosters drew upon a premodern Spanish backdrop of ease and romance, promoters of peninsular Florida largely eschewed its human-made history as a destructive mess of European trading, Indian Wars, slavery, and sectional strife. In the words of Manatee County booster Samuel Upham, "Florida . . . has, during the past 350 years, been hustled about from pillar to post like a shuttle-cock."[124] Instead, promoters focused on the allure of Florida's tropical nature, which promised another form of escape from industrial America.

Playing on the antimodernist fantasies of northerners, Florida boosters depicted their state as a therapeutic alternative to the "overworked," "active business country" of the North.[125] Brinton's guide warned: "The harassing strain of our American life, our over-active, excitable, national temperament" made advisable a "timely and judicious change of climate," and Florida was an ideal destination.[126] Sidney Lanier, who was commissioned by the Atlantic Coast Line Railroad in 1875 to write a travel guide, wrote, "The question of Florida is a question of an indefinite enlargement of many people's pleasures and of many people's existences as against that universal killing ague of modern life—the fever of the unrest of trade throbbing through the long chill of a seven-months' winter."[127] This emphasis on tropical forms of leisure was a particularly Floridian phenomenon and one that applied especially to the Florida peninsula. Whereas boosters of the state's panhandle region tended to draw upon the "Old South" imagery of cotton plantations and aristocratic planters that pervaded literature that promoted tourism to the postwar South, boosters presented the peninsula as a more exotic proposition.[128] Links with the Caribbean contributed to the region's tropical imagery, and Florida excursion companies encouraged tourists to visit Havana and Nassau, often after seeing Key West—a town where "the number of Cubans and Spaniards seen, the queer and incessant jargon of foreign tongues add much towards its tropical and non-American appearance."[129] Promoters compared Florida's climate to that of Cuba and Barbados to reinforce ideas of the peninsula as a place that resembled the Caribbean tropics as much as the American South.[130]

As had happened in California, the rise of a new part of Florida contributed to intrastate divisions that were at once cultural, economic, and political. While the panhandle had been home to most of Florida's population and wealth before the Civil War, the peninsula came to the fore as a tourist destination in the postwar decades, sparking tensions between the older "cotton" counties and the peninsular counties (including six new counties that were formed in 1887).[131] Promotion fed into evolving intrastate identities as boosters more clearly delineated between Florida's different regions and attractions. In the three climatic sections of the state James Wood Davidson's 1889 guidebook identified ("Northern Florida," "Semi-tropical Florida," and "Subtropical Florida"), "Semi-tropical Florida" covered the majority of the peninsula, marked off at the north by a diagonal line from Cedar Keys to Fernandina and at the south by Lake Okeechobee. "Semi-tropical Florida enjoys an equability decidedly greater than does Northern Florida," Davidson explained.[132]

The lure of tropical nature drew tourists down into the peninsula. The Clyde Steamship Company, a leading tour boat agency, explained how "passengers have their first glimpse of tropical Florida" as ships from New York approached the St Johns River, adding that that glimpse was "fascinating and picturesque."[133] For these visitors, Palatka, a winter resort town on the St. Johns River, offered "green foliage and golden fruit [that] give the locality a picturesque and semi-tropical appearance." Beyond the town, where the river "contracts," the "tropic heavens smile upon the weird and wondrous scene [that] thrills the traveler's soul."[134] These tropical locales could be safely reached because of modern technology, promoters assured their readers, assuaging any fears northerners might have about abandoning civilization completely. The cover of an 1882 tourist guide, *Illustrated Florida*, presented a jungle-like coastal setting of palm trees, birds, and alligators in which a steamship floated in the background—a necessary reminder that the "accessories of civilization" navigated this tropical corner of the United States (Figure 2.5).

Visitors to the peninsula imbibed the ideal of tropical adventure. As renowned novelist Elizabeth Stuart Phelps traveled by train to Florida in 1876, she mused: "Now we have fairly set our faces towards the tropics. Do I consider St. Augustine . . . as situated in the tropics? . . . [I replied] that I am open to conviction on the matter, but that I certainly supposed that Florida was—perhaps it *would* be more accurate to say semi-tropical."[135]

Gendered formation narratives informed the selling of tourism to Florida's tropic of hopes. These often supported a patriarchal ideal in which white men combated effete overcivilization through virile activities such as hunting and women were "released" from the supposedly unwomanly and neurasthenia-inducing demands of urban modernity. "In no other country are the daughters (the future mothers of the nation) so *rapidly* educated [and] stimulated to abnormal mental exertion," one tourist guide explained.[136] This lamentable consequence of American progress had created a "rapid increase" in "the number of nervous women" in the North, while falling birth rates reinforced the fear that Anglo-American women were being abnormally affected by modern life.[137] The near-tropics of Florida offered vital reinvigoration. Brinton found much to admire in the potential effects of the state's climate on American women: "A

Figure 2.5. In the 1870s and 1880s, steamships carried tourists deeper into the Florida peninsula, which offered scenes of tropical exoticism and the wildlife that made hunting a popular
winter sport in the state. *Source*: Dodge Art Publishing Company, *Illustrated Florida* (Buffalo: Dodge Art Publishing Co., 1882). From the P. K. Yonge Library of Florida History,
George A. Smathers Libraries, University of Florida.

warm climate promises aid where medicines are utterly ineffectual. I mean in
marriages not blessed by offspring. Most readers know how early females are
married in the tropics. Mothers of fourteen and sixteen years are not uncom-
mon. Heat stimulates powerfully the faculty of reproduction."[138] White tourists in Florida could expect this environment-induced fertility to be passed on
to their own bodies. This idea implicitly raised problematic issues relating to
other effects of tropical "heat," given the tendency for Euro-Americans to see
"tropical races"—African Americans in particular but also Latin Americans—
as sexually licentious and unrestrained.[139] For Helen Hunt Jackson, the "heat"
of the tropics "stimulated" in its inhabitants not only fertility but certain baser
instincts: passions that potentially endangered Victorian sexual and gender
codes. But boosters such as Brinton located the "tropicalization" of northern
women in Florida's climate within a clear political framework: "The wives of the
French colonists in Algiers are notably more fertile than when in their Northern homes."[140] For French colonists in Algiers, he substituted American tourists
in Florida. Although the latter were not colonial rulers, they could nevertheless
derive environmental benefits from tropical relocation without succumbing to
the degeneracy of the natives.[141]

Heightened female fertility in the tropics of Florida shaped the thinking of another promoter who, in an 1888 pamphlet, featured it as part of a lengthy comparison of Florida and southern California. "The climate of Southern California is masculine, while that of Florida is feminine," he wrote. "The climate of Southern California will benefit the male sex more readily, while that of Florida acts more speedily upon females."[142] Perhaps he based this rather curious analysis on the gender division of population in the two states. Because of the Gold Rush, California in 1850 had been predominantly male (over 90 percent). Despite the evening out of the ratio in subsequent decades, males still constituted 60 percent of the state's population in 1880. The population of Florida, by contrast, was a nearly even split between the sexes (Table 2.1). This particular promoter's statement was hardly representative of Florida tourism boosters in general, who advocated the ways that their state "acted" upon both male and female tourists, notably improving "the worn-out man of business [who] will find the necessary relaxation from 'brain-fag'" in myriad "opportunities to take outdoor exercise, plenty of sunshine, pure and bracing air," and other, more violent, pursuits.[143]

Tropical Florida was sold to male tourists as a "hunter's paradise": a wilderness where men could temporarily leave behind the plush surroundings of the hotel and indulge in uncivilized, reinvigorating pursuits.[144] "Here," declared a pamphlet for the Hotel Ormond, "civilization and the wilderness sit cheek by jowl."[145] The masculine renewal Florida offered supported what Richard Slotkin has described as the American faith in "regeneration through violence."[146] Ideas of the state's tropical wildness tantalized tourists in Florida: a female visitor commented "that you are in the tropics when you get among things that bite."[147] For male visitors frustrated with urban lives that divorced them

Table 2.1. Percent population by gender, California and Florida, 1850–1900

Year	California		Florida	
	% male	% female	% male	% female
1850	92.4	7.6	52.5	47.5
1860	71.9	28.1	51.9	48.1
1870	62.3	37.7	50	50
1880	59.9	40.1	50.6	49.4
1890	57.7	42.3	51.6	48.4
1900	55.3	44.7	52.1	47.9

Source: Carter et al., Historical Statistics of the United States: Millennial Edition, 1:27, 213.

from the formation narratives of frontier America, boosters depicted an animal bounty awaiting conquest throughout "the Heart of Tropical Florida."[148] On steamers down the St. Johns, Indian, and Ocklawaha Rivers, male tourists shot at all manner of creatures, including alligators, whose numbers were rapidly reduced along those waterways. A typical experience on the Ocklawaha was described by a tourist from Chicago: "The scenery becomes more tropical, the palms appear on the banks, the white herons and egrets on the flats, and the alligators in the river—causing great excitement among the newcomers, and a general discharge of rifles from the upper decks, most of the bullets of these raw sportsmen glancing harmlessly from the mailed sides of the great saurian as he flounders into the stream."[149] Although female visitors such as Harriet Beecher Stowe objected to the blood sports, hunting became integral to Florida's appeal to tourists. Railroad and steamship companies promised a "Paradise for Sports-men" where "the tourist, with a passion for hunting, may find good sport" in the "succession of forests, prairies, 'hammocks,' swamps and marshes."[150] Two New York "sportsmen" who called themselves the "Alligator Brigade" were annual vis-itors to the St. Johns River, where, on one trip, they killed deer, wildcats, wild hogs, and at least twelve alligators.[151] By 1890, alligator hides and teeth were estimated to be worth $40,000 yearly to Florida's economy.[152] But the draw of hunting "things that bite" as well as birds was of greater significance to the state. Along with fishing—guidebooks informed tourists that they could "get far away from all signs of civilization on many of Florida's streams"—hunting supported the selling of Florida as a tropical site for masculine regeneration.[153]

High-profile visitors such as Thomas Edison and Henry Ford, both of whom purchased property in Fort Myers on the west coast of the peninsula, drew attention to Florida as a haven for sufferers of neurasthenia and seasonal ailments. In March 1885, an ailing Edison traveled to Fort Myers, where he recovered his health. "The Electrical Wizard's Health Improving with Florida Air," the *Boston Globe* reported.[154] Edison bought fourteen acres by the Caloo-sahatchee River and hosted famous guests such as Harvey Firestone and Henry Ford. The publicity generated by such events helped launch a local tourism industry in Fort Myers, which quickly grew into a town.[155] In 1892, Edison's father, Samuel, whose health was affected by the harsh climate of his Michigan home, stayed at his son's Florida property, where, the *New York Times* reported, he could benefit from "the balmy breezes of the sunny South."[156] The senior Edison was part of the growing phenomenon of winter visitors who traveled farther into the Florida peninsula.

As had happened in southern California, the promotion of Florida as a semi-tropical escape from overcivilization fueled interest in real estate and internal improvements in the state, including a southward expansion into the peninsula. The state's railroad facilities grew rapidly between 1880 and 1885, when predominantly northern investment produced more than 1,000 miles of tracks across the state.[157] The length of time it took to travel from New York to Jacksonville was shortened to as little as thirty-six hours and made more comfortable with luxury trains such as the Florida Special. Although figures from promotional literature are hardly reliable, one pamphlet estimated that 164,000 visitors registered at Florida hotels in the winter of 1885—a somewhat deceptive figure in that individual tourists often stayed in multiple hotels while in Florida—almost half that of the state's resident population.[158] Northerner Henry Sanford, founder of the central Florida town bearing his name, hailed the internal improvements as confirmation of his "long time predictions about Florida as the winter resort for health and pleasure of the people north of it. . . . The movement toward Florida to-day, I am satisfied, is but a driblet in comparison with the stream which, in steadily increasing volume, must inevitably pour down upon the only bit of semi-tropical country under our flag."[159] This latter claim, of course, chose to ignore Florida's West Coast rival, where promoters were hailing the "peerless, lovely golden valleys of Semi-Tropical California."[160]

Taking advantage of the extended railroad links, tourists increasingly ventured beyond the Jacksonville–St. Augustine route to experience tropical parts of Florida firsthand. From 1882, travelers heading from the St. Johns River to Titusville rode the Jacksonville, Tampa and Key West Railway's Tropical Trunk Line. Tourists in Kissimmee in south-central Florida stayed in the town's new Tropical Hotel. "Anyone having a fondness for exploration may reach within a few hours from Kissimmee as tropical, luxuriant, and weird a wilderness as there is this side of Africa," a pamphlet declared.[161] Rockledge on the Indian River offered Tropical House, a hotel for 150 guests that advertised "boating, fishing, oysters, hunting, rocky shore, superb scenery, together with the finest Oranges, Bananas, Pineapples, and Guavas."[162] Rooms were $2.50 per night. Tourists purchased and built winter homes in new resorts such as Winter Park, Maitland, and Longwood, which, a state guide explained, were being "filled with the cottage homes of wealthy Northerners, who here spend the months from November to May, in the midst of orange groves, flowers, and the other surroundings of the semi-tropics."[163] Pleasure tourism increasingly matched health-seeking as the motive for travel to Florida. "It is no longer the invalids who have the monopoly in the migration southward," wrote Oliver Crosby in his 1887 guidebook. "It has become the fashion for people who can afford it to either own a cottage in an orange grove, or engage rooms at a hotel in our wonderful climate."[164]

This shift moved the state into fiercer competition with southern California, where promoters responded to Florida's popularity with often-bitter apprais-als.[165] An 1885 guide to the Southern Pacific's new Sunset Route to California featured a sage old traveler lecturing a naïve younger man on where to go for winter: "As I have said to you, dozens of times, drop Florida, at once and for-ever. . . . It amazes me unspeakably to witness the annual exodus of northern people to Florida as soon as the holidays are over."[166] The narrator targeted Florida's social and environmental drawbacks, declaring that tourists were bet-ter off wintering in California, where they would be "free from the petty extor-tions and annoying financial snares which are the inevitable accompaniment of hotel life in Florida," where it was unpleasantly moist.[167] Southern California promoters used the language of tropicality to both sell their state and denigrate their rival, playing especially on fears that Florida had a damp, energy-sapping atmosphere.[168] The *Los Angeles Times* stated matter-of-factly that "the climate of Florida is admittedly inferior to that of Southern California."[169] This was a two-way street. Complaining that the Pacific state's boosters "scruple not at anything that will build up California's reputation," including "defaming Florida and seeking to poison the public mind against her," Florida promoters used the same tactics, often depicting California as desperately arid.[170] The profuse nature to be found in Florida, declared a writer in the *Dispatch*, was better than "a land barren of vegetation and fairly parched for want of water."[171] A degree of envy underpinned these criticisms, which intensified during southern California's boom in land prices in the 1880s. Florida's sellers complained that "the Californians evidently find it necessary to work their little boom for all it is worth while some of Florida's tourists[,] for a change, have taken advantage of the low rates to take a look at that State."[172] That year northern railroads ominously reported "The California Movement—People Going to Southern California, Instead of Florida."[173]

However, the 1880s was the decade when Henry Plant and Henry Flagler—two northern capitalists turned railroad and hotel developers—gave new impe-tus to tourism in Florida. The "Rhodeses of the American tropics," in C. Vann Woodward's apt phrasing, enjoyed a healthy intrastate competition. While the Plant System linked up the peninsula's Gulf Coast, reaching the small town of Tampa in 1885, where Plant had built the ornate Tampa Bay Hotel, Flagler accumulated existing tracks and then built new lines down the state's Atlan-tic coast, constructing the luxuriant Alcazar and Ponce de Leon Hotels in St. Augustine in 1888 before extending links to southern Florida, where he helped found Palm Beach and Miami.[174] Like the Southern Pacific Company in the West, the Plant Company and Flagler's Florida East Coast Railway Company incorporated railroads, passenger departments, land companies, and hotels into vast operations.[175] The hotels became social and sporting symbols of Florida. Tourists at Flagler's Alcazar Hotel could take part in the Tropical Tennis Championship.[176] An Indiana tourist wrote home that Aladdin's lamp could not have compared to the sight of the Tampa Bay Hotel's 1,000 rooms lit up with electric lights in the midst of "gorgeously tropical grounds."[177] By virtue of its relative proximity for tourists, visiting Florida was cheaper than was California. In 1894, the cost of traveling from Chicago to Florida was less than one-fourth of the cost of traveling from Chicago to the Pacific coast.[178] By the turn of the century, Florida's coastal hotels were being celebrated as the final links in an American "chain of pleasure palaces which stretches from the tropics to the frontier of the land of snow and ice."[179]

Figure 2.6. Florida river vistas were used to entice tourists, as were spectacles of impoverished African Americans, often children. *Source: Beauties of the Ocklawaha and Tampa* (Philadelphia: J. Murray Jordan, 1890). From the P. K. Yonge Library of Florida History, George A. Smathers Libraries, University of Florida.

These resorts were constructed at the same time that Jim Crow segregation began in Florida, and Plant and Flagler's companies enticed wealthy white northerners by linking tropical leisure with African American subservience. They were far from alone in showing southern blacks as exotic figures for white consumption. Tourists observed, often in racist terms, how young African Americans and fruits were the 'chief productions to the visitor' in Florida resorts such as St. Augustine.[180] The inclusion of an African American child in a Florida steamship company's sequence of images advertising tourism on the Ocklawaha River was typical in promotional images of this era (Fig. 2.6).

The large hotel companies expanded this advertising motif, casting black children and servants as features that enhanced the leisure experiences of An-

glo-Americans. Although white visitors were not advised to tour black neigh-borhoods in Florida in the same way they were encouraged to see Chinatowns and "Spanish Towns" in southern California, African Americans were almost as prominent as exotic fruits and flora in the selling of Florida's tropic of hopes. A typical Plant Company pamphlet advertised Florida's "finest health and plea-sure resorts" with pictures of a pineapple, palm leaves, and three smiling African American children—a collection of tropical "types" that associated Florida with contented African Americans and first-class hotels (Figure 2.7).

The Plant Company photograph of African American boys who were dressed in ragged clothes yet were apparently happy with their lot provided implicit reassurances of a stable racial hierarchy for white tourists who entered a "winter playground" where black poverty existed alongside, albeit segregated from, the luxurious white-only resorts. Promoters sought to delineate a modern role for blacks in Florida with frequent depictions of African American servitude that reinforced images of white leisure. The cover of a Flagler railroad pamphlet of-fered the words "The East Coast of Florida is Paradise Regained" and showed two African American porters who held out a bag of golf clubs and a suitcase. The image suggested that tourists could expect grinning obedience from blacks on the hotel's Eden-like grounds (Figure 2.8).

The racial undertones of Florida tourism were perhaps most evident in the phenomenon of "Afromobiling." In the 1890s, Afromobiles—rickshaw-type carts that tourists sat in while being pushed or pulled by African American hotel employees—became a popular form of transportation from the hotel to the beach, town, or golf course.[181] Images of Afromobiling proliferated in promo-tional materials for south Florida locations.[182] A dialogue in an 1891 pamphlet for the Hotel Ormond revealed the antimodern thrill of the experience:

"What makes us go?" inquired a woman's voice from the depth of our car.

"It's not an underground cable," said a man on the rear platform, cran-ing his neck to look at the ground.

"Nor an electric," said another, looking skyward for the wire.

"It's a small beast," exclaimed a third, peering over the dash-board.[183]

The "small beast" was in fact an African American man, whose pedaling powered the vehicle and enabled the leisure travelers to thoroughly revel in the experi-ence. In Flagler-developed Palm Beach, where motor cars were prohibited from its founding in 1893, Afromobiling became an iconic attraction at the exclusive resorts that capitalists such as Jay Gould and writers such as Henry James vis-ited.[184] Boosters fetishized the experience of "a horseless carriage propelled by

Figure 2.7. By the 1890s, the Plant System of railroads traversed the Gulf Coast of the peninsula. Henry B. Plant's companies used images of grinning African American children in advertisements for their railroads and hotels, a motif that masked the harsh realities of Jim Crow. *Source: Map of the Plant System—5094 Miles* (Buffalo: Matthews, Northrup & Co., n.d.) From the P. K. Yonge Library of Florida History, George A. Smathers Libraries, University of Florida.

Figure 2.8.Florida's first golf course was built in 1897 in Palm Beach, and golf soon became hugely popular among guests at luxuriant hotels. Black caddies and hotel porters provided the labor that supported tropical leisure. *Source:* Florida East Coast Railway, *Florida East Coast: The East Coast of Florida Is Paradise Regained* (Jacksonville: The Florida East Coast Railway Company, 1904). From the P. K. Yonge Library of Florida History, Department of Special and Area Studies Collections, George A. Smathers Libraries, University of Florida.

a motor with a smiling charcoal face."[185] Afromobiling became an enactment of the desires of whites for explicit forms of racial hierarchy in Florida. As Harrison Rhodes wrote in a 1917 guidebook to "Vacation America," Palm Beach's "most characteristic sport is the wheel chair—the Afro-mobile, so-called from the black slave of the pedal who propels you."[186]

Florida was thus sold to tourists as an American state that satisfied colonialist appetites for tropical pleasure and racial dominance. Through racial, environmental, and gendered imagery, promoters created an image of wintering in Florida's coastal resorts as a brand of escape from "busy" America—a luxuriant experience that, as one northern visitor exclaimed, could "excite in the mind visions of life in the orient."[187] But promoters always sought to control these fantasies by placing them within the security of modern America. Thus, tourists who purchased winter homes in Florida were said to have found the best of both worlds: "such luxuries of the Tropics with [the] comforts of the Temperate Zone!"[188]

In the late nineteenth century, formation narratives of American renewal linked California and Florida as seasonal semi-tropical destinations for white tourists. Growing anxieties about overcivilization in the urban North gave impetus to representations of two corners of the United States that offered the tropical features of primitivism and leisure. Southern California's boosters cultivated a Spanish fantasy past that encouraged visitors to luxuriate in a romantic history based on ruined missions, Franciscan friars, and dark-eyed Spanish ladies. They converted the poverty of modern Mexicans into a tourist attraction.[189] But the promotional constructions of a precapitalist Spanish society supported intense capitalist development of the region. Los Angeles swelled from a population of 11,000 in 1880 to 50,000 ten years later, and freedom from overcivilization became a precursor to business investment and building construction. As T. D. Stimson, a Chicago investor in California, wrote in 1894, southern California had "transformed from a somewhat isolated health resort into a beautiful and prosperous region, where health, pleasure, and business may be found in combination."[190]

Peninsular Florida competed successfully with southern California as both a winter resort and America's most tropical proposition.[191] The Florida East Coast Railway enticed tourists to come south to experience "America's tropical kingdom."[192] As discussed in the next chapter, this emphasis hurt the attempts of Floridians to attract white settlers who were reluctant to inhabit "torrid" climates. For tourists, however, Florida's tropical qualities conveyed strong attractions, among them "a moral, as well as a physical benefit, [achieved] from this communion with the primitive world."[193] The railroad companies that constructed luxury hotels down the state's coastlines disseminated colonialist representations of African American servitude that added to the reputation of Florida as a tropical paradise for white leisure. Tourists contributed to this tropical-racial imagery and sometimes exposed the virulent racism lurking at its base. In 1894, while southbound on a train heading down Florida's east coast, Harold W. Raymond wrote about how "the foliage lost its memories of the temperate zone and became wholly tropical" and "the negroes in the smoking car going South to shovel sand on the new road were filling the air with happy song.... The Florida 'nigger'—he calls himself that—is the happiest member of his race."[194]

Although it is impossible to quantify the influence of promoters in attracting people, the tourism industries expanded dramatically in California and Florida, both of which became prime destinations for American health and pleasure seekers.[195] As the *Los Angeles Times* reported in 1891, "Florida is the leading competitor of California as a winter resort in the United States."[196] In both states, seasonal tourism acted as an engine of economic growth, creating increased tax revenues and internal improvements, while affluent visitors purchased lands and winter homes.[197] In 1899, the California State Board of Trade remarked with envy that approximately 200,000 tourists visited Florida in each season, bringing at least $10 million into that state.[198] Southern California, it was estimated, received over 100,000 visitors each year shortly after the turn of the century.[199] Even as they competed with and often denigrated one another, southern California and Florida benefited from a rivalry that not only provided healthy competition—the promotion and growth of "Semi-Tropic California" inspired the sellers of "Semi-Tropic Florida" and vice versa—but also legitimized the transformation of two exotic wildernesses into America's "winter playgrounds."[200] In the process, their promoters shaped national conceptions of leisure as a vital activity. By 1900, the American "middle class had established vacationing as a requirement for its physical health and for its spiritual and emotional well-being as well."[201] Southern California and Florida were crucial to this shift, promising not only ease from harsh winters but also release from the worst effects of overcivilized modernity. The formation narratives of American renewal in internal tropics propelled the development of southern California and peninsular Florida into the twin leisure capitals of America. "There seems [*sic*] to be two favored sections in our great big United States where climate, health[,] as well as pleasure seekers go;" a Florida magazine observed in 1905: "California (Southern California) and Florida (Southern Florida), two little bits of land in all our Western hemisphere, where one can feel free from a killing frost and where they can get a breeze from the tropics."[202]

3

The Fruits of Labor

Boosterist Visions of Republican Renewal and Semi-Tropical Agriculture

Reaching beyond efforts to attract health and pleasure seekers, visions of semi-tropical America pervaded the selling of settlement and agriculture in California and Florida. Designed to add to the permanent population and increase the number of acres used for agriculture in each state, this literature was dominated by conceptions of labor rather than leisure. Railroad agents, landowners, and agricultural writers envisioned fecund lands where dedicated settlers could produce rare, profitable crops and achieve independence in areas distant from the industrialized Northeast, where America's free labor ideology appeared to be increasingly threatened.[1] Boosters of California and Florida engaged with an agrarian myth of the West that cherished the expansion into and cultivation of "virgin" lands where individuals could improve on their own through hard work.[2] Promoters modified this discourse by asserting that such efforts would be especially rewarded by the special environments and semi-tropical products of southern California and peninsular Florida. They claimed that the distinctive regions upheld traditional republican ideals of a "society of economically progressive, socially equal, and politically competent citizens."[3] Of its ten- to forty-acre tracts that were available for from $1.25 to $5 per acre, the Florida Land and Improvement Company declared, "Any enterprising man, even if his means are limited, can buy a farm, which in a few years, by good management and industry, will make him independent."[4] Agricultural prosperity would improve underdeveloped regions: "Small farms secure a thrifty, settled section," wrote William H. Martin of the California Immigrant Union. "What a revenue to the industry and wealth of the State . . . would be secured, if some inducement could be made to those who are 'living from hand to mouth,' to take up these valuable little spots, and make for themselves permanent, happy homes!"[5]

This chapter analyzes the promotion of semi-tropical agriculture as the basis for republican societies in California and Florida. A complex blending of idealism and self-interest defined this promotion, which was more inclusive than the literature that promoted tourism. Promoters targeted potential migrants from across classes, welcoming "all moral, intelligent, and industrious men and women," although, as populations and land values rose, they increasingly stressed the importance of "some capital" for settlers interested in horticulture.[6] Land boosters articulated capitalist and agrarian motivations, arguing that settlement (of the right kind) promised economic and social benefits. "It is the proportion of increase [in population] that gives activity to business, and profit to the ownership of land," explained the Southern Pacific Railroad.[7] The railroads not only benefited from selling tickets and land but also gained the new shipping freight that was crucial for their long-term profits.[8] Financial considerations were relevant to all land promoters, who featured economic data, such as crop values, in their literature. Yet many boosters cared for more than just bottom-line incentives; they shared ideals about the kinds of societies that would develop in their states. "We are all immigrants, or their descendants," wrote Florida's commissioner of immigration in 1879. "We give immigration credit for all we are or hope to become."[9] Promoters of immigration to Florida and California saw themselves as facilitators of progress and often excoriated crooked real estate speculators who promised "the Eden of garden-spots—the one Paradise of the earth" because they undermined "the conscientious chronicler of sober truth."[10] As David Vaught has written, horticulturists in California "believed they were cultivating not only specialty crops, but California itself. Their mission was to promote both small, virtuous communities *and* economic development."[11] The dollar and the dream were fused in the promotion of land in semi-tropical America. Striving to entice migrants and colonies, boosters constructed formation narratives of republican citizens operating small farms in California and Florida.

Boosterist assertions that independent farming was possible were a nationwide phenomenon; Kansas, Colorado, Georgia, and Texas were sold as especially suited to successful agriculture.[12] Many of these promoters joined the Farmer's Alliance and the Populist movement that attacked the evils of corporate wealth and sought local "transformation by boosting real estate values, strengthening links with the market, and developing the commercial structure of a modern agricultural society."[13] Although—aided by a decade of bountiful rainfall from the mid-1870s that encouraged farming on the Great Plains—the number of farms in the United States nearly tripled between 1860 and 1890, rural poverty was widespread, and the children of farmers increasingly migrated to cities. Agrarian discontent grew into the Populist movement of the 1890s.[14] Boosters of the West and the South drew upon the core U.S. ideologies of republicanism and continental expansion that hailed the social worth of the independent farmer, but they were also driven by fears about the effects of urbanization and industrialization in the North. In a perversion of core values, urban industrial employers had begun to present "free labor" as the freedom to contract for wages in the labor market rather than ownership of productive property.[15] For many, this shift away from the independence of landownership was inseparable from the traumas of unprecedented levels of economic depression and labor strife, including a nationwide railroad strike in 1877, the Haymarket Riot in 1886, and the Pullman strike in 1894.[16] In the context of class conflict and concentration of wealth, the republican ideal of the United States as a healthy, meritocratic society of producers—in which most men, ideally, owned property—seemed like an outdated dream.

As republican ideals underwent a painful divorce from northern realities, they were projected onto other environments that included southern California and peninsula Florida. These regions were considered to be "new" to white American settlers and were untouched by divisive industrialization, and their once-maligned remoteness became a virtue for promoters who advocated the "connection between agriculture and civilization."[17] As the next chapter shows, irrigation in California and drainage in Florida—technological processes that supported agricultural growth—complemented this boosterist narrative in the Progressive Era. The focus here is on promotional visions of semi-tropical agriculture as an occupation through which "an industrious, economical and sober man, with or without a family," could "raise himself into independent . . . circumstances."[18]

Land companies and state boosters in California and Florida constructed commercial semi-tropical variants of America's agrarian mythology. Southern California and peninsular Florida were sold as places where agricultural ventures could succeed based on individual effort and skill. Lauding reports that "the tendency of the agriculturists" in the state was "toward small farms," the *Florida Dispatch* pointed to California as another place where "the farmers who earn most money per acre are those who have twenty or thirty acres in grapes and other fruit."[19] Land promoters thus recalled the nation's myth of the garden while focusing their hopes on the newness of semi-tropical agriculture.[20] Like

Florida, California was said to be "new," and "the fact that it is new inspires us with the hope, and imparts to us a faith" that "one of the most favored countries of the earth" could emerge there.[21] Both states were said to be peculiarly suited to prosperous small farming and a virtuous citizenry. Because of southern California's natural fertility, long summers, and mild winters, "the productive capacity of the country and its power of supporting a dense population are very great," J. P. Widney wrote.[22] The tendency was toward a "more thorough subdivision of land"; twenty acres, "especially in the fruit districts," was deemed sufficient for the "united labors of a large family."[23] The vision was mirrored in Florida, where the Bureau of Immigration reported that "people are rapidly learning that whether they propose cultivating fruits or vegetables, small tracts well tilled are vastly more profitable than larger areas indifferently cultivated or partially neglected. The small places are the most profitable, and the most satisfactory to the owners."[24]

Agricultural progress was inextricably bound to the tropical qualities of the states. According to promoters, their specialty semi-tropical products, especially citrus, would give producers a virtual monopoly in national markets. As one Florida railroad agent put it, "Agriculture is immensely profitable in Florida because Nature has established for her farmers a certain monopoly."[25] A West Coast grower wrote, "Southern California represents an industry of a character peculiarly its own. Only one other State in the Union—Florida (and perhaps another on a small scale—Louisiana)—is engaged to any extent in the cultivation of semi-tropical fruits."[26] If this distinctiveness posed its own problems—nineteenth-century settlers often sought an area that was climatically and topographically similar to their home state and were intimidated by the unfamiliar requirements of raising food in California and Florida—it was also proof of the unmatched potentialities of the two states as agricultural producers.[27] Here promoters borrowed from Jeffersonian conceptions of political economy: a desirable agrarian society could remain prosperous and healthy so long as it had market connections to a more populous "metropolitan" area.[28] The metropolitan market that purchased products from the agricultural region would sustain the latter's independent constituency without exporting its own social problems. As Joyce Appleby has shown, this republican vision was in fact a profoundly commercial one that championed market-oriented agriculture over purely self-sufficient farming.[29] Land promoters of southern California and Florida revived this Jeffersonian doctrine.[30] Rarely did they depict agriculture in terms of self-sufficiency; instead, they said, settlers and growers would produce rare crops to be shipped to and sold in northeastern and midwestern cities, thereby obtaining a steady income that would support their communities.[31] At a time when industrial dominance in the North was creating starker divisions between workers and employers (and rampant capitalism was increasingly associated with social inequalities), boosters of the semi-tropical states resurrected the republican vision of "a free society of independent men prospering through an expansive commerce in farm commodities."[32]

But the sellers of California and Florida had to confront existing assumptions that seemed to contradict their ideas of self-directed semi-tropical labor. These included white conceptions of hotter regions as enervating places (for whites, at least) where high fertility induced idleness and what little work was done had to be coerced.[33] Responding to the "erroneous idea" that "the mild climate of California begets that lassitude and indisposition to labor so common to tropical climates," N. P. Chipman of the California State Board of Trade stressed that settlers "engage here indoors and outdoors in all the occupations found in the temperate zone . . . and with all the zest and ambition that distinguish the American people elsewhere."[34] As a former slave state with a humid environment, Florida suffered even more than California from misconceptions about the relationship between the climate and labor. State promoters felt the need to warn off potential settlers "who imagine they shall have nothing to do here, but to lie in the shade and eat oranges and bananas, as they fall dead-ripe at their feet," since, in fact, "industry, energy, and perseverance are essential to success, even in this genial climate."[35]

Although both states had tropical characteristics, California and Florida were not identical prospects. While promoters in each state tapped into a historic faith in open land as the seedbed for republican independence, California had the stronger position: it was part of the West that dominated America's most celebrated formation narratives.[36] For Frederick Jackson Turner, "expansion westward with its new opportunities" and "perennial rebirth" had "furnish[ed] the forces dominating American character."[37] Whereas California took strength from this western mythology, Florida faced disadvantages in its efforts to attract settlers because of the South's comparatively "un-American" associations with landed aristocracy, economic stagnation, and military defeat.[38] Florida was also vulnerable to claims that its heat was so great it could harm health. As John F. Richmond of the Sumter County Agricultural and Fruit Growers' Association wrote in 1882, "Many intelligent Americans believe to this day that Southern Florida, though desirable in winter, can be nothing but a sickly burning furnace in summer."[39] Southern California promoters pounced on these ideas. The *Riverside Press and Horticulturist* proclaimed in 1887 that "as a citrus fruit country, Florida is officially and practically taking a back seat. As a winter resort, Florida is to-day playing second fiddle to California. As a place of summer residence the State was always a failure."[40]

Their rivalry notwithstanding, California and Florida both benefited from visions of semi-tropical agriculture as the foundation for new societies that would be relatively undisturbed by the death knells of republicanism that were being heard in the North—namely, the growth of cities, industrial unrest, and the consolidation of wealth in just a few hands.[41] Promoters of both states articulated national anxieties about the diminished prospects for independence based on individual ability. As a Florida immigration agent wrote of the North, "Concentrated capital and keen competition in the progressive centers of trade make the struggle for existence more arduous and the chances for advancement by mere industry and intelligence become fewer every day."[42] Praising the state's fruit-growing industry in 1889, the California State Board of Trade declared, "What [man] seeks after all and above all is a region where his labor is worth most to him."[43] Semi-tropical agriculture rewarded individual labor while requiring less actual physical work; it was "a business demanding no exhaustive labor."[44] Fruit-growing would thus be a pleasurable occupation that was far less arduous than farming elsewhere. "The possessor of a few acres in orange trees," Benjamin Truman explained, "is lifted above the ordinary drudgery of farm labor."[45] But for promoters, "labor" referred not only to manual work but also to the broader concept of the energy and skill individuals directed toward achieving independence from the soil. This viewpoint simultaneously celebrated widespread land ownership and agricultural production and sought to elevate the producer above the drudgery of traditional farming. This was possible because cheap hired labor was available in both states: Native Americans, Asians, and Mexicans in California and African Americans in Florida performed much of the harvest work. White developers desired them, but as field laborers rather than citizens. The images boosters presented of republican settlement provides insight into how racial stratification was made palatable to white settlers. Formation narratives of Anglo-American independence were intertwined with allusions to nonwhite laborers who were available to—yet excluded from—the progressive (read: white) civilizations that were emerging in the two states.

For J. De Barth Shorb, the president of southern California's Horticultural Society in 1880, prosperous agriculture was the lifeblood of republican health. "Where wages are derived principally from the soil, and more especially from the farm owned by the man who has made the wages, you can consider that country safe—free from communism, free of internal revolution, and in but little danger of foreign invasion."[46] Agriculture—and a healthy version of it—would be king in California and Florida, two states that, as America had once done, promised to shed the dead skin of older societies. As the *Los Angeles Times* declared, "Florida is not as other countries. There is no land on the face of the earth, unless it be Southern California, which enjoys the same advantages— the same immunity from heat and cold" and "the same resources of agricultural production"; these two semi-tropical states were "distinct and superior to all other sections of the universe."[47]

Semi-Tropical California for Settlers

California's semi-tropical agriculture was promoted in tandem with the social and physical transformation of the state—especially the shift to diversified horticulture that expanded with irrigation and improved marketing from the 1870s. In analyzing these developments, some historians have highlighted rigid capitalist policies, including the employment of migratory, often nonwhite, workers, a practice that led to industrialized agriculture in California.[48] Kevin Starr and David Vaught, in contrast, argue that a distinctly agrarian-republican self-image characterized California growers, for whom horticulture was separate from sordid northeastern "manufacturing."[49] These conflicting interpretations of California's agricultural identity reflect the diversity of the crops grown in the state, which led to myriad forms and notions of production. When one uses the boosterist literature for the region as a lens, however, the contrasts emerge in a more integrated way. Combining republican and colonialist strains, boosters sold semi-tropical California as a renewing opportunity for independent agriculture, yet they also equated renewal with Anglo-led development and accepted and promoted racial hierarchy as part of this progressive agricultural future.

Visions of semi-tropical agriculture emerged in the depressed 1870s. Agriculture, ironically, was at the root of the state's socioeconomic malaise. California had moved on from the vagaries of gold mining. As one promoter wrote, "the *prosperous* business . . . is not now, as formerly, mining, but agriculture." But precisely what kind of agriculture that would be remained uncertain.[50] In the 1870s, wheat became the state's leading crop.[51] In California's central valley, grain developed into a profitable crop; California's annual production was six times the combined total of that of Oregon and Washington.[52] Yet California wheat production was characterized by large, absentee-owned farms that employed crowds of "tramp" laborers who worked for low wages.[53] The wheat industry appalled journalist Henry George, who wrote a series of pieces from his home in San Francisco that attacked land monopoly and wealth concentration as the perverse consequences of capitalist "progress" and questioned the opportunities for "personal independence" in a future, industrialized California.[54] In his 1879 polemic *Progress and Poverty*, George charged that with the sharper division between "the House of Have and the House of Want, progress is not real and cannot be permanent. The reaction must come."[55] So it did in San Francisco, where a cut in the wages of railroad workers inspired radicalism led by Dennis Kearney and a newly formed Workingmen's Party—local signs of the nationwide hardening of class conflict.

Chinese immigration also undermined California's ability to attract settlers. In San Francisco, Kearney-inspired whites participated in intense agitation against Chinese immigrants.[56] According to railroad promoter B. B. Redding, the publicity given to the "Chinese Question" meant that whites in other states were "led to believe that the small farmer and farm-laborer cannot succeed in this State."[57] A Los Angeles newspaper editor spoke for many whites on the West Coast when he combined racism and nativism to depict the Chinese presence as a direct threat to California's democratic future, concluding that "the welfare of our race and of Republican government in this State demands the exclusion of the Chinese."[58] Spurred by California politicians, both major political parties pursued exclusion in their national platforms, an effort that culminated in 1882, when Congress passed the Chinese Exclusion Act, which barred Chinese nationals from entering the U.S. for a decade and denied citizenship to Chinese who were already in the states.[59] The act, which was well received by whites in California and was renewed in 1892, provided the political basis for the selling of California to white farmers as a place where semi-tropical agriculture rather than wheat would be the defining crops.

For many promoters, the realities of the industrialization of California wheat production were decidedly at odds with the agrarian ideals and socioeconomic benefits they associated with the production of fruit and vegetables. Wheat farms were often vast mechanized operations worked on by hundreds of "tramp" laborers, like the Glenn ranch on the Sacramento River which, in 1879, covered 45,000 acres and employed a "rank and file . . . army" of 500 men at harvest.[60] For railroad agents such as William H. Mills, fruit culture promised higher land values and more shipping freight because fruit could be harvested and transported more frequently than wheat. Furthermore, unlike grain, semitropical agriculture emphasized the distinctiveness of California's environment. "Horticulture, prosecuted under the unrivalled advantages that attend it here, leaves us without a competitor," Mills wrote. "Upon this substantial and enduring basis, the entire industrial structure [of the region] will eventually rise."[61] This "industrial structure" would be defined by small farms—the very antithesis of what was needed to produce California wheat, which even Charles Nordhoff disdained as "not a pleasant system of agriculture, nor one which can be permanent."[62] Southern California, in particular, promised a better kind of progress characterized by prosperous small farms and republican stability. "The industries connected with the orchards, vineyards and gardens of California have an inherent tendency of segregation [of land-holding]," Mills wrote. "Ten acres of orchard, vineyard or garden will afford profitable employment equal to that required upon one thousand acres of ordinary wheat land in this State."[63] If their conservatism and vested interests meant that California land boosters shied away from the land tax proposals of George and loathed the activism of Kearney, they also shared in popular fears that a few wealthy owners would achieve a monopoly on land and that social disintegration would follow and strove to encourage small farms as the basis of a healthier civilization.[64] Fruit-growing on twenty -to forty-acre tracts combined agrarian and capitalist impulses. Writing in 1878, Charles Shinn expressed the Californian hope that "our era of wheat growing and large farms is to change into an era of diversified interests and small, healthy farms, worked by their owners."[65]

To realize this change, California promoters tapped into the American faith in the West as "the spatial site for revitalizing national energies."[66] Westward expansionism provided latent source material for boosters such as former mayor of Los Angeles E. F. Spence, who wrote in the *Californian*, "The emigrating trend of the American farmer is westward," and with the "deplorable . . . tendency among the people to congregate in the cities" in the East, California stepped forth as the ideal home for "the progressive farmer of today. . . . The course of the Star of Empire, civilization and population, has long been toward the West; but here on the bosom of the broad Pacific that star fades away and . . . the typical pioneer, the explorer, the scientist and the progressive American must stop because they can go no further." There, they would build up a superior agricultural civilization because "nowhere else in the world is labor more generously rewarded or the intelligent tiller of the soil receives a readier or richer recompense."[67] William Martin of the California Immigrant Union described small farming as the "natural" western system. He wrote that "the great success of the Western States in rapid improvement and large laboring citizenship lies in the fact that they could offer to the emigrant small farms" from which "a man of small means could . . . get a good start towards independence and wealth."[68] That independence, Martin posited, was particularly attainable in southern California because of its rare agricultural prospects. "Less laborious" than cereal farming, California's "semi-tropical fruit culture" had the "world for a market" and promised improved chances "for a man who has neither a profession nor a lucrative trade, nor much capital, to become independent."[69] Martin, a respected booster, had a successful career as a promoter of semi-tropical America. He was later employed by Florida land companies because of his work in California, after which he returned to the West Coast to work for the San Diego County Immigration Association.

However, one problem with the promotion of southern California as a mecca for agriculture still existed: Anglo-Americans had previously considered the region a "barren, sandy, and desert waste."[70] This culture also fed into American notions of Latin improvidence. "The land was looked upon as only fit for grazing," J. P. Widney wrote, as "the old residents . . . gravely argue[d] that agriculture could not be made to pay."[71] The postconquest influx of white Americans placed increasing pressure on the "old residents," who were forced into expensive litigation to prove that they owned the lands they held under Mexican law.[72] The Californios' precarious status was further weakened by devastating droughts from 1862 to 1864 that killed off cattle, accelerating the dispossession of their holdings.[73] Souvenir guidebooks described "the transition from the native Californian to the Anglo-Saxon element," a change that brought "the new stir of life and activity infused into hitherto torpid and dormant arteries."[74] In the eyes of boosters, the descendants of the Californios were equally "dormant." The Mexican "is not very fond of work, but when it is absolutely necessary to buy candles and pay the musicians for a dance, or buy whiskey, you can rely on him for working as long as the necessity lasts." Compared with energetic Americans, "slowness" was "one of the marvels" of "Mexican work."[75]

Land promoters emphasized agricultural evolution as the destiny of a state now under Anglo-American control. "The old Californians knew but little of the comforts and pleasures of civilized life and cared less," stated the *Pacific Rural Press* in 1886. "But by-and-by came a different people—an industrious, thrifty, civilized people," who arrived from the East to "plant oranges and lemons and vines and . . . build up new and pleasanter homes in this new Italy, of the Pacific slope." Anglo agriculturalists' displacement of the Mexican cattle economy signaled the advent of "modern civilization, with its system of land sales, mortgages, etc., [that] captured both land and cattle, and opened up the country to a new life and a new industry."[76] This "new life" would be supported by irrigation, a process that, promoters asserted, would further break up large Mexican and U.S. landholdings. Promoters believed that irrigating land would raise taxes and land values, thus making it expensive to cling to large parcels. Thus, they argued, irrigation would contribute to the selling off of extensive domains into smaller parcels of land ideal for orchards and gardens, thereby, in theory, producing "the very reverse of monopoly in the land."[77] The result would be middle-class communities of landowners who were independent, prosperous, and close to nature. "It is irrigation, if anything," T. W. Haskins wrote, "that will overcome the growing tendency of people in this country to leave the country and crowd into already congested cities."[78]

Railroad expansion and the settlement of Anglo colonies underwrote the hopeful visions of semi-tropical agriculture in southern California. An 1870 land company prospectus declared, "For the growth of all the semi-tropical, and some of the tropical fruits, there is no country in the world better fitted than the valleys and foothills of the southern portion of this State," which had been "hitherto comparatively neglected."[79] Settler interest in the region had begun even before the completion in 1876 of the Southern Pacific's link between San Francisco and Los Angeles. In 1875, the *Los Angeles Herald* received hundreds of letters of inquiry about southern California from people in Illinois, Nebraska, Michigan, and Minnesota.[80] In Los Angeles, local businessmen formed a chamber of commerce and commissioned A. T. Hawley to write a pamphlet about the county to mark the arrival of the railroad. Hawley's text described increasing land values and foresaw the positive impact of the railroad on the ability of growers to dispatch crops to market.[81] Aware of the skepticism of easterners about the region, Hawley put the potential of southern California in the context of free labor ideology. "I believe that no section of the country offers greater inducements to the industrious, capable seeker after a home, than Los Angeles County."[82] The region had an "almost unlimited" "capacity for production," Hawley claimed, and a "soil and climate unsurpassed for the production of Semi-tropical and ordinary fruits" that needed only "the labor and energy of thousands of families."[83]

The settlement of Anglo colonies reinforced the republican imagery promoters of the region created. Anaheim, Pasadena, Riverside, and numerous other towns in southern California began as colonies: groups of northeastern or midwestern families who banded together to purchase enough land for each family to own a small farm, suggesting a form of settlement that combined economic independence with republican unity. After a severe winter in 1872, a group of Indiana families resolved to organize a cooperative movement and migrate to a milder climate; they considered both southern California and Florida.[84] They chose southern California because they believed it offered fertile soils without the threat of disease or enervation they might have to contend with in Florida. According to a later pamphlet on Pasadena, "Some one of the group had received a letter from a visitor to Southern California" which "told of the warm, genial sunshine, of the trade winds sighing through the orange groves . . . and of the immunity from malaria, yellow fever and other epidemics."[85] They founded the town of Pasadena, which, along with other citrus colonies, became a symbol of southern California's agricultural civilization of independence in a kinder climate. Remarking upon the "social elements," "religious principles," and "temperate habits" of the Pasadena colonists in an 1883 guidebook, *A Southern California Paradise*, George Bancroft wrote: "*These* they transplanted to their new homes, and if watched with the same care . . . they will thrive and bear much good fruit."[86] Semi-tropical fecundity and specialty crops, boosters asserted, made this "colony system" profitable, but the social benefits were also important. The Southern Pacific Company promoted colonies as part of their land policy, which, as land agent Jerome Madden wrote in 1890, "has always been, and is now, to encourage the settlement of its land in small tracts, by persons who will live on and cultivate them."[87] One promotional source claimed that "living on 20-acre farms in a colony is more like living in the suburbs of a city than in a lonely rural community."[88] Thus, "immigrants settling in Semi-Tropical California will not find themselves in a wilderness," as an emigrant magazine explained, but in "a civilized community."[89] The colony system was hailed as "one of the most beneficent of all modern contributions to the comfort, prosperity, and happiness of the human family."[90]

For all the eulogizing of the new colonies, California's fruit culture was still a fledgling industry that faced challenges related to both growing and marketing crops. As late as 1878, Charles Shinn noted that one of the "peculiar drawbacks" of the region's agriculture was the "limited market for perishable produce." The market for the goods southern California growers produced in that decade was limited to San Francisco because it took several days to carry the products to the Midwest and the East.[91] "Distance from market must always fetter more or less the fruit industry of the Pacific slope," a Florida promoter claimed.[92] But he was wrong. In 1877, the first railroad carload of oranges was shipped east (to St. Louis), a precursor to the expanded marketing of California fruits in midwestern and northeastern cities that occurred with new railroad facilities and the development of refrigerated cars in the 1880s.

In the 1870s, techniques for growing citrus remained experimental, though. Southern California settlers were thoroughly unaccustomed to the region's soils and climate. In 1877, growers formed the Southern California Horticultural Society and published journals to improve their prospects as horticultural pioneers. As the secretary of the Southern California Immigration Association wrote, "Farming has to be learned over again in Southern California," a region that was "certainly quite unlike the eastern part of the United States in almost everything that can be mentioned"—which, of course, was the heart of its appeal.[93]

Florida was the notable exception. In the 1870s, Florida was widely considered to be the superior of the two states for the production of citrus fruits.[94] Southern California growers looked to their Florida counterparts for guidance and expertise, corresponding as producers who recognized, as one put it, "the similarity, in many respects[,] of the climate and productions of California and Florida."[95] Florida growers subscribed to California's *Rural Press* just as West Coast growers read the *Florida Dispatch* and the *Florida Agriculturist*. When Floridians proposed that a "national convention of Semi-Tropical Fruit-Growers" be held in Washington, D.C.—a "move [that] directly interests Florida, Louisiana and Southern California"—Californians responded positively, declaring that "as the Florida Fruit-Growers Association is probably the oldest organization of the kind within the three States it should take the initiative in calling the Convention."[96] Through advertising, growers in both states worked to increase demand in the North for fruits that had long been considered luxuries.[97] They also shared agricultural techniques and experience; Thomas Garey's *Orange Culture in California* was recommended in Florida to "progressive orange-growers . . . who desire to become familiar with the advanced ideas and the best practice of our California neighbors."[98]

Southern California's leading promotional journal from 1880 to 1883 was *Semi-Tropic California*, a monthly that was published as an "emigration paper" by the Southern California Horticultural Society.[99] Edited by horticulturist Nathan C. Carter and former Kansas immigration agent George Rice, the journal, which initially expressed concerns that immigration to the West Coast continued to flow predominantly to northern California, Oregon, and Washington Territory, "devoted [itself] to the development of Southern California" through agriculture.[100] The region's scant population was attributed to the legacies of Mexican landholding and ranching that were finally being overcome through irrigation and subdivision.[101] In the first six months of publication, 30,000 issues of *Semi-Tropic California* were disseminated east of the Rockies and the publishers reported receipt of "nearly one thousand letters and postals" from readers who wanted to know more about the region.[102] In its pages, southern California was cast as a "Semi-Tropic Land" that "brought together in magnificent profusion the most perfect specimens of . . . the temperate zones, with equally as perfect ones of the semi-tropic and tropic."[103] This natural bounty supported republican settlement in the form of "hundreds of thousands of opportunities, where a man with a family and little or no means" could "acquire a comfortable home in a few years" if he was persistent and planned carefully.[104] Carter and Rice (who went on to become secretary of the Southern California Immigration Association) advertised their own land in their magazine, including a tract named the "Semi-Tropic California Colony." They presented the land they hoped to sell as thousands of acres that were ideal for growing grapes and oranges, land where "homes of peace and plenty can be made by those who will bring at least $1,000 in money and strong arms and willing hearts to *work* and wait" for the orchards to bear fruit.[105]

The magazine also reported the 1880 visit of President Rutherford B. Hayes to California, including Los Angeles. The first presidential trip to the Pacific Coast was a major boost for southern California. It occurred as the nation was emerging from the depression of the 1870s, and it publicized the almost-complete railroad links with the East that heralded an end to the region's remoteness—what Benjamin Truman described as California's "now relative nearness to the 'States.'"[106] After Hayes had given a public address in Los Angeles commenting on "how Californians have come to consider their State a part of the Union," Alexander Ramsey, his secretary of war, spoke of "the richness of the soil ... and ... beautiful climate."[107] The presidential party's affirmation of the agricultural potential of southern California amplified the claims of boosters that the region only needed further settlement to prosper.[108] Observing that America's "rural spirit" was "dying out" in the East, H. M. La Rue, president of the 1879 California state fair, stressed that "the ultimate object for which we toil and strive is to build up an enduring civilization" founded upon agriculture. California's semi-tropical environment made such a future possible. The "genial climate" and "natural beauty of our scenery, where ... every fruit [will] ripen" meant that "the occupation of farming will ever be attractive and ennobling" on the West Coast.[109] The message was summed up by the *Sacramento Record-Union*: thanks to its climate and soil, California was "the Farmer's Paradise."[110]

Successful colonies became active proponents of this semi-tropical vision. Riverside, which was founded in 1871 by midwesterners, was "extensively advertised throughout the United States" by the Riverside Land and Irrigation Company, which was organized in 1875 by landowners who hoped "that an intelligent and prosperous community shall be established upon their territory."[111] The company targeted "northern and eastern people" in pamphlets describing Riverside's railroad links (the Southern Pacific's Colton station was seven miles away), a "delightful, bracing atmosphere," and impressive orange and lemon crops: 200,000 trees by 1879. In contrast to other warm areas in the United States where disease was a threat—including the "orange-producing districts of Florida" that had been hit with yellow fever—Riverside displayed "perfect immunity" and a low death rate. Moreover, the colony enjoyed a year-round climate that did not induce laziness. "At no time ... was the heat so oppressive as to interrupt outdoor labor, or labor of any kind," the settlers claimed. On a small tract, a farmer could grow fruit as part of a "young and prosperous community" that had attracted some 600 settlers by 1875.[112] Elsewhere the land company advertised its 15,000 acres for "semi-tropical fruit-growing and beautiful and healthful homes" with the pledge that "no lands . . . [would be] sold but to actual settlers."[113]

The republican imagery used to advertise Riverside was inseparable from colonialist assertions that white settlers there could obtain cheap nonwhite labor. The harvesting of fruit in southern California was an intensive seasonal emergency, and even on a small farm hired help was useful, if not vital.[114] White field workers were preferred but they were also scarce, more expensive, and eager to move on. Native Americans instead filled the labor needs. A contributor to the *Pacific Rural Press* visited Riverside in 1872: "There are no roving tribes of Indians in Southern California, but there are a few Catholic Indians, converted by the early missionaries from Mexico, who are peaceable and many of them industrious, and who perform much of the labor here."[115] In its pamphlets, the Riverside Land and Irrigation Company explained how "Indian labor of a reliable character can be obtained as farm hands at 75c per day and board"— less than half what white field hands were paid.[116] The "independence" (or lack thereof) of these Native Americans was not discussed. In his 1886 guidebook, Theodore Van Dyke stated that contrary to eastern concerns, "the Chinese and the Indians are not . . . any drawback." As a minority group prevented by law from further arrivals, the Chinese were useful laborers in the region's developing agricultural sector. "[T]he Chinaman is no meaner than [the white man], and is much cheaper"—although, he added, "no one considers a Chinaman half a substitute for a reliable white man."[117] Racial hierarchy underpinned the selling of semi-tropical colonies such as Riverside as ideal agricultural prospects for white Americans.

Although racial heterogeneity had benefits for growers, California promoters explicitly cast semi-tropical agriculture as the product of white American enterprise. Ignoring the critical labor performed by Native Americans, Mexicans, and Chinese, Charles H. Shinn, the editor of the *California Horticulturist* and a prodigious promoter, referred to semi-tropical agriculture in an 1881 magazine article as an unprecedented "Anglo-Saxon" venture. From his base in San Francisco, Shinn admired the southern counties that were becoming better known through promotional pamphlets and citrus fairs in Riverside and Los Angeles. Shinn took these things as proof that "the irrepressible American has entered a new field—that of intensive horticulture, in a semi-tropic land."[118] Southern California's climate made it superior to lands further south such as Mexico and Central America. While those regions produced similar products, "there is less danger from that direction than people imagine," Shinn wrote. "Orange groves are not planted in a day, nor will New England colonies choose waste wildernesses under a foreign flag when they can live in Southern California on the border of two climatic zones." Indeed, "soil, climate, and location combine to make the semi-tropic fruit center of the world in Southern California."[119] For boosters such as Shinn, California's southern border was not the only difference between a "waste wilderness" (such as Mexico) and a "coming . . . land of almost ideal homes" (southern California). The constituencies who controlled these lands also were crucial to the differences in development of the two regions. Shinn saw California's "tropic south-land" as an uplifting location for "New England colonies" and indicated that the residents of the birthplace of American republicanism could be relocated to an environment that suggested the tropics. Republican society would thus be imported, producing a semi-tropical revitalization of U.S. traditions that were coming under threat in the industrial Northeast. "Let us hope," Shinn concluded, "that in Southern California there will be no million-peopled metropolis, crime-laden, terror-haunted by specters of infamy, and shaken by thousand-spindled machineries." Shinn contrasted this dark vision of modern industry with the sunny agricultural future of the "Saxons" of southern California, who needed only to "develop their distinctive industries as to virtually control the world's markets." California's tropic of hopes thus represented a vital republican alternative to industrial America: "Whole communities of men shall rest, each one under his own orange tree, and blessed in his own garden. Thus, in our own way, we are solving a problem which has perplexed the world. We are shaping a reply to warrior, and social reformer, and nihilist."[120]

The redemptive qualities of semi-tropical agriculture were reiterated by the California Immigration Commission, a Chicago-based organization heavily financed by the Southern Pacific Railroad that focused its efforts on the Midwest. Tropicality adorned the cover of the commission's 1883 guidebook in the shape of a horn of plenty from which bananas and pineapples spilled out. *California: The Cornucopia of the World* was written by commission officer Isaac N. Hoag (Figure 3.1).

As he marketed railroad land priced from $2.50 to $20 per acre and more expensive private land, Hoag stressed the agricultural benefits of a semi-tropical land. "To the farmer, California's climate is at once health and wealth, security and certainty. . . . All animal and vegetable life and growth is strong and healthful and vigorous under its peculiarly benign, resuscitating and perfecting influence."[121] Compared to the arduous labor of midwestern farming, where "tornadoes, cyclones, thunder and lightning" or "scalding hot, sunstroke days in summer" could "destroy crops or delay work in the field," southern California

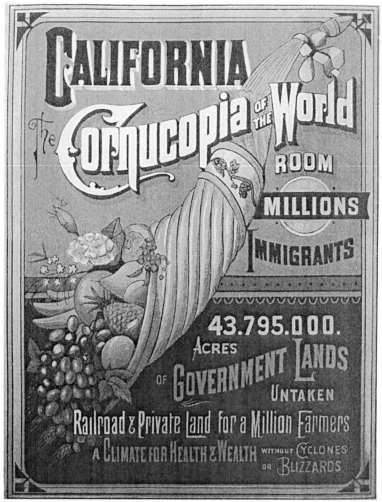

Figure 3.1. California's tropical cornucopia of products, led by citrus, was said to offer millions of Americans opportunities for prosperity on small farms. *Source:* Isaac N. Hoag, *California, the Cornucopia of the World: Room for Millions of Immigrants* (Chicago: Rand McNally, 1883). Courtesy of Department of Special Collections, Charles E. Young Research Library, UCLA.

offered pleasurable, prosperous agriculture. Hoag contrasted California with Illinois, claiming that if the states somehow swapped climates, Illinois land would be immensely more valuable because it would have "a monopoly [on] the semi-tropical fruit products of the United States."[122] Instead, California had that distinction, and citrus cultivation was spreading within the state, such that "we have now a 'Semi-Tropical California' extending from San Diego to within one hundred miles of the line of Oregon."[123]

This growth of "Semi-Tropical California" in the 1880s was attributable to the new railroads and to new promotional techniques, including displays at expositions. After the development of refrigerated railway cars in the 1880s, the Southern Pacific and Santa Fe Railroads began shipping semi-tropical crops to northeastern markets.[124] The California State Board of Trade explained the significance of these changes: "As methods of handling improve and rates of freight cheapen, fruit can be sent in larger quantities and be sold cheaper, and still leave a good profit."[125] Because of competition between railroads, the cost of shipping fruit fell from $3.38 per pound in 1871 to $1.37 per pound in 1888. Once the market expanded, fruit cultivation promised a prosperous, small-farming society: wine and fruit yielded an average income of $104 per acre, compared to $19 per acre for grain.[126] "In California you could hardly say that the average wheat farm was less than 640 acres," the Board of Trade stated, but "the farm unit in fruit culture under irrigation is not more than twenty acres," which meant that "thirty-two families shall occupy the land that one occupied before."[127]

Individual settlers in southern California both reinforced and undermined the images the boosters promoted. "Pioneer," an easterner who settled in Ventura County, wrote favorably of the county's agricultural progress, which included citrus-producing foothill "gardens" of from five to forty acres and a new railroad link that would be completed in 1886. Although Ventura County was less renowned than other counties in the region, it offered to "the industrious settler" the opportunity "to procure a good home in a desirable locality."[128] But settlers also warned those back East against notions of easy independence. "I can understand how some of the States' people meet with disappointment on coming to California," wrote Calvin Fletcher in an 1880 letter to the *Indiana Farmer*, explaining that some settlers had failed, in part, because they clung to the agricultural methods of their home states.[129] Other concerns for settlers of limited means included increasing land values in certain citrus regions and the need to produce other crops while semi-tropical orchards matured.[130] As the California State Board of Trade informed settlers, budded citrus trees came into full bearing at five years from planting and seedlings at eight, at which point each tree would produce three to five boxes of fruit (or between 432 and 720 oranges).[131] Many of these issues were acknowledged in booster literature, which continued to attract settlers to the West Coast. Pamphlets about California that were sent to Champaign, Illinois, for example, led ten families to send two representatives to the Pacific state, where they registered with the State Board of Trade with a view to purchasing land and migrating to California.[132]

The railroads advertised southern California and its semi-tropical agriculture at expositions in the Northeast, the Midwest, and the South that were attended by thousands of visitors. At the 1885 World's Fair in New Orleans, California won the gold medal for the best display of citrus fruit—an award that commentators deemed "a magnificent advertisement for the State."[133] A West Coast booster explained, "Our most formidable competitor was Florida, which had the advantage of nearness to the place of exhibition, and made great efforts to carry off the prize."[134] In 1889, promoters initiated California on Wheels, a train that carried the state's fruit on "a tour of two seasons [and] visited all the leading cities and most of the smaller towns in the northern part of the United States." The train was seen by 1.5 million people.[135] Exhibition trains, organizers noted, were not new: the Canadian Pacific Railroad and the Northern Pacific Railway were already using them, as was the Chicago, Milwaukee, and St. Paul Railroad, which "had a car sent out from Florida" that "was meeting with grand results."[136] But California on Wheels, with its oranges and vines, conveyed a specific promotional message. As Los Angeles booster C. A. Warner commented, the easterner viewing the displays "will realize the fact that he can come out here on a farm of ten acres, and can farm with great deal better results than he could farm on 160 acres [in the] East."[137] Fruit exhibits supported the assertions of boosters that "a semi-tropical climate, with plenty of water for the soil, gives land a greater value for agriculture than all the rains that a temperate climate can possibly afford. Such a climate has California. Such supply of water has California, and these circumstances are rendering her truly the farmer's country."[138]

In a change from earlier decades, migrants in the 1880s moved to southern California in greater numbers than to the northern parts of the state. Reduced railroad fares in the 1880s enticed thousands of Americans to southern California, the population of which, over the decade, increased by 136,981. (In contrast, the Sacramento Valley grew by only 11,779 in the same decade.)[139] The six counties of southern California constituted only 7.5 percent of the state's population in 1880, but by 1890, they accounted for nearly 17 percent, and this figure continued to rise.[140] Semi-tropical agriculture was vital to this settlement. As J. P. Irish of the State Board of Trade's Immigration Committee reported in 1895, "The counties which show the most advancement in wealth [and population] are those in which the principal product is fruit."[141]

Formation narratives of republican settlement played a fundamental role in the emergence of semi-tropical California as a desirable region for agriculture on small farms. "What Southern California needs above all other things," an 1888 pamphlet declared, "is a large influx of industrious and intelligent tillers of the soil"—settlers "whether possessed of much or little capital" who brought with them the intrinsic American qualities "of brawn, energy, and persistent faith in the glorious possibilities of this sun-kissed land."[142] For many settlers, the glorious possibilities were realized. Through the 1880s, land values in orange colonies such as Riverside rose significantly, and southern California developed a reputation in the East as expensive. Charging that this belief was "mistaken," A. A. Ward, a settler from Ohio, described in 1888 how, in general, "the actual need, after landing, is but little, if any[,] greater than in most of the western states." Ward argued that in southern California, a man, "if industrious[,] can make money on ten acres, plenty of it."[143] The notion that industry would be rewarded was thus embedded in the selling of southern California. America's West Coast tropic meant renewed hope for an independent republican citizenry. In the words of a settler from Indiana, California was a state where a person's agricultural endeavor met with results and, thus, "you will find your social position just what you deserve" in a "sunny land where through time a worthy race will claim foothold."[144]

Semi-Tropical Florida for Settlers

Florida land boosters, like their counterparts in southern California, advertised semi-tropical agriculture as a unique opportunity for independence for Americans "rich or poor, who come to our State with willing hands, a frugal mind, and an honest purpose."[145] Promoters of the peninsula state also engaged with the myth of the West as a means of attracting settlers. Recalling the traditional cry of "Go West, young man," Helen Harcourt declared in her 1889 guidebook that "Florida . . . with her sunny smile and warmth of welcome, stepped forward into the light, offering far more than all the much-vaunted West could bestow."[146] Such claims distanced Florida from many of the negative associations with the plantation South. For promoters, semi-tropical fruit culture was a healthier agricultural alternative, one that brought Florida "closer" to California.[147] Nonetheless, Florida was inextricably fused to the South, and it was more difficult for Florida promoters to sell the vision of a renewing agriculture than it was for their counterparts in California. As land surveyor and editor of the *Florida New-Yorker* John MacDonald wrote in 1883, "Few of our northern people" have "had any faith in either the people or the lands of the South," especially since "Westward, Ho! was the cry" of U.S. expansion.[148]

The economic realities of the postbellum South made matters worse, and Florida was cash poor even among the defeated Confederate states. In 1870, the average value of a farm's land and buildings in California was $5,953; in Florida, it was $777.[149] In the absence of available capital, the State Bureau of Immigration was forced to rely on private advertisements and contributions from counties to fund its annual guides to the state's land prices, soil types, and "social conditions."[150] Like California, Florida suffered from legal controversies about who owned land, some of which dated as far as back as the Spanish period. In addition, the Internal Improvement Fund, the body in charge of state land, was unable to provide grants to railroad developers because of a legal injunction related to an unpaid debt that lasted until 1881.[151] Florida's existing railways were "in a condition of financial chaos and physical decrepitude," with scarcely 400 miles of tracks statewide, none of which penetrated into the peninsula.[152]

For northerners, the Civil War cast a psychological shadow over the state. "In our correspondence," immigration commissioner J. S. Adams wrote, "the question is often asked, 'Is it safe for a Northern man to come to Florida?'"[153] Adams, of course, answered that it was, but the fears of northerners about Florida were not that easily assuaged, particularly as Reconstruction brought federal military rule to the former Confederacy and southern resentment against "carpetbaggers" from the North grew.[154] "There is nothing that has operated so disastrously to the cause of southern immigration as the disorders that have grown out of the late war," immigration commissioner Dennis Eagan wrote in 1873, although he claimed that Florida had avoided the "anarchy and disorder which have convulsed many of the other Southern States."[155] This was not the case: Reconstruction-era Florida was rife with political and racial violence that targeted African Americans and white Republicans.[156] Whatever their political leanings, Florida boosters in the 1870s faced considerable obstacles when it came to convincing whites to migrate there and labor on their own farms. How, northerners queried, could they make their fortunes in a land where labor had been degraded by slavery, where they might be brutally harassed, and where the climate perhaps sapped energy and resolve?

Agriculture was both part of the problem and a remedy. Where the agricultural problem in California was wheat, the problem in Florida was cotton. Adams gave the following dismal description of cotton-raising in Florida: "The pre-eminence given this crop, and the prevalence of slave labor . . . have all combined to crush out all diversity of occupations not directly tributary to and concerned in the raising of cotton. . . . Whether or not cotton has been 'king,' it has certainly been a social tyrant" that had "prevented the formation of those small villages as centers of population" that "in the Northern States, [develop] the essential instruments and means of social progress."[157] Florida's cotton belt ran through the northern counties of Jackson, Leon, Madison, and Gadsden, where the majority of whites and blacks had lived before the war. For decades after the war, the area was associated with the "old regime" of staple-crop culture, albeit in the new form of sharecropping.[158] Peninsular Florida was a different proposition, however. Although planters had long viewed it skeptically as "a comparatively unoccupied waste of thin, sandy land," it proved suitable to rarer

crops.[159] "In no State of the Union can so extensive a variety of valuable productions be successfully cultivated as in Florida," Adams wrote, clarifying that
while "most of the crops grown in the temperate zone flourish in the northern
portion of the State," virtually "all the Peninsula is adapted to the cultivation of
semi-tropical fruits."[160] Echoing southern Californians, he thus proclaimed for
Florida "a monopoly" in the "growth of tropical and semi-tropical Fruits" that,
"when fairly developed, will make her one of the richest and most important of
the United States."[161]

Moves toward commercial semi-tropical agriculture began during Reconstruction. In 1870, northern capitalist Henry Sanford founded Sanford in central Florida and began advertising its land as ideal for growing citrus crops.
Although he himself struggled financially, Sanford brought a colony of Swedes
to the region and inspired later developers to enter the peninsula.[162] New settlers succeeded in growing citrus and sending small quantities by ship to the
Northeast. They also published the *Florida New-Yorker*, a periodical that promoted orange culture in the Big Apple.[163] Also in the 1870s, Jacksonville's *Florida Agriculturist* began as a horticultural journal devoted to "the cultivation of
the grape, peach, orange, lemon, [and] citron," among other fruits. It educated
settlers about growing techniques and challenged northerners who "sneer . . . at
the sand and low lands of Florida."[164] The *Florida Agriculturist* asserted that
Florida was coming into its own as a land of fruit growers—a valid point in the
sense that the state's semi-tropical fruits had never before been grown for the
market. The periodical compared Florida to other supposedly "barren places
[that] have, as soon as the products to which they were best adapted . . . been
introduced . . . proved to be far more profitable than fields apparently of superior fertility." Florida would thus be the latest example of America's "*manifest
destiny*," through which once "wild and uninviting" regions "become populous
and would remunerate the labor bestowed upon" them as soon as the particular
adaptations that were needed to make the land prosper had been identified.[165]

"Semi-tropical" became the term Florida land boosters preferred. From 1875
to 1878, the state's leading promotional journal was the *Semi-Tropical*, a Jack-
sonville-based monthly edited by former state governor Harrison Reed. The
journal, an advertisement explained, "intended to be a worthy exponent and
representative of the intelligence and practical industry of the State, which, in
climate, soil, resources, and advantages, presents unequalled and peculiar attractions . . . for immigration and settlement."[166] Florida's formation narrative
of semi-tropical independence was set in contrast with a North where honest
agricultural effort—that mainstay of Jeffersonian America—had been stripped
of its dignity and worth. J. F. Bartholf of Manatee County observed that "it is to

be regretted that there is so much fastidiousness and aristocratic pride in this hundredth year of our republic. . . . It is contrary to the principles of a republic to make distinction in the classes of its citizens. A man who labors with his muscles is as much entitled to respect as one who seeks existence by his mental powers alone."[167] Settlers who grew fruit and vegetables in Florida could "successfully cultivate" "true manhood and statesmanship."[168] Some Floridians saw great advertising potential for the state in its semi-tropical products. One contributor to *Semi-Tropical* called for a horticultural display at the Philadelphia Centennial so Florida could exhibit "the beauty of her semi-tropical verdure" to potential settlers.[169]

The tropical connections between Florida and California were increasingly apparent. On the West Coast, growers read and praised Reed's *Semi-Tropical* as a magazine that was "ably conducted," and the *Florida Dispatch* reported—often approvingly—on the development of agriculture in California, especially citrus agriculture.[170] Competing with California at expositions around the country, Florida organized a semi-tropical fruit display for the 1885 New Orleans World's Fair that, according to the display commissioner, General Sebring, helped "send 20,000 fresh settlers to the State."[171] The lower cost of rail fare to and from California inspired Florida boosters at an 1887 convention to call on Florida's railroads to copy the policies that enabled "California [to] ship her products to any part of the country at a paying rate of freight" and "provide immigrant sleepers."[172] With regard to the promotion of the West Coast and the work of the Southern California Immigration Association in particular, a Florida editor declared, "California has set a good many fashions that Florida would do well to imitate."[173] Imitating their California counterparts, Florida boosters in 1889 sent out display trains of citrus fruit entitled Florida on Wheels.[174]

Cordial relations turned sour as the states competed for settlers. Harrison Reed, for example, was riled in 1877 by the continuous "receipt of pamphlets, maps, and circulars setting forth the advantages of California, particularly the southern portion of it, for settlement and cultivation."[175] In response to a circular by the Riverside Land and Irrigation Company, Reed produced an article that purported to be an examination "of the comparative advantages of California and Florida for the profitable investment of labor and capital, and the pursuits of agriculture, horticulture, or any branch of industry."[176] His conclusions fell firmly in Florida's favor. While Florida's soils were somewhat inferior, he wrote, that state was preferable to the aridity of southern California, which meant additional expenses for water for irrigation. In addition, southern California lacked the abundant forests that in Florida provided settlers with convenient timber. Florida lands, moreover, were cheaper and closer to northeastern markets. Thus Florida "can offer the industrious man of small means superior advantages for acquiring a home."[177]

Reed articulated two common themes in Floridian critiques of California: its remoteness and expense. Floridians explained that "good orange lands in Florida have always sold at much lower prices than in California" and that their state was far closer to major markets than California was.[178] These were both true enough. S. Powers, a Florida settler who had lived for six years in California, noted in 1887 how "land here costs only one-half to one-fifth of what it does in California," a statement that is supported by data on land prices in both states.[179] In addition, the products Florida farmers grew had less distance to travel to reach northern cities and were ready for market several weeks earlier in the season than fruit grown in California.[180]

Arguments over whose citrus was better were also pervasive, though this was by no means the only field of battle between the two states.[181] In an 1888 pamphlet published by the Alachua County Immigration Association, Rev. George Watson included in his "points of honest comparison between the two localities" topics as diverse as topography, water, "night air," fuel, types of fruit, distance from markets, and cost of living.[182] His thirteen-point list of comparisons invariably praised Florida, which had "far superior" citrus fruits (although, in a rare admission, Watson conceded that California's grapes and nuts were superior). His longest point, however, invoked republican ideals. Southern California was prohibitively expensive—a "land for the rich and luxurious classes"—whereas Florida, while it had "unlimited capabilities for the use of wealth," was "emphatically the land for the poor," the place where people of small means, through hard work, could achieve independence on their own few acres, which were "sufficient for a home and orchard."[183] Florida boosters such as Watson thus worked to undercut the republican imagery that had been crafted for southern California while selling their own state as the true location where labor would be rewarded.

The barbs cut the other way, of course, and deeper. Florida was often denounced as a land unfit for white laborers. Dr. Frederick Lente, an advocate of Florida's climate, reported "certain unfounded ideas and prejudices [about Florida] which have become deeply-rooted in northern communities," among them notions of a stifling, swamplike atmosphere.[184] Northerners who had migrated to California emphasized such points. William Olden hailed California as a desirable homeland that provided "the fruits and luxuries of both the tropics and temperate zones," but he warned that because of its seasonal heat and diseases, Florida was not a place to "make a home, but only a temporary stopping place during the winter."[185] A yellow fever panic in Jacksonville in 1888 and later outbreaks unsettled northerners who were considering Florida for permanent residency.[186] Even if one avoided illness, the summer heat could diminish year-round productivity. As Seth French, a Civil War veteran from Wisconsin who became both a successful grower in Orange County and Florida's commissioner of immigration, wrote in 1879, "Most Northern people believe that our climate is oppressively warm in summer, and also imagine that white persons can not labor, either physically or mentally—or, at least, do not; that the Southron has but little industry or energy, and that the Northern immigrant soon loses his former addition and activity."[187]

French described a formation narrative that worked directly counter to the hopes of Florida's sellers and settlers who had come from the North and Midwest, and they fervently challenged its accuracy. The livability of the state's summer "climate has proved itself in the experience of thousands, brought up elsewhere," wrote one migrant who had settled near Jacksonville in 1876.[188] The settler did, however, highlight the many failures of recent immigrants to the state who had focused solely on growing oranges without considering how close they were to a market or the importance of having paying crops for the five to eight years it took an orange grove to mature. Truck gardening was critical to the survival of settlers during that initial period in the life of a citrus grove.[189] "In all cases I would advise him, as soon as he pitches on his piece of land and builds his home, to commence on a small garden of vegetables, for it saves a great deal of money," another Florida settler wrote in 1878 to potential migrants in Maryland. "He can then lay out his little nursery bed to raise his orange, lemon, and lime trees, as they take a long time to come into bearing." Agriculture in Florida's farming paradise had to be learned: "It takes time and labor and perseverance to make an orange grove and to learn the many kinds of cultivation which tropical and semi-tropical fruits require," the settler explained from personal experience.[190] Land surveyor John Mac-Donald reiterated how important it was for landowners to understand the agricultural and commercial requirements of the new environment: "Many have failed in Florida, but always on account of their own mismanagement."[191] But MacDonald himself was proof that natives of cold climates could prosper in Florida. A Canadian by birth, he had worked in Wisconsin and Michigan before coming to Florida in 1876 with damaged lungs. After he recovered, he purchased land and set out 400 wild orange trees, which "failed on account of my own inexperience" with semi-tropical horticulture. A stubborn agriculturist, MacDonald then found success with citrus in Orange County and became a leading proponent of the region's attractions as a destination where northerners could achieve the republican ideal of independence. "It is true we have no millionaires yet who made their fortunes here," MacDonald wrote, "but that is the best feature in it, because it almost insures success to the majority," led by the thousands of "intelligent, industrious Northern men of small means [who] are comfortably situated on permanent homes."[192]

Southern sociopolitical legacies troubled Florida boosters less after the Compromise of 1877 ended Reconstruction and southern Democrats once again captured political offices in "Redemption" regimes. For all but the most ardently Republican boosters—such as Macdonald, who briefly left the state, upset that "a few ignorant demagogues amongst the Democrats threatened the total expulsion of Yankees"—Democrat George Drew's gubernatorial victory in 1876 represented a relief, if not a triumph: it ended the sectional antagonisms of Reconstruction under which "progress [was] impossible."[193] An article in the *Cincinnati Enquirer* that was reprinted in the Florida press announced that across the South "all the machinery of law and good order are in full and successful operation," particularly "since the despicable carpet-bag *regime* has been supplanted by intelligent and honest home government."[194] Such biased and damning verdicts of Reconstruction overlooked the achievements of the black and carpetbag Republican state governments in the South, which included the creation of a system of public school education where virtually none had existed before, but reflected a broad northern acceptance of southern charges that black suffrage had been, at best, a misguided policy.[195]

Sectional reconciliation became a mantra among Florida boosters. The damaging "beliefs" in southern backwardness that French lamented were countered by assertions that Florida was becoming a "Northern colony" and "a Northern State as regards population, so many Northerners are now residing there."[196] This exaggeration carried an important nugget of truth. From a tiny population during the antebellum years, peninsular Florida had grown through arrivals from the Northeast and Midwest (as well as the South). The population in the citrus-growing counties of Sumter and Orange increased from a combined total of 2,536 in 1867 to 12,262 in 1880.[197] The in-migration began before 1876, but post-Reconstruction boosters saw it as proof of the abatement of sectional strife that Redemption supposedly offered. The state's southern-born population, whether they were native to Florida or migrants from other southern states, were said to "look with intelligent interest at the incoming tide of immigration, and welcome it heartily," since "they wish to see the State developed in that way." Opinions about politics and race still divided many southerners and northerners, but they could agree about a desire to capitalize on Florida's growth. Though southern-born Floridians might "resent with some ardor ... the missionary spirit that seeks to change, asking them to discard the old and adopt the new—a tone . . . that offends the inherent conservatism that marks this people," boosters stressed that "the straight-forward man that means business is always cordially welcomed."[198] In his 1887 guide, Oliver Crosby, a settler from New England, stated that "Political Sectionalism is no longer a drawback to Northern emigration to Florida, if indeed it ever was except in a few isolated, intensely Southern communities. . . . Northern men need not fear that they may blunder into such a community."[199] The state's immigration guide for 1882 explained that Polk County was exempt from "the deep political bitterness and old war prejudices that have proved so detrimental to society in other localities," while a booster for Sumter County flatly declared, "The war between the sections is over."[200]

Also over were the attempts of Radical Republicans to protect the rights of freedmen in the South. Redemption governments imposed a white supremacist society on the state that Florida boosters invariably supported in lily-white visions of settlement. Yet as economic developers, they also recognized that African Americans, who constituted nearly half the state's population, were vital to Florida's economy as railroad workers, laborers, and farmers. Indeed, immediately after the Civil War, state agencies strove to attract blacks, especially in order to fill labor needs, and thousands of African Americans had arrived from other southern states.[201] As Leon Litwack has written, "Florida [seemed to be] the 'land of plenty'" for blacks, "where homesteads were plentiful, wages high, and laborers scarce."[202] In his 1874 *Florida Settler* guide, Eagan praised, albeit faintly, this "migration of colored labor" as being "only the more intelligent and thrifty class of colored men—those who are possessed of some means, and have prudence and foresight enough to take care of it."[203] Many white Floridians, Eagan knew, feared that this development could mean "the permanent predominance of the colored element," which would hinder progress, scare off capital, and raise a "race-feeling."[204] Eagan, however, countered that blacks were well suited to Florida's climate and were progressing as free citizens, thus forming a welcome addition to a state that offered "plenty of room" and "a golden opportunity for every industrious colored man to grow independent."[205]

Such positive views of African American migrants to Florida essentially died with the end of Reconstruction. Through the 1880s, blacks in the state strove to regain lost political power. They did maintain influence in some municipal governments, particularly in southern Florida, but they faced a strong push toward white supremacy from the state's leaders.[206] The new Democratic governor, George Drew, a New Hampshire man who had made a fortune in Florida's timber industry before the Civil War, told the *New York Tribune* after his election victory: "The curse of this section is the thieving propensity of the blacks. . . . Only a few save any money. . . . They are great spendthrifts, and the worst thing is to pay them regularly."[207] In the 1880s, as Democratic governors Drew and William Bloxham targeted settlers and investors from the North, Florida promoters hailed the republican opportunities for white settlers while they simultaneously depicted African Americans as fundamentally inferior and worked to disenfranchise them as citizens. Whites were promised great rewards for their labor in the peninsula. Colonel A. K. McClure's 1886 guidebook to the South pointed to "the new Florida that has been developed within the last few years that I regard as the most inviting part of the whole continent for the small farmer who can adapt himself to its climate and the simple but systematic method of culture that here produces the best results for labor to be found in any State of the Union."[208] Articulating the formation narrative of republican prosperity in his 1879 pamphlet *Semi-Tropical Florida*, Seth French wrote, "We want immigrants of kindred races, that we may be a homogeneous people. . . . We do not wish to be misunderstood on this point; we do not want immigrants for subordinate positions, but, on the contrary, invite them to locate, and become the owners of their homes in fee simple forever; we want them to become citizens, and have with us equal political privileges and responsibilities in all the obligations imposed upon citizens under a republican government."[209] To emphasize French's point that Florida was looking for farmers, agrarian imagery adorned the cover in the form of a grower harvesting oranges (Fig. 3.2).

The cause of Florida boosters was aided in 1880 when former president Ulysses S. Grant toured the state on a journey that also took him into the Caribbean and Central America.[210] In a symbolic act, Grant turned over the first spade of earth for the South Florida Railroad that would eventually link Tampa and the Gulf coast with Jacksonville.[211] Like Hayes's trip to southern California—which took place the same year—Grant's visit to and declarations about Florida were of great benefit to its promoters. Grant marveled at Florida's size—"an area greater than New York, Massachusetts, and Connecticut combined"—and declared that the state "is capable of supplying all the oranges, lemons, pineapples, and other semi-tropical fruits used in the United States, and one hundred million dollars of sugar [that are] now [being] imported."[212] The state merely awaited an influx of energetic settlers to take advantage of its natural fertility. "With deposits of fertilizer under it and above it sufficient for many generations," Florida only wanted "people and enterprise, both of which it is rapidly obtaining." Grant also affirmed the notion the promoters put forward of a tropical expansion of the republican ideal of self-sufficient citizens: "Florida

Figure 3.2. The cover of a guide to Florida by commissioner of immigration Seth French, an orange grower himself, featured a semi-tropical farm and farmer, a response to growing interest in the North in horticulture as the basis for an independent existence in Florida. Seth French, *Semi-Tropical Florida: Its Climate, Soil, and Productions* (Chicago: Rand, McNally & Co., 1879). Courtesy of University of West Florida University Archives and West Florida History Center.

to-day affords the best opening in the world for young men of small means and great industry."[213]

Grant's report was initially published in the *Philadelphia Ledger*, but it was reproduced in numerous publications disseminated by promotional bodies.[214] If the southern state's soil was inferior to that of, say, Illinois or Iowa, it was "perfectly adapted to the climate and semi-tropical productions of the country, and will yield a more bountiful return to the good husbandman than any other soil on the face of the globe," proclaimed the Florida Land Agency.[215] Whether Grant's appraisal influenced Philadelphia capitalist Hamilton Disston to purchase 4 million acres of state land the following year is unknown, but Disston's land companies repeated Grant's description of a land that upheld free labor ideals.[216] One reproduced Grant's words in their entirety before expanding on them: "On general principles a start in Florida costs no more and often less than in the west. . . . *Everything depends upon the man*; some have tact to turn everything into cash, while others walk over dollars without knowing it. Energy, industry and common sense are needed, and pay as well in Florida as anywhere in America."[217] After the Disston purchase, the state government was freed of its debt and granted millions of acres of land to northern-owned railroads. By 1890, Florida's railway mileage had increased fivefold to 2,489 miles and the Jacksonville, Tampa and Key West Railway alone had obtained 2,000,000 acres of land.[218]

Promoters who wrote for land and railway companies continued to evoke republican rhetoric to sell their Florida domain. George Barbour, who first came to Florida as a correspondent for the *Chicago Times* on Grant's 1880 tour, was sufficiently enamored with the state to settle there, initially as "commissary" for the South Florida Railroad, a role that involved overseeing the expansion of the railroad. Citing "the multifarious inquiries addressed to the State Bureau of Immigration," Barbour became convinced of "a real demand for an adequate and trustworthy descriptive work on Florida" and set out to produce one, with the blessings of the state governor and the commissioner of immigration.[219] Barbour interpreted Florida as a state hindered by a southern past and yet eminently capable of the progressive development "of all our Western States."[220] In fact, Barbour claimed, because of its rapidly increasing steamship and railroad facilities and relative closeness to markets, the peninsula offered superior advantages to the "far-off, bleak, inhospitable West." Defining "Semi-Tropical Florida"—by which he meant most of the peninsula—as "the region where many of the products of both the temperate and tropical climates may be found growing side by side," Barbour hailed a land that "probably produces the greatest variety of marketable and profitable

crops of any region in our country."[221] Typical of the growing confidence of
Florida land promoters in the 1880s, Barbour placed Florida firmly within
U.S. traditions of republican expansion, in which "living without labor is not
possible, and here as elsewhere the great law prevails, that in the sweat of
his brow shall man eat his bread." While accepting that the "experiment of
a man, especially with a family, transferring all his interests and hopes from
a temperate to a semi-tropical region, is necessarily a trying one," Barbour,
like his travel companion Grant, saw Florida as a tropic to be settled by worthy American farmers. He described the state as "beyond all other regions of
America the most favored for poor people with little capital but of industrious disposition, able and willing to work."[222]

Prominent California booster William H. Martin stressed Florida's similarities with southern California in his new position as a booster for Florida land
companies. In 1881, after the Florida Land and Improvement Company, which
was in charge of the Disston lands, appointed him as their land commissioner,
Martin traveled through peninsular Florida "with a view of attending to the
subdivision and colonizing" of the company's lands, including 120,000 acres
in Orange County that were on sale for from $2 to $10 per acre.[223] Promoting
small-scale citrus culture, Martin used the exact same tropes he had used to sell
California, even declaring that "in all my travels through the State of California, I
have never seen as many orange groves as I saw in Orange County [Florida]."[224]
Under Martin's direction, the company's pamphlets contrasted Florida's meritocratic agriculture—where "everything depends upon the man"—with the
industrial North, where "the better classes" were "now crowded so compactly
in our large cities or working out subsistence in manufacturing villages and
towns." In Florida's "developing enterprise" northerners could discover "the sure
reward of thrift and well-directed energy."[225] Settlers would have to adapt, but
the fruit of their labor would make it worthwhile. An 1886 treatise on orange-
growing explained that northerners who had settled in Florida could "learn [cit-
rus cultivation], and even learn to love to work. The sweet sleep and refreshing
rest under the soothing anodyne of labor would come without the learning.
After a while would come the noble independence of a free man. Try it, young
man, try it! Come from the crowded city to the country! Come South, come to
Florida!"[226]

In the vision of such boosters, this "free man" was white. Like French's vision
of a "homogeneous people," the images many boosters created were racially exclusive. In many cases the assumption that "northerner" meant "white person"
was implicit, as with D. H. Jacques' statement in his 1877 pamphlet Florida as
a Permanent Home: "Poor men [in the North], whose means are too limited

to enable them to buy and stock a farm, where lands are dear and building improvements expensive . . . provided they have industry, energy, pluck, and perseverance, can vastly improve their condition, and the prospects of their families, by coming to Florida."[227] Yet African Americans struggling with the same financial limitations, and more, in Florida, were depicted as thriftless and lazy—a damning characterization in promotional literature that repeatedly stressed that Florida "holds forth her hand in hearty welcome . . . [to] the poor, honest man . . . who comes to her seeking a comfortable home, and is neither ashamed nor too lazy to work for it."[228] For land promoters in the post-Reconstruction years, the state's freedmen were precisely those "too lazy to work for it." Yet paradoxically, promoters presented African Americans as ideally suited for brutish fieldwork. "While the African is as necessary in clearing away forests and in hard manual labor as the Irishman is at the North," Oliver Crosby wrote in 1887, "now that he is free he has no idea of working more than is barely necessary to keep him in pork and grits."[229] Indeed, "with all the progress claimed for the colored man, it will be ages before the negro as a rule is a thrifty, honest laborer." Incoming white settlers, therefore, need not fear competition from the African American population since the "average southern darky" was "utterly shiftless and devoid of honor"—a failure in free labor terms.[230] These racist depictions denied the efforts of black citizens to pursue economic and social independence in the face of white supremacy in Florida, including the inhabitants of Eatonville, in Orange County, who incorporated the first all-black town in the United States in 1887.[231] But such boosterist views shaped the attitudes of incoming whites who might have felt differently in the North: according to Crosby (perhaps speaking from experience, since he had come from New England), the "most ardent but honest Republicans often broaden their views [on racial equality] after a visit to the land where the Fifteenth Amendment means something."[232] By "broaden their views," Crosby meant that northerners would see the folly of universal male suffrage after a prolonged stay in the white-controlled South.

Leading promoters such as James Wood Davidson were politically active in efforts to repeal the racial equality laws instigated by Reconstruction governments. A reporter in New York who became a fruit grower in south Florida, Davidson was held in such esteem by his neighbors that he was chosen as Dade County's representative to the State Constitutional Convention in 1885. The new constitution created a poll tax and other restrictive measures that began the process of disenfranchising African Americans in Florida. Davidson published a book in 1889, by which point few African Americans in the state could vote, that became a standard guide to Florida and cast racial hierarchy as a profound benefit to the state's development. "During the period between 1865 and 1876 these slaves worked faithfully in the plantation of politics," Davidson wrote; "but at the latter date a second emancipation changed their status slightly, and since then they have been working somewhat more and voting rather less, and are doing vastly better in all important respects. So also is Florida prospering. The future fortunes of the negroes are largely in the hands of the controlling race, and they themselves will probably have little to do in shaping it; and doubtless the less they have to do with it the better."[233]

Following Reconstruction, the de facto and de jure subordination of African Americans in Florida reinforced the images promoters offered of a society of independent landowners. The two strains of republicanism and colonialism were compatible in their minds because of the pervasive belief of whites that African Americans lacked the character to succeed in a free labor environment. In Barbour's verdict, "The negro . . . will not play a permanent or prominent part in Florida. In moderate numbers, no doubt, he will always be found there, but his shiftless, incompetent, and indolent ways will not long be endured by the class of vigorous and thoroughgoing Northern and Western men who constitute the bulk of the immigration to Florida at present."[234] In a similar vein, Helen Harcourt lamented the lack of productivity of "the present generation of free-born colored ladies and gentlemen" who were "of a far different class from the faithful old slaves of yore." Harcourt believed that for white settlers, "a comfortable competence" "is . . . here waiting for the self-chosen ones, who elect to take advantage of the gift so freely offered to those who have manhood enough to grasp it and make the best use of it."[235] For Harcourt, the impoverishment and disenfranchisement of African Americans were justified, if not inevitable. In Florida's tropic of hopes, racial hierarchy and republican opportunity flourished side by side. Boosters proclaimed that "the code of morality . . . does not stand high among the majority of the colored race" and promised the "vast army [of whites in the North] who struggle on from day to day, overworked, underpaid, or not paid at all" that "every energetic man may make a reality for himself if he will but seize and hold Florida's royal bounty."[236]

In the late nineteenth century, promoters of California and Florida shared in and responded to an increasing sense of unease among Americans in the North and Midwest who sensed that the opportunities for landed independence that were available to their forefathers had diminished. They projected the agrarian myth onto southern California and peninsula Florida, semi-tropical regions that provided special opportunities for small farmers. A trend toward smaller farms was evident in both states: the average acreage per farm in California fell from 481 in 1870 to 397 in 1900 and, in Florida, it decreased from 231 in

1870 to 106 in 1900.[237] California had a distinct advantage over Florida in this ideological competition, as promoters were able to merge "western" and tropical traits in their descriptions of the state's emergent agriculture. Although initially southern California growers looked to Florida for expertise, the West Coast region grew rapidly in the 1880s as railroads facilitated the development of agricultural colonies.[238] In contrast, Florida's climate and racial composition hindered the efforts of its promoters to induce immigration through similar visions of rewarded labor. As the *Florida Annual* reported, "One of the most common inquiries made concerning Florida's climate, by men from sections further north, is whether a man from such places can 'work out' in Florida sun with impunity."[239] Concerns about migrating to a state that was home to a large population of African Americans (who constituted 46.5 percent of the state's total in 1880) compounded the reluctance of northerners to relocate to Florida. In the 1880s, promoters increasingly depicted blacks as little more than manual workers who were incapable of succeeding in a free labor environment and were being necessarily supplanted by independent white citizens. While the "African" in Florida was little more than a "Bulldozer," Oliver Crosby explained, the industrious white settler could "become more of a man than he ever could in a populous Northern district."[240]

Boosters in both states produced critiques of urban-industrial "progress." They constructed formation narratives of improved communities based on agricultural prosperity. "We have practically a monopoly of the semi-tropical fruits in the United States," Isaac N. Hoag wrote. "Florida is the only formidable competitor of California in these fruits, and both states together can not [*sic*] supply the demand."[241] A monopoly on the markets for semi-tropical products would give lasting life to a superior republican existence. Californians echoed the Florida booster who called to those in the North living "the precarious life of a salaried clerk, book-keeper, or salesmen, shut in-doors all day and every day . . . earning barely enough to keep up appearances before the world," to claim "the free, manly life of the farmer or fruit-grower, breathing God's pure air, uncontaminated by the dust and smoke of cities, living a life of comfort and freedom from care, even if one of honest daily toil, and storing up for the future a sufficient independence for himself and his family."[242]

Into the 1890s, boosters of California and Florida strove for an agricultural future for their states that combined commercial development and republican independence. Their faith in semi-tropical agriculture meant that citrus growers and horticulturists in both states were rarely die-hard Populists. While horticulturists in both states articulated the agrarian rhetoric and tariff protectionism of Populism, they directed their energies less into political protest and more into activities that took advantage of the uniqueness of their products, including forming cooperatives such as the Southern California Fruit Exchange (1893) and hosting booster events such as the 1890 Semi-Tropical Exposition in Ocala, Florida.[243]. In southern California, increased land values reinforced beliefs in the region's special agricultural progress and diminished the appeal of Populism; consequently, "small wheat growers in isolated rural regions made up the bulk of California's relatively weak Populist movement."[244] For promoters, southern California's semi-tropical agriculture represented the prosperous foundation for a society that bypassed unhealthy modern tendencies toward urban crowding and rampant industrialism. "The middle classes of California will always draw their living from the soil," a leading promoter wrote in 1891, since "manufacturing will not develop to any great extent for many years to come" and "the products of which the State appears to have a natural monopoly promise to support a dense population, spread over the country in colonies, on small farms, and in loosely built towns."[245] California's tropic of hopes was thus an exception in the nation: "No other part of the United States is developing under similar conditions," the booster concluded, "and hence the economic history of California has the importance of a new experiment."[246]

The formation narrative was identical in peninsular Florida, which also developed into a distinctive agricultural region. As MacDonald wrote, "Our country can never be a manufacturing country," but instead showed "the tendency . . . to village life" and settlement in "groves and gardens."[247] Through the production of fruits and vegetables, Florida moved in new directions that separated its economy from that of the rest of the South.[248] This separatism was partly why Populism never took hold in Florida either, although the city of Ocala, surprisingly, was chosen to host the National Farmers' Alliance Convention in 1890.[249] As historian Robert McMath has noted, "The same mix of boosterism and social criticism that characterized the California Alliance was to be found among the Floridians who hosted the Ocala meeting."[250] Local organizers of the convention advertised their state to the visitors from the Midwest at a semi-tropical exposition that displayed the state's fruits and vegetables.[251] As in California, Florida's agricultural sector was presented as qualitatively different from the declining fortunes of "traditional" American farming: it was located in a region on the rise, where new "orange and lemon groves and vineyards are pushing forward" the possibilities of semi-tropical settlement.[252] The *Daily Alta California* acknowledged in 1890 that Florida was more than a match for California in a proposed "semi-tropical contest" to be held in Chicago.[253] While they shared the agrarian ideals of Populism, California and Florida promoters saw and sold their states as lands apart: American tropics, home to prosperous small farms that upheld both capitalist and republican progress. By the 1890s, California and Florida were successfully competing with Mediterranean countries in the production of semi-tropical fruits for the U.S. market.[254] The future would thus be one of "American Fruit for Americans": a patriotic development for which "the semi-tropical Americans [of California and Florida] bless their opportunity."[255]

4

Desert and Swamp

The Conquest of Tropical Nature in the Progressive Era

Around the turn of the twentieth century, as agricultural development further altered the physical and social conditions of their states, promoters of southern California and peninsular Florida looked to untouched internal domains as new sites for settlement, tourism, and agricultural expansion. Although these undeveloped regions were topographical opposites—one was too dry and the other was too wet—they presented similar challenges to boosters who envisaged the conversion of "forbidding" nature into homelands that could be marketed for their tropical fertility.[1] As Floridian Fred Pfeiffer asked rhetorically, "The places where only silence and barrenness in one instance, and richest vegetation in the other, held reign, are yielding to constant application of scientific energy, and when the work shall have been finished, what will have been accomplished?"[2] Promoters answered this question with myriad depictions of reclaimed farmlands for prosperous white settlers, cultivating visions of republican independence that softened the racial and labor hierarchies in both states. Long viewed as wastelands that stood outside the developed coastal corridors of the two states, California's interior desert and Florida's swamp thus became the final frontiers of conquest in the two semitropical states.

This chapter analyzes the promotion of irrigation in California and drainage in Florida, in particular, California's Imperial Valley and the Florida Everglades. In both locations agricultural boosters, landowners, chambers of commerce, and state and railroad agents formulated foundation narratives to entice settlers and visitors to areas that had long been denigrated as savage and inhospitable. Such narratives have pervaded ideas of American expansion since the late eighteenth century, as historian David Nye notes: "The foundation stories that white Americans have told about the reconstruction and habitation of a new space are secular stories about what in many cultures are religious matters: how a group comes to dwell in a particular space, and how it wields power to transform the land and make a living from it."[3] The focus here is not on the technological aspects of irrigation and drainage but how these processes and landscapes fit in the evolving promotion of the two states as a tropic of hopes for Anglo-Americans. With a generation of development behind them, tourism promoters of California and Florida evinced a growing fascination with the unreclaimed landscapes and with Native Americans as human symbols of "savage" environments that were said to be disappearing from modern society. While boosters enticed tourists to these areas as part of a wilderness vogue in the postfrontier United States, land developers in both states hailed the reclamation of wild nature and the creation of fertile "winter gardens" for American settlers. One promoter called the Everglades "an Outdoor Paradise for the Farmer [and] the Fruit Grower," while a California newspaper wrote that the work in the Colorado Desert "will convert what has been an uninhabited desert into a tropical garden spot."[4]

The Imperial Valley and the Everglades can be seen as exaggerated microcosms of their states. They offered an intensified version of the desert-swamp dichotomy that had shaped the rivalry between California and Florida for decades. Furthermore, the claims of boosters that the Imperial Valley was a model of development for the Everglades were part of a broader trend in which Florida boosters increasingly looked to the West Coast and the growing sophistication and success of California's promotional organs and horticultural cooperatives. With the confidence that came with having pulled ahead of Florida in their rivalry as producers of semi-tropical fruits, California promoters in 1902 remarked, "We have learned much in past times from Florida, and can now pay her back in the horticultural lore built upon our natural capacities."[5] The Imperial Valley's higher levels of production and settlement compared to the Everglades were in keeping with southern California's commercial superiority over Florida. This inequality notwithstanding, promoters of both states inherited earlier visions of semi-tropical agriculture as a profitable occupation for small farmers and applied them to untapped internal domains.

By the 1890s, southern California and peninsular Florida were considerably more inhabited and well known than they had been a generation earlier. Between 1880 and 1890 the populations of southern California and peninsular Florida rose from 64,371 to 201,352 and 71,010 to 147,695, respectively, while the value of farmland and buildings increased in California by 266 percent and in Florida by 365 percent.[6] Their interior lowlands, which had yet to be settled by white Americans, had become new focal points for promotional efforts. But boosters of Imperial Valley and the Everglades built upon the preexisting formation narratives of semi-tropical agriculture, for which irrigation and drainage were already components. In more developed parts of California and Florida, successful attempts at irrigation and drainage had contributed in the 1880s to localized increases in population and land values, while promoters articulated neo-Jeffersonian visions of progress in which reclamation was a "civilizing agent" that supported small-farming settlement.[7] Together, they contributed to growth in both regions. By 1890 each state was producing over 1 million boxes of citrus fruit annually, or approximately 72 million pounds of fruit.[8] Land prices rose in prime semi-tropical fruit areas such as Los Angeles County, California, and Orange County, Florida, often to prohibitively expensive levels. Ambitious developers thus turned to deserts and wetlands that had intimidated their predecessors but now represented fresh resources. In both cases, the ability to control water seemed to be the necessary next step to opening up new land for semi-tropical agriculture.

California and Florida were also part of a greater reclamation story in post-frontier America.[9] Across the West and the South, the reclamation of desert and swamp lands was infused with an ethos of utilitarian conservationism that saw nature as a set of resources to be used prudently by humanity.[10] "The rise of peoples from savagery to civilization" was the reason for a "steadily increasing growth of the amount demanded by . . . man from the actual resources of the country," President Theodore Roosevelt declared at a 1908 White House conference on conservation. Roosevelt noted that "but little land fitted for agriculture now remains unoccupied save what can be reclaimed by irrigation and drainage."[11] The Reclamation Act of 1902 initiated federal funding for irrigation projects.[12] Like other Progressive Era reformers, advocates of reclamation were concerned with mediating the effects of industrial society on individual lives.[13] Ironically, although the cost and scale of reclamation increasingly necessitated government support, boosters presented it as a renewing force for independent citizenship.[14] "A few years ago our farm boys were flocking to the cities in thousands," John L. Matthews wrote. "But as the cost of living has gone up, as the control of business has centered in vast corporations, as the life of man in the city has come to be more and more guided and controlled for him, there has been a revulsion and young men and young women turn to the country again, seeking independent livelihood." Irrigation and drainage, it was claimed, would open up "a healthier and stronger home life for the upbringing of independent Americans."[15]

In contrast to other reclamation promoters in the U.S., however, boosters of the Imperial Valley and the Everglades focused on the distinctive "tropical" qualities of the land in these two locations. Indeed, the hotter and harsher environments of the Imperial Valley and the Everglades compared with, say, Los Angeles County or the St. Johns River area pushed promoters to make more emphatic claims, and the word "tropical" began to appear more often instead of the "semi-tropical" that had been used in previous decades. This language was influenced by the actual expansion of the United States into the tropics during this period: the controversial acquisition, under different guises, of Hawaii, Puerto Rico, Cuba, and the Philippines.[16] In the depressed 1890s, U.S. expansionists desired tropical territories as markets for surplus U.S. goods and as strategic possessions, but they were widely regarded as unsuitable places for Anglo-Americans to live. In addition, the new possessions of the United States were places that undermined cherished concepts of republican identity.[17] "It is a matter of universal experience that democratic institutions have never on a large scale prospered in tropical latitudes," Senator Carl Schurz wrote of the proposed annexation of Hawaii.[18] Creating a self-aggrandizing distinction between republican and imperial forms of growth, promoters of western irrigation declared that "the business of the commonwealth is to strengthen itself, and this can be done by internal expansion."[19]

The Imperial Valley and the Everglades, however, were sold by their promoters as unique lands that were both tropical *and* republican, lands that married the fertility of the tropics with virtuous independent living. Describing the social effects of irrigation, Imperial Valley booster A. J. Wells wrote: "It is the development of natural resources; it involves national prosperity; it adds stability to national life. The most valuable citizen, other things being equal, is the man who owns the land from which he makes his living. The wandering laborer, the restless miner, the lonely herdsman, add little to the strength or safety of a community. But attach one of these men to the soil, let him own a small farm and he becomes a citizen who can be depended on and will add to the stability of those institutions which we most highly prize."[20] Everglades promoters echoed these notions; for them, drainage reclamation in a fertile climate meant "the production of happy and prosperous homes" for nearly 400,000 families.[21] Observers elsewhere reinforced these claims. "'Back to the Soil' is a progressive moment," wrote a San Francisco journalist, who cited both the "great movement . . . to drain the Everglades of Florida and open up the land to settlement" and "southeastern California [where] the desert is being made to bloom like the rose." Americans could "break away from city conditions [and] the daily grind of work that never gives independence" in exchange for small farms that, in sustaining a middle-class population, "make the people of the entire community healthful."[22] Boosters sold the reclamation of the Imperial Valley and the Everglades as virtuous conquests that were far preferable to overseas imperial expansion because they opened fertile regions for white Americans: "back to the land" settlers who could become independent on semi-tropical farms that formed the backbone of stable communities.[23]

This was a vision that distorted the realities of agricultural production as it formed in the Imperial Valley and the Everglades, where land corporations became heavily invested in the selling of tropical real estate. Promoters of the reclaimed lands in southern California and southern Florida continued to hark back to traditional republican ideals even at a time when more sophisticated grower cooperatives employing intensive "specialized farming" contributed to a hardening division between landowners and farm laborers in both states.[24] As Steven Stoll has written of California agriculture, "the falling status of rural labor coincided with the gradual realization on the part of growers that specialized horticulture demanded a detestable kind of work. Cheap labor evolved to the point that it finally defined anyone with no other options in the economy."[25] This, primarily, meant ethnic and racial minorities, especially Mexicans and Asians in California and African Americans in Florida. Even as boosters such as Wells sold reclamation in terms of a process that replaced the "wandering laborer" with the independent settler, migratory labor by poorly paid ethnic and racial minorities became a permanent fixture in both domains.[26] Boosters reinforced the marginalization of migrant laborers by focusing on the agrarian prosperity enjoyed by Anglo-American settlers and developers, who were cast as the vital agents of change that would convert "worthlessness to wealth."[27] According to the boosters, the skill and ambition of the new landowners, if not their sweat and brawn, were the distinctly American traits that would transform the Imperial Valley and the Everglades from desert and swamp into progressive tropics. Land companies and the agents of corporations in southern California and southern Florida thus audaciously co-opted (and corrupted) republican ideology in order to sell their domains and attract white Americans to societies stratified by race and class.

Irrigation in California's Imperial Valley

The desert had an ambivalent status in the selling of California. Early white settlers in the state invariably described its deserts as ugly and barren: for some, they constituted "an American Sahara, devoid of all agricultural possibilities."[28] Tourists described their displeasure while crossing the desert en route to the Pacific coast. It was a "hopeless country," wrote Elizabeth Custer, who loathed the "heat and dust of the Mojave."[29] Yet, encouraged by promoter-journalists such as Charles Fletcher Lummis and George Wharton James and by the desert-themed literature of writer Mary Austin, Americans developed an appreciation for the desert landscape of the southwest.[30] For example, the Santa Fe and Southern Pacific Railroads boosted sites such as the Grand Canyon.[31] Tourists began to report the unique, primitive appeal of the "Southwestern Wonderland."[32] "There is always something cosmic and elemental about the desert," stated the Santa Fe Passenger Department in 1899. "We seem to be transported into some earlier geologic time . . . and herein lies the wonder of it!"[33]

Both health tourism and ideas of racial primitivism contributed to the new appreciation of the nation's desert. The desert climate was repeatedly cited as a reason why southern California was better than Florida. Responding to queries about the environment from easterners, a San Diego doctor explained that while southern California's scant winter rains accounted for "the lack of that luxuriant vegetation that many expect to find in a semi-tropical country," this was in fact a benefit because it contributed to the most healthful atmosphere in the semi-tropic zone.[34] Build a sanitarium in the desert, Mary Vail noted, and it would become "a source of wealth with as much certainty as if the attraction were a gold mine or a fertile plain."[35] Health spas and resorts had much to offer the weary tourist from the East: the "atmosphere is so light, so clear, so tonic," wrote Lummis, who also praised the desert's many "scenic wonders of the first magnitude."[36]

First among these "scenic wonders" were Native Americans. California promoters sensed a "source of wealth" to be mined in the association in the white imagination between primitive wilderness and nonwhite peoples. The Santa Fe Railroad advertised its lines with Native American–themed posters and exhibited Pueblo and Zuni Indians for tourist groups on the transcontinental trains. Tourists in California were promised encounters with "strange tribes of the desert [who] greet them in intervening wild spots, offering quaint wares of pottery and fabrics of half-barbaric pattern."[37] An expiration date was often placed on these encounters with "half-barbaric" landscapes and peoples. For Lummis,

"The American Indian . . . unquestionably the most picturesque human figure that has walked the earth since the Renaissance . . . is rapidly becoming extinct," and artists and tourists needed to come soon to the Southwest to be able to "study" them.[38] Morbidity infused this fascination. In one telling example, "The Desert Maiden," a short story about a Mojave Indian girl that was featured in a promotional magazine, showed a photograph that symbolized a vanishing race: an old, terribly emaciated Native American. The caption was "The Sick Mojave."[39]

For land developers, southern California's deserts were a wasteland to be "redeemed" by irrigation.[40] "Though they love their land with passionate fervor, they have been told that it was a desert," Charles H. Shinn commented in 1881 of the region's boosters, in reference to reports in the East that seized on occasional droughts to deride southern California's prospects.[41] Irrigation took on prominence in the promotional literature as both a material process that turned arid lands into productive ones and an allegorical one that crafted an American homeland from "a region of drought and barrenness."[42] In 1870, few farmers irrigated because they saw the process as an expensive luxury, but over the next decades, southern California experienced a boom in irrigation as new settlers who saw reliable access to water as crucial to agricultural success set about harnessing rivers and artesian sources of water.[43] By 1878, some 200,000 acres had been irrigated, and by 1890 that figure had increased by 500 percent to 1,004,223.[44] "Irrigating canals or ditches are already to be seen carrying water . . . in every direction through the valleys," wrote I. N. Hoag of the California Immigration Commission in 1883, "and wherever this water is used on the land, the once apparently worthless desert is made to bloom and blossom like the rose."[45]

The effects of irrigation were evident in California's growing "orange empire."[46] The number of bearing orange trees increased from 41,000 in 1870, to 280,000 in 1880, to 1.2 million in 1890, and California was a close second to Florida in total output.[47] In 1887, the state of California passed the Wright Act, which created local irrigation districts controlled by land owners. Settlers also headed in far greater numbers than before to newly irrigated areas in the southern part of the state. The California State Board of Trade hailed "horticulture and irrigation" as "the prime factors in the progress of the State in material wealth."[48] The population of seven northern and central California counties (Alpine, Calaveras, Del Norte, El Dorado, Marin, Mendocino, and San Luis Obispo) was 41,131 in 1870—virtually the equivalent (40,849) of seven southern counties (Fresno, Kern, Los Angeles, Merced, San Bernardino, San Diego,

Tulare).[49] By 1890, the northern group of counties, which were still largely unirrigated, had grown to only 67,778 residents, whereas the southern group, where irrigation was most widely practiced in the state, had 250,283 inhabitants. San Diego County, one of the most remote southern counties, had changed significantly with a new railroad link and an increase in irrigated lands from 5,000 in 1870 to 35,000 acres by 1890.[50] The Pacific Coast Land Bureau, which owned large tracts in the county, explained that 30,000 people were "now living where but a few years ago the world thought there was nothing but a fifth rate cattle range, if anything."[51]

For William E. Smythe, who wrote *The Conquest of Arid America* (1895), southern California stood out as a success story in irrigated transformation.[52] Smythe's verdict made clear that the vigorous promotion efforts of the previous generation had paid off: "Probably the public is more familiar with the orange-colonies of southern California than with any other institutions in the arid West."[53] Thanks to its boosters, the former desert colony of Riverside was now renowned for its irrigated groves and prosperous community, where "landownings are divided into five- and ten-acre lots" and "the civic institutions are fully equal to the highest New England standard." Although the land in southern California was increasingly expensive, the region's citrus colonies symbolized for Smythe an enticing alternative to an East of "overgrown cities and overcrowded industries" and the high unemployment and labor protests that followed the banking collapse of 1893. Two years after Frederick Jackson Turner stated his frontier thesis, Smythe saw in the national economic "stagnation" the shadow of the closed frontier: the end of a fruitful "policy of peaceful conquest over the resources of a virgin continent." However, Smythe was optimistic that frontiers created by humans could remedy these industrial wrongs and provide new formation narratives for Americans. Thus he pondered "how the American character will be modified and transformed when millions of people shall have finally made their homes in the arid regions, under conditions as yet untried by Anglo-Saxon men."[54] Southern California, in particular, provided "an extreme illustration of the value of water in an arid country," even though Smythe was quick to point out that its natural conditions were unique.[55] The experiences of Colorado and Utah, he wrote, were more representative of most of the American West "because southern California is semi-tropical and therefore not fairly representative of average possibilities."[56] Irrigation, however, was crucial to the selling of California as an exceptional tropic. Americans were persuaded that southern California avoided the tropical dampness that supposedly created unhealthy populations.[57] But its promoters continuously asserted that aridity and tropicality were not mutually exclusive: a desert land that was sufficiently irrigated could be as fertile as a rainforest (Egypt was frequently cited as an example).[58] The irrigated colony of Redlands thus offered "a climate that is dry, warm and yet not enervating."[59] "The most wonderful thing about California is the fact that although it has a semi-tropical temperature it has not a semi-tropical rainfall," one writer declared in a typically one-sided comparison of California and Florida. "As a consequence, there is hardly any natural tree-growth in the great valleys, and hence no swamps, insects or malaria."[60] The dry tropical climate of California was compatible with energetic progress.[61] In 1894, former governor of New Mexico Territory Lionel Sheldon, a Los Angeles resident, wrote that "there are some countries where heat and moisture are so great that vegetation grows so rapidly and in such rankness as almost to defy human effort to control or subject it." In those places, "there is a tendency to luxurious life which is obstructive to growth of civilization."[62] Although Sheldon did not refer directly to Florida, his description of rampant "vegetation" and "rain and heat" resonated with reservations about southern Florida, which, while perfectly suited to the "luxurious life" of winter tourism, was deemed potentially too "rank" for progressive settlement. By contrast, through the irrigated "control" of its deserts, southern California had become a civilized semi-tropical land.

Racial improvement was embedded in the selling of irrigated California. Riverside's chamber of commerce explained how before the colony's midwestern founders arrived, the region had been "a possible paradise treeless and barren, without life or beauty—a desert."[63] In reality there had been "life" in the region, as the chamber acknowledged: "Their distant neighbors [were] Spaniards and Indians," but "their own habitations [were] the first to be made by a white man," whose enterprise was manifest in modern orange groves and gardens of "palm and pomegranate, olive, persimmon and fig," all of which gave a "semi-tropical richness" to the surroundings. Through the arrival of white settlers, the land had been converted "from a desert waste to a garden, from a voiceless spot to a peopled plain, from a dream to realization."[64] At the International Irrigation Congress held in Los Angeles in 1893, promoter Harry Ellington Brook declared, "Irrigation has here made a country such as can be seen nowhere else, which supports in comfort, and even luxury, more people to the acre than the soil supports in any other country peopled by the Anglo-Saxon race."[65]

Visual representations reiterated the message, such as a cartoon pamphlet distributed at the 1893 World's Fair entitled "Irrigation and Its Results" that depicted California's environmental, social, and racial conversion. The image showed scenes before and after irrigation: the region had been transformed from a desolate frontier landscape with a single cactus that was inhabited by Native Americans and a cowboy to a tropical garden (verdant beneath a banner for "Irrigation") that was home to two white women and a white child (Fig. 4.1).

The "results" of reclamation were clear: Anglo-Americans (notably, women and children) in a fertile landscape were separated from the primitive desert of Indians and ranchers. Garden imagery connected to ideas of human fertility and controlled breeding was prominent in the growing eugenics movement that saw southern California as an ideal land for "improvement" of the white race.[66] For the region's boosters, irrigation made health-giving gardens possible, another signifier of peaceful Anglo-American conquest. In his 1899 guidebook published by the Santa Fe Railroad, Charles Keeler wrote of Riverside, "In this section as in so many other districts of southern California, which were found a desert occupied by a scanty, unprogressive Mexican population, and which have been made by Saxon industry perennial gardens of verdure and bloom, the irrigating ditch has been the magic wand of transformation."[67]

Figure 4.1. California promoters organized an impressive state display and reams of literature for the 27 million visitors to the Chicago World's Fair in 1893, including visual messages designed to persuade potential settlers from the Midwest of the environmental and racial triumphs irrigation had wrought in southern California. *Source:* Harry Ellington Brook, *The County and City of Los Angeles in Southern California* (Los Angeles: Times-Mirror Company, 1893). Courtesy of Department of Special Collections, Charles E. Young Research Library, UCLA.

Land reclamation fed into colonialist ideas of human reclamation. Whites in California strove to uplift the "inferior" natives who had been incapable of transformation themselves. The Sherman Institute, a boarding school that was founded in Riverside in 1901, sought to reeducate Native Americans to prepare them for integration into U.S. society. (Similar Americanization programs were set up to assimilate Mexicans, Chinese, Japanese, and Filipinos in Progressive Era California.)[68] Cited by boosters as an example that countered national criticism of white treatment of Indians, the project was championed by *Sunset* magazine—a monthly started by the Southern Pacific Railroad in 1898 to promote its western domain to settlers and tourists—as "striking proof that there still lurks in the national consciousness a keen sense of moral obligation ... to make useful citizens of the American Indians and to raise them to a place of intelligence whereon they may compete successfully with their Anglo-Saxon brothers."[69] "Useful citizens" meant industrious Indians who contributed to Anglo conceptions of progress. At the Sherman Institute, which emphasized education in industrial and service trades, native customs and languages were suppressed. An Indian agent reported of Native American children attending Sherman that "they cannot help but gain some ideas, when they go to Riverside or other thrifty towns, by seeing what industry can accomplish."[70] The institute also became a site that boosters promoted. "Pleasure-seekers" in Riverside were encouraged to visit not only the "fifty-six square miles of orchards within the city limits" but also the "Sherman Institute—the Carlisle Indian School of the Pacific."[71] In that sense, the program was an extension of the irrigation story. Groups of "progressive" whites took it upon themselves to convert Native Americans who, like desert lands, would "be trained in the spirit of Americanism, and, so far as possible ... imbued with the energy and industry ... that has made America the greatest nation."[72]

By the time the Imperial Valley became a focus of promotional energies at the turn of the century, the economy of semi-tropical California had been transformed and land values in many counties had increased sharply. Such consequences had been predicted: as early as 1883 the *Rural Californian* produced an "emigration paper" that stated, "We believe—no panic or calamity interposing—that in the next ten years it will be very difficult to buy any desirable lands with water, suitable for orange or raisin growing, in southern California, for less than $1000 per acre."[73] Although self-serving and somewhat overblown, these claims had proved prescient by the mid-1890s, when horticulture had become a lucrative enterprise and California's orange crop alone brought $3,000,000 into the state.[74] The Southern California Fruit Growers' Exchange, a producers' cooperative that was formed in 1893, enabled members to get better prices in the marketplace. Members also strove for changes in tariff protection and freight rates and innovations in fruit distribution, including refrigerated railway cars. A pamphlet distributed at the World's Fair reported "a general impression [in the East] that Southern California land is so expensive as to be beyond the reach of all but the well-to-do."[75] At $100 to $200 per acre—the prices the Semi-Tropic Land and Water Company of Rialto, California, quoted in 1890—such impressions were becoming rooted in reality (Fig. 4.2). While land prices varied tremendously, depending on location, soil type, and water supply, semi-tropical agricultural tracts were invariably more expensive. In 1893 unirrigated land for grain, alfalfa, or deciduous fruits cost $30 to $100 per acre while quality irrigated citrus lands sold for not less than $250 per acre.[76]

To some extent, increased land values imperiled the formation narratives of republican citizenship embedded in the promotion of semi-tropical agriculture in California. Significant capital became a prerequisite for most settlers. Some promoters acknowledged as much: "Great advances in land values certainly bring great advantages," a rural writer commented, "but they also produce results which are detrimental to the men of comparatively small means who

Figure 4.2. Land companies such as the Semi-Tropic Land and Water Company of San Bernardino County, California, advertised small parcels of irrigated semi-tropic land with "special inducements to purchasers for actual settlement." Source: *Lands of the Semi-Tropic Land and Water Company, San Bernardino County, California* (San Francisco: Britton & Rey, 1890). Courtesy of The Bancroft Library, University of California, Berkeley.

are seeking homes. And this class form [*sic*] the bone and sinew of the population."[77] Yet land promoters also saw in increasing land prices confirmation of their region's agricultural exceptionalism and social progress. Many were landowners who benefited personally from higher real estate values and wealthier settlers. The Southern California Immigration Association, which was formed in 1886, warned, "While not disposed to discourage the immigration of those who have some means and evince a disposition to avail themselves of the opportunities afforded by a new country, the association does not hold out flattering inducements in favor of southern California as a 'poor man's country.'"[78] These promoters emphasized that the region's (and Florida's) market monopoly of semi-tropical agriculture had effectively been passed on to its real estate prices. Given that "a man can do better on ten acres here than on 160 acres in the East," Henry Ellington Brook declared, "ten acres of Southern California land ought to be cheap at ten times the price of Eastern land, with our climate in the bargain."[79]

Vigorous growth in the production of semi-tropical crops during a decade of national depression supported such claims. For example, between 1890 and 1900, the total number of semi-tropical fruit trees in California increased from 1.8 million to 8.9 million.[80] Yet promoters clung to their visions of semi-tropical California as a region that was more truly republican than the industrial Northeast. Citrus leader Riverside, for example, where land was priced at hundreds of dollars per acre, was featured frequently in *Sunset* magazine as a success story in terms of republican values. "Riverside is the richest city in the world, has the largest per capita income," wrote J. P. Baumgartner. "Yet it has no millionaires and no paupers." The increasing wealth of producers of semi-tropical agricultural products was, in fact, a healthy evolution that was producing prosperous middle-class communities, Baumgartner claimed. The irrigated settlement had "an even and equitable distribution of wealth naturally incident to the character of the industries in which the people are engaged, resulting in almost ideal social conditions."[81]

For promoters of southern California, the growth of Riverside and other irrigated sections augured well for the potential of the Mojave and Colorado Deserts. Hotter and drier than the coastal and foothill counties, these inland valleys had been largely overlooked by developers during the 1880s boom, and the depression of the 1890s had halted irrigation plans in those areas.[82] They remained unreclaimed and were inhabited only by small numbers of Native Americans. Nonetheless, promoters began to see the deserts as future homelands. An 1893 pamphlet opined, "Twenty years ago, Riverside, the center of California orange production, was a barren, sandy, and desert waste. Twenty years hence, the Mojave and Colorado basins will support a dense population. Water will be the magic element to effect this marvelous change."[83] Hailing in 1896 "the men of [California's] southern valleys" who had achieved a "conquest of the desert" and "made the small farm unit supreme," Smythe also pointed to the Colorado Desert as the next site for republican expansion.[84] With improved conditions in the national economy after 1898, the irrigated acreage in California increased by nearly 20 percent in four years, including the Salton Sink, part of the Colorado Desert.[85]

The area was renamed—branded—the Imperial Valley by the private California Development Company, which, in the late 1890s, asserted an unauthorized water right to the Colorado River and set out to irrigate, subdivide, and sell valley lands.[86] Located in southeastern California, the Imperial Valley consisted of an area of desert somewhat larger than the state of Delaware. Located some 200 feet below the Colorado River, the valley was forty miles by sixty and had an average yearly rainfall of only three inches.[87] One scholar has described the Imperial Valley as "a desert pit or oven."[88] But the valley also contained a potentially irrigable area of over 400,000 acres, and that is what gripped the imagination of Smythe when he toured the area in 1900 for *Sunset*. The interior desert promised quasi-tropical lands at much cheaper prices than elsewhere in the state. Once reclaimed, Smythe wrote, the Colorado Desert would become "a new civilization" with "the little farm" as its cornerstone.[89] Socially the valley would be like Riverside—a dense country of "independent" settlers who would "realize . . . all the best possibilities of country and of town life"—but, unlike Riverside, where prices ran upward of $300 per acre, the newly reclaimed desert lands would be offered for $10 to $15 per acre, a price the average American could afford that even included a perpetual right to water. "There are thousands of eastern people who desire to live in California, and are only prevented from doing so by the mistaken idea that all land in this country is high-priced," Smythe explained. When the Imperial Valley was inhabited by a community of settlers on small farms, it would resemble a "twentieth century Damascus, [but] fairer than that in the Syrian desert," since it would be full of "the life of a new time and blessed with American liberty."[90]

Land developers predicted myriad benefits once the Imperial Valley was irrigated. One of the first would be that it would revise the initial impressions of incoming visitors. Despite the growing interest in the unredeemed desert, promoters pointed out that tourists on the San Diego & Eastern Railroad had to endure a long stretch of dusty air; closed, hot carriages; and desolate views. Once they could see "the restful green verdure" of irrigated lands, however, "the new route to California will be a wonderful improvement over the old."[91] Entering the state near Calexico, the tourist would traverse forty or fifty miles "of fields of green with alfalfa and other crops" and witness that "the temperature along the desert is almost tropical"—although (and this was important) also "endurable out of doors."[92] Advertisements appeared for new pleasure and health resorts in Imperial Valley settlements, such as Silsbee on Blue Lake.[93] Imperial County also had attractions for the new automobile driver. Imperial Avenue, which in plans would be lined with farmers' cottages and shade trees, would extend forty-five miles from the Southern Pacific Railroad to Calexico. Boosters predicted that it would have a future equal to such celebrated boulevards as Magnolia Avenue in Riverside and Euclid Avenue in Ontario.[94]

The Imperial Valley was sold first and foremost as a land that promised republican independence through its farms: the "'free home for every family' [that] is the American ideal."[95] The California Development Company and its colonizing body, the Imperial Land Company, promoted the reclamation project in magazines and pamphlets, describing the valley as the new frontier for "men of limited means, who would be very glad to secure a tract of good, fertile land" with water rights.[96] By 1901, the towns of Imperial and Calexico had been founded, schools had been opened, and farms had been laid out. Landowners began publishing the *Imperial Valley Press*, a boosterist newspaper that borrowed heavily from the tactics promoters had used to sell semi-tropical California. Citing the "rules laid down" by leading railroad and state government promoter William H. Mills "on how to build up a community" in southern California, the valley's developers boldly stated: "Now watch Imperial grow."[97] In a magazine targeting homeseekers, the Imperial Land Company depicted a lady who was irrigation incarnate; her wand transformed the land "From Desert to Garden" (Fig. 4.3).

For the California Development Company, however, the "magical" conversion of this "desert pit" into fertile land for agriculture proved an overwhelming task: as Carey McWilliams wrote, "The scale was too vast, the commitments too immense, the problems too enormous."[98] In 1905, after the California Development Company had cut into the banks of the Colorado River to provide water to irrigate the valley, the river flooded one of the artificial cuts and rushed down the steep slope into the Imperial Valley and then on into the Salton Sink (which would become the Salton Sea). The private speculation company, facing bankruptcy, were forced to turn to the Southern Pacific Railroad for assistance.[99] The railroad, which owned land and railroad lines in the area, launched a massive, protracted damming operation that, after two years, prevented the river from destroying the entire reclamation project.[100] The selling of the Imperial Valley then resumed under the far steadier guidance of the Southern Pacific

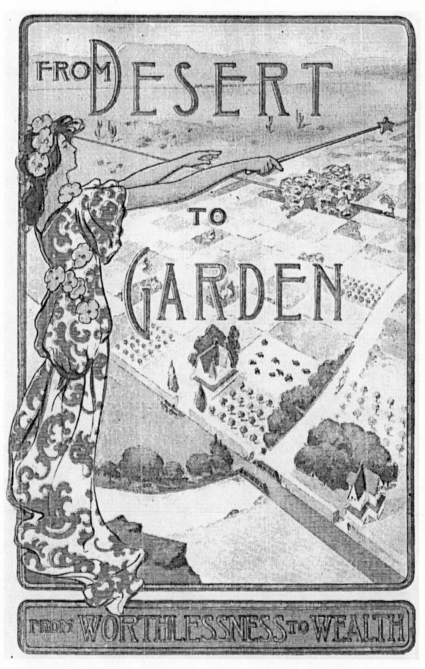

Figure 4.3. Promoters of California's Imperial Valley suggested that the wealth produced through irrigation would foster republican communities of independent landowners. *Source: California Homeseeker* 1, no. 3 (April 1902). Courtesy of the San Francisco History Center, San Francisco Public Library.

Company, which had by then been promoting southern California as a superior semi-tropic for thirty years. Two organs of the company, *Sunset* magazine and its Home-seekers' Bureau, led the selling of the Imperial Valley after 1907. The Southern Pacific's Passenger Company had already published *Semi-Tropic California*, a pamphlet that included alluring descriptions of newly reclaimed desert colonies such as Indio, which "originally . . . had nothing of outward appearance to redeem it" but now was proof of "how it is possible to transform a barren desert into an Eden."[101] The irrigated town of Indio combined an "absolutely dry and pure" atmosphere with "a scene of dense tropical growth." The town of Salton, located further south in the valley, "needs no greater incentive than water to rival the tropics in productiveness."[102] Starting in 1906, the Southern Pacific offered discounted one-way rates to colonists traveling to southern California. It was estimated that on one Monday in November 1907, 7,000 passengers reached Los Angeles using this special rate, many of whom continued on to the Imperial Valley to start new homes there.[103]

Building on the earlier colonialist ideas of white expansion into "tropical" California, the local press linked Imperial Valley settlements to British colonial development in Egypt.[104] The *Imperial Valley Press* cited a recent U.S. Geological Survey that found the valley suitable for irrigation works similar to those the British had constructed in North Africa. With its "semi-tropical climate" and potential "diversity of agricultural products," the Imperial Valley was an "an occidental Egypt" in the United States, the newspaper claimed.[105] Racial conquest was written into the vision for the Imperial Valley; it had been settled by "the first white men [who] trekked across the barren wastes and founded this vast inland agricultural empire."[106] Promoters attributed the fructifying of the land to Anglo-American skill. "In January, 1901, there was not a living white man on all the desert waste," wrote Otis B. Tout of the Sunset Magazine Home-Seekers' Bureau, while another pamphlet stressed that the region had been one of "drought and barrenness in which only a few Indians roamed, finding scanty subsistence by a rude kind of agriculture in spots along the river moistened by the overflow."[107]

Valley boosters in the town of El Centro organized a promotional parade in July 1909 that championed Imperial Valley as "the American Nile country" and distributed 400 copies of a booster publication, the *Desert Farmer*, replete with images of irrigated farms.[108] The colonialist ideology of Imperial Valley promoters sometimes stretched to a Lamarckian belief that conquest of the land would also civilize the wilds, that human development of the desert could actually alter its climate. Envisaging the creation of a "humid strip" from southern California to Texas, these boosters predicted that "the heat of the desert will be nullified" by the evaporation of vast acreages of watered lands. Extremes of desert temperature would be modified—the minimum raised and the maximum lowered—ultimately leading to improved conditions for a semi-tropical American civilization.[109]

Republican independence in the reclaimed desert was a pervasive theme, transplanting to Imperial Valley the ideal of irrigation articulated at the 1893 International Irrigation Congress in Los Angeles, where Smythe claimed that the two key terms were synonymous: "Irrigation and Independence."[110] Imperial Valley, promoters asserted, was "distinctly a farming region" where "agriculture . . . [was] the basis of abiding prosperity for towns."[111] Responding to the vigorous sales pitch, white settlers introduced a range of crops to the desert soil. By 1908, nearly 300,000 acres in the Imperial Valley were under cultivation and crops worth over $2 million were being produced. Fifteen thousand people lived in an area that extended from Indio to Calexico and Imperial County had been established as California's newest county.[112] By the winter of 1910, the 3,500 farms under cultivation in the valley had a combined acreage of approximately 350,000: an average of 100 acres per farm that was less than a third of the average acreage of farms across the state.[113] The Imperial Valley was sold as a sustaining republican homeland: a region where "what a man can do to better his condition will be measured chiefly by his energy and his ability." Building upon the ideals of agrarian independence in semi-tropical California, boosters stated that nowhere would "intelligent effort . . . win more independence and satisfaction in the return than in the valley."[114]

But developers and settlers in the Imperial Valley increasingly looked to employ cheap migrant laborers as a means of maximizing profits from their reclaimed farms. The potential profitability of the Imperial Valley lands was evident in 1914, when the Southern Pacific sold 44,000 acres of valley land to a syndicate of 200 Los Angeles businessmen who then marketed the property as a prime location for citrus and cotton farms.[115] While its land boosters continued to use republican rhetoric, the Imperial Valley exemplified California's hardening divide between business-minded landowners and landless field workers.[116] In the early twentieth century, "the individual grower [in southern California] . . . functioned as a businessman involved more with a bureaucratic cooperative and less with actual farming itself." Hand-picking and packing fruit invariably was "reserved for other nationalities, and, to a lesser extent, poor Anglo-Americans."[117] Older notions of living on and working one's own land in semi-tropical California were increasingly absent in the Imperial Valley. Boosters often characterized this change as a positive move toward "scientific" farming. "This new agriculture requires brains, and that success is conditioned upon intelligence," explained A. J. Wells. "The man who merely works never gets on. If working could take the place of thinking, every mule might get rich."[118] From the beginning of white settlement in the valley, Native Americans in the Colorado Desert were used as a cheap work force.[119] The Imperial Valley visions of independent white settlers were intertwined with an acceptance of the fact that human "mules" would be needed for labor in the desert pit, a colonialist mentality that gave new depth to the boosterist representation of the Imperial Valley as the "American Nile Valley."[120]

A shift in the Imperial Valley toward cotton production accelerated landowners' reliance on a racialized migrant workforce.[121] One advocate of the valley's cotton-producing potential promoted it in 1910 as "just like Dixie Land."[122] White settler-landowners could prosper by employing nonwhite laborers at cheap wages, in particular "Indians and Mexicans" who could "be had in large bands in the valley." Japanese workers were also available, but they demanded higher wages and were "exceedingly independent and intractable." There was some discussion of bringing into the valley "the picturesque negro, with his music and drollery."[123] Reflecting the racist mindset of such promoters, Japanese "independence" was conceived of as an impediment to the prosperous independence of white landowners, who, in their search for cheap labor, also turned to "Hindus" (Asian Indians) who were shipped into the Imperial Valley at short notice from the San Joaquin Valley.[124] Mrs. Sarah F. Wiles, described as "California's first woman cotton planter," joined other valley growers in bringing in "Hindus, who worked not only faithfully, but were willing to work for what the growers could afford to pay them," an eastern newspaper reported.[125] In the Imperial Valley, few landowners in the valley actually worked their fields in the desert heat when they could afford to pay someone else to do stoop labor.[126] Some successful planters initiated a sharecropping scheme, in which their holdings were leased out in ten-, twenty-, or fifty-acre plots, and the renter shared half and half with the owner.[127] Employment agencies were formed that specialized in bringing in and overseeing Mexican cotton pickers for Imperial Valley planters.[128] In 1914, as a result of landowners' access to this inexpensive and racialized work force, the Imperial Valley was producing 16,500 acres of cotton, a crop worth $1.4 million.[129] The crop was harvested by increasing numbers of Mexican migrant workers who traveled from harvest to harvest and worked for low wages. These laborers were social and economic outsiders in a self-styled republican land where, its boosters stated, "thousands of clean-living, clean-thinking, healthy, sane, cheery Americans . . . have come into the desert to make ten blades of grass grow where none grew for ages."[130]

The tropical fertility of the Imperial Valley remained at the forefront of the promotional message. Boosters made the tropical productivity of the Imperial Valley the crucial selling point, as they had done for California's coastal and foothill counties in earlier decades. The valley's unique rewards made the harsh climate and realities of labor palatable. The California desert, developers proclaimed, had been made into an American tropic of realized hopes, "the best piece of agricultural land occupied by white men on the face of the earth."[131] "This section of the Golden State is as rich as the Valley of the Nile," land advertisements explained. "With plenty of water and wafted by the warm breezes of a semi-tropical climate," it produced twelve crops per year, including cantaloupes, alfalfa, citrus, tomatoes, and cotton.[132] Imperial County's eight chambers of commerce, which were formed as a means of increasing land values and attracting more settlers, advertised the "Rare Fertility of Wonderful Imperial Valley," which rivaled "in production the most luxuriant growth of tropic climes" (Fig. 4.4).

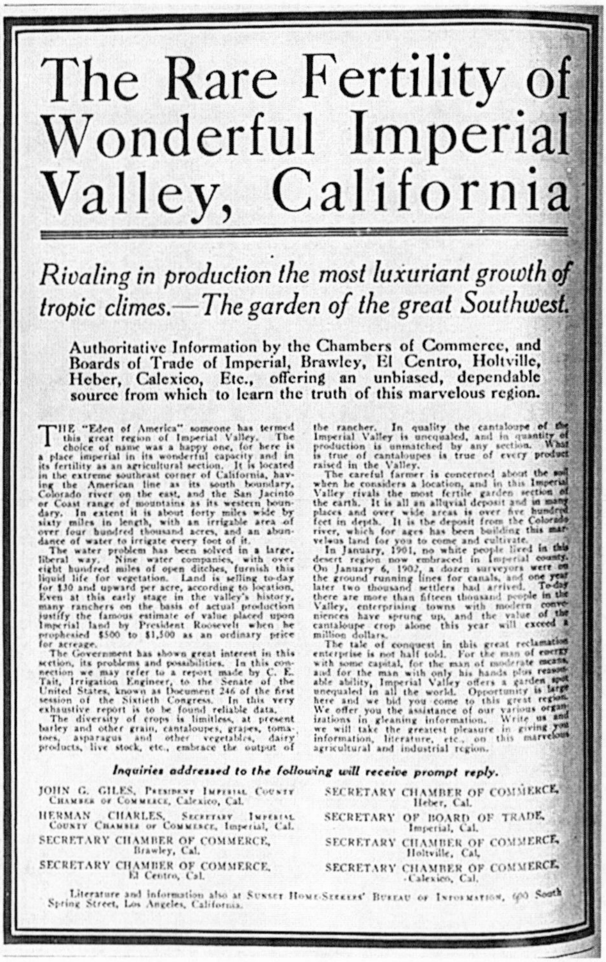

The Rare Fertility of Wonderful Imperial Valley, California

Rivaling in production the most luxuriant growth of tropic climes.—The garden of the great Southwest.

Authoritative Information by the Chambers of Commerce, and Boards of Trade of Imperial, Brawley, El Centro, Holtville, Heber, Calexico, Etc., offering an unbiased, dependable source from which to learn the truth of this marvelous region.

THE "Eden of America" someone has termed this great region of Imperial Valley. The choice of name was a happy one, for here is a place imperial in its wonderful capacity and in its fertility as an agricultural section. It is located in the extreme southeast corner of California, having the American line as its south boundary, Colorado river on the east, and the San Jacinto or Coast range of mountains as its western boundary. In extent it is about forty miles wide by sixty miles in length, with an irrigable area of over four hundred thousand acres, and an abundance of water to irrigate every foot of it.

The water problem has been solved in a large, liberal way. Nine water companies, with over eight hundred miles of open ditches, furnish this liquid life for vegetation. Land is selling to-day for $30 and upward per acre, according to location. Even at this early stage in the valley's history, many ranchers on the basis of actual production justify the famous estimate of value placed upon Imperial land by President Roosevelt when he prophesied $500 to $1,500 as an ordinary price for acreage.

The Government has shown great interest in this section, its problems and possibilities. In this connection we may refer to a report made by C. E. Tait, Irrigation Engineer, to the Senate of the United States, known as Document 246 of the first session of the Sixtieth Congress. In this very exhaustive report is to be found reliable data.

The diversity of crops is limitless, at present barley and other grain, cantaloupes, grapes, tomatoes, asparagus and other vegetables, dairy products, live stock, etc., embrace the output of the rancher. In quality the cantaloupe of the Imperial Valley is unequaled, and in quantity of production is unmatched by any section. What is true of cantaloupes is true of every product raised in the Valley.

The careful farmer is concerned about the soil when he considers a location, and in this Imperial Valley rivals the most fertile garden section of the earth. It is all an allqvial deposit and in many places and over wide areas is over five hundred feet in depth. It is the deposit from the Colorado river, which for ages has been building this marvelous land for you to come and cultivate.

In January, 1901, no white people lived in this desert region now embraced in Imperial county. On January 6, 1902, a dozen surveyors were on the ground running lines for canals, and one year later two thousand settlers had arrived. To-day there are more than fifteen thousand people in the Valley, enterprising towns with modern conveniences have sprung up, and the value of the cantaloupe crop alone this year will exceed a million dollars.

The tale of conquest in this great reclamation enterprise is not half told. For the man of energy with some capital, for the man of moderate means, and for the man with only his hands plus reasonable ability, Imperial Valley offers a garden spot unequaled in all the world. Opportunity is large here and we bid you come to this great region. We offer you the assistance of our various organizations in gleaning information. Write us and we will take the greatest pleasure in giving you information, literature, etc., on this marvelous agricultural and industrial region.

Inquiries addressed to the following will receive prompt reply.

JOHN G. GILES, President Imperial County Chamber of Commerce, Calexico, Cal.

HERMAN CHARLES, Secretary Imperial County Chamber of Commerce, Imperial, Cal.

SECRETARY CHAMBER OF COMMERCE, Brawley, Cal.

SECRETARY CHAMBER OF COMMERCE, El Centro, Cal.

SECRETARY CHAMBER OF COMMERCE, Heber, Cal.

SECRETARY OF BOARD OF TRADE, Imperial, Cal.

SECRETARY CHAMBER OF COMMERCE, Holtville, Cal.

SECRETARY CHAMBER OF COMMERCE, Calexico, Cal.

Literature and information also at Sunset Home-Seekers' Bureau of Information, 600 South Spring Street, Los Angeles, California.

Figure 4.4. At the turn of the twentieth century, the Imperial Valley was promoted as the "Eden of America," a tropical and republican homeland for white settlers. *Source: Sunset* 21, no. 5 (September 1908): 11. Courtesy of Social Sciences and Humanities Library, University of California, San Diego, California.

Calling upon settlers to purchase land for $30 and more per acre, boosters wrote, "The tale of conquest in this great reclamation enterprise is not half told."[133] Yet an important environmental conquest had largely been achieved. As A. J. Wells wrote in 1914, "The old prejudice against the desert is gone, as with water it puts on another face and becomes amazingly productive."[134] Excursions of "home-seekers" who were brought to Imperial County to see the new farms and labor arrangements were said to be "greatly impressed" with the "American Nile Valley" and its array of crops.[135] Although the region was divided into predominantly white landowners and non-Anglo migrant laborers, promoters clung stubbornly to their script of republican independence for the worthy and continued to claim that the irrigated desert was the "Land of Promise Fulfilled." They presented the Imperial Valley as a homeland for Americans who were "working with the spirit of conquerors, with buoyant hope and confidence in the future."[136] The booster ideal was articulated by a member of a group of 100 businessmen who traveled to the Imperial Valley with the San Diego Chamber of Commerce in 1910. He stated, "I admire your country and I foresee the greatest future for this section that one could desire, but still more do I admire your sturdy men who have fought back the desert, made the forces of nature their slaves and make a paradise of this once arid region."[137]

Draining Florida's Everglades

Promoters of peninsula Florida confronted the problem of a swamp.[138] For many nineteenth-century Americans, Florida's environment suggested disease, lethargy, and damp wastelands "not in any degree to be connected with agricultural pursuits, healthful residence, or the enjoyments of prosperity."[139] Southern California promoters occasionally contributed to this devastating perception. When Floridians attempted to deride California's citrus industry, the *Los Angeles Times* curtly responded, "Hark from the Swamps a Doleful Sound."[140] Some Florida boosters found selling material in precisely this distinction. "Many will refer to the vast amount of waste land in Florida in the shape of swamps, everglades, ... etc.," wrote Rev. George D. Watson in an 1888 immigration pamphlet, "but southern California has a far greater waste in its rainless Mojave Desert [and] would gladly give millions of wealth for a few of the little lakes, tens of thousands of which begerm [sic] the territory of Florida."[141] Florida settlers needed fertilizer, Watson wrote, but California settlers needed water. The difference was that water in the West was much more scarce and expensive than the fertilizer that was obtainable from the "muck and peat beds" of Florida.[142] Such arguments were not enough to persuade Americans who feared swamps even more than they did deserts. As one Floridian lamented in the 1880s, "It is customary to assert that the climate of California is bracing and stimulating ... and that of Florida is sluggish and soporific."[143]

But Florida's wetlands were similar to the southern California desert in the sense that both occupied an ambivalent position in promotional imagery as both tourist attraction and impediment to settlement. As development moved southward into the peninsula in the 1890s, tourism promoters increasingly saw unique value in the Everglades and in their only human inhabitants, the Seminole Indians, as an exotic attraction for adventurous tourists. At the same time, draining southern Florida's swamps became an obsession of would-be developers, who saw an opportunity to conquer an intimidating environment and add vast new fertile acreage to America's East Coast tropic of hopes.

Like irrigation in the West, mastery of the wetlands was an expensive and drawn-out process in the development of Florida. In 1850, when the federal government granted "swamp and overflowed" lands to the states for drainage and reclamation, Florida received 20 million acres, or about 60 percent of its land mass, the majority of which was located in the peninsula.[144] Reclamation was virtually nonexistent for decades, however, proscribed by the Civil War, by the turbulence of Reconstruction, and then by complex litigation that prevented the Internal Improvement Fund—the body that controlled state land—from granting swamp land to private developers. In the 1880s, southern Florida was still widely perceived as being agriculturally worthless, an unwanted American frontier: the population of Dade County in 1890 was just 861.[145] The region was also home to the state's remaining Seminole Indians (perhaps 200 lived in island dwellings in the Everglades). Some promoters still blamed their resistance to removal in the first half of the nineteenth century for southern Florida's relative dearth of white residents.[146]

The selling of southern Florida received impetus from Philadelphia capitalist Hamilton Disston's purchase in 1881 of 4 million acres in the region. Disston immediately began trying to drain the swamp lands.[147] The scheme had limited results. Although the $1 million purchase relieved the debt of the Internal Improvement Fund and thereby freed the state government to attract railroad developers, this development was controversial: Populists in the state charged that corporate interests were being favored at the expense of homesteaders. The national banking collapse of 1893 brought the enterprise to a temporary halt, and Disston's death three years later precluded its resumption. The total area that had been permanently drained was no more than 50,000 acres.[148] Nonetheless, the project inspired promoters of southern Florida and challenged the beliefs of northerners that the land was an unredeemable swamp. As Lake Okeechobee was higher than the Everglades, Disston's plan was to lower the lake by cutting canals into it that would carry excess water from Okeechobee into the Atlantic and the Gulf of Mexico.[149] After cutting dredges around Lake Okeechobee, Disston's engineers demonstrated that the water table could be lowered—albeit at great expense—and that reclaimed lands would produce viable crops that included winter vegetables and sugarcane.[150] Disston's land companies also vigorously encouraged small-scale farmers to buy land, which they initially offered for $1.25 to $5 per acre. A former deputy commissioner of the U.S. Department of Agriculture reported a "great . . . rush of settlers to the 'land of perpetual June' from the North," an event that resulted in increasing property values.[151] Between 1880 and 1885, the total population of the five peninsular counties where Disston's land companies were most active rose from 24,547 to 45,588.[152] Moreover, Disston's purchase rehabilitated the state's credit, which in turn made major railroad construction possible in Florida. The number of railway miles in the state swelled from 518 in 1880 to over 3,200 by 1900.[153] Some railroads offered discounted rates to new settlers. In 1896, for example, one-way colony excursion rates from Chicago to Florida were reduced to $18 by the Illinois Central.[154] As the state department of agriculture later reported, after Disston's deal, "Florida entered upon an era of internal development that has made her one of the most prosperous in the South."[155]

The Disston drainage project encouraged boosters to present visions of the future transformation of southern Florida. Governor William Bloxham, who oversaw Disston's purchase and was decidedly biased in its favor, was nonetheless justified in describing it as "an advertisement such as we never had" for "our resources and climatic advantages."[156] The drainage of southern Florida, promoters responded, would open up a unique environment for U.S. expansion. Ignoring the persistent claims that California was also semi-tropical, an 1885 Florida guidebook hailed the drainage scheme as "the reclamation of millions of what are suspected to be the richest lands on the continent, and they constituting wholly the only bit of semi-tropical territory over which our nation's flag waves."[157]

Into the 1890s, the southward progress of development in Florida drove new ambitious plans to reclaim the Everglades, a vast watery prairie of nearly 3 million acres below Lake Okeechobee.[158] The Everglades, which were almost unexplored by whites, had a special place in the American imagination as a domestic wetland of unsurpassed exoticism. Its "possibilities, in an agricultural or commercial point of view," as an 1884 guidebook put it, were "as utterly unknown as those of the interior of Africa."[159] The Everglades were a daunting but logical frontier for Florida boosters who had successfully attracted settlers and tourists to the northern and coastal counties of peninsular Florida. In 1892, James Ingraham, who was already a significant player in the state's socioeconomic growth, crossed the Everglades with a company of men as part of an exploratory mission to assess their potential for drainage.[160] As a close subordinate of Gulf Coast railroad magnate Henry Plant, Ingraham served as president of Plant's South Florida Railroad. Shortly after Ingraham completed his Everglades tour, Plant's rival, Henry Flagler, hired him as vice-president of the Florida East Coast Railway Company. In his new position, Ingraham oversaw the promotion of hundreds of thousands of acres of land the state had granted the company during the construction of the railroad.[161] Ingraham saw the Everglades as the next frontier of tropical development and became one of many promoters who pushed for drainage and future settlement there.[162] As an agricultural paper explained in 1903, "Our pioneers laid down the rails for traffic and pleasure 400 miles down the Atlantic coast, penetrating a savage jungle hitherto believed to be uninhabitable," and they had now reached "the very verge of the Everglades."[163]

Natural events further encouraged this southward push to the Everglades. In the winter of 1894–95, a freeze struck the peninsula and citrus orchards throughout central Florida were killed. The state's orange crop fell to virtually none from 6 million boxes (a figure that would not be reached again until 1909).[164] The freeze ended Florida's predominance over California as an orange producer.[165] Indeed, its effects were recognized in southern California, where a contributor in the *Los Angeles Times* asked whether commercial orange growing in Florida would be revived any time soon. A long delay would make southern California "the only section in the United States in which citrus fruit may be raised, year after year, as a safe business proposition."[166] The Florida freeze also affected competition for tourists. "Florida has been a strong competitor of California for the winter tourist business," the writer explained, because the southern part of the state had the important advantages of lower transportation rates to and from major northeastern cities and "more of a tropical character of climate" and "vegetation" than did southern California. Yet guests at Florida hotels were "compelled to remain in steam-heated rooms" during the freeze, and the writer envisaged that "a large proportion" of the southern state's winter travel "will be diverted to Southern California, for some years to come."[167] Florida's freeze thus provided further evidence that southern California was moving ahead in the interstate rivalry. "Southern California is the semi-tropical region of the United States par excellence," West Coast boosters purred.[168]

For all these setbacks, however, the freeze also encouraged Florida railroad and land developers to press further south, beyond a notional "frost line" in a route that took them to the edges of the Everglades. In the first decade of the twentieth century, the wetlands became the focal point for extensive reclamation schemes and a new battlefield between corporate and populist elements in Florida, where an immense amount of state land—approximately 17 million acres—had already been granted to railroad companies by the state's Democratic Party administrations after Reconstruction.[169] As in California, where the Southern Pacific Railroad's so-called octopus drew public indignation because of its influence in state land development and politics, Florida was rife with anti-railroad and anti-corporate sentiment that shaped the rhetoric of governors William S. Jennings (1901–5) and Napoleon Bonaparte Broward (1905–9).[170] Jennings succeeded in convincing the federal government to cede the Everglades to the state, and Broward became the figurehead of the drainage scheme. He was elected because of his campaign pledge to reclaim the Everglades as a frontier for homesteaders rather than as bounty for "land grant corporations."[171] "The call of Everglades," Broward declared, was to bring "the landless man to the manless land."[172] This promise, as one scholar writes, Broward "proved unable to keep."[173] The expense of drainage forced the state to sell considerable acreage in the Everglades to private developers, including 500,000 acres to Colorado capitalist Richard J. Bolles of the Florida Fruit Lands Company, which was based in Kansas City. This is but one example of how the Everglades were sold to large corporations in the 1910s and 1920s. Ironically, in both California and Florida the often-despised railroads were significant promoters of reclamation schemes, and railroad and corporate developers borrowed heavily from the promotional imagery of reclamation for republican citizens that their populist detractors had constructed.

Napoleon Broward and his supporters saw drainage as both a conservationist and a republican measure: as a means of harnessing unused natural resources and cultivating independent citizens. But there was also a colonialist bent to this vision. Broward sent an open letter to the people of Florida in which he compared the future Everglades to Egypt, where "the British Government[,] undeterred by the item of expense or the fear of failure, built the great Assouan Dam which harnessed the Nile floods and made them obedient."[174] To realize this vision, Broward created the Everglades Drainage District and funded the state's initial efforts through a tax on southern Florida lands, a move that raised the ire of large landholders such as Flagler, whose viewpoint was articulated in the Florida newspapers he owned such as the *Times-Union*. But in 1906 the state engineers began work on the massive task of lowering the water table and opening up the Everglades for settlement. The state's first dredges were cut into Lake Okeechobee, designed to draw away to the ocean the water that otherwise drained into the Everglades, as the engineers followed the example set by Disston's men two decades earlier as well as the logic behind Broward's declaration that "water will run downhill!"[175] In recognition of his reclamation efforts, Broward was named president of the National Drainage Congress and traveled with President Roosevelt to inspect drained land in the Mississippi Valley. Broward cited national motives for draining the Everglades: it would benefit the country because they would become the ultimate "home of the sugar cane in the United States."[176] A fellow Everglades enthusiast lauded Broward as a "masterful promoter" of the "work which will convert a vast, useless waste into what promises to be the most productive part of Florida, if not . . . in the whole United States of America."[177]

As dredging continued, both state and private promoters claimed that the drainage of the Everglades amounted to a conquest of tropical wilds that would populate southern Florida with independent farmers. Magazines published by railroad and corporate landowners—such as the *Florida East Coast Homeseeker*, which the Flagler Company began publishing in 1899—explained that peninsular Florida's "waste places have been settled up by a strong, courageous people" who would do the same in the Everglades.[178] Flagler's Model Land Company was in charge of selling his 210,000 acres in swampy southern Florida.[179] Settlers who enjoyed success became local celebrities and case studies. Walter Waldin, for example, an Iowan who migrated to Dade County in 1899, bought land bordering on the Everglades, and began growing winter vegetables, was hailed in a 1907 article as a fine example of "the farmer and fruit grower" who had joined "the independent list."[180] Waldin, who went to southern Florida to "learn the secret of truck growing in the tropics," won prizes for his vegetable displays at the Dade County fair and earned a substantial income from his produce. Not inconsequentially for those who supported white settlement in the Everglades, his land rose rapidly in value. "Follow Mr. Waldin's methods," the magazine explained, "and you can succeed."[181] Waldin himself became an active booster. In Miami newspapers, he contrasted farming in southern Florida with farming in the Midwest, arguing that the peninsula's climate and special crops ("tropical fruits" and truck vegetables) made far superior agriculture possible.[182] In 1910, Waldin put his 60-acre farm on the market for $17,000 and pursued a full-time career as a land promoter. He wrote *Truck Farming in the Everglades*, a book that, in addition to advertising his own "Beautiful Everglades Plantation," promulgated the vision of reclamation as both a "money-making investment" for the individual and a virtuous social cause. Citing the national back-to-the-land movement, Waldin praised the thousands of Americans who wanted to "avail themselves of the valuable opportunity to secure a home and a livelihood in this superb climate."[183]

Building on the semi-tropical links between Florida and California, boosters of southern Florida actively encouraged connections between the state's incipient drainage scheme and the irrigation of the West. While promoters of drainage took inspiration from the newly available acreage irrigation created—"what irrigation is doing for the West . . . drainage promises to do for the East," wrote a journalist in 1907—they also posited that drainage was a cheaper way of creating new land for settlement: drainage, it was claimed, cost less than $5 per acre, compared to the $30 per acre cost of irrigation.[184] Broward argued, erroneously, that reclamation of the Everglades could be done for as little as $1 per acre.[185] Other promoters expressed bold claims that Florida's drained lands would be cheaper and more fertile than irrigated land in California, while "the greatly superior climate of the Everglades district is revealed by . . . comparisons between South Florida and southern California."[186] While southern drainage enthusiasts called for the federal government to fund the draining of the South's wetlands on a scale to match its funding of western irrigation, other promoters emphasized the transformative effects reclamation could have on a region.[187] In the *Florida East Coast Homeseeker*, former governor Jennings attributed his faith in the Florida drainage project to traveling to California and witnessing the effects of irrigation. "Never before had I appreciated the full value of water. As the train went on, mile after mile . . . through waterless plains, my eyes were opened to the possibilities of the Everglades."[188] State chemist R. E. Rose, a former superintendent on the Disston scheme, explained that "the rich, undrained muck or swamp lands in Florida" were similar to "the wonderfully fertile arid lands of the West," in that both had rich soils that had mistakenly been considered "unproductive . . . simply for want of air [or] water."[189] Man and technology, however, were righting these natural "wants" in both swamp and desert, thereby opening up prime tropical real estate.

For John Gifford, southern California provided an enticing glimpse into what southern Florida could become. Gifford, a former assistant professor of forestry at Cornell University, became a prolific author on conservation and reclamation in the early twentieth century. He was particularly interested in the tropics, having "devoted his life to the study of conditions in tropical and semi-tropical countries, and Southern Florida in particular."[190] In a series of his essays on drainage that was published by the Everglades Land Sales Company, Gifford pointed to the success of southern California irrigation as a marker for Florida and the Everglades. He wrote that "in Southern California the hand of man has produced a highly developed and attractive region with no resources except vim and climate" and noted that "obstacles . . . [were] met on every hand." Southern Florida had "the resources, but the vim has been lacking." The region had been "reposing since the Seminole war," not due to "laziness" but from "indulging our love of leisure." But the time had come for reclamation. Articulating a formation narrative that merged frontier and Progressive mythologies, Gifford concluded that it was "this grappling with nature which develops the latent forces within the man. The coming age is to be an age of conquest, the conquest of nature, the reclamation of swamp lands and the irrigation of deserts."[191]

California's Imperial Valley also served as a model for southern Florida's wetlands. Confronting continuing skepticism about the Everglades, Rose wrote, "This [is] by no means the first instance in which the Soil Experts of the Government have condemned as worthless some of the most productive soils in America; a notable instance was the condemnation of the soils of the 'Imperial Valley of California,' pronounced worthless for agricultural purposes by the U.S. authorities [in 1902], and now noted as one of the most productive regions of America, as are the Everglades."[192] As in the Imperial Valley, ideas of human-created climate change appeared in musings on the "possible effect of the draining of the Glades upon the climate of South Florida."[193] Some boosters prophesied that drainage would create 3 million acres of prairie-like land in which any extremes of heat would be modified, a civilized tropical domain "swept by cool winds from gulf to ocean."[194]

In hailing this total conquest of nature, promoters of the Everglades such as Gifford frequently moved beyond the semi-tropical metaphor earlier state boosters had favored and hailed a thoroughly tropical expansion (as the title of the leading Everglades magazine, *Tropic*, attested).[195] Explicitly and implicitly, Everglades promoters juxtaposed their internal tropic with the tropical territories the United States had taken in 1898. Settlers were called upon to come to the Everglades to join in the "progress of America's Latest Empire."[196] In a railroad magazine, Professor H. W. Wiley contrasted the sugar-producing qualities of the Everglades with "Hawaii, Porto Rico, and the Philippines," while Gifford pointed out that the Everglades were "larger than Porto Rico or Jamaica."[197] This discourse sometimes reiterated that Florida was an Anglo-American tropic: drainage, a 1911 guide to Miami and its hinterland espoused, represented the achievements of the "white man conqueror," who alone had "scientifically harnessed" the swamps.[198] Emphasizing the difference between Florida and the overseas protectorates, the Everglades Land Sales Company of Kansas City promoted its vast acres in southern Florida as being in "The Only Truly Tropical Section of the United States."[199]

Advances in medical and agricultural science aided these claims to a tropical climate. By the first decade of the twentieth century, important developments in science had made the image of southern Florida as a tropical place for new settlers less problematic. In 1898, research proved that malaria and yellow fever came from mosquito bites, thus discrediting the idea that these diseases came from the watery vapors of swamplands.[200] Although the prevalence of mosquitoes in wetlands meant that health concerns were not wholly removed, the implications for the future of Florida—and the wider South—were significant. A 1912 editorial highlighted what it meant for southern Florida: "Sanitary science has abolished [the worst terrors of the tropics] in the subtropical South."[201] This new knowledge made it easier to sell Florida as America's tropic of hopes. In 1904, the U.S. Department of Agriculture conducted a biological survey that concluded that there were, in fact, "three regions in the [continental] United States which belong to the Tropical Zone": southern Texas by the mouth of the Rio Grande, Arizona and California along the Colorado River, and southern Florida. John Gifford wrote that "the first two are hot and arid" while "the other is humid and pleasant throughout the major portion of the year," concluding that southern Florida was "the only tropical part of this country which can be reached by rail."[202] Finally, Americans were consuming ever-larger amounts of tropical fruit, such that "bananas, oranges, grapefruit, limes and pineapples" were becoming "almost as staple as wheat and corn."[203] Earlier fears that such fruits would be overproduced diminished amid this greater demand, and land that was suitable for the cultivation of tropical "staples" became desirable.[204] "The sterile soils of Florida and the desert lands of California have yielded the largest quantity of the best fruit," Gifford wrote in 1909.[205]

At the same time, southern Florida boosters also found selling points in the unconquered qualities of the Everglades and its only inhabitants: the Seminole Indians. Like their California counterparts, promoters of tourism in southern Florida highlighted the exoticism of the unredeemed swamp. This strategy was often inextricably bound to ideas of racial primitivism.[206] For decades, Florida pamphlets had featured swamps and alligator scenes, and a common motif was the image of an African American baby in the mouth of the reptile. Among the "Florida Products" depicted in a standard guide to the state's east coast were a swamp, fruit, and a black child.[207] A southern booster later lamented that such photo guides had unfortunately fostered "the nation's impression that Florida was largely a land of alligators, swamps and negro babies."[208] Everglades boosters, however, amended this trope by focusing more and more on the Seminoles, creating a promotional literature that, paradoxically, romanticized the Native American inhabitants of the "unredeemed" wetlands while it also championed the reclamation project that was under way. By the first decade of the twentieth century, with Flagler hotels accommodating 40,000 guests annually, excursion companies began to take tourists into the Everglades, promoting the trips as safe

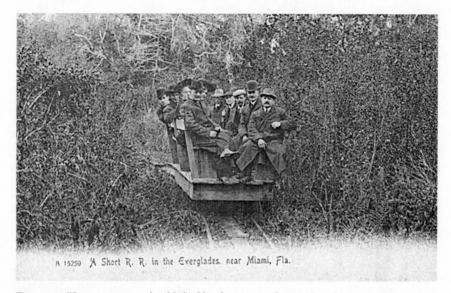

A 15259   A Short R. R. in the Everglades. near Miami, Fla.

Figure 4.5. This 1902 postcard published by the New York City–based Rotograph Company depicted the new tourist experience of forays into the Everglades. Courtesy of HistoryMiami Archives and Research Center, Miami, Florida.

encounters with a tropical wilderness.[209] Postcards showed off the open railroad cars that carried tourists from Miami into the fringes of the Everglades (Fig. 4.5).

The Seminoles recognized the threat these incursions posed to their way of life. As one investment guide to Florida noted in 1898, the Seminoles "will rarely ever act as guides, and try to discourage parties in exploring the Everglades."[210] Yet the tours proved increasingly popular, particularly as drainage of the Everglades appeared more feasible and made that particular tourist experience seem like an endangered one. The Florida East Coast Hotel Company advertised the Everglades tours as journeys through time as much as through space: "From Miami a small boat will carry the curious visitor up into the wildest stretches of the Everglades, the last of the waste lands east of the Mississippi which remain unreclaimed, and which have held for years all the mystery and romance . . . which [the] mind can conjure up. Here he may catch a glimpse in their native haunts of the Seminoles, the sole remaining remnant of the Indian tribes that once roamed over Dixie."[211]

Florida promoters cast the Seminoles, like their Everglades home, as the purest remnants of the American wilderness. This involved a significant turnabout in white conceptions of the state's Native Americans.[212] In earlier decades, the Seminoles were feared as a mixed-race band that had combated the American military. As late as the 1880s, they were denigrated as "refugees, runaways, vagabonds," a group that was comprised of a "general mixture of Indian bloods" and "hundreds of runaway negroes." But by the early decades of the twentieth century, boosters had stopped emphasizing the Seminoles' links to runaway slaves.[213] Instead, Florida East Coast Railway agent Willard L. Bragg praised the remaining Seminoles, who never signed a treaty with the U.S. government, as the most "dignified" and "pure" Native Americans left in the nation. According to Bragg, the Seminoles were superior to what he called "notoriously immoral" Western reservation Indians because they chose to live independently. In an inaccurate statement that glossed over a past many whites in the Jim Crow South were uncomfortable with, he also praised them for having blood that was "practically pure and undefiled from mixture with any other race."[214] Suitably cleansed of any unsettling links to racial mixture, the Seminoles were rapidly embedded in itineraries of white tourists in southern Florida. Responding to the growing interest in them and recognizing the dangers to their livelihood that drainage presented, Seminoles turned to selling souvenirs to tourists: "unusual specimens of handiwork" that added "just the touch of weirdness which is needed to make complete the ensemble of the picture," as one promotional pamphlet explained.[215] Other Seminole Indians relocated to newly formed tourist camps near Miami and the Everglades, where they were famed for their alligator wrestling. Later on, they founded tourist camps along the Tamiami Trail.[216] Boosters hailed the Seminoles as a vital resource in southern Florida's tourism economy. A 1925 article in *Suniland* magazine showed how whites had reimagined the Native Americans. Dismissing as fallacy the historical fact "that the Seminoles are a mixed race due to inter-marriage with fugitive slaves which escaped from Southern plantations and ultimately settled in the Everglades," the author stressed that "Uncle Sam's scientists . . . report that the remnant redskins now living in southern Florida are 'of pure blood, fine physique, and dignified mien.'"[217] While still considered a less civilized race—the article's title was "Savages of Southern Sunshine"—the Seminoles had become a purified and unthreatening one, befitting the New South vision of racial separation. Moreover, they were a financial asset to the state: "These picturesque Indians are worth a million dollars to Florida in advertising value."[218]

For Everglades land developers, however, the displacement of these "wild" Native Americans formed an inevitable part of the internal expansion made possible by reclamation. Indeed, putting "waste" lands to use could bring about improvements for their "primitive" inhabitants. Inspired by the works of California horticulturist and eugenics expert Luther Burbank, a Florida writer explained, "This is what we do when we take wild stock like the negro or Indian, and bring it up from infancy in close contact with and under the special influence of a high state of civilization . . . to form an improved variety."[219] Reclamation was deemed a necessary step to making the Native Americans productive citizens. "The poor Seminole; what of him?" Gifford wrote. "The time will soon come when he will have to put on pants and go to work on the land, join his relatives in Oklahoma, or die from the effects of too much bad whiskey."[220]

Drainage itself became a tourist attraction. Visitors who traveled from Miami and Fort Lauderdale were "very interested" to see the dredges at work in the Miami and New Rivers.[221] Tourists thus simultaneously enjoyed the transformation of the wetlands made possible by the technology of the dredges and the vanishing lifestyle of the Native Americans who lived in the Everglades—all with the nostalgic understanding that the former would bring about the end of the latter. "The mystery and poetry which has surrounded [the Seminoles] ever since the great wars of the nineteenth century," Harrison Rhodes wrote, "is gradually being dissipated. It is probable [that] the draining of [the] Everglades and the settling of the country will be the last chapter of their history."[222] Rhodes was proved wrong, of course, but he was far from alone in this view. The point was more harshly made by a 1911 Miami guidebook that juxtaposed a photograph of an "Everglades Drainage Canal" with that of a "Seminole Indian's Grave," implying that the one gave way inevitably to the other.[223]

But for all their grand hopes of conquering the tropical environment, boosters of Florida drainage experienced great disappointments. Broward's plan for a public drainage program that would open the Everglades to settlers proved unrealistic, scuttled by the challenges and expenses of draining such a vast area. By 1910, two-thirds of the land had been sold by the state to private companies: the Internal Improvement Fund was in desperate need of cash if the state was to keep its promise to drain the wetlands.[224] Moreover, the drainage scheme struggled to gain legitimacy in the eyes of nation. The skepticism of northerners and midwesterners about the Everglades was exacerbated by federal government reports that questioned the fertility of much of the reclaimed soils.[225] Federal engineer James O. Wright's 1909 report, which argued for the feasibility of drainage and was widely cited in promotional literature, was criticized by other scientists.[226] In 1912, Congress held a six-month investigation into Everglades drainage. The findings were inconclusive but hardly encouraging.[227] Southern Florida developers were also accused of gross misrepresentation of the region's potential and faced ongoing setbacks in the mechanics of drainage.[228] "On paper the everglades are the garden spot of the whole earth," charged a writer in the *Boston Globe*. "In reality they are mostly a submarine region which appeals more to amphibious than to land animals."[229] Damaged but undaunted, drainage boosters continued to disseminate photographs designed to demonstrate the conquest of the swamp (Fig. 4.6).

Figure 4.6. This photograph used one new technology to prove the reliability of the results of another technology: the newly drained land is solid enough to support the weight of an automobile. *Source*: "A Neglected Opportunity," *Florida East Coast Homeseeker* 13, no. 11 (November 1911): 413. From the P. K. Yonge Library of Florida History, Department of Special and Area Studies Collections, George A. Smathers Libraries, University of Florida.

Witnesses came forth to testify to the environmental transformation. Thomas E. Will, a former editor for the American Forestry Association, was one of many Americans to be seduced by the dream of tropical farms on reclaimed land. He had become intrigued by the Everglades through the writings of Gifford in 1909. Will traveled to southern Florida, wrote articles on the Everglades, and formed the "first Everglades Farming Association," an organization that sponsored the transportation of buyers of Everglades lands from the northeast to Zona, Florida, on the South New River Canal.[230] In 1911, H. B. Stonebrook, of Pasadena, California, bought twenty small farms in the Everglades and foresaw that "happy, prosperous homes will be established of a diversified and most representative type of American citizenship." Settlers would be drawn together by a "common interest—that of securing a home in this rich new country, of semi-tropical climate."[231] Describing a new farm in 1910, another promoter wrote, "This is a scene on the once despised Everglades, the supposed home of venomous snakes, reeking in malaria and unfit for human habitation. It has been said that man can never improve on nature; but one view of this magnificent place contradicts that."[232] *Everglade Magazine*, which was begun in 1911 by local landowners, pushed for legitimacy by calling on prospective settlers to read the works of experts such as Walter Waldin and John Gifford in order to understand the changes that were taking place in southern Florida. "To study and then to practically apply is the best way to learn to use your Everglade land. Men like Gifford and Waldin are blazing the way."[233] Everglades land companies and the state brought in newspaper editors from across the country who reported positively on the region.[234] Earl E. Moore, editor of the *Plaindealer* of Cleveland, Ohio, wrote, "I had a hazy idea the [Everglades] was an impenetrable swamp," but he discovered instead "a wonderfully rich, fertile field, of which Florida may well be proud and in the cultivation and development of which thousands of families are to attain independent wealth."[235] Noting that "homeseekers are more and more preferring the natural life of the country to the artificial life of the city," Baltimore editor Day Allen Wiley stated that Americans could "live this life . . . in the Everglades of Florida," where "the drainage canal is making . . . a home land in truth." W. J. Etten, managing editor of Michigan's *Grand Rapids News*, was sufficiently impressed to purchase 100 acres of Everglades land himself.[236]

Corporate promoters in the 1910s continued to hark back to traditional republican ideology based on small farming as a means of furthering their plans for the Everglades. "The Everglades assume such a condition as will permit of perfect farming," the Everglade Land Sales Company of Chicago boasted. It cited a state government authority that predicted that the population of the Everglades would reach 250,000 within five years. The land company depicted its payment plan as a republican measure, one that "enabled any man to own a home in the Everglades." It advertised its five- to forty-acre tracts at $40 per acre. By April 1910, the company had sold 15,000 farms in the region.[237] Corporate developer Richard Bolles, who at one point owned 900,000 acres of Everglades land, promoted the reclamation project with the slogan "More land for the people—that is the keynote of national progress."[238] "Back to the land" ideals infused the selling of southern Florida farms. "To the city man, living on a salary, often in a dark or stuffy office, always an underling, working in a narrow groove, dependent on today's wages for tomorrow's food, the independent countryman's life must appeal, for he is a free man, master of himself," Waldin declared.[239] An advertisement for the Walter Waldin Investment Company featured an image of an idyllic landscape of small truck farms being admired by two onlookers dressed in suits—presumably city men in pursuit of the agrarian promise of the Everglades. Their sharp attire indicated that they were gentlemen farmers, for whom business savvy rather than field work was most important. This image was increasingly cultivated by boosters of southern Florida (Fig. 4.7).

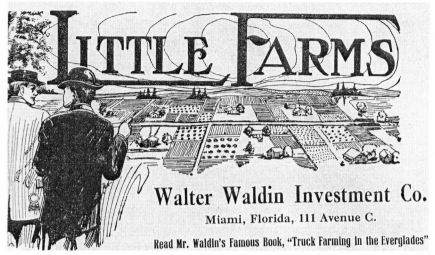

Figure 4.7. Land corporations such as the Walter Waldin Investment Company sold re-claimed Florida land to settlers. *Source*: Advertisement by Walter Waldin Investment Company in *Florida East Coast Homeseeker* 14, no. 7 (July 1912): 273. From the P. K. Yonge Library of Florida History, Department of Special and Area Studies Collections, George A. Smathers Libraries, University of Florida.

Indeed, the older ideas of working one's own small plot in semi-tropical Florida were being replaced by colonialist representations of progressive white communities that could make use of disenfranchised African American workers. In the fertile Everglades, promoters stressed, the outdoor labor of landowners was not what would determine agricultural prosperity. As Walter Waldin informed his readers, one of the attractions of truck farming in the Everglades was that landowners "frequently hire all work done" and that "our profits will certainly average more than twice as much [as in the Midwest]."[240] These expectations were possible because of the white South's control of black labor: the *Florida Agriculturist* informed readers that the state was "nearly 60 per cent white, with brain from forty States," alongside "the plastic muscle of the negro."[241] Southern Florida periodicals such as *Tropic* magazine featured photographs of blacks working in reclaimed fields and asserted that white settlers could prosper without having to do the hardest work themselves.[242] Once technological conquest of the swamp made "civilized" settlement possible, promoters made it clear that southern Florida was a tropic where whites would have the ascendancy. Racial hierarchy was built into the transformation of the environment. The Florida Land Development Company, for example, advertised five-acre tracts in the "Everglade Gardens" of Okeechobee Park with the following attractive array of features: "Most Productive Soil in Existence. Cool Summers. Mild Winters. Pure Water. Perfectly Healthy. No Swamps. Few Insects."[243] But another attraction appeared in the advertisement's small print: "No negroes own land in Okeechobee Park." The specificity that no blacks *owned* land was significant. "Negroes" were available to the agriculturists in Okeechobee Park as laborers, but they did not own land and thus were not considered citizens of the healthful community being formed in this "Mid-Winter Garden of America."[244]

In the Progressive Era, promoters of southern California and peninsular Florida turned to the reclamation of lands long perceived as harsh and worthless, describing processes that would create new frontiers and new formation narratives for U.S. settlers. In the deserts of southern California, irrigation made possible the expansion of prosperous agriculture and encouraged visions of a region that could supply a tropical cornucopia of products. Drainage was equally significant in the selling and development of southern Florida. In both cases, Anglo-Americans were persuaded that undeveloped land could be transfigured into productive domains for republican society. Once the Imperial Valley and the Everglades had been "conquered and inhabited," as one booster put it, they would be sites of "true cooperation" that brought settlers together through the prosperous cultivation of distinctive fruits and crops.[245] Whereas, on one side of the continent, Imperial Valley was both a "modern miracle" of environmental improvement and a "land of promise for rich and poor," on the other coast, the drainage of the Everglades was "the ultimate changing of a hitherto worthless watery waste into a land of happy homes, productive farms and thriving communities."[246]

By the 1920s, however, these depictions of republican settlement appeared very hollow. By then, land ownership in the Imperial Valley was concentrated in the hands of a few, as control of water sources and the rising cost of land increasingly benefited wealthy owners who built up their acreage.[247] As Donald Pisani has written, "Irrigation became the ally, instead of the enemy, of land monopoly and concentration."[248] To be sure, the boosterist promises of fertility were not mistaken. In 1925 the Imperial Valley's cotton crop was worth $13 million and covered 200,000 acres of reclaimed desert.[249] But the earlier selling visions of Smythe and other reclamation boosters that a middling farming society would form in California's tropical desert had faded in the face of a rigidly hierarchical agricultural landscape. Large-scale corporate developers effectively co-opted traditional republican ideals to continue selling the valley to realize their own goals. But Imperial Valley promoters also contributed to this shift by stressing the exemption from field work that white landowners in the region could enjoy.[250] Sharecropping systems and control of migratory nonwhite labor were increasingly apparent in descriptions of the Imperial Valley.[251] By the 1920s, the Imperial Valley's cotton and other semi-tropical crops were picked predominantly by Mexican laborers, whose efforts to obtain better-than-starvation wages were met with fierce resistance by the valley's growers.[252] As one agricultural historian writes of the Imperial Valley, "With its large-scale production, absentee corporate ownership, labor-intensive crops, and seasonal reliance on an army of nonwhite immigrants, the valley's agriculture represented industrialized farming in its most extreme and unalloyed form."[253]

In the Everglades, drainage developers faced repeated setbacks in their attempts to remove water and settle farmers. Even though promoters had made tens of thousands of sales, fewer than 1,000 people actually lived in the Everglades in 1920. New towns in the Lake Okeechobee district, such as Okeelanta and Clewiston, were prone to flooding with heavy rains.[254] But the Imperial Valley still remained an example to emulate.[255] Frustrated at the lack of progress made in drainage, the *Miami News* editorialized, "If the men in charge of the public improvement work in Florida could be taken to Imperial Valley, where the desert has been transformed into garden lands selling for $150 to $300 an acre, and could see what faith and engineering skill have accomplished, they would return to the Everglades reclamation work, ashamed of the years that have been frittered away."[256] In 1922, James Ingraham put the blame elsewhere, charging that the federal government had unfairly prioritized irrigation in California over drainage in Florida.[257] In the mid-1920s, the Everglades began to attract renewed attention and greater financial support from the federal government. It became an important sugar-producing area; 10,000 acres were cultivated around Lake Okeechobee.[258] By 1925, farming activities were being conducted in approximately 1,000 square miles of Everglades land, with truck farming the leading industry.[259] Growers mostly employed migratory African American laborers, many from Georgia, to work their truck and sugar farms.[260] "Unskilled labor is supplied generally by negro help, and is secured locally," a 1920s guide to industry in Florida explained.[261] Moving on from the visions of a society of middle-class farmers, promoters now stressed the need for capital: because of the cost of ditching and diking farms to supplement the drainage system, "development of Everglades farm lands is a job for capital in large sums" rather than for "the individual small farmer."[262]

Reclamation in the first decades of the twentieth century fundamentally altered both the physical and the imagined landscapes of semi-tropical California and Florida. The catastrophic environmental damage wrought by these conquests was scarcely an afterthought for developers, who envisaged their work in terms of capitalist and republican progress. In time, more and more observers would take a very different view, realizing, as Stephen Whitfield has written, that "the natural attractions that enraptured so many residents and transients [were] endangered" by the relentless pursuit of economic growth.[263] For boosters, however, the desire for profit and the utilitarian conservationist mentality made reclaiming California's desert and Florida's swamp a necessary and celebrated form of American expansion. Indeed, for many promoters, the conquest and transformation of America's internal tropics were precisely what distinguished their civilization from those of other nations that harbored backward swamps and deserts. They symbolized the different abilities of nations and peoples to subdue and harness harsh environments, to put nature to proper use. For boosters such as John D. Gifford, the ongoing story of internal reclamation was ultimately one of American greatness: whereas foreign tropical countries that were "so richly supplied with nature's gifts" remained "undeveloped," it was "those regions where the most is supplied by the hand of man, as in California and Florida, [that] have progressed the most."[264]

5

"New Edens of the Saxon Home-Seeker"

Los Angeles, Miami, and Semi-Tropical Urban Life

In the first decades of twentieth century, cities became increasingly prominent in the promotion of southern California and peninsular Florida, and Los Angeles and Miami emerged as iconic destinations for those who sought America's tropic of hopes. To an extent, this involved a shift in emphasis, if not an apparent contradiction, since the promotional imagery had long emphasized how the fecundity of nature in the two states offered settlers and visitors alternatives to an increasingly urban, industrial nation. Cities did not fit well with this vision. Although belief that America's agrarian ideal was attainable was on the wane by the turn of the century, it had long described urban centers as "sores on the body politic" and praised small farmers because they lived apart from the vices of city life.[1] Boosters in the two states often shared this view, declaring with gusto that California was becoming "*the great* agricultural State of the Union" or that Florida was "essentially an agricultural state."[2] Although such statements were not inaccurate, urban development and promotion grew in significance in both states, where semi-tropical agriculture was maturing into capital-intensive farm businesses that were beyond the scope of what many Americans could afford. Boosters thus moved beyond a straightforward critique of urbanization and lauding of agriculture (although these elements remained) and began to emphasize the cities of the states they boosted as new and distinctive settlements.[3] Conceptions of national identity were changing: consumerism was growing, and promoters targeted a growing constituency of middle-class Americans who valued relaxation and contentment just as highly as they valued hard work and economic gain. As a result, California and Florida were sold as unique, open, sunny cities that promised a modern way of life that was cleansed and improved by semi-tropical nature.[4]

This chapter focuses on the selling of Los Angeles and Miami as they became the most widely promoted cities in southern California and peninsular Florida. Scholars have highlighted links between the cities. A 1999 collection of essays that focused on both cities noted, "Though they are situated a continent apart, Miami and Los Angeles are perhaps more like each other than like other American cities. At the same time, they retain obvious individual identities."[5] The essays dealt with the growth and relationship of the two cities from the 1920s to the 1990s, however, providing limited insight into the earlier period (from the turn of the century up into the 1920s) when the booster tropes were first formulated.[6] In that earlier period, the two cities competed with and distinguished themselves from one another. Both cities were imagined as near-tropical entities that were environmentally and socially different from and preferable to the industrial metropolises of the North and Midwest, replacing factory smoke, crowded streets, and fierce competition with neighborhoods of homeowners, pleasant avenues, and outdoor existences. Like their predecessors who promised independence through agriculture, boosters who promoted urban life in southern California and southern Florida articulated a long-standing criticism of the relentless pace of northern capitalism and city life and suggested that the acquisition of wealth was not all that Miami or Los Angeles offered. While the cities were promoted as sites of financial opportunity, offering both increasing land values for new homeowners and undeveloped commercial fields for businessmen, they were also sold as places that would change the character of residents for the better, places where a less cutthroat and more leisurely lifestyle was the norm. They would be sites of urban "playgrounds" where, as Charles Dudley Warner wrote, "the vital forces of modern life are not enervated, but have added to them something of the charm of a less anxious and more contented spirit."[7]

The growing significance of Los Angeles in California and Miami in Florida was part of the national trend toward urbanization. Between 1865 and 1920, the U.S. population changed from mostly rural to predominantly urban as both available land and agricultural prices declined (sometimes precipitously) and cities increasingly offered greater opportunities for socioeconomic mobility.[8] Cities lured rural Americans, in particular young people, with the promise of improved economic prospects and an escape from the isolation of farm life.[9] By 1890, two out of every three persons in the state of New York lived in towns, while Chicago had swelled from a frontier outpost to a metropolis of over 1 million residents.[10] Urbanization also created cultural dislocation: it wrenched countless U.S. citizens from smaller, rural communities and thrust them into complex urban scenes where they encountered foreign-born immigrants and industrial employment.[11] Commentators worried about the effects on the American people of northern cities that sprawled with industrial factories and high-rise buildings and attracted vast numbers of "undesirable" immigrants from southern and eastern Europe. In the eyes of many native-born whites, these new arrivals were utter foreigners who did the lowest-paying unskilled jobs and thus drove down wages, supported corrupt political "bosses," and inhabited dirty, congested slums.[12] Many native-born people who had reached the middle class abandoned the city completely. Taking advantage of new transportation facilities, especially streetcars, they sought out suburban locations—near to but outside business districts and working-class neighborhoods—as places to buy homes and settle.

The ambivalence of Americans toward cities shaped the selling of Los Angeles and Miami as distinctive, suburban settlements that combined progressive civilization with healthful nature: cities that softened the frantic pace of modern life and offered new formation narratives to urban Americans. Their promoters echoed the main points of the contemporaneous city beautiful movement, in which civic planners in Boston, Denver, and other cities used aesthetics and architecture in their efforts to cultivate moral and civic virtue in urban populations.[13] But promoters of Los Angeles and Miami focused particularly on the tropical qualities of their cities and the effects of tropicality on urban life. Former mayor E. F. Spence depicted Los Angeles as a city apart: "modern" with "buildings that would be a credit to any city of the East" but also a place with "something strange about it all. It is the verdure that is tropical in all the term implies; every yard has its palms, bananas or other tropical trees and plants."[14] Twenty years later, Miami was boosted in almost identical terms, for its "rich splendor, its harbor, its tropical aspect, its climate," which made it "the most perfect city in the United States."[15] Depictions of Los Angeles and Miami in the early twentieth century were organic evolutions of the selling of California and Florida as semi-tropical lands. Republican ideals based on small-scale agriculture were adapted to suit cities where citizens could become independent through the ownership of a suburban home with a verdant garden. Civic and corporate boosters who hawked urban homes, lots, and hotels argued that leisure and labor could thus coexist in harmonious balance in Los Angeles and Miami.

Los Angeles preceded and exceeded Miami. Founded as a Spanish pueblo in 1781, the City of Angels grew slowly for a century. It was home to just over 10,000 people in the 1870s. The city's boom in the 1880s created a population explosion, and by 1890, the population had increased to 50,000. All of this happened six years before Miami was incorporated as a city. In subsequent decades, in-migration, geographical expansion, and urban vegetation fueled a view of Los Angeles as "the Most Progressive Metropolis of the Twentieth Century."[16] For the city's leading promoters, such as Charles Fletcher Lummis, "progress" was indicated not only in the growth of commerce and population (vital as these markers were) but also in the perception that the city was an example of a higher civilization in the United States. A formation narrative of improved urban citizens was created around the city's climate, its natural resources, and the racial composition of its inhabitants. White residents, the modern majority in Los Angeles, could cultivate a better kind of existence there: "In this motherly climate the race now foremost in the world will fairly outstrip itself in achievement; and most of all in what is best of all—the joy of life," Lummis wrote.[17] Poverty need not exist except in exotic ghettoes, which boosters cast as remnants of southern California's "romantic past" and which were, in any case, removed from the suburban neighborhoods they promoted. Los Angeles would thus be home to a middling population "with means, leisure and incentive for culture," a city with no "undesirable classes," "no 'Shanty-towns' and no 'North Ends.'"[18]

Miami was smaller and less industrial than Los Angeles. It was incorporated as a city in 1896, after Henry Flagler's Florida East Coast Railway reached Biscayne Bay. The images its promoters presented owed a great deal to images promoters had used for Los Angeles. A writer in the *Miami Metropolis* who was typical of south Florida boosters commented in 1912, "I called Miami the Los Angeles of Florida [and] have now no reason to take this back, for Miami is certainly doing herself proud."[19] Miami was sold as a "young" city that was unlike immigrant-ridden northern metropolises. It was presented as a quasi-tropical urban space where the Anglo-American population could experience contented lives without losing their enterprising qualities. "What particularly strikes one at Miami," the *Metropolis* writer explained, "is the spirit of hustle and boost, the splendid streets, the fine residences, with their ornamental gardens, the stately royal palms and the waving cocoanut trees, all of which typify semi-tropical Florida."[20] The capitalist "spirit of hustle and boost" was mediated by the regenerative qualities of open streets, tropical foliage, and fine homes. As in Los Angeles, racial separation was an essential part of the image boosters presented of a middle-class city composed of republican citizens. Even though African Americans (who constituted between 25 and 40 percent of Miami's population in the period 1900 to 1930) were vital to the city's development, laws and city policies mandating segregation ensured that boosters could present Miami as a product of "white man's ingenuity [and] science."[21]

Both cities were characterized by racial exclusion and class stratification, yet promised a superior urban existence for white residents. Developers in southern California relied on Mexicans and other racial-ethnic groups and developers in Florida depended on African Americans to provide the labor that was needed to build new infrastructure and service booming tourism trades. Segregation was accomplished through de facto and de jure polices of racial zoning, which were normalized in promotional representations of racially-ordered semi-tropical cities. For boosters, the natural and human-made environments thus combined to make California's "City of Angels" and Florida's "Magic City" unique: each one "lies in a land of perpetual summer" and "promises every advantage without any of the disadvantages of urban life."[22]

Semi-Tropical Los Angeles

The selling of Los Angeles focused on how the city's semi-tropical environment influenced urban life. This vision, which crystallized around the turn of the century, relied on a growing emphasis on suburban settlement in southern California.[23] After the Gold Rush, settlers had moved into San Francisco, creating in the Bay Area a thriving port that by 1870 was the fourteenth largest city in America and the undisputed center of industry and wealth on the Pacific Coast.[24] Southern California, meanwhile, remained a distinctly pastoral region in which Los Angeles, a journalist recalled, was "considered one of the toughest cow towns in the Southwest."[25] In 1880, San Francisco's population was 21 times bigger than that of Los Angeles.[26] But with new railroads, tourism for health, and agricultural development on the outskirts of the city, Los Angeles grew rapidly in the next twenty years, contributing to a statewide trend of urban development. California had more urban than rural inhabitants for the first time in the 1890s (Table 5.1). In the two decades after 1900, the size of California's urban and rural constituencies pulled sharply apart, increasing by 200 percent and 55 percent, respectively. By the 1920s, the Pacific state, including southern California, was a thoroughly urban-dominant society.

In this period, Los Angeles became the urban center of semi-tropical California, having won over San Diego as the terminus for the first direct railroads into the region and the site of a real estate boom in the mid-1880s. Los Angeles was subsequently promoted as a qualitatively distinctive American city, although initially boosters claimed a predecessor of sorts in New Orleans, another semi-tropical city.[27] Los Angeles and New Orleans were physically connected in 1883 by the Southern Pacific Railroad's southern branch. With a population of over 200,000 at the time, New Orleans also suggested the growth

Table 5.1. Urban and rural population of California, 1870–1930

Year	Total Population	Urban		Rural	
		N	%	N	%
1870	560,247	208,437	37.2	351,809	62.8
1880	864,694	370,611	42.9	494,083	57.1
1890	1,213,398	589,464	48.6	623,934	51.4
1900	1,485,053	776,820	52.3	708,233	47.7
1910	2,377,549	1,468,419	61.8	909,130	38.2
1920	3,426,861	2,326,959	67.9	1,099,902	32.1
1930	5,677,251	4,160,596	73.3	1,516,655	26.7

Source: Carter et al., Historical Statistics of the United States: Millennial Edition, 1:213.

potential of much-smaller Los Angeles. The natural environment of the two cities seemed quite similar to many observers. A Los Angeles Times writer explained how both cities had a semi-tropical climate, a "softness of . . . verdure and . . . beauty of . . . vegetation." In addition, both had long been populated by people who originated from other countries, which made them exotic places within the borders of the nation. "In New Orleans the traces of French occupancy are as plain as, if not plainer than, the remnants of Spanish-American population and Spanish-American habits in Los Angeles."[28] However, the exoticism of both cities was being reshaped by the presence of white Americans. "Slowly and surely, Anglo-Saxon selfishness and push are encroaching upon all that once was Spanish or French in either city. The adobe of California will be in the near future a thing of the past, and the French boutique will only be found on the other side of the Atlantic."[29] But Los Angeles was firmly cast as a superior kind of semi-tropical city.[30] New Orleans was associated with outbreaks of yellow fever and "oppressive" summers, but Los Angeles had a healthful and livable climate and mild summers. Although Los Angeles was drier than New Orleans, it also had more "intensified" semi-tropical flora. "Here the verdure is greener, the flowers brighter-hued, the trees more stately, [and] the fruit more luscious than in its sister city."[31]

The promotional work of developing the city's identity was led by the Los Angeles Chamber of Commerce, an influential body that was formed for the second time in October 1888, after the collapse of the real estate boom. Recognizing the interconnectedness of the infrastructures of the city, the tourism industry, and the agricultural sector, the city's business elite organized to fund and develop the selling of Los Angeles and its hinterland. They wanted to "foster and encourage commerce," to "induce immigration and the subdivision, settlement and cultivation of our lands," and to "assist in the development of the material resources of this region and generally to promote the business interests of this section."[32] Within a few years, the group included over 500 of the "leading businessmen, capitalists and professional men of the city" and had disseminated 165,000 pamphlets and 50,000 bulletins throughout the Northeast.[33] By 1899, the Chamber of Commerce had over 1,000 members and observers were praising the efforts of the chamber, which had prepared materials for hundreds of eastern magazines and newspapers and had sent out nearly 1 million pamphlets that described southern California, especially Los Angeles.[34]

The exhibit hall at the Chamber of Commerce became a popular destination for tourists.[35] It provided information about the region's resorts, citrus lands, and business openings. Civic promoters successfully pushed to expand the winter tourism trade into the summer, and Los Angeles was increasingly depicted as an "all-year" resort that was the hub of southern California: the "starting point" for tourists who would enjoy the city's verdant parks, "semi-tropic" seaside hotels, and "palm-shaded avenues [that] make outdoor life a daily delight."[36] Visitors often returned to southern California as settlers and investors, and tourists were encouraged to take note of the way the region's climate and nature improved urban life. The *Los Angeles Bulletin* noted that city homes were often surrounded by "orange groves, broad-leaved banana trees, and all the other charming indications to point to the fact that the climate is semi-tropical."[37] The Chamber of Commerce hailed the "Open Air Life" of Los Angeles that was impossible in frigid eastern metropolises.[38] Transferring the region's agricultural exceptionalism to its urban areas, the *Los Angeles Times* stated: "Life in the cities of Southern California is just as attractive in its way, and as different from life in the cities of the East, as is country life in this section from that of the farmer in the States beyond the Rockies."[39]

Boosters connected the garden characteristics of Los Angeles to the vision of development through small farming that earlier boosters had disseminated. Urban growth in southern California involved the formation of suburbs after many small farms—those republican symbols that were the hallmark of the initial promotions of the region—failed in the early twentieth century, unable to compete against larger corporate farms. In San Diego, for instance, "as small farms failed and landholders sold off their excess acreage, subsequent developers planned and built large suburban communities on rural lands that were in close proximity to urban San Diego. . . . The citrus orchards were plowed under by developers [and] tract homes grew up in their place."[40] Real estate compa-

nies such as the Western Avenue Land and Water Company—owners of tracts
of land along electric trolley lines to Gardena and Redondo—advertised that
"Money in Small Farming" could be made in "Suburban Los Angeles": a city
"growing toward the ocean" which offered "Interurban Electric car lines, rapid
transit, low fares, perfect soil and climate" and "the advantage of outdoor life and
independent health restoring employment."[41] Promoters used tropical imagery
to promote urban centers where residents could find rebirth in a life lived in
harmony with nature. As one advocate of the city's growth wrote in 1895, "It
has been done by the brains and energy of the typical American—here, for the
first time in American history, fully free to expand to full potency, to work with
Nature and not against her."[42]

The newness of Los Angeles was a central theme in the literature that promoted it. The city was always cast as young, natural, and untainted by industry
or history. This view, of course, ignored its Mexican past. When that past was
acknowledged, it was presented as inherently flawed. For example, the *Los Angeles Times* explained how "the blood of the old Los Angeles was slow and sluggish." The Los Angeles of the recent past had been home to a few "aristocratic"
Californios and a "substratum of society [who were] cloddish and rested on
the dead level of content." People spent their days at the old mission church or
at cockfights and rodeos. They "heard never the whistle of the locomotive or
the rumble of the street-car." "All of this is past," the *Times* assured its readers.
White Americans had introduced technological progress to the city without
ruining the softer, more "feminine" traits that set it apart from the frantic, "masculine" centers of industrial America. "Bright, lovely, modern Los Angeles was
born, cradled in the fragrance of the orange, and rejoicing in the sunshine of
semi-tropical skies. . . . The blood ran quick in her veins. It was not blood native
to the soil, but it was the warm, stirring blood of American progress."[43]

Thus brought to life, "modern" Los Angeles promised renewal to Americans
because it offered a desirable natural environment and was free of the huge manufacturing plants of the East and the supposedly un-American immigrants who
worked in such places. This booster paradigm was clearly articulated in the pages
of *Land of Sunshine*, a semi-literary monthly that was started in the middle of the
depressed 1890s and was initially funded by the Los Angeles Chamber of Commerce. Lavishly illustrated, the magazine became a particularly eloquent and conservative voice among the loud chorus of Los Angeles boosters. In its own words,
it was a publication "fit to stand as a type of Southern California culture."[44] It was
supplied to major libraries throughout the East and quoted in the dailies of New
York, Boston, and Chicago. The magazine had an estimated 50,000 readers after
just one year.[45] Key to its success was its editor, Massachusetts-born Charles F.

Lummis, a mercurial individual who had walked from Ohio to the West Coast in the 1880s and had developed a deep faith in the regenerative qualities of southern California. Lummis was an evolutionist and an amateur ethnologist who wrote extensively about the "primitive" traits of indigenous peoples in the American Southwest and Latin America (whom he referred to in colonialist terminology as "my brownies"). He wrote passionate formation narratives in which Anglo-American society would become more rounded and fulfilled in California's semi-tropics.[46] His editorials offered theories about evolution, race, and the climate that promoted southern California and its metropolis, Los Angeles, as the future apex of American republicanism and contentment. Firm in his belief "that every living creature is very much the handiwork of its environment," Lummis posited that southern California represented a "radical change" in American history: whites inhabiting a semi-tropical environment marked "the most fascinating and novel sociologic problem ever set to be worked out."[47] White Americans had not only domesticated the environment but were now becoming products of it. An article entitled "A Semi-Tropic Crop" emphasized this point with a photograph of a smiling white baby amid fruits and vegetables. This human "crop"—like the re-

Figure 5.1. Promoters of southern California disseminated formation narratives about the new "semi-tropic crop" of Americans being born there. *Source:* "A Semi-Tropic Crop," *Land of Sunshine* 2, no. 6 (May 1895): 97. Courtesy of Mandeville Special Collections Library, University of California, San Diego, California.

gion's fruits—served as a glorious eugenic advertisement of what happened when Anglo-Americans and a semi-tropical climate were combined.[48] Los Angeles and its surrounding communities were evidence that "here, for the very first time, the Saxon has made himself fully at home in a perfect type of the semi-tropics."[49]

For civic boosters, both the human-created and the natural characteristics of Los Angeles benefited residents. *Land of Sunshine* repeatedly informed readers that the city had avoided the trap of the "great manufacturing interests" that "employ thousands of half educated foreigners, such as are to be found in many eastern sections."[50] When petroleum was discovered near Los Angeles in the 1890s, promoters acknowledged that it would inevitably lead to new manufacturing enterprises, but they stressed that Los Angeles "never will be strictly" a manufacturing city, since it owed its commercial growth primarily to tourism, a prosperous agricultural hinterland, and suburban home-seekers.[51] The construction of Los Angeles harbor at San Pedro, which began in 1899, encouraged boosters to dream "of Los Angeles as a great commercial and manufacturing city," but they continued to differentiate between their city and eastern metropolises.[52] Boosters of Los Angeles claimed that the city had "no distinctly foreign element" because it attracted few "uncultured" or "illiterate" migrants.[53] Indeed, boosters attributed the modern "birth" of Los Angeles to an incoming population of enterprising white Americans who had turned immigration into an unmitigated good: an "idle" Mexican population was being replaced with progressive whites from the Midwest and Northeast. Thus, at a time when New England was suffering from what one booster characterized as an "invasion" of unskilled European immigrants who had "seriously lowered the mean of culture," Los Angeles was becoming a truly American city, where "politically and socially the good citizen is not ruled" by foreign groups and voting blocs.[54]

Lummis spoke for the city's corporate boosters when he described a type of urban growth that was both capitalist and republican and fostered a healthy American community.[55] A self-proclaimed "republican" who advocated southern California's worth as a middle-class society that avoided northeastern "extremes of poverty and riches [and] a vast horde of half-educated or perhaps ignorant laborers," Lummis repeatedly praised the composition of Los Angeles's growing populace. "This is no penal colony; we are not crying for 'population at any cost.' The immigration we wish—and emphatically the only kind we wish—is of a refined, intelligent class."[56] Lummis thus participated in the rampant nativism of the period, as did other boosters. He hailed the Americans who came to Los Angeles as the "livest of 'live Americans,'" citizens who "have decreed that here shall be a great city—and a perfect city to live in."[57]

Spatial and technological developments in Los Angeles were critical to hopes for an ideal semi-tropical city. In addition to the city's desirable landscape, its transportation systems, and its "untainted" politics, its spatial openness—including more widely dispersed residences and extensively decentralized business districts—distinguished Los Angeles from the major metropolises of the United States.[58] Across the nation, reformers argued that streetcars were a safety valve for urban congestion, and in this regard, Los Angeles was a model. It had developed an extensive network of interurban trolley lines that ran throughout the Los Angeles Basin.[59] The Southern Pacific's Henry E. Huntington had constructed and amalgamated this affordable transportation resource.[60] By 1895, the city had nearly 100 miles of street railways. A strong local good roads movement promoted the development of a second interurban transportation network at a time when the number of automobiles on the road was increasing.[61] Both of these networks supported rapid growth in the region. In 1910, one Los Angeles newspaper declared that "Southern California is the automobilists' Paradise."[62] Los Angeles was also the first American city to have streets lit wholly by electricity.[63] Municipal restrictions on building height encouraged the spread of growth outward and pushed up land values. Los Angeles grew from 29 square miles in 1890 to 85 in 1910—a size that was exceeded at the time only by New York, Chicago, and Philadelphia.[64]

Boosters celebrated the city's spatial expansion. They characterized it as an open city that provided an alternative to the crowded conditions of older eastern cities. In Los Angeles, one city guide explained, "There are no congested districts, no grouping of human beings in dark, poorly ventilated, crowded quarters, no unsightly flats, but homes, homes, homes on every hand on large lots with lawns, and trees and flowers in luxuriant abundance."[65] Los Angeles offered a balance between commercial development and nature: the city's business progress and its tree-lined roads, parks, and gardens were equally pervasive in the promotional literature.[66] The "typical" Los Angeles garden was shown to be a miniature park in itself, as in a photograph of a large house from a 1908 guide that explained, "Semi-tropic in climate, Los Angeles offers exceptional opportunities to the homebuilder" (Fig. 5.2).

Boosters sold Los Angeles using the unique formation narratives it offered urban Americans. In particular, civic promoters engaged with a broad change in American values. Middle-class citizens increasingly sought relaxation as well as work in the new belief that personal fulfillment was as important as economic security.[67] Los Angeles boosters targeted an older, wealthier class of Americans who were attracted more by the city's leisure and lifestyle attractions than by the search for employment.[68] "No other city in the Union has so large percentage of residents who are not in active business, who brought money with them, or

Figure 5.2. Urban boosters of semi-tropical California highlighted the verdant gardens that could surround new suburban homes in their region. However, the homes that were typically on show were affordable only to elite and upper-middle-class Americans. *Source:* Southern Pacific Company, *California, South of Tehachapi: From Notes by the Agents* (San Francisco: Southern Pacific Passenger Department, 1908), 10. Courtesy of the California History Room, California State Library, Sacramento, California.

live upon an income from elsewhere," Lummis reported in 1895.[69] The lifestyle possibilities of the semi-tropics thus came to the fore, shaping expectations of personal contentment and improvement that had origins in the winter tourism boosterism of earlier decades. But the formation narrative was now transplanted to the city, where residents could live better lives. It was repeatedly explained that in spite of all their material progress, eastern Americans had not yet figured out how to be happy. If they inhabited a semi-tropical city, they could learn to "enjoy life," not least because "a fiesta is so logical a thing to a decent climate."[70] Worthwhile living, like citrus, was a natural product of the climate. "Home life in Southern California" enabled residents to relax in their own "lawn and semi-tropic garden."[71] "Fruit and sunshine are good for body and brain and soul," wrote renowned author Charlotte Perkins Stetson in a piece on southern California.[72] In a clean, semi-tropical city, Americans would be free to live for pleasure and realize the republican dream of the "pursuit of happiness." Thus, in Los Angeles, boosters declared, "New people are being molded from old stock."[73]

In 1896, Charles Dudley Warner astutely described the implications of the environmental and racial alchemy that was occurring in semi-tropical Los Angeles in a magazine article entitled "Race and Climate."[74] Co-author with Mark Twain of *The Gilded Age*—a best-selling 1873 novel that satirized the greed and corruption of modern America—Warner had by the 1890s become a renowned travel writer, an expert on "all the Lands of the Sun." His editor claimed that he was "especially fitted to speak in a literary way on the influence of climate on man."[75] The reference to "all the Lands of the Sun" indicates how Americans continued to view southern California as part of a climatic spectrum that stretched beyond national borders. Most "lands of the sun" were, however, equated with nonwhite races, enervation, and social instability. These issues formed the basis of Warner's discussion. His thesis asked whether "a white man, and particularly an Anglo-Saxon white man," could thrive in southern California. Would whites flourish and bring further progress to civilization, released from the restrictions of traditional colder climates, or would they become softened and lazy by the warm climate, resembling "inferior" Latin races? In short, "Is it necessary to freeze and thaw a man, alternately, in order to get the best out of him?"[76] The query carried huge sociopolitical significance. In "tropical islands" in the Caribbean, where the white man "is always thawed to the point of perspiration," Warner stated, whites had "no rights which the black man is bound to respect." In fact, under a tropical sun the white man was made to feel that he belonged to "an inferior race" and lacked the energy "to resist this prevailing impression." The climate performed a kind of racial inversion that was unimaginable in colder regions, sapping the "energy" of the white man and elevating the black man, who, although "lazy, as he commonly is," remained "vigorous and prolific" in spite of the heat. The concern in the context of the future of southern California was obvious. "The evolution of civilization" had not taken place in mild climates but in places where nature was "apparently hostile." This was "especially true of what we call the Anglo-Saxon strain, which is the dominant force in the United States," but one that "has never attempted to establish itself on any large scale in the tropics, and we have no evidence of what it might do there."[77]

In semi-tropical California, however, Warner proclaimed, racial hierarchy would not be subverted by environment. The region was both semi-tropical and fit for Anglo-Americans, in part because it was "more stimulating than any other semi-tropical climate I am acquainted with." This opened up the possibility that a new type of Anglo-American society and lifestyle could develop that combined the bygone Spanish-Californian civilization that had been "conducive to the enjoyment of life" with the American drive that could fuel the "energetic progress of the world." Warner, a well-known critic of the material excesses of industrial America, hoped that whites in semi-tropical California would "strike out for themselves a middle and a better way," producing a society full of "Anglo-Saxon vitality" modified by climate whose citizens who were less driven by business and more directed by the contentment of leisure.[78] They would not "sink into indolence" or "be in any degree thriftless." Instead, citizens could inhabit a city of tropical parks and gardens, where the "grace of life," the "ease of living," and the "enjoyment of existence" could balance their "restless," material instincts.[79] "Many people have a hope, almost amounting to a belief," Warner concluded, "that the Anglo-Saxon energy and spirit in the setting of the peculiar climate of Southern California will produce a new sort of community." Sold through the racist lens of Anglo-American superiority and progress, America's West Coast tropic would not only "raise the best fruit in the world in abundance to supply a continent" but also "have a people as beautiful as their fruit . . . so that it can justly be said, 'by their fruits ye shall know them.'"[80]

Race interacted dynamically with class in boosters' ideas of an improved human crop in semi-tropical Los Angeles. In part because of the unprecedented number of labor conflicts in the United States in the 1890s, foreign-born migrants from Southern and Eastern Europe, in particular, became associated with union organizing and political radicalism.[81] They therefore represented a threat to the economic power of the capitalist elite. Los Angeles promoters frequently stressed that there was no problem of "troublesome" foreigners or class conflict in their semi-tropical city, unlike in eastern cities. The city's "foreign" peoples were well-behaved: "Although there is a large number of Mexican and Oriental residents in Los Angeles," a city newspaper explained in 1905, "one of the peculiarities that the stranger first notices is the lack of any breach of order in the crowded streets."[82] The city was populated mostly by "enterprising" white Americans, guides to the city reassured potential visitors, reflecting the fact that the majority of new residents in the city were native-born Americans, many from the Midwest. In 1900, just 18 percent of Los Angeles' white population was foreign-born (compared with 37 percent in New York, 35 percent in Chicago, and 30 percent in San Francisco), while 41 percent of the city's native-born population had been born in the Midwest.[83] One booster claimed that "public opinion in Los Angeles has no sympathy with strikers and boycotters."[84] Would-be settlers were assured at the turn of the century that owning their own home was within their reach and that this would create a city that was true to older values of republican independence: "Los Angeles, like Philadelphia, is a city of homes. There is probably no city in the country where so large a proportion of people of moderate means own their homes, or are acquiring them by installment payments. This, of itself, is a guarantee for commercial peace and good government."[85]

The city's commercial elite, however, also strove for an open-shop policy toward labor as a means of ensuring "commercial peace."[86] A leading advocate for the open shop was booster Harrison Gray Otis, the editor of the *Los Angeles Times*, who saw it as a core factor in the city's forming identity. This anti-union stance set the city apart from San Francisco, a staunch union town, where influential white-only unions ensured that closed-shop practices persisted across most manufacturing industries.[87] In Los Angeles, by contrast, aside from a flurry of organizing around 1910, unions were kept down by the well-financed Merchants and Manufacturers Association and the Chamber of Commerce.[88] The city's open-shop practices were cited as evidence of its healthier civilization. The Chamber of Commerce stated that "our manufacturers and the business men in Los Angeles enjoy the great advantage of being free from those troublesome and demoralizing labor disturbances, which are so common in most of the large manufacturing cities of the country."[89] Opposing the progressive drive toward protecting workers through unionization and regulation, Otis and other Los Angeles boosters called for a culture of "industrial freedom"—that is, freedom for employers to negotiate with non-unionized workers. For Otis, "Among all of [the city's] splendid material assets, none is so valuable, morally, and materially, as her possession of that priceless boon, industrial freedom."[90] Indeed, Los Angeles was cast as an example to the nation: this "just and constitutional doctrine" ought to be followed by "any and every patriotic community in the United States."[91]

Opposing open-shop practices, then, was deemed "un-American." This stance made it possible for employers to oppose trade unionists as dangerous subversives. It also supported a system in which Los Angeles businesses obtained cheap labor from nonwhite groups, often immigrants. Native Americans, Chinese, Japanese, Filipinos, and Mexicans all did necessary menial work and accepted other low-paying, non-unionized jobs while white employers championed the "just" doctrine of industrial freedom. Throughout the Progressive era, the need of employers for inexpensive workers existed uneasily with the hopes of boosters for a superior white American stock in semi-tropical California. Stanford University president David Starr Jordan observed in 1907 that on "the Pacific Coast everywhere—farmers, fruit-growers, canners, lumbermen, housekeepers, road builders—everywhere there is a demand for cheap, coarse labor—a demand which the white men cannot meet."[92] Los Angeles developers increasingly sought out Mexicans to do the "coarse" labor needed in an expanding city, particularly after the Mexican Revolution began in 1910, when thousands of Mexicans came to the city in search of better economic prospects.[93] Mexican migrants performed much of the manual work in Los Angeles in nonunionized jobs, and the city soon had an economy that was stratified by race.[94] A 1920s city report declared matter-of-factly that manual labor in Los Angeles was "the occupation of the Mexican," who showed "an indifference to physical hardships and a supreme satisfaction in doing the menial."[95]

Representations of contented Mexicans served an important function in the selling of Los Angeles. They helped deny the emergence of a modern Mexican working class in a city that was promoted on the basis of its homogenous, republican citizens. Los Angeles boosters effectively sought to control the city's Mexican presence—both literally and figuratively—by highlighting instead a premodern Latin past, a romantic Spanish heritage epitomized in La Fiesta de Los Angeles, an annual parade and four-day carnival in the city that was first organized in 1894 by the city's Merchants Association. The parade became a leading and lucrative tourist attraction for the city.[96] Along with displays of Chinese and Native Americans, the Fiesta played upon the city's Spanish heritage by featuring missionaries, caballeros, and senoritas, who, as one observer wrote, "present vividly a picture of another century," of Los Angeles's "old dreamy past."[97] According to another visitor from Chicago, Los Angeles's Fiesta was "the survival of an old Spanish tradition," but it was an Anglo-constructed version.[98] The city's boosters thus encouraged white Angelinos and tourists to live out fantasies of Latin leisure even as they marginalized contemporary Mexicans in their vision of the city's future.[99] Urban modernity was to be found only in white neighborhoods: according to the Southern Pacific's Passenger Company, the region had "the most modern and active of cities and some quaint and sleepy Spanish pueblos."[100] "Sonoratown," the area where most Mexicans lived in Los Angeles, was excluded from the images of "typical" Los Angeles residential streets. Instead it became an exotic destination for white tourists and residents, for many of whom the "Los Angeles of the older days" was like "the fragments of a half-forgotten dream," a romantic reminder "that here half a century ago another civilization existed."[101]

The separateness of ethnic and racial minorities in the promotional literature for Los Angeles was reinforced by the city's spatial expansion. As Los Angeles expanded outward from the old Spanish plaza, white settlers chose new residential districts that were too expensive for or were closed to Mexicans and other nonwhite people.[102] E. F. Spence observed this shift as early as 1891: "In former days the principal part of the city was about the old plaza, upon which the Pico house and Mission fronted, and now in close proximity to Chinatown; but the city of to-day seems to be reaching out toward the sea; its suburbs being many miles to the south and west, containing fine avenues, magnificent residences, and many public parks that are fast becoming places of great beauty and interest."[103] Because ethnic and racial minorities could not afford to live in the suburbs, they had to settle on the eastern fringe of the city and areas close to the plaza.[104] In that sense, portrayals of the city's new subdivisions as racially exclusive were realistic. As Lummis wrote, "Barbed wire would not keep out undesirable classes, but the price of land will—$300 an acre is as tall a fence as is needed around any community."[105] The Los Angeles of boosterist literature quickly became a city of gardened suburbs connected by a growing network of roads and public railways that was inhabited by white homeowners. Promoters claimed that "no huddling of people in the residence parts of the city" existed.[106] In fact, Lummis wrote, Los Angeles was "a standing riddle to the cooped East."[107] In the pointed words of Lummis, southern California and its leading city had become "the new Eden of the Saxon home-seeker."[108]

The selling of Los Angeles contributed to a remarkable period of growth for the city, which doubled in population in the 1890s (from 50,000 to 102,000) and trebled in the 1900s (to 319,000). The city's spectacular growth resurrected sectional tensions in California. Los Angeles boosters commented that San Francisco leaders clung to the "self-satisfied assumption that San Francisco is California."[109] And promoters of northern California, envious of the success of the southern part of the state, proposed that a bureau be established in Los Angeles to direct immigrants to central and northern parts of the state.[110] In the first decade of the new century, a flurry of meetings and debates were held about whether or not to divide the state. Southern California boosters complained of unfair taxation and limited representation in the state legislature, which was dominated by northern Californians.[111] A member of the Los Angeles Chamber of Commerce stated, "The north predominates. The authorities do not understand our situation, conditions and our needs. Therefore we do not get just representation."[112] As southern California leaders demanded greater political power in the state, they cheered on the expansion of Los Angeles, which surpassed San Francisco in the 1910s as California's largest city. By 1920, Los Angeles was home to 577,000 residents. The geographical size of the city had also grown to 440 square miles. Los Angeles was thus the most extensive city in United States by a large margin: New York, the second-largest, occupied only 299 square miles.[113] Automobile tourism, which was increasingly popular, introduced a new theme in the selling of the city. Los Angeles County, a 1924 pamphlet stated, contained "over 4,444 miles of improved roads connecting mountain and ocean and winding through beautiful valleys filled with orange groves."[114] By 1930, one million tourists were visiting Los Angeles each year, of which an average of 150,000 stayed on as residents.[115]

The growing city of Los Angeles continued to be promoted as a semi-tropical American location. "Climate has exerted a profound influence upon the destinies

of mankind," boosters declared, and in Los Angeles this meant architecture, gardens, and customs that referred to other semi-tropical locations. "Suggestions
of Japan, as well as India and Spain, are seen in the environs of Los Angeles,"
read the caption for a photograph of suburban bungalow homes. *Sunset* magazine hailed the city's culture as a "blending of the two ... great civilizations"—the
colder northern strain that "worships the process of producing rather than enjoy-
ing the product" and the warmer southern strain that meant the "joy of living."[116]
The emergence of the film industry in Los Angeles added another layer to the
images boosters presented. By 1915 there were sixty motion picture studios in
southern California, and they were producing 75 percent of the nation's films.[117]
While the film industry indelibly associated Los Angeles with a glamorous, affluent lifestyle, it also promoted the region's unique status. "No wonder that Los
Angeles has become 'Capital of the Moving-Picture World,'" Lummis wrote in
1915. "Not only can the firm operators work here all the year round; they can 'stage'
Palestine, Italy, Colorado, Egypt, or almost any temperate or tropic land."[118]

The language Lummis chose here is telling. For its promoters and its film-
makers, Los Angeles was an American city that was "staged" in a tropical setting.
By the time Mexican immigrants began to arrive in significant numbers in the
1910s and 1920s, Los Angeles had been successfully recast by its promoters as
an Anglo-American city.[119] A guide that was printed for the 1915 Panama-California Exposition in San Diego summed up the transformation. Los Angeles, it
explained, "originally ... was inhabited only by Mexicans and aboriginal Indians,
but the onward march of immigration and progress brought to its confines men
and money from the eastern states, until now this class of desirable citizens is so
multitudinous that the original and foreign element is very little in evidence."[120]
Just as the "original" element had become "foreign" in Los Angeles, healthier
white Americans were now its "native" population: the ever-improving offspring
of a city that was "famed the world over for its magnificent blocks and palatial
homes, together with its semi-tropical verdure in tree, flower, shrub, and fruit,"
an urban homeland that married semi-tropical life and Anglo-American independence.[121] Indeed, Los Angeles, echoed the city's *Herald* in 1905, was earning a
reputation as "the Paradise of the World": a city of "tropical palm and palmetto,"
yet one where "the white man has absorbed the place, as he ever does, and his
ideas characterize the city."[122]

Semi-Tropical Miami

In the early twentieth century, Miami emulated and chased Los Angeles. The
city's boosters cultivated images of urban life that were similar to the ones Los

Angeles's boosters drew upon. Although Florida became increasingly urban-ized, it trailed behind California by some distance. In 1910, Florida's largest cities were Jacksonville (57,700), Tampa (37,800), Pensacola (23,000), and Key West (19,900). The combined total of these four cities was less than half the population of Los Angeles. Miami was home to only 5,500 residents.[123] Flori-da's urban growth was slight—at least thirty years behind that of California.[124] However, urban growth was increasingly important in Florida. It rose from 10 percent of the state's population in 1880 to over a third in 1920 to more than 50 percent by 1930 (Table 5.2). The population of Dade County, including Fort Dallas (later Miami), rose from 861 in 1890 to 4,955 in 1900 and 42,753 by 1920. Most of the county's residents lived in and around Miami.[125]

Although Miami was promoted as the urban apotheosis of Florida's tropics, it was hardly representative of the state's cities, which were characterized by their diversity. Nevin O. Winter's 1918 guide summed up the contrasting repu-tations of some of Florida's prominent cities. In the panhandle, Tallahassee, the small state capital, had been the "chief city of the state in slave-holding times." It was an Old South town that was distinct in character and history from newer cities in the peninsula. Jacksonville, the "metropolis of Florida," was a manufac-turing center and the gateway to the peninsula; it received most incoming trains to the state. Promoters romanticized St. Augustine, once the capital of Spanish Florida, as a relic of Spanish settlement where the American visitor could feel "that he has been suddenly transferred into some half-forgotten city of the long ago." At the tip of the state, Key West was an isolated port that was closely tied to Cuba in trade and customs, as were neighborhoods in Tampa, where a thriv-

Table 5.2. Urban and rural population of Florida, 1870–1930

Year	Total Population	Urban		Rural	
		N	%	N	%
1870	187,748	15,275	8.1	172,473	91.9
1880	269,493	26,947	10	242,546	90
1890	391,422	77,358	19.8	314,064	80.2
1900	528,542	107,031	20.3	421,511	79.7
1910	752,619	219,080	29.1	533,539	70.9
1920	968,470	353,515	36.5	614,955	63.5
1930	1,468,211	759,778	51.7	708,433	48.3

Source: Carter et al., Historical Statistics of the United States: Millennial Edition, 1:192.

ing cigar industry and a large Cuban population had developed. Tampa also grew into the commercial center of Florida's Gulf Coast and a popular destination for home-seekers. "A drive out through the residence section is interesting," the guidebook stated, "and one finds that Tampa is becoming a city of bungalows like the California cities." Miami, however, was the city that emerged as the self-styled "Magic City" of the peninsula. It was distinctive not only because it was "the most southerly city on the mainland of the United States," but also because it was Florida's answer to Los Angeles.[126]

From its inception in 1896, when Henry Flagler was inspired by the 1895 freeze to extend the Florida East Coast Railway to Biscayne Bay, Miami was primarily a "resort town."[127] A proliferation of guidebooks for the east coast of the peninsula produced by the hotel and railroad companies emphasized the opportunities for sport, leisure, and socializing in Palm Beach, Lake Worth, and Miami. Winter tourism formed the lifeblood of the new city, and Miami's Hotel Royal Palm was promoted as the southernmost "link in the chain of pleasure palaces which stretches from the tropics to the frontier of the land of snow and ice."[128] To attract the growing numbers of winter guests, guidebooks featured photographs of Miami's palm-lined "tropical avenues," beaches, and golf links.[129] "The lure of the tropics is not a misnomer," a tourist from Kansas wrote in 1910. "The drowsy, sun-lit days, and the gorgeous nights are like succeeding pages in the book of enchantment. No wonder the spendthrift tourists come trooping to Miami on Biscayne Bay."[130]

While the city was primarily sold and identified as a tourist destination, settlers also came to Miami in its formative years and became some of its leading promoters. Ethan V. Blackman, who was born in New York State in 1845, was an orange grower and a Methodist preacher in Lake County, Florida, in the 1880s and 1890s who headed further south after the freeze of 1895. "When Miami was discovered," a fellow booster wrote of Blackman, "he followed the course of the railroad into that sub-tropical section and grew up with the country."[131] Blackman served as editor of Flagler's *Florida East Coast Homeseeker* and for over twenty years managed the Dade County Fair, which advertised Miami and the agricultural potential of its environs. Blackman made investments in Miami real estate that provided him with a substantial income. By the 1920s, he was living in the Miami subdivision of Riverside Heights and was still an active booster, journalist, and member of the city's Chamber of Commerce. The latter organization was then under the presidency of Everest George Sewell, who surpassed even Blackman as a figurehead in Miami promotion. Born in Georgia in 1874, Sewell settled in Kissimmee before moving to Miami in 1896, where he opened the first men's clothing store in the new city. In 1900 Sewell initiated

Miami's first civic organization, the Merchants Association. He proposed the elaborate fifteenth anniversary celebrations for the association in 1911, and, four years later, as chair of the publicity bureau of the Chamber of Commerce, he oversaw expensive advertising campaigns for Miami. "No citizen of this community has given more lavishly of his time and fine abilities to the great cause of civic advancement," a booster pamphlet proclaimed.[132]

Boosters such as Blackman and Sewell created a backstory for Miami that presented it as a city carved out of tropical coastline through the money and vision of Henry Flagler. Prior to the railroad magnate's intervention, "It had been a long, weary Rip Van Winkle sleep that enveloped this tropical section," Blackman wrote.[133] Such sentiments echoed claims that Los Angeles had been "dormant" prior to Anglo development in the 1870s and 1880s—although there was a difference in what slumber implied here. In southern California, it defined Spanish-Mexican landowners as woefully unproductive; in south Florida, it described an essentially pre-human history, with the exception of the Seminole Indians. In the promotional literature, Miami, with "scarcely . . . a trace of civilization" beforehand, had "awakened" with the arrival of the railroad and the opening of the Royal Palm Hotel, which soon became its social hub.[134] Boosterist images of Miami's climate, tourist attractions, real estate, and lifestyle became inseparable from the city's identity. As F. Page Wilson, a settler in the 1890s, recalled, "Miami has always been a publicity-conscious city. Perhaps under its economic circumstances it was bound to be. It had to sell, not automobiles or other products, but itself, its homes and way of life."[135]

In that regard, Miami's connection to Los Angeles was profound. The "Magic City" came into being at precisely the time that southern California boosters were beginning to promote Los Angeles as a "New Eden of the Saxon home-seeker," a city where Americans would become "re-inventors of the lost art of content."[136] The two cities shared a vision of semi-tropical life that was impossible in the colder, crowded, industrial metropolises of the North. Indeed, if anything, the emphasis on pleasure and leisure was even more prominent in Miami, which lacked the broad economic base that developed in Los Angeles. Miami's self-image was an intensified version of the depictions of tropical luxuriance that had been used to sell coastal Florida for decades. Thousands of promotional pamphlets for Miami described a city on the fringes of the tropics. It was the "hub of a wheel, each of the spokes of which leads to some lands where life and conditions are very different from those which obtain in the United States."[137]

Miami inherited lingering concerns about living in south Florida year-round. As city booster C. H. Ward commented in 1915, "The most difficult task has been to convince the home-seeker that the summer climate is desirable."[138] Initially, Miami developed into a city where the number of winter visitors exceeded the permanent population by a factor of ten or more. In 1913, for example, approximately 125,000 tourists visited the city, which had only 11,000 residents.[139] The city's leaders eagerly promoted its hotels and sporting and leisure pursuits even as they strove to entice a larger permanent population. More year-round residents would provide a stable citizenry, create new businesses, and drive up real estate prices. But the distinctions between tourism and settlement became blurred. As a 1920s publication by the *Miami Herald* stated, "Primarily, Miami aspired to be no more than a winter resort, but with the coming of the thousands of visitors to the hotels and apartment houses, homes began to dot the city in every direction, and soon a permanent population marked the way for just as permanent business and other institutions that serve to make a complete city."[140]

To attract residents, Miami boosters, like their Los Angeles counterparts, focused on the benefits of the climate, the city's agricultural hinterland, and investment opportunities.[141] In 1897, Blackman and fellow residents started the Dade County Fair, which grew into a much-anticipated annual event that displayed both the agricultural and human products of south Florida. Alongside crop exhibits, boosters organized eugenically symbolic "baby shows" where healthful white infants were put on display to celebrate the new generation of Americans being produced in the semi-tropics.[142] "It was remarked by many of the tourists that they had never seen so many handsome babies at a baby show," a journalist reported. "This, like all the products of Dade county, is the best."[143] Growing national interest in the possibility of draining the Everglades also contributed to Miami's growth. South Florida boosters stressed that Miami and Dade Counties would share in the "increased business, trade and land values, which will inevitably follow the advent of the many new immigrants from the north" into the reclaimed wetlands, and numerous companies invested in reclamation were based in Miami.[144] A few years after the Spanish-American War, the Florida East Coast Railway informed potential investors that "Miami, this new metropolis of the far South, is the gateway . . . to all that wonderful region which has lately come under the protection of the American eagle."[145] Such statements reflected the boosters' desire that Miami would come to have a much greater significance than a winter resort. "Miami, from the very beginning, has been marked with a progress unknown to any other city in the State, if not in the United States," promoters proclaimed.[146]

Corporate boosters in Miami looked to Los Angeles as both a symbol and a model. Many Floridians were interested in learning from the experiences of Californians. In 1909, the state's leading citrus growers formed the Florida Citrus Exchange, a cooperative that sought to improve distribution by emulating the California Fruit Growers' Exchange. Florida growers brought in experts from California to ensure that their cooperative followed "as closely as practicable the lines of the organization" in California, which was "one of the most successful organizations of its kind in this country."[147] West Coast boosters also impressed Floridians.[148] In the 1900s, the California Promotion Committee—a statewide umbrella group for local chambers of commerce—urged citizens to contribute to advertising campaigns with the faith that "time, energy, money and system are required to make a city beautiful. Well ordered streets, clean yards, attractive buildings and homes are all conducive to a more satisfied feeling on the part of residents, and are inducements to visitors to locate."[149] California had more chambers of commerce and promotional organizations than any other state and stood out as an inspiration for Florida.[150] As a booster in the *Florida East Coast Homeseeker* wrote in 1907, "The State of Florida might learn some very valuable lessons from the pushing, energetic people of the State of California," where "the counties and State spend large sums of money in advertising, while cities, towns and individuals contribute their dollars to this great end."[151]

Los Angeles in particular inspired boosterist efforts in Miami. The latter's periodicals and promoters frequently ran headlines such as "Miami Destined to Become Los Angeles of Eastern U.S." and "Miami's Future Brighter than Los Angeles."[152] By 1910, when Miami was home to less than 6,000 people, Los Angeles had expanded to a population of nearly 320,000. Los Angeles thus symbolized a desired future for Miami developers, one of whom wrote that "it is pleasant to have travelers see a resemblance between Miami and Los Angeles— there is no doubt that the Magic City has a citizenry, also, which is planning to build for the future."[153] Occasionally envy spilled over in these comparisons and Miamians cited vital statistics to suggest that their city was healthier than Los Angeles or building statistics that showed faster rates of construction in south Florida.[154] Yet the disparity in size meant that, in general, Los Angeles presented a target to aim for more than a rival to beat. A new resident of Miami who had previously lived in Los Angeles wrote in 1913 that "if Los Angeles could grow to a population of 400,000 in fifteen years Miami can and will do the same and more."[155] The city's corporate boosters took direct lessons from the Los Angeles Chamber of Commerce. The president of the Miami Board of Trade, Isidor Cohen, traveled to Los Angeles in 1912 and reported back about "the profusion of flowers" in that city as an "asset" that should be matched in Miami. So was the Los Angeles Chamber of Commerce building, which showed off county "exhibits of all kinds" to visitors.[156] "Miami," Cohen concluded, "could do well indeed to emulate California in this and several other respects."[157] Inspired by promot-

ers, visitors and new residents in Miami affirmed the "resemblance" between the
two cities. Erstwhile Populist spokesman and presidential candidate William
Jennings Bryan, who came to the city to give a lecture and then purchased a
home there in 1912, declared that "Miami will be the Los Angeles of Florida."[158]

Despite these assertions, the spatial characteristics of Miami were in fact
quite different from those of Los Angeles. While the latter grew into a vast
open city of suburbs, Miami hugged the coastline and remained relatively com-
pact until its boom in the 1920s. City boosters highlighted improvements in
urban transportation, including bus services, a trolley system, and better side-
walks—twelve miles of concrete sidewalk were built within the city limits in
1914 alone.[159] Yet the downtown sector was surrounded on three sides by the
Miami River and Biscayne Bay, and after a quarter-century the city covered just
fifteen square miles.[160] In the 1920s, Miami became one of the most congested
cities in the nation in terms of traffic.[161] Such notable physical differences did
not prohibit Miami boosters from looking to California, however. Instead, the
growth of Los Angeles offered a useful goal for Miami. A 1915 newspaper article
with the headline "Miami's Resources Unparalleled" typified how parallels with
Los Angeles were used to bolster the city's development. "Miami has 20,000
people at the present time," it stated. "Many visitors characterize it as the Los
Angeles of the southeast and it does not seem at all improbable that Miami's
population will exceed 100,000 within a few years."[162] Ten years later, the city
had hit that mark and, although it was no match for Los Angeles's spatial expansion, it had grown outward to sixty-two square miles.[163]

Underpinning all of the comparisons of Miami with Los Angeles was the
formation narrative of a renewing urban environment for Americans. This
boosterist ideal of evolved urban life in tropical Florida was articulated by William F. Blackman, president of Rollins College in Winter Park, in a 1903 address
that was reprinted in the *Florida East Coast Homeseeker* after the publication's
editor had invited Blackman to "come to Miami and see . . . what was being accomplished."[164] Like Charles Dudley Warner in southern California, Blackman
saw south Florida as the future site for a well-rounded American civilization.
Northerners, he chided, were still erroneously disturbed at the prospect of living near the tropics. "It is generally thought that a continuous residence in this
warm country makes men lazy and shiftless, and that no one can make great
achievements surrounded with tropical or sub-tropical conditions." The construction of Miami, however, belied those fears that "in the tropics, and at their
verge, men will only dream and loiter." Blackman pointed to the ancient civilizations of the Mediterranean, where "human life" had been "splendid and fruitful."
Yet a slowing of the hectic pace of American life was perhaps not a bad thing.

"Doubtless there is here, beneath a more vertical sun—and ought to be—some slackening of speed in the race of life; but then, we have more days, and longer, every year, in which to do our work than our Northern neighbors have, as well as a more responsive Nature to work upon." Furthermore—in a statement that would have seemed sacrilegious to most northerners only a few decades before—Blackman boasted of south Florida's potential to create new Americans who were defined by their capacity to enjoy life rather than the virtues of work. "Is it so certain that speed and struggle are better than safety and sanity, that labor is more sacred than is leisure?" His message, echoed by Miami's corporate boosters, was that the free labor model was no longer dominant or even necessary—and certainly not in a semi-tropical city. There, Americans were learning that leisure and contentment could form the basis of improved communities. "What if it be true," he concluded, "that the vocation of this Southland is, in part, to temper the consuming ambition of the North, to steady and flavor and enrich and recuperate our American life in these days of unexampled strain after wealth and power?"[165]

But corporate promoters also cited Miami's economic growth as an important signifier of the city's improvement. For boosters, progress was found in the assessed value of real estate that rose from $120,000 in 1897 to $820,000 in 1905 to $12,259,400 in 1915. In addition, the population increased from 480 in 1897 to 15,592 in 1915.[166] The message was clear: the once "sleeping" city was evolving into a buzzing American marketplace. Miami, E. A. Waddell wrote, boasted "as many modern improvements as can be found in any city four times its age in the United States," proving that "we have . . . an up-to-date, go-ahead class of people."[167]

However, Miami's rise heightened long-running sectional tensions in Florida, and south Florida promoters increasingly pushed for greater representation in the state government. At times they called for the state capital to be moved to Gainesville or Orlando and even debated (like their southern California counterparts) the possibility of dividing the states.[168] As one booster wrote in the 1920s, "The contest for political control of the State" was not between Republicans and Democrats but between "the conservative, settled old regions of North and West Florida and the newly developing country of the Florida peninsula," led by the Magic City.[169] Home to only several families in 1895, Miami by 1920 had a permanent population of 30,000 that was augmented during the winter season by a transient group of over 100,000.[170] As Miami boosters pushed for greater political and investment capital for their city, they sought to assuage the fears of northerners about supposed south Florida lethargy. George Chapin, a promoter-historian of the area, wrote in 1914 that the fact "that such a city can

and does exist in the tropical portion of Florida will give the world a new conception of the energy that is building up the most southern of all the states."[171]

Miami promoters asserted that the tropical city made a superior urban lifestyle possible.[172] They presented Miami to older and wealthier white Americans
as the perfect city for a comfortable, semi-retired life that combined modern
amenities with fertile natural resources. "Miami is drawing to itself thousands
of the better class of American citizens, men and women of education and
character, thus building a citizenship" of "people who have made their wealth
elsewhere" and were "seeking Miami in ever-increasing numbers for either a
winter or a permanent home," C. H. Ward wrote.[173] Many of the city's home-
seekers were wealthy, and promoters recognized Miami's connection to a broad
shift from producer to consumer conceptions of American identity. As a Miami
resident later wrote of its growth, "A contributing factor no doubt lies in the
changed attitude of many classes of our people. The long rough work of subdu-
ing a continent about completed, they turned more and more to the joys of a
fuller, freer, more natural life in the open."[174] The emergence of a film industry
in Florida—in Jacksonville, Tampa, and Miami—encouraged hopes that the
southern state might rival California as the motion picture capital of America.[175] In architecture, too, Miami mimicked Los Angeles: faux Mediterranean
themes and palm-lined residences typified the "homes in this metropolis of the
subtropics."[176] Real estate developers such as the Montray Corporation of New
York showed off Miami houses surrounded by vegetation—the urban symbols
of Florida's tropic of hopes (Figure 5.3).

The marketing of Miami also promulgated the racial and class hierarchies
that were central to the city's development. Miami was a product of the Jim
Crow South. Across Florida, most African Americans had stopped being able
to vote within a decade of the amendments to the state constitution in 1885 that
had created the poll tax and other measures designed to disenfranchise them.[177]
Physical and legal segregation of the races in public transportation, civic spaces,
and housing became pronounced in the 1890s, and the 1896 Supreme Court rul-
ing of "separate but equal" in *Plessy v. Ferguson* gave legal sanction to Jim Crow
policies. Miami's promoters presented a New South of hard racial divisions. Ignoring the high rates of lynching and physical intimidation that whites inflicted
on blacks in Florida, the 1904 Florida state immigration guide stated that "social
equality between the races is not tolerated, and is impossible; miscegenation
is prohibited by law, and the gulf that marks the social boundary between the
white race and the black, is as broad as the universe, and as fathomless as the
infinitudes of space. Yet, the relationship between the races is of the most kindly
and friendly order."[178]

Figure 5.3. The "typical" Miami homes featured in the promotional literature chambers of commerce and real estate companies generated in the 1910s and 1920s were, in fact, class-specific elaborate houses and mansions that were always adorned with the palm trees of a tropical environment. *Source:* Earl Royce Dumont, *Miami* (Miami: Montray Corporation, 1921). From the P. K. Yonge Library of Florida History, Department of Special and Area Studies Collections, George A. Smathers Libraries, University of Florida.

African Americans were kept out of the white neighborhoods of Miami from the founding of the city through custom, and beginning in the early 1900s, they faced formal legal exclusion.[179] As was the case in other Florida cities, Miami's "Colored Town" was anything but equal to white neighborhoods in terms of housing, schools, or health care.[180] Most African Americans were unable to afford to buy or build their own homes and were forced to pay the high rents charged by white absentee landlords for housing that was "substandard by every definition." Historian Wali Kharif notes that "some [African Americans] lived in run-down shanties and shacks" that looked nothing like the "typical" Miami homes of booster literature.[181] The city's impoverished black neighborhoods were excluded from promotional guidebooks not least because their very existence undermined statements that Miami "has built up a solid, loyal, homogenous people, united in one object, that of not only building a city beautiful in material things, but one in which education and culture are encouraged."[182] These sentiments were written by and for the city's white population, just as the "East Coast of Florida has the ideal climate for the white man," according to F. J. De Croix.[183] Miami was hailed as a beautiful "white city" because of its architectural style, which incorporated the white of Mediterranean housing, but that language also unwittingly expressed the racial vision of the city's boosters.[184] For example, a representative and extensive city guide published in 1921 made no mention of Miami's black population at all.[185]

Yet Miami attracted blacks, including thousands of Bahamians who were drawn to south Florida by jobs on railroads, in housing construction, in the fruit and vegetable industries, and in service occupations in hotels and restaurants.[186] By 1920, nearly 5,000 Bahamians lived in Miami; they constituted half of the city's black population and almost a sixth of the urban total.[187] Miami developers depended on this marginalized population and did not entirely erase the city's black population from the literature they generated. But promoters presented blacks as locked into subservient roles that did not threaten civic prosperity and the leisure of whites.[188] A 1920s guide included a modern aerial view of the city paired with a photograph that showed "the Beginning of Miami in 1896": a group of suited white men—including E. G. Sewell—stood in front of a number of African American men who were engaged in the physical work of clearing Biscayne Bay. Articulating the colonialist ideal of a two-tiered society, promoters made a critical distinction between the men based on race: the whites were "a group of pioneer settlers" whereas the blacks were "a gang of workmen" that was "soon increased by hundreds." Promoters thus attributed the classic American quality of pioneer settlement to the white founders of Miami and reduced the contributions of the city's African American residents, who were as much pioneers and settlers as the whites, to manual labor.[189] Boosters were well aware that the hardening of racial control under Jim Crow made Florida and its cities a more appealing destination for many whites. A 1903 *Chicago Times-Herald* article stated that "the negro problem, if not settled, is in progress of settlement," thereby ending a "source of irritation" and encouraging the "overflow of [white] humanity from the busier and more active hives of the world [to the South]."[190]

Promoters also represented southern Florida as a region that was free from the immigrant groups that supposedly ran the political machines of northern industrial cities. Miami, like Los Angeles, was said to be free from "the foreign element which is flocking, in large numbers, to our shores and obtaining control of the Northern cities."[191] In fact, Miami's major "foreign element"—native-born and foreign-born blacks—were subjected to legal and extralegal codes that ensured racial hierarchy. In 1920, the efforts of African Americans to register to vote in Miami were met with violent reprisals by the Dade County chapter of the Ku Klux Klan. Members of the Klan chanted "Git back nigger. Go back to Nigger town."[192] Recalling the racist treatment and dilapidated housing he endured in the city, a Bahamian migrant wrote, "Colored Miami certainly was not the Miami of which I heard. It was a filthy backyard to the Magic City."[193]

Working to obscure the harsh realities of racism and poverty blacks experienced in their city, Miami's boosters focused on uplifting formation narratives for whites based on the city's lifestyle. They promised potential settlers "an out-of-door life the year round [that] makes the city one of the greatest ports for the pleasure-loving element."[194] In 1915, E. G. Sewell of the Chamber of Commerce advertised Miami throughout the North. His efforts included placing a large electric sign at Forty-Second Street and Broadway in New York that informed "the shivering New Yorkers in January that it is 'June in Miami.'" This was part of a nationwide public relations campaign that ultimately made Miami the best advertised city in the South. "Real life of Miami is out in the open," the Chamber of Commerce explained.[195] Miami's promoters promised their target audiences a new generation of urban citizens. In a book of poems about south Florida, George Merrick, the developer of the luxury subdivision of Coral Gables, wrote of the "Heirs of Tropic Spring": "Oh! To be born in this sweet southern spring-time is to be the heir of its joy; the child of its play."[196] The visual imagery the Chamber of Commerce promulgated made it clear that Miami's "heirs of Tropic Spring" were white. Pictures showed whites golfing, swimming, and driving through the city's verdant avenues that were the result of a vigorous local good roads movement.[197] The pamphlets always emphasized that Miami's tropical environs made possible a new urban existence for Americans. A typical Chamber of Commerce guide featured an oceanside scene of white men and women walking, driving, and returning from the tennis courts, surrounded by automobiles, steamships, airplanes, and a modern hotel, all set in the midst of tropical palms. Confirming the uniqueness of the city, the text praised Miami as "the epitome of the charm and lure of the Southland" that

INTRODUCTION

Miami, the epitome of the charm and lure of the Southland, beckons to young and old, rich and poor. Who can resist her smiling welcome as she perches, gem-like, on the finger which Florida dips so daintily into the blue southern waters, clothed in the romance and mystery of the tropics, basking in everlasting summer, her beauty enhanced by the richness of verdure and flower? Her hospitality is unbounded, she has become the cynosure of all eyes and to visit this fair city is to find ·· The Tourist's Delight ·· The Motorist's Mecca ·· The Fisherman's Paradise ·· The Yachtsman's Rendezvous ·· The Golfer's Joy.

Figure 5.4. In 1917, the Miami Chamber of Commerce boasted that Miami was the "fastest growing city" in the United States, a "cosmopolitan city" that ranked with the French Riviera as a leisure destination. *Source: Miami, the Land of Palms and Sunshine* (Miami: Miami Chamber of Commerce, 1917). Courtesy of Special Collections, University of Miami Libraries, Coral Gables, Florida.

"perches, gem-like, on the finger which Florida dips so daintily into the blue southern waters, clothed in the romance and mystery of the tropics" (Figure 5.4). Placing American modernity in the context of tropical nature, Miami's sellers verbalized the hope that "no other region, in any part of the world, can show so happy a blending of the joy of life with the business energy that creates material progress and modern civilization."[198]

The selling of Miami as a joyous and recuperative site contributed to its transformation from trading outpost in the 1890s to one of the nation's fastest-growing cities in the 1920s. Corporate boosters used this ideal to sell city lots and increase the value of urban land, always maintaining that Miami offered a qualitatively different American city. As one real estate company put it, "A metropolis, such as is New York City, is not the kind of metropolis Miami wants to be"—not a city "packing buildings together like sardines in a box" and "crowding apartments and streets with millions of people representing every nationality." Such a vision "would mean . . . sacrificing to commercialism everything that makes Miami the most comfortable and the most delightful community in the world."[199] In the eyes of promoters, Miami was a city that "happily combines business aggressiveness and progressiveness with a wholesome appreciation of what it means to be a community" of "beautiful homes, surrounded by ample space, decorated with tropical shrubbery, flower and vegetable gardens." Such a city could produce "home-loving, intelligent, progressive, honorable" citizens.[200] Los Angeles had already paved the way as a semi-tropical city that was home to a white community of republican citizens; Miami had only to follow its California rival. Thus, as a civic booster declared in 1920, Miami was "destined to be the great city of Florida and of that section of the country, ultimately being to that region what Los Angeles is to Southern California, to which its growth and characteristics are very similar."[201]

Through the Progressive Era, corporate promoters of southern California and south Florida fashioned new urban identities, casting Los Angeles and Miami as distinctive cities that escaped the instability of older, industrial American cities associated with labor unrest and immigrants who refused to assimilate. For boosters, tropicality and Anglo-American enterprise combined to produce evolved cities that were neither crowded nor debilitating but were instead healthful, progressive, and conducive to a contented, outdoor lifestyle. Los Angeles was sold by a hyperactive Chamber of Commerce that oversaw its rapid growth into one of the most spatially expansive in the United States. New industries based on oil and the film industry contributed to the diversified economy of the city. In 1899, when Miami was just three years old, Los Angeles had swelled to 108,000 people, and those who attended the National Education Association's annual meeting that year were told to expect "a busy place, and handsome withal"—a "metropolis whose *ensemble* is thoroughly modern. The business push, so unexpected in a semi-tropical climate, reminds one of Chicago." Attendees were assured that "not alone is Trade worshiped": "the Beautiful also finds ample expression" in the flower-lined streets and neighborhoods and the cottages and gardens that testified to a city with tropical claims.[202] Miami boosters saw in Los Angeles a symbol for their own city's future. If Miami lacked the impressive spatial expansion of Los Angeles and was more reliant on winter tourism, its boosters found that tourism was a legitimate means of attracting permanent citizens.[203] The natural environment was the key, celebrated in pamphlets such as one published by the Chamber of Commerce in 1919 that stated that the city's "climate, location, [and] resources have made Miami, Florida, what she is today, the acknowledged jewel of the Southland, the most talked-about and the fastest-growing city in the South."[204]

Indeed, in the 1920s Los Angeles and Miami were the two most publicized cities in the United States. Both were sites of growing economies and booming real estate markets.[205] Miami benefited from growing levels of automobile traffic on the Dixie Highway, which was completed in 1927 and connected south Florida to the Midwest. Florida promoter Charles Fox highlighted the significance of the highway for south Florida, noting that increasing numbers of visitors were driving into the state each winter. This migration was a very modern phenomenon that depended on good roads and low-priced cars, but Fox saw it in terms of a reinvigorated form of U.S. expansion, as "the counterpart . . . of those former movements which are so symbolic of the glorious traditions of the American pioneering spirit."[206]

Depicting their city as a modern inheritor of the nation's historic expansive impulses, Miami's promoters attracted thousands of Americans to south Florida's tropics through well-financed national advertising campaigns. For example, in March 1924, the Florida Development Board spent $400,000 on publicity in northern newspapers.[207] As Miami's population soared (a 238 percent increase in population from 1920 to 1925), the city's promoters made feverish comparisons with Los Angeles: "Florida to-day is approximately where California was in 1900," exclaimed one. "There will be as good reason for industries to spring up here as there were for those industries that sprang up at Los Angeles to sustain an otherwise illogical community of a million or more souls."[208] Booster Richard H. Edmonds drew a "simile" between the earlier settling of the "Los Angeles section" by midwesterners who went there "with the idea of settling down quietly for the balance of life" but soon invested in local businesses, and the "similar conditions" that "exist in Florida at this time," as the "fairly well-to-do people from the West and North are likewise moving here either for permanent residence or for the winter."[209]

Tropicality infused rivalry between the two cities. George Merrick's gated community of Coral Gables in Miami, for example, was promoted as a city in the "heart of the American tropics" that was designed with a unique merging of architectural styles that Merrick termed "tropic Mediterranean."[210] Los Angeles was prominent in the developer's mind: "A great city, Los Angeles, was brought into being on the far side of the Continent from the congested East, which furnished its population," Merrick told the *New York Times* in 1925. "Economically, should not Miami, which is comparatively a New York suburb . . . grow in vastly greater ratio and extent?" Merrick made his feelings clear that Miami, not Los Angeles, was the truly tropical city of the United States: "The lure of the tropics is a great and definite thing alone to build upon. The Miami area and thence on south to Cape Sable . . . comprises absolutely the only American tropics, and in that great fact Miami owns and will forever hold a priceless American monopoly. We are 600 miles south of the southernmost tip of California."[211] Tellingly, Miami's success sparked a significant response from Los Angeles promoters, who acknowledged the "keen competition from Florida" and formed the All Year Club of Southern California as a rival booster organization.[212] In 1925, a Los Angeles consulting firm called for "a campaign which will at least cause the public to give California as much consideration as it does Florida."[213] From his south Florida home, William Jennings Bryan felt it was "certain that Miami will one day surpass in size and prosperity the Magic City of Southern California—and it will probably be within the lifetime of many who are now living."[214]

In a replay of the experience of Los Angeles in the mid-1880s, the dramatic public interest in Miami led to a real estate boom in 1925. Promoters contributed to soaring real estate values. While they focused on the city's ability to produce healthier, happier citizens, they also whetted the appetites of Americans by referring to the economic bonanza that could be had in Miami simply by buying and reselling lots. "People must have places in which to live. They must have land—land, above all," declared a typical Miami booster, explaining that land values always rose following the discovery of a "commonly desired spot." "That is what is happening to Miami, and will continue to happen. That is why there is no surer value than Miami real estate."[215] Tropical characteristics underwrote this "common desire" for urban lots: "A climate the like of which does not exist outside of the semi-tropical zone, and of this section Miami is the metropolis and must remain so for all time."[216] The lure of profitable semi-tropical real estate sparked a frenzy of land-selling and get-rich-quick schemes in 1925. The Miami "land boom resembles something between fantasy and farce, miracle and merry-go-round," the *New York Times* commented, which called the land boom "the latest and most violent form of winter sport."[217]

Just as the boom in Los Angeles had suddenly ended, Miami's real estate values collapsed under inflated prices, and the ensuing financial bust damaged the city's reputation.[218] In its wake, frustrated south Florida boosters responded to skepticism about the region by referring once again to southern California's earlier experiences as a road map for Miami: "Only recently similar forecasts were being broadcast of the ultimate fate of Los Angeles and all southern California," undaunted boosters Frank Stockbridge and John Perry wrote in 1926.[219]

The *Los Angeles Times* sent "well wishes to the Everglades State," noting that not only did the two states share a "semi-tropical climate" but that Florida's boom-and-bust cycle had been "matched here" and had eventually led to "steady development."[220] Indeed, in the fallout from the failure of the real estate market and hurricane damage in 1927, Miami promoters found solace in pointing again to the West Coast. As one guide declared, "The experience of Los Angeles will be more than duplicated in the growth of Miami."[221] By 1930, the Miami Chamber of Commerce's slogan of "100,000 population by 1925" had finally been realized—albeit five years late.[222] The city had grown from 30,000 people in 1920 to 110,000 in 1930.[223] In early 1929, the year of the Wall Street crash, the *New York Times* reported that Miami "which three years ago was deserted by disillusioned land speculators and two years ago was shattered by hurricane winds . . . has experienced a reversal of fortune."[224]

The promotional imagery of Los Angeles and Miami exemplified the ways that southern California and peninsular Florida were sold as tropics of hope for white Americans. According to their boosters, both regions and both cities married republican ideals of homogeneous, home-owning communities with colonialist divisions based on race and class. Indeed, the one depended on the other. De facto and de jure policies of segregation by race in employment and housing underpinned the selling of Los Angeles and Miami. Both affluent cities relied on the labor of ethnic and racial communities that were marginalized politically and economically—Mexicans in California and African Americans in Florida. Promoters naturalized these racial stratifications with optimistic depictions of city development that focused on suburban tropical neighborhoods that offered the republican ideal of independent and happy citizens. They described Miami's destiny as "controlled" by "two purposes": "the utilitarian and aesthetic," creating an urban center of "progressive business activity and at the same time a wholesome and attractive city of homes."[225] The model for Miami was Los Angeles, a city that had reinvented ideas of American urban life, where, as the Chamber of Commerce stated in 1928, "We Americans are becoming an outdoor people."[226] By the 1920s, the once-strange environments of the semitropical states presented Americans with redemptive cities of gardened independence, locations where urbanization meant not decay but rebirth. Thus, for Florida promoter Arthur Brisbane, the future of the two states was not "cities of crowded windy streets, but cities that will cover hundreds of square miles, spreading over hills and valleys, [and] with beautiful roads." In a day to come, "Those now living will see in California and in Florida, cities greater than any now on earth."[227]

Conclusion

Beyond America's Tropic of Hopes

Writing in 1903, a settler in Florida penned a letter in which he confessed how, for years back in Ohio, he had dreamed "of a land of flowers" resplendent with "orange, grapefruit and lemon trees" surrounding a "neat cottage with its wide well-shaded porches." He explained that "I only knew of two countries where my wishes could be gratified: California and Florida."[1] This book has argued that ideas of tropicality on offer within U.S. borders infused the selling of California and Florida and that those tropical ideas were successful. Although scholars have marginalized this discourse, the semi-tropical imagery promoters constructed of California and Florida from the 1870s into the 1920s played significant roles in recasting popular conceptions of both states and attracting settlers, tourists, and investors to previously disdained environments that now offered distinctive attractions. In the 1870s, southern California was seen as an intimidating and remote desert, fit for cattle and little else.[2] In the decades that followed, it was reimagined as a fertile land of unmatched possibilities for American society. Through the work of its boosters and growers, growing semi-tropical fruit replaced gold mining as the state's iconic industry: "The emblem upon [California's] seal should not be the miner's pick and the crouching bear," southern California promoters declared, "but the clustering grape, the orange, the olive, and the broad leaves of the banana, drooping under the warm rays of the southern sun."[3] In turn, American attitudes toward California changed fundamentally. The East, as a San Francisco journalist observed in 1910, now "looked upon California as a semitropical state, whose chief horticultural product was the orange and lemon."[4] Well-funded programs to promote agriculture, tourism, and urban life successfully attracted many new residents, and southern California's population rose from fewer than 50,000 residents in 1880 (5 percent of the state's population) to 2.8 million people in 1930 (half of the state's total).[5]

Florida underwent a similar rehabilitation, from a place that was dismissed as swampy backwater to a hotbed of capitalist development. By the 1920s, hundreds of thousands of visitors visited the peninsula each year by rail and car, creating the demand for a string of "beautiful, modern cities in semi-tropical settings."[6] In 1870, Florida was home to only 187,748 residents, but by 1930, over 1.4 million lived in the state, half a million of which had arrived in the 1920s, during Florida's land speculation boom. On this latter growth, one guidebook writer declared, "Florida is being overwhelmed with a great wave of outside people who appreciate its possibilities and who will build up just as they have done in California, another empire."[7]

If the writer unwittingly (but accurately) confirmed that California had outdone Florida in preceding decades—by then, Los Angeles was the fifth largest city in the nation and Los Angeles County was the wealthiest producer of farm crops in the nation—he also demonstrated the intimate connections between the two states that their boosters had long cultivated.[8] These links clustered around the notion of safe, quasi-tropical environments that provided for healthier and more prosperous republican communities, thus reinvigorating core American ideals that were under threat from industrialization, urbanization, and agricultural decline elsewhere in the nation. Above all, the semi-tropics of California and Florida offered enticing new formation narratives for white Americans: those "outside people" who saw in the new "empires" growing up in the fertile corners of their nation unique opportunities for personal and social reinvigoration. The tropical imagery paid off. In the first decade of the twentieth century, California rose to first among the states in terms of the number of native white settlers it attracted (a position it would continue to hold through the century). Although Florida was not in the top ten in the 1900s in this regard, it rose to fourth in the 1910s, when it attracted 84,500 white American migrants (compared to California's 538,000). In the 1920s, Florida rose to third. By the 1930s and beyond, California and Florida placed first and second, respectively, as the two leading states to which white Americans relocated.[9]

In that sense, by the 1930s the promotional imagery of semi-tropical California and Florida had effectively done its work. As the nation reeled from the effects of the Wall Street crash, Americans regarded California and Florida as the most desirable states to live in, even though both states suffered severely during the Depression. South Florida was already hurting before 1929 because of the collapse of Miami's real estate boom and a series of hurricanes that had battered the state's Atlantic coast. Meanwhile, potential migrants from the Midwest were warned against trying to settle in California, and for the first time, writers, film-makers, and photographers began to challenge the hegemonic imagery genera-tions of boosters had produced.[10] But the very success of the boosterist trope of California and Florida as a tropic of hopes for white Americans also augured a change in focus. Promoters no longer needed to provide broad descriptions of the climate, geography, and environment of the two states. Hence, in the 1930s, the use of the term "tropical" appeared far less frequently in the literature that boosted southern California and peninsular Florida. Although the term still appeared in outsider pieces on the states—"Semi-tropical countries are most ideal for writing, such as Florida and California," commented a journalist in the *New York Times*—their promoters had far less need to fashion narratives of white adaptation in exotic nature.[11] The conversion of remote, underpopu-lated lands into fertile, populous gardens had been achieved, and boosters now focused on images of outdoor life in thoroughly modern and developed civi-lizations. Above all, the falling away of the language of tropicality indicated a fundamental conquering of natural environments that had once intimidated whites. Because industry and population had effectively domesticated Califor-nia and Florida, the environments and climates of the two states were no lon-ger deterrents in any real sense. In the words of one Los Angeles booster, the city's "environs" were "the all year round playgrounds for the American Business Man and his family," while Florida state commissioner of agriculture Nathan Mayo hailed the conversion of the peninsula from "a vast wilderness inhabited by a wild race" into a state that was home to "a million of the descendants of Europeans."[12] The damage done by these transformations to the natural eco-systems of California and Florida was immense and lasting.[13] But in getting those regions settled, and in convincing growing numbers of Americans of their special worth, the selling of semi-tropical California and Florida undoubtedly succeeded.

This can be seen also in the influence of the tropical tropes used to promote California and Florida on the imperialist ideology of the Soviet Union in the 1930s. In 1934 the Moscow magazine *Ogonyok* published an extensive and color-ful pamphlet entitled *Soviet Sub-Tropics*, which promoted the southern border-lands of the Soviet Union, especially the Transcaucasus.[14] The American inspi-ration for the pamphlet's vision was explicit. The writers were obsessed with the notion of "catching up [with] America," especially its semi-tropical states. They hailed Azerbaijan as "finer than the lands of California," while the head of the newly formed Soviet Department of Sub-Tropical Cultures declared, "Let's Create a Soviet Florida!"[15] This Soviet "sub-tropical" plan formed part of Joseph Stalin's vision of "socialism in one country"—a model of development that rejected internationalism and aimed to create a completely self-reliant state in which the republics of Russia and Ukraine hosted the major industry and politics while the more marginal Transcaucasus were "a place of luxury, health, and sunshine for Soviet workers."[16] The development ideals in California and Florida, of course, had been very different from the Soviet Union's goals for its own semi-tropics: in the United States, those goals centered on republicanism rather than socialism and on how independent health and wealth fostered improved capitalist communities. Yet they invoked the similar notion that "sub-tropical" regions provided valuable internal diversity for the nation, and the transformations of semi-tropical California and Florida thus formed a model for the Soviet version.

More problematically, the images boosters used to promote semi-tropical California and Florida also fed into the boosting of the actual tropical acquisitions of the United States (Hawaii, Puerto Rico, the Philippines, and Cuba) in 1898. Advocates of U.S. imperial expansion in the late nineteenth century faced strong opposition to the notion of taking tropical colonies, most fervently on the grounds that the latter were racially and socially unfit environments for American society.[17] Pro-expansionists, however, looked to California and Florida as examples of the potential benefits to be gained by taking Spanish or tropical colonies.[18] In 1892, John L. Stevens, U.S. Department of State minister to the kingdom of Hawaii, was concerned about the growing importation of Japanese workers, which he saw as a precursor to Japan's taking control of Hawaii. Stevens cited the white settlement of California as a model for how the federal government could annex and "Americanize the islands." In a cable to Secretary of State John Foster, Stevens explained that the United States should take ownership of Hawaii and then offer "small lots for . . . [U.S.] settlers and freeholders," which would bring about the "permanent preponderance of a population and civilization which will make the islands like southern California," thereby "bringing everything here into harmony with American life and prosperity."[19] Indeed, the pointed comparison between America's continental, "semi-tropical" states and potential overseas colonies was made frequently after the Spanish-American War, as politicians and writers defended the new tropical protectorates in terms of Manifest Destiny: a natural continuation of the expansion of the United States that had earlier encompassed California and Florida.[20] Republican Murat Halstead, a newspaper editor and an advisor to President McKinley, having cited the ongoing relevance of the Monroe Doctrine and Manifest Destiny, explained that "Spain is losing the last of her American islands as she lost all her American continental empires."[21] Guides to the U.S.'s new tropical "possessions" borrowed liberally from the language that had been used to describe Florida and California earlier in the nineteenth century. Trumbull White, author of *Our New Possessions* (1898) and *Puerto Rico and Its People* (1938), defended America's "moral right and manifest destiny" to take the islands and to "dominate in commercial influence and in all things for the uplifting of a swarming population of alien races."[22] As boosters had done in the selling of former continental "waste places," these supporters of U.S. imperialism emphasized the growing influence of the rule of white Americans—a triumph of race over environment. "Tho Honolulu is a tropical town in every respect," John Musick wrote in a treatise on Hawaii, "it is impossible for one to be on shore an hour without realizing that, after all, the controlling forces in this wonderful land are not tropical but American."[23] Descriptions of Hawaii's attractions sounded eerily reminiscent of descriptions of Florida and southern California a few decades earlier. Indeed, the writer repeated word for word Edward King's 1874 description of Florida: "This is the Kanaka life in the land of sunshine. *This is the south, slumberous, voluptuous, round, and graceful.*"[24] But it was California rather than Florida that was the true inspiration for advocates of U.S. expansion. Halstead wrote: "The example that, above all, vindicates the policy of annexation—not excepting Louisiana, Florida, or Texas—is California."[25]

Even though U.S. anti-imperialists tried to deny continuity between earlier continental expansion and the new overseas acquisitions, the connections were profound. While the newer "commercial" expansion contrasted somewhat in purpose with older expansion for the purpose of settlement, both were legitimized by the rhetoric of Manifest Destiny, which assumed that the displacement of indigenous, non-white peoples was part of white American progress. With typical bluster, Theodore Roosevelt mocked the anti-imperialist claims that the policy of "1899 is to destroy the fundamental principles and noblest ideals" of America with the false logic that such "doctrines condemn your forefathers and mine for ever having settled in these United States."[26] For Halstead, overseas tropical expansion was the logical step forward for a mature republic: "That consolidation which we call nationality, and which, with guarantees of popular liberty in republicanism and democracy, has in it the enduring and dominating substance of imperialism, that overcomes and expands and constructs and goes on to greater destinies." Americans should thus take pride in "the mighty magic of our fortune that transforms all that becomes ours. It was so with Louisiana, California, and the rest. It will be so with Cuba and Hawaii."[27]

The tropical links between California and Florida, on the one hand, and the U.S. protectorates in the Pacific and the Caribbean, on the other, were hard to miss. By the turn of the twentieth century, the transformations of the natural environments of Florida and southern California had generated great interest in semi-tropical agriculture. Both locations stood out as symbols of the Anglo-American development of exotic, sun-kissed domains. Writing in 1898, E. J. Wickson, professor of horticulture at the University of California, pointed out how with "rapidity American insight reversed the Spanish conception of the value and adaptations of the country, and American energy and ingenuity made practical and profitable use of them."[28] Intentionally or not, such statements supported the conceptual link Halstead and numerous other pro-expansionists made between former Spanish possessions that Anglo-Americans had "made practical and profitable" and noncontiguous islands such as Cuba where a similar process could take place.[29] For decades, California boosters had been providing formation narratives of South American lethargy versus Anglo endeavor that reinforced the imperialist argument. "Because the Spanish occupants [of California] were inert it has been supposed that the climate is enervating and conduces to sloth and idleness," an 1899 pamphlet by the California State Board of Trade declared. But "the habits of the Spaniard are no criterion for the wide-awake, alert American," since "the Spaniard has hung along the latitudes of the tropics for so many centuries that it would take many generations to breed out his natural inertia."[30] For advocates of U.S. imperialism, the ongoing development of California and Florida provided evidence that white Americans were a very different "breed" from tropical inhabitants and were more than capable of harnessing new fertile environments. In the context of the pervasive booster message of Anglo-Americans harnessing the semi-tropical potential of California and Florida, the acquisition of tropical colonies in the 1890s was a culmination of the ideological currents of late-nineteenth-century American expansion.[31]

Nonetheless, several leading California and Florida boosters bitterly criticized the nation's tropical expansion.[32] They did so for numerous reasons that included racism, concern about competition in the production of agricultural goods, and "moral" opposition to overseas imperialism. Charles F. Lummis provides a good example. In the pages of *Land of Sunshine*, Lummis railed against

America's imperialist ventures, writing in 1896 that the Cuban rebellion consisted of "negroes" who were the "worst elements in the island," led by ruffians whom he equated disdainfully with U.S. labor leader Eugene Debs.³³ After the Spanish-American War, Lummis warned that the "Imperial Trend" potentially meant "the sacrifice of California," since "we cannot keep out nor fine the products of our new 'possessions,' which raise the same things that California does" or shut out "subjects of the United States, as we can—and have been obliged to—the alien Chinese."³⁴ Tellingly, Lummis envisioned a strict dichotomy between the "healthy" farming of southern California and the coerced labor that would develop in the tropical colonies: the California "men who have farms, fruit ranches, sugar-beet fields, [and] garden homes" would be ruined by the "cheap products of Hawaii, Porto Rico [sic] and the Philippines" that would be raised by ignorant "coolies."³⁵ This distinction ignored the labor and racial realities that were emerging in California's agricultural sector. But it presented California and Florida to the rest of the nation as products of republican rather than imperialist designs. Indeed, for Lummis, Halstead's logic of linking Florida, Texas, and California to the 1898 tropical acquisitions amounted to a kind of heresy: a historical misreading of republican expansion as imperial conquest. "Jefferson Expansion was to get room for American settlers; McKinley Imperialism is to make room for a few speculators," Lummis wrote in 1900.³⁶ This blinding faith in continental republicanism was critical to the selling of California and Florida as democratic homelands that were congruent with American traditions.

Boosters of southern California and peninsular Florida thus marked out their states as the semi-tropical edges of U.S. republicanism and white society: beyond these boundaries, the social and racial "climates" became increasingly murky. Referring to the frequent comparisons visitors made between southern California and Palestine, the Los Angeles Chamber of Commerce stressed, "Unlike Palestine, however, Southern California is not a melancholy reminder of its former greatness, but a center of active, aggressive American enterprise; a region in which the best thought and energy of the American people are finding their crowning development, under the most genial clime in which the Anglo-Saxon race ever wooed the favors of Mother Earth."³⁷ A 1918 guide to Florida argued that the state had "first lured the red man from the more inhospitable North and he was followed by the white man," after which "Latin contended with Latin for its mastery, and, in turn, with the Anglo-Saxon and Anglo-American."³⁸

Even as California and Florida boosters clearly distinguished between their republican states and the "backward" tropics, support for U.S. commercial expansion in Central and South America and the Caribbean became more prominent in the promotion of both states after 1898. U.S. capitalists sensed the profits to be made in the new tropical protectorates. Shortly after the Spanish-American War, Florida railroad magnate Henry Flagler invested in a 360-mile railroad in Cuba, which also attracted the venture capital of Southern Pacific railroad owner E. H. Harriman.[39] California and Florida boosters increasingly emphasized how their states could benefit capitalists who wanted to take advantage of the new opportunities the tropics provided, and they presented Los Angeles and Miami as ideal locations for the corporate bases of such investors. As Harry Ellington Brook wrote in 1901, "It is not difficult to foresee a time when Los Angeles may become headquarters for Americans investments" in "the Spanish-American countries between the United States line and the Isthmus."[40] Costa Rica, for example, offered fertile real estate at "absurdly low" prices "in proportion to the value of the products," while the "natives"—a "simple, kindly people, who are satisfied with little"—would "under American overseers . . . make good laborers" at only 50 to 75 cents per day. From their base in Los Angeles, American investors could thus initiate "a peaceful conquest of that section" of "Tropic America."[41] Stanford University president David Starr Jordan similarly endorsed the southward expansion of U.S. commerce and industry. In 1899, he envisaged "the peaceful invasion of Mexico" through the "spread of American ideas" and capital, the "ultimate result" of which would be "to change Mexico from a paternal despotism to a self-governing republic"—such that, in 100 years, it could be "an Anglo-Saxon republic instead of a Spanish one."[42] Boosters presented Florida as "the natural gateway to the West Indies," since "the great peninsula, like a huge finger, directs the way to fertile regions beyond, awaiting American capital and enterprise."[43] Although tongue in cheek in tone, an 1898 letter from "California to Hawaii" published in the *Pacific Rural Press* was on the money in observing how Florida boosters looked to benefit financially from Cuba and Californians did the same with Hawaii, adding a fresh layer to the semi-tropical rivalry of the two states: Florida was overheard telling Louisiana, "'Say Lou, have you heard that Cal proposes to have that sandwich [Hawaii] all to herself, as a stand-off to my new semi-tropical combination with Cuba?'"[44]

Semi-tropical California and Florida had thus come to the fore as fortuitously located states for the untapped resources of the Pacific and the Caribbean. Promoters in both states eagerly supported the Panama Canal, recognizing the new investment opportunities it offered. In Florida, Flagler's railroad company completed an expensive overseas link from Miami to Key West in 1912 with a view to tapping into the trade that passed through the canal. The *Miami Herald* declared that the railway would "connect this country with the islands of the sea and [convey] the great traffic from the Panama."[45] Boosters stressed the commercial significance of Miami in the coming "union of North and South America in a confederacy of commerce," in which once-peripheral Florida would be "a great central state."[46] Tampa boosters held a twelve-day Panama Canal Celebration in 1910.[47] In 1915, on a far grander scale, California promoters organized two major expositions to commemorate the completion one year earlier of the Panama Canal, which had encouraged investment in the state's ports and cities.[48] The fairs, which were held in San Francisco and San Diego, focused on the canal's benefits for California investors. *Semi-Tropic California*, a guidebook that was published for the Panama-California Exposition in San Diego, directed the attention of "the American pioneer" to Central and South America as "the world of new opportunity." Racial stereotypes again were used to support the vision of commercial expansion. Although Latin Americans "will not work like people of northern lands," they "are most happy in making others happy," including the more energetic "North American" developer.[49] By the early twentieth century, semi-tropical California and Florida were being reconfigured by their boosters as stable stepping-stones for American investment in the fertile but underdeveloped tropics of Latin America.

And yet, throughout the heyday of American imperialism, California and Florida were successfully sold to new settlers using the older, cherished ideals of democratic republican progress. For their champions, southern California and peninsular Florida married the social and material benefits of a "self-governing republic" to the powerful natural potency of the tropics, bringing to life seductive formation narratives of independent white citizens who enjoyed prosperity and virtuous living in fertile farms and suburban cities. Corporate promoters in the two states, however, increasingly corrupted the rhetoric of republicanism as they pursued profits and legitimized the control of poorly paid nonwhite inhabitants as the foundation for these semi-tropical paradises. In that sense, far from being unique, California and Florida perpetuated the same patterns of racial domination and the pursuit of wealth that characterized the rest of the nation. These would play a significant role in future developments in both states, as Mexican and Afro-Caribbean immigrants came in greater numbers to southern California and peninsular Florida, respectively, where they did the backbreaking manual labor that whites were unwilling to do, often living in segregated neighborhoods far away from the prosperous white communities boosterist visions celebrated. The selling of America's tropic of hopes consistently carved out space for hierarchies of race and class within the uplifting images of republican communities in California and Florida. As Charles F. Lummis wrote of white settlers who were coming to the West Coast, "They find it not only the most independent but the most fascinating home-life in the world . . . It has something of kingship—and the most virulent republican approves of a monarchy when he can be the monarch."[50]

Notes

Introduction

1. "Semi-Tropic America," *Los Angeles Times*, August 13, 1882, 3.

2. See, for example, *Falfurrias*, *"the Land of Heart's Delight," in Semi-Tropical South Texas;* and Dennett, *Louisiana as It Is: Its Topography and Material Resources.*

3. Quotation from Benton, *Semi-Tropic California*, 1. See also Williamson, *Florida Politics in the Gilded Age, 1877–1893*, 170. For some examples of the titular use of "semi-tropical" in California promotion, see Truman, *Semi-Tropical California*; the Los Angeles periodical *Semi-Tropic California*; and *Semi-Tropic California—Citrus Fruit Area of the State*. For Florida, see French, *Semi-Tropical Florida*; and the Jacksonville periodical *Semi-Tropical* (1875–77).

4. Brook, *Irrigation in Southern California*, 16.

5. Hopkins, *Common Sense Applied to the Immigrant Question*, 3, italics in Hopkins.

6. George Canning Hill, "Florida for the Winter," *New England Magazine* 4, no. 3 (March 1888): 210.

7. I use the terms "Anglo" and "Anglo-American" in this book interchangeably with "white" but acknowledge that this terminology obscures as well as reveals. For example, German or Italian Americans were white but did not consider themselves "Anglo." In the context of California and Florida promotion, however, the term was used broadly to differentiate whites from native and non-white inhabitants: Mexicans, Native Americans, African Americans, and Asians. Several modern scholars also apply the term in this way in studies of these states: see Deverell, *Whitewashed Adobe*, 9.

8. Sanchez, *Becoming Mexican American*; Chan, *This Bitter-Sweet Soil*; Ortiz, *Emancipation Betrayed*.

9. Spickard, *Almost All Aliens*, 23–25.

10. Wood, *The Creation of the American Republic*, 53–54.

11. The finest study of California boosterism remains an unpublished 1973 Ph.D. thesis: Orsi, "Selling the Golden State." See also Starr, *Inventing the Dream*; Kurutz and Kurutz, *California Calls You*; McWilliams, *Southern California Country*; Davis, *City of Quartz*; and Deverell, *Whitewashed Adobe*. For Florida, see Rowe, *The Idea of Florida in the American Literary Imagination*; Thompson, "Florida in American Popular Magazines," 1–15; and Spivack, "Paradise Awaits," 429–38.

12. Degler, "In Making Historical Comparisons Focus on Common National Issues," 21. See also Woodward, *The Comparative Approach to American History*, xi–xiii.

13. For an interesting study of Florida's self-imagery as a "rerun" of California, see Whitfield, "Florida's Fudged Identity," 7–29.

14. "Florida and California," *Daily Alta California*, July 23, 1883, 2.

15. Foote, *Regional Fictions*, 3.

16. Marchand, *Advertising the American Dream*, xvii; Mohl, "Shadows in the Sunshine," 66.

17. Woodward, *Origins of the New South*, 492.

18. Los Angeles Chamber of Commerce, *New Facts and Figures concerning Southern California*, 20.

19. For a study of western promoters, see Wrobel, *Promised Lands*.

20. Marchand, *Advertising the American Dream*, xix, Marchand's italics.

21. Postel, *The Populist Vision*, 297. See also Wills, *Boosters, Hustlers, and Speculators*.

22. Hoag, *California: The Cornucopia of the World* (1883 edition), 54–55.

23. Orsi, *Sunset Limited*.

24. Starr, *Inventing the Dream*, 165.

25. B. B. Redding, "Immigration and How to Promote It," *Californian* 5, no. 25 (January 1882): 60.

26. Mayo, *Florida, an Advancing State*, 99.

27. Today the U.S. census bureau defines the Northeast as New England and the mid-Atlantic states of New York, Pennsylvania, and New Jersey. The Midwest includes Wisconsin, Michigan, Illinois, Indiana, Ohio, Missouri, North Dakota, South Dakota, Nebraska, Kansas, Minnesota, and Iowa.

28. Los Angeles Chamber of Commerce, *New Facts and Figures concerning Southern California*, 19.

29. Barbour, *Florida for Tourists, Invalids and Settlers*, 238.

30. See Patterson, *The Mosquito Crusades*.

31. "Florida and California," 2.

32. "Semi-Tropic America," 3.

33. George W. Cable, "Dr. Sevier," *Century* 27, no. 3 (January 1884): 422.

34. "Semi-Tropic America," 3.

35. Starr, *Inventing the Dream*, 45.

36. Sackman, *Orange Empire*, 29–30.

37. Examples of this abound. See, for example, E. J. Wickson, "Our Debt to Semi-Tropical Gardening," *Pacific Rural Press*, January 30, 1897, 70–71; Sylvester Baxter, "A Great Modern Spaniard," *The Atlantic Monthly* 85, no. 510 (April 1900): 559.

38. Nordhoff, *California for Health, Pleasure, and Residence*, 172.

39. "Eating Oranges," *Los Angeles Times*, February 24, 1890, 6.

40. "Itinerant," "In the Semi-Tropics," *Los Angeles Times*, March 29, 1885, 4. See also Elizabeth Bacon Custer, "Memories of 'Our Italy,'" *Land of Sunshine* 3, no. 2 (July 1895): 51–56.

41. Starr, *Inventing the Dream*, 45.

42. For a study of how ideas of expansion, freedom, and racial dominance shaped filibustering in the antebellum United States, see May, *Manifest Destiny's Underworld*.

43. Wood, *Empire of Liberty*, 7; Shalhope, "Toward a Republican Synthesis," 49–80.

44. Nye, *America as Second Creation*, esp. 1–20.

45. Ibid., 5–6.

46. Ibid., 11.

47. Spickard, *Almost All Aliens*, 23.

48. Tolderness, *Peoples and Problems of India*, 7–8.

49. Ibid., 8.

50. Wiebe, *The Search for Order*, xiii.

51. Lears, *No Place of Grace*.

52. LaFeber, *The New Empire*, 1–61.

53. See Wrobel, *The End of American Exceptionalism*; and Kasson, *Civilizing the Machine*, 183–234.

54. Turner, *The Significance of the Frontier in American History*, 1–2.

55. Foner, *Free Soil, Free Labor, Free Men*, 13–17.

56. Arnold, "'Illusory Riches,'" 6–18. See also the chapter "Inventing Tropicality" in Arnold, *The Problem of Nature*, 141–68.

57. Kenny, "Climate, Race, and Imperial Authority," 695. See also Kidd, *The Control of the Tropics*.

58. Charles Dudley Warner, "Race and Climate," *Land of Sunshine* 4, no. 3 (February 1896): 104.

59. Love, *Race over Empire*, 25.

60. In the late nineteenth century, the related argument was also made that people from hotter, tropical climates had never migrated to colder countries and never would, although the arrival into the North of Italians, Greeks, and southern blacks, for example, challenged this environmental-racial assumption. See "Senator Stewart of Nevada for Expansion," in Halstead, *Pictorial History of America's New Possessions*, 610.

61. Senator Carl Schurz quoted in ibid., 67.

62. "Semi-Tropical California," *Chicago Daily Tribune*, May 4, 1875, 3.

63. "California and Florida," *Sacramento Daily Union*, December 2, 1887, 2.

Chapter 1. "Our" Tropical Lands

1. "Poor Florida!" *Pacific Rural Press*, October 1, 1887, 260.

2. Hyde, *An American Vision*, 122–23.

3. Jacobson, *Barbarian Virtues*, 110; Arnold, "'Illusory Riches,'" 6–18.

4. Starr, *Americans and the California Dream*, 57–58. "Mining camp" quotation from Orsi, *Sunset Limited*, 133.

5. Covington, *The Seminoles of Florida*.

6. "Florida and California," *Daily Alta California*, July 23, 1883, 2.

7. Foner, *Free Soil, Free Labor, Free Men*, 301–17.

8. Ibid., 16–17.

9. Forbush, *Florida*, 3.

10. Nordhoff, *California for Health, Pleasure, and Residence*, 12.

11. Commissioner of Lands and Immigration, State of Florida, *Florida: Its Climate, Soil and Productions*, 57, italics in original.

12. Rolle, *California*, 14–15.

13. Weinberg, *Manifest Destiny*, 49–54, 89.

14. Senator John Randolph quoted in Harcourt, *Home Life in Florida*, 22.

15. Rogin, *Fathers and Children*, 197.

16. "Florida and the High Cost of Living," *Florida Farmer and Homeseeker* 26, no. 7 (July 1914): 190.

17. The 1851 Land Act, which Congress created to adjudicate land disputes between Californios and Anglo-American squatters, "effectively disposed Californios of approximately 40% of their

lands held before 1846." Douglas Monroy, *Thrown among Strangers*, reproduced in Chan and Olin, *Major Problems in California History*, 133. See also Rifkin, *Manifesting America*, 149–96.

18. Farnham, *Life, Adventures, and Travels in California*, 363.
19. Griffin-Pierce, *Native Americans*, 103.
20. *California Souvenir Views.*
21. Love, *Race over Empire*, 31.
22. Ibid., 32, 28.
23. Starr, *Americans and the California Dream*, 52–53.
24. Saxton, *The Indispensable Enemy*, 60–66.
25. Orsi, *Sunset Limited*, 105, 133.
26. Bean, *California*, 182–83; Stephen Powers, "California Saved," *Atlantic Monthly* 28, no. 169 (November 1871): 602.
27. Hopkins, *Common Sense Applied to the Immigrant Question*, 3.
28. Ibid., 4–6.
29. Ibid., 4, 17.
30. McWilliams, *California: The Great Exception.*
31. Rolle, *California*, 217.
32. Ibid., 217–32.
33. Rae, *Westward by Rail*, 264–65.
34. Hopkins, *Common Sense Applied to the Immigrant Question*, 4.
35. Ibid., 16.
36. Rolle, *California*, 270; Bean, *California*, 154–55. See, for example, Bret Harte, "Luck of Roaring Camp," *Chicago Tribune*, March 27, 1870, 6.
37. Robert J. Gregg, "The Climatic Advantages of San Diego," *San Diego Union*, October 20, 1883, in California Scrapbook Collection, vol. 21, San Diego County California Pamphlets—Immigration Association of California, 22, Special Collections, California State Library, Sacramento, California.
38. Saxton, *The Indispensable Enemy*, 60–100.
39. Hopkins, *Common Sense Applied to the Immigrant Question*, 21.
40. Ibid., 20, Hopkins's italics.
41. Ibid., Hopkins's italics.
42. Ibid., 19–22.
43. Ibid., 3–4.
44. Ibid., 18, Hopkins's italics.
45. Nordhoff, *California for Health, Pleasure, and Residence*, 18.
46. Orsi, *Sunset Limited*, 130–65.
47. "New Publications: 'California: For Health, Pleasure, and Residence," *New York Times*, October 18, 1872, 2.
48. Lindley and Widney, *California of the South*, 280.
49. Nordhoff, *California for Health, Pleasure, and Residence*, 11, my italics.
50. O'Connor, *Nordhoff's West Coast*, 5–6.
51. Richard Henry Dana quoted in Barron, Bernstein, and Fort, *Made in California*, 51.
52. O'Connor, *Nordhoff's West Coast*, 7.
53. Painter, *Standing at Armageddon*, 25–26.
54. Charles Nordhoff, "The Misgovernment of New York—A Remedy Suggested," *North American Review* 113, no. 233 (October 1871): 321–43.

55. Ibid., 321–22.

56. Nordhoff, *California for Health, Pleasure, and Residence*, 12.

57. See the chapters "Southern California for Invalids," "Semi-Tropical Fruits in Southern California," and "A California Cattle Rancho" in ibid.

58. Ibid., 128.

59. For a discussion of "push" and "pull" factors in migration, see Daniels, *Coming to America*, 17–22.

60. Nordhoff, *California for Health, Pleasure, and Residence*, 18.

61. Ibid., 155.

62. Ibid., 162.

63. Ibid., 123.

64. Ibid., 157.

65. Ibid., 181.

66. Ibid., 90–91.

67. Ibid., 177.

68. Kurutz, *Benjamin C. Truman*, 24. By "occident," Truman presumably meant "West" or "Western hemisphere," but the term reflected his tendency to romanticize California. Writing in 1903, he declared that "Semi-Tropical California" "captivates seekers after occidental homes." Truman, *Southern California*, n.p.

69. Truman, *Semi-Tropical California*, 12.

70. Ibid., 29.

71. Ibid., 14.

72. Ibid., 27.

73. Ibid., 27.

74. Ibid., 26.

75. Ibid., 46.

76. Major William McPherson, quoted in ibid., 38.

77. "Florida versus Southern California," *Los Angeles Herald*, December 2, 1880, 2.

78. Truman, *Semi-Tropical California*, 12.

79. Tebeau, *A History of Florida*, 191–92, 221–38.

80. For the socioeconomic problems of the postwar South, see Rabinowitz, *The First New South*, 2–37.

81. Carter et al., *Historical Statistics of the United States*, 4:4–61.

82. Pozzetta, "Foreigners in Florida, 165.

83. Commissioner of Lands and Immigration, State of Florida, *Florida: Its Climate, Soil and Productions*, 3.

84. Ibid., 14.

85. Ibid., 6.

86. Delaware was the least populated.

87. Carter et al., *Historical Statistics of the United States*, 1:180, 213, 217.

88. On the struggles of southern states to attract immigrants, see Woodward, *Origins of the New South*, 60–61, 86–89.

89. John Lee Williams, "Notice to Emigrants," from *The Territory of Florida* (1837), in O'Sullivan and Lane, *The Florida Reader*, 76.

90. Ibid., 76–77.

91. Ibid., 77.

92. Commissioner of Lands and Immigration, State of Florida, *Florida: Its Climate, Soil and Productions*, 7.

93. See Boyd, "The Seminole War," 3–115.

94. Long, *Florida Breezes*, 1.

95. Richmond, *Sumter County, Florida*, 11.

96. Quoted in Baptist, *Creating an Old South*, 27.

97. Williams, "Notice to Emigrants," 77.

98. Thomas Jefferson quoted in Smiley, "The Quest for the Central Theme in Southern History," 310.

99. Williams, "Notice to Emigrants," 77.

100. Commissioner of Lands and Immigration, State of Florida, *Florida: Its Climate, Soil and Productions*, 14.

101. On Florida during Reconstruction, see Shofner, *Nor Is It Over Yet*.

102. Florida Department of Agriculture, *Fifth Census of the State of Florida*, 15.

103. Ibid., 12–16.

104. Ibid., 13.

105. See Stowe's introduction in Munroe, *The Florida Annual*, 6–7; and Stowe, *Palmetto Leaves*, reproduced in O'Sullivan and Lane, *The Florida Reader*, 140.

106. Harriet Beecher Stowe, "Our Florida Plantation," *Atlantic Monthly* 43, no. 259 (May 1879): 641–50.

107. Stowe, *Palmetto Leaves*, 35–38.

108. See Hedrick, *Harriet Beecher Stowe*, 338; Stowe's guidebook even receives scant analysis in a book about the author's time in Florida: see Foster and Foster, *Beechers, Stowes, and Yankee Strangers*.

109. Gerson, *Harriet Beecher Stowe*, 192.

110. For an analysis of the ongoing process of sectional reconciliation, including the importance of tourism, see Silber, *The Romance of Reunion*.

111. Quotation in O'Sullivan and Lane, *The Florida Reader*, 140.

112. Belmore Florida Land Company, *Florida, the Land of Sunshine, Oranges, and Health*, 1.

113. Crosby, *Florida Facts Both Bright and Blue*, 85.

114. Stowe, *Palmetto Leaves*, 38.

115. On the dangers of malaria in Florida summers, see ibid., 129–30.

116. "Letter No. 2, Gainesville, Fla. April 6, 1860," in Byrne, *Florida and Texas*.

117. Stowe, *Palmetto Leaves*, 26.

118. Ibid., 140, 128.

119. Ibid., 36.

120. See "Florida," *New York Tribune*, December 5, 1861, 4; and "Florida for the Contrabands," *Chicago Tribune*, December 11, 1861, 2.

121. Litwack, *Been in the Storm So Long*, 308–9.

122. Ambrose Douglass, quoted in ibid., 177.

123. "From the Land of Flowers," *Christian Recorder*, December 28, 1872, quoted in Ortiz, *Emancipation Betrayed*, 18.

124. Ortiz, *Emancipation Betrayed*, 2–50.

125. Foner, *Reconstruction*, 429.

126. H. A. Massey, "Trip to St. Augustine," *Atlanta Constitution*, March 25, 1876, 3.

127. Stowe, *Palmetto Leaves*, 243, 284, 286.

128. Ibid., 279.

129. Foner, *Reconstruction*, 46–48.

130. Ibid., 46–48.

131. Stowe, *Palmetto Leaves*, 283.

132. Ibid., 280.

133. Ibid., 284–85.

134. Ibid., 269.

135. Ibid., 281–82.

136. Foner, *Reconstruction*, 449.

137. "Illustrated Books of Travel," *The Examiner*, December 25, 1875, 1447.

138. King, *The Southern States of America*, 405.

139. Ibid., 382.

140. Ibid., 417.

141. Ibid., 393, 417.

142. Ibid., 408.

143. Ibid., 380.

144. Ibid., 380–407.

145. Ibid., 419.

146. Shofner, *Nor Is It Over Yet*.

147. King, *The Southern States of America*, 404.

148. Nordhoff, *California for Health, Pleasure, and Residence*, 11, my italics.

149. William Henry Bishop, "Southern California I," *Harpers* 65, no. 389 (October 1882): 713.

150. Harriet Beecher Stowe quoted in Ortiz, *Emancipation Betrayed*, 29.

Chapter 2. A Climate for Health and Wealth

1. Jacobson, *Barbarian Virtues*, 50–56.

2. Bishop Haven, "The American Damascus," *Semi-Tropic California* 3, no. 1 (January 1880), 11.

3. Belmore Florida Land Company, *Florida, the Land of Sunshine, Oranges, and Health*, 1.

4. Hoag, *California: The Cornucopia of the World* (1883 edition), 55. For wages, see Painter, *Standing at Armageddon*, xix–xxvi.

5. "Floridiana—Immigration Meeting: Noteworthy Gathering of Representative Men from Over the State," *Florida Dispatch* 7, no. 32 (August 8, 1887): 666.

6. Mayo, *Florida, an Advancing State*, 164. On the importance of tourism to the West, see Pomeroy, *In Search of the Golden West*.

7. "California and Florida," *Los Angeles Times*, May 19, 1891, 4.

8. Letter by Margaret Etheridge Maynard reproduced in Octave Thanet, "Six Visions of St. Augustine," *Atlantic Monthly* 58, no. 346 (August 1886): 187.

9. Van Dyke, *Southern California*, 221.

10. Dr. A. A. Ward (Del Mar, San Diego County) to Mr. Holabird (Southern California Horticultural Society), undated letter [ca. 1888], Folder "San Diego Chamber of Commerce, Correspondence, 1888–1900," Charles B. Turrill Papers as Manager, San Diego Chamber of Commerce, 1878–1890, California Historical Society.

11. Keeler, *Southern California*, 9.

12. Aron, *Working at Play*, 3–10.

13. Foner, *Reconstruction*, 461; Hays, *The Response to Industrialism*, 47.

14. Wiebe, *The Search for Order*, 12; Lears, *No Place of Grace*, xii.

15. Strong, *The New Era*, 79.

16. Beard, *American Nervousness*, vi–ix, 94.

17. See the introduction in Lears, *No Place of Grace*. For other influential articulations of such fears, see Thomas, *Alternative America*.

18. Beard, *American Nervousness*, 97.

19. Aron, *Working at Play*. For nineteenth-century tourism to the far West, see Hyde, *An American Vision*.

20. Bird, *Dressing in Feathers*.

21. Beard, *American Nervousness*, 120.

22. Charles Dudley Warner, "Editor's Study," *Harper's Monthly* 89 (October 1894): 800, quoted in Lears, *No Place of Grace*, 52.

23. "Mr. Church's View in the Arctic Region," *New York Times*, March 29, 1861, 4.

24. Hughes, *American Visions*, 161.

25. "The Influence of Climate," *The Old Guard* 4, no. 3 (March 1866): 163.

26. Baur, *The Health Seekers of Southern California*; "A Winter Cure," *Semi-Tropical* 1, no. 3 (November 1875): 141.

27. "Bethesda."

28. See Rogers, *Climate in Pulmonary Consumption*; Shaw, *California as a Health Resort*; Lente, *The Constituents of Climate*; Kenworthy, *Climatology of Florida*; and the table in Davidson, *The Florida of To-Day*, 109.

29. Kropp, "'All Our Yesterdays.'"

30. Charles H. Shinn, "With the Spanish Californians," *Interior* (November 6, 1890): n.p., in Charles Howard Shinn Papers, Bancroft Library, University of California, Berkeley.

31. A. G. Chandler, "Letter from Florida," *Indiana Farmer* (November 12, 1887): 16; Tyler, *Where to Go in Florida*, 26.

32. Munroe, *The Florida Annual*, 45.

33. "Itinerant," "In the Semi-Tropics," *Los Angeles Times* (March 29, 1885): 4.

34. "The Effect California Climate Has Upon Easterners," *Los Angeles Times*, June 24, 1886, n.p., California Scrapbook Collection, volume 12, Los Angeles County—Immigration Association of California, 120, California State Library.

35. Starr, *Inventing the Dream*, 83.

36. Warner Bros., *Southern California*, 146.

37. Charles Dudley Warner, "The Golden Hesperides," *Atlantic Monthly* 61, no. 363 (January 1888): 56.

38. Rosaldo, "Imperialist Nostalgia," 107–22.

39. Los Angeles Chamber of Commerce, *New Facts and Figures concerning Southern California*, 19.

40. A. Thorne, "Railroads and Sunshine," *Land of Sunshine* 4, no. 3 (February 1896): 153.

41. Nutting, *To the Pacific Coast via the Sunset Route of the Southern Pacific Company*, 14.

42. William Henry Bishop, "Southern California III," *Harpers* 66, no. 391 (December 1882): 713.

43. A typical article explained that Yosemite Valley promised "the delights of a week's or a month's [worth of] shooting among our hills and forests." "Sportsmen's Targets," *Sunset* 1, no. 4 (August 1898): 53.

44. Hoag, *California: The Cornucopia of the World* (1883 edition), 18.

45. Brook, *The Land of Sunshine*, 9.

46. The secretary of the northern California citrus fair in 1886 declared that the exhibit of semi-tropical productions was "undeniable proof that the northern half of our State is as truly semi-tropic in climate as Los Angeles or Florida"; H. Latham, "Northern California Citrus Fair," *Daily Alta California*, 12 January 1886, 8.

47. Lindley and Widney, *California of the South*, 62.

48. Shepard, *Semi-Tropic California*.

49. "Our Own State," *Daily Alta California*, June 17, 1884, 8.

50. Vail, *"Both Sides Told," or Southern California as It Is*, 5.

51. Johnstone, *"By Semi-Tropic Seas"*; *California Souvenir Views*.

52. Kate Sanborn, "In Southern California—Kate Sanborn's Experiences and Opinions," *New York Times*, August 7, 1893.

53. *Facts and Figures concerning Southern California and Los Angeles City and County*, 4.

54. *Semi-Tropic California* 3, no. 4 (April 1880): 5.

55. "Exile," "Florida and California," *Florida Dispatch* 1, no. 14 (June 26, 1882): 213.

56. H. H. [Helen Hunt Jackson], "Outdoor Industries in Southern California," *Century* 26, no. 6 (October 1883): 803. The article was reproduced in an 1892 travel book by the same author: Jackson, *Glimpses of Three Coasts*, 3–29.

57. H. H., "Outdoor Industries," 803.

58. Ibid.

59. These Warner Bros. were not connected to the Warner Bros. film studio in Hollywood.

60. Statement made by C. A. Warner, of Warner Bros., Los Angeles, at a meeting of the San Diego Chamber of Commerce on August 14, 1888, Folder "Records of Advertising Southern California, 1888," Charles B. Turrill Papers as Manager, San Diego Chamber of Commerce, 1878–1890, California Historical Society.

61. Warner Bros., *Southern California*, 37.

62. Ibid., 9, 37, 146.

63. *Los Angeles Mirror* (January 8, 1887), n.p., Los Angeles County—Immigration Association of California, 120, vol. 12 in California Scrapbook Collection, California State Library.

64. Van Dyke, *The Still Hunter*; Van Dyke, *The Rifle, Rod, and Gun in California*.

65. "Southern California," *New York Times*, July 5, 1886, 3.

66. Van Dyke, *Southern California*, 207.

67. Ibid., 215.

68. Starr, *Inventing the Dream*, 48.

69. Van Dyke, *Southern California*, 22.

70. Kropp, "'All Our Yesterdays.'"

71. McWilliams, *Southern California Country*, 21–75.

72. Shinn, "With the Spanish Californians."

73. Kropp, "'All Our Yesterdays,'" 19–21.

74. Mathes, *Helen Hunt Jackson and Her Indian Reform Legacy*, 81.

75. Shinn, "With the Spanish Californians."

76. Jackson, *Ramona*, 106–7.

77. "The Original Ramona," *Washington Post*, December 15, 1898, 9.

78. *The Mentor: Southern California, the Land of Sunshine* 4, no. 21 (December 15, 1916): 10. Charles F. Lummis is the author of this untitled article.

79. Keeler, *Southern California*, 90.

80. McWilliams, *Southern California Country*; Gutierrez, "Significant to Whom?" 524.

81. Camarillo, *Chicanos in a Changing Society*, 41.

82. Ibid., 41–52.

83. Deverell, *Whitewashed Adobe*, 28.

84. Bishop, "Southern California III," 47.

85. Ibid., 47.

86. Carter, *The Missions of Nueva California*, 1.

87. Carter, *Some By-Ways of California*, 187.

88. H. H., "Outdoor Industries," 820.

89. Jackson's use of "orientalism" here seemingly refers to her idea that peoples from the "Orient" shared with the Californios a lifestyle less driven by material accumulation and more by contented living. See ibid., 807, 820.

90. Lindley and Widney, *California of the South*, 101–2.

91. J. Torrey Connor, "Only John," *Land of Sunshine* 4, no. 3 (February 1896): 111.

92. For the influence of Mardi Gras, see Stanonis, "Through a Purple (Green and Gold) Haze," 109–31.

93. "La Fiesta de Los Angeles," *Land of Sunshine* 4, no. 6 (May 1896): 269.

94. Charles F. Lummis, "In the Lion's Den," *Land of Sunshine* 4, no. 1 (December 1895): 43.

95. Jacobson, *Barbarian Virtues*, 50–51.

96. Harry Ellington Brook, "Olden Times in Southern California," *Land of Sunshine* 1, no. 2 (July 1894): 27.

97. Ibid., 30.

98. Lindley and Widney, *California of the South*, 61–100.

99. Dumke, *The Boom of the Eighties in Southern California*.

100. Charles Turrill, General Manager, San Diego Chamber of Commerce, to the Editor of the *Times-Democrat*, New Orleans, Louisiana, August 16, 1888, Folder "San Diego Chamber of Commerce, Correspondence, 1888–1900," Charles B. Turrill Papers as Manager, San Diego Chamber of Commerce, 1878–1890, California Historical Society.

101. Warner, "Golden Hesperides," 48–49.

102. M. E. W., "A Home in Southern California," *Land of Sunshine* 1, no. 6 (November 1894): 117.

103. Grace Ellery Channing, "The Basket of Anita," *Scribners* 8, no. 2 (August 1890): 206.

104. "Off for the Winter," *Chicago Tribune*, December 9, 1894, 14.

105. Birney H. Donnell, "La Fiesta De Las Flores—The Annual Playtime of Southern California," *California Homeseeker* 1, no. 4 (May 1902): 226.

106. Brook, *The Land of Sunshine*, 9.

107. I. N. Reed, "Southern California Attracting Much Attention," *Chicago Tribune*, May 22, 1892, 46.

108. Keeler, *Southern California*, 135.

109. "The Woman in California," *California Homeseeker* 1, no. 3 (April 1902): 129.

110. Elizabeth Bacon Custer, "Memories of 'Our Italy,'" *Land of Sunshine* 3, no. 2 (July 1895): 51.

111. Brook, *The Land of Sunshine*, 10.

112. Ibid., 58.

113. "Exile," "Florida and California," 213. The letter was reprinted in "Twin Sisters—Comparison and Contrasts between Florida and California," *Los Angeles Times*, August 1, 1882, 3.

114. Ibid.

115. See Willis, *Health Trip to the Tropics*; "The Region of the St. John's," *New York Times*, March

2, 1871, 6. For how northern visitors in the antebellum period collected souvenirs of the South, including "uncollectible" souvenirs such as the tastes and smells of Florida citrus, see Plaag, "'There Is an Abundance of Those Which Are Genuine,'" 24–49.

116. Report of Surgeon-General Lawson of the United States Army, quoted in Robinson, *Florida: A Pamphlet Descriptive of Its History, Topography, Climate, Soil, Resources, and Natural Advantages*, 13.

117. Surgeon-General Lawson's report in Davidson, *The Florida of To-Day*, 54–55; see also Byrne, "Letter No. 1," *Florida and Texas*, 5.

118. Richmond, *Sumter County, Florida*, 6.

119. Mayo, *Florida, an Advancing State*, 99.

120. George Canning Hill, "Florida for the Winter," *New England Magazine* 6, no. 3 (March 1888): 209–16.

121. King, *The Southern States of America*, 378.

122. Regarding St. Augustine's reinvention as a Spanish renaissance city after the defeat of the Confederacy, see Hillyer, "Designing Dixie."

123. Brinton, *A Guide-Book of Florida and the South*, 32.

124. Upham, *Notes from Sunland*, 49.

125. Kenworthy, *Climatology of Florida*, 9, quoted in Davidson, *The Florida of To-Day*, 57; Cox, *Dreaming of Dixie*; Silber, *The Romance of Reunion*, 80–82.

126. Brinton, *A Guide-Book of Florida and the South*, 57, 115–31.

127. Lanier, *Florida*, 12–13.

128. Silber, *The Romance of Reunion*, 66–92.

129. "Extreme Southern Florida," *Florida Dispatch* 1, no. 3 (April 10, 1882): 6. For travel itineraries, see Florida East Coast Railway, *Florida: A Trip from Jacksonville to—Havana*.

130. Robinson, *Florida: A Pamphlet Descriptive of Its History, Topography, Climate, Soil, Resources, and Natural Advantages*, 10.

131. Tebeau, *A History of Florida*, 274–92.

132. I. N. Reed, "Southern California Attracting Much Attention," *Chicago Tribune*, May 22, 1892, 46.

133. Clyde Steamship Company, *Beautiful St. John's River*, 2.

134. Lee, *The Tourist's Guide of Florida*, 131, 146.

135. Elizabeth Stuart Phelps, "Going South," *Atlantic Monthly* 37 (January 1876): 29, Phelps's italics.

136. "Bethesda," n.p., italics in original.

137. Ibid.

138. Brinton, *A Guide-Book of Florida and the South*, 119.

139. Pike, *The United States and Latin America*, 54–59.

140. Brinton, *A Guide-Book of Florida and the South*, 119.

141. Brinton went on to become a leading American ethnologist and expert on the so-called hierarchy of peoples. He wrote in his 1890 book *Races and Peoples* that "the European or white race stands at the head of the list, the African or negro at its foot": Brinton, *Races and Peoples*, 8.

142. Ashby, *Alachua, the Garden County of Florida*, 19.

143. Kenworthy, *Climatology of Florida*, 10, quoted in Davidson, *The Florida of To-Day*, 57.

144. On the relationship between hunting and white supremacy in the New South, see Giltner, *Hunting and Fishing in the New South*.

145. *Hotel Ormond* (1891), 2, Brochure 4173, Florida Ephemera Collection, George A. Smathers Libraries, University of Florida Library, Gainesville, Florida. (Hereafter Florida Ephemera Collection.)

146. Slotkin, *Regeneration through Violence.*

147. Phelps, "Going South," 29.

148. See Henshall, *Camping and Cruising in Florida; Views of Florida;* Clyde Steamship Company, *Beautiful St. John's River,* 1.

149. "Florida: A Tour through East Florida," *Chicago Tribune,* May 10, 1870, 2.

150. Richardson, *Florida: The East Coast and Keys,* 24. See also Eacker, "Gender in Paradise," 495–512.

151. "Hunting Days in Florida," *New York Times,* May 30, 1897, 17.

152. White, *Jacksonville, Florida, and Surrounding Towns,* 21.

153. Presbrey, *Florida, Cuba, and Jamaica,* 22. See also Robinson, *Florida: A Pamphlet Descriptive of Its History, Topography, Climate, Soil, Resources, and Natural Advantages,* 41.

154. "Edison at Fort Myers," *Boston Globe,* February 28, 1887, 5.

155. Alberta Eisman, "Thomas Edison's Florida," *New York Times,* June 24, 1990. See also Albion, *The Florida Life of Thomas Edison.*

156. "Thomas Edison's Father," *New York Times,* January 24, 1892.

157. Varnum, *Florida, Its Climate, Productions and Characteristics,* 3.

158. Gulf Coast Land Company, *The Gulf Coast of Florida,* 13.

159. General Henry S. Sanford, "The Rush for Florida," *Florida Dispatch* 1, no. 6 (May 1, 1882): 83.

160. "Proceedings of the Southern California Horticultural Society," *Southern California Horticulturist,* 1, no. 1 (September 1877): 16.

161. Presbrey, *Florida, Cuba, and Jamaica,* 12.

162. "Tropical House, Rock Ledge" advertisement in Lee, *The Tourist's Guide of Florida,* 212.

163. Munroe, *The Florida Annual,* 44.

164. Crosby, *Florida Facts Both Bright and Blue,* 80.

165. "California vs. Florida—The Tide of Winter Travel Sets Strongly towards the West," *Daily Alta California,* May 28, 1887, 1.

166. Nutting, *To the Pacific Coast via the Sunset Route of the Southern Pacific Company,* 15.

167. Ibid.

168. Hosmer McKoon, "Our Glorious Climate," *Land of Sunshine* 1, no. 1 (June 1894): 15.

169. "California and Florida," *Los Angeles Times,* 4.

170. "A Very Knowing Man," *Florida Farmer and Fruit Grower* 1, no. 8 (February 23, 1887): 60.

171. "California vs. Florida," *Florida Dispatch* 7, no. 22 (May 30, 1887): 464.

172. W., "California and Florida," *Florida Dispatch* 7, no. 23 (June 6, 1887): 486.

173. "The California Movement," *Lewiston Evening Journal,* October 26, 1887, 1.

174. Woodward, *Origins of the New South,* 110; Braden, *The Architecture of Leisure;* Bramson, "A Tale of Three Henrys," 112–43.

175. Mormino and Arsenault, "Introduction," xviii.

176. Youngs, "The Sporting Set Winters in Florida," 57–78.

177. A. C. Harvey, "Letter from Florida," *Indiana Farmer,* May 27, 1893, 1.

178. "Off for the Winter," *Chicago Tribune,* December 9, 1894, 14.

179. Florida East Coast Hotel Company, *East Coast of Florida,* 60.

180. H. A. Massey, "Trip to St. Augustine," *Atlanta Constitution,* March 25, 1876, 3.

181. For a study of the racial dynamics of the tourist activities that were popular in a northern resort town, see Simon, *Boardwalk of Dreams*.

182. See the front cover of the brochure for *The Magnolia, St. Augustine, Florida* (1900), Brochure 155, Florida Ephemera Collection; and *Florida* (Raymond-Whitcomb Tours to Florida and Cuba, 1920), 9, Brochure175, Florida Ephemera Collection.

183. *Hotel Ormond* (Ormond, 1891), Brochure 177, Florida Ephemera Collection.

184. James, *The American Scene*, 449–50.

185. Winter, *Florida: The Land of Enchantment*, 248.

186. Harrison Rhodes, "In Vacation America," reproduced in *St. Cloud Tribune*, January 11, 1917, 3.

187. King, *The Southern States of America*, 401; Hill, "Florida for the Winter," 220.

188. Ingram, *Florida: Beauties of the East Coast*, 52.

189. See the chapter on "La Fiesta de Los Angeles" in Deverell, *Whitewashed Adobe*, 49–90.

190. T. D. Stimson, "Sunshine and Eastern Capital," *Land of Sunshine* 1, no. 1 (June 1894): 15.

191. Hardy, *Down South*, 115–16.

192. Florida East Coast Railway and Florida East Coast Hotel Company, *Florida East Coast Railway and Hotels*.

193. Tyler, *Where to Go in Florida*, 3.

194. Harold W. Raymond, "In Pineapple Fields," *Washington Post*, February 18, 1894, 16.

195. "The Resistless Tourist," *San Francisco Call*, October 16, 1898, 6.

196. "California and Florida," *Los Angeles Times*, May 19, 1891, 4.

197. See K. H. Wade, "Marvelous Progress," *Land of Sunshine* 1, no. 1 (June 1894): 14.

198. Chipman, *California . . . Its Resources and Advantages*, 44.

199. "Why Tourists Come Here," *Los Angeles Herald*, October 28, 1906, 4.

200. "Lower California as a Winter Resort," *Florida Agriculturist* 1, no. 46 (November 14, 1874): 364; William Winter, "The California Movement versus Florida Apathy," *Florida Times Union*, June 5, 1887, 2.

201. Aron, *Working At Play*, 5.

202. "The Tide of Travel," *Florida East Coast Homeseeker* 7, no. 1 (January 1905): 6.

Chapter 3. The Fruits of Labor

1. Painter, *Standing at Armageddon*, xxx.

2. Richardson, *The Death of Reconstruction*, 230. For the agrarian myth of the West, see Smith, *Virgin Land*.

3. Appleby, *Capitalism and a New Social Order*, 50.

4. Florida Land Improvement Company, *Florida, Its Climate, Soil, and Productions*, 2.

5. Martin, *Supplement to All about California*, 7.

6. "Letters from the East," *Los Angeles Herald*, May 8, 1875, 4; "Southern California Immigration Association," *Los Angeles Times*, January 1886, California Scrapbook Collection, vol. 12: Los Angeles County—Immigration Association of California, 58, California State Library.

7. Madden, *California: Its Attractions for the Invalid, Tourist, Capitalist, and Homeseeker*, 18.

8. Orsi, *Sunset Limited*; Brown and Hudson, "Henry Flagler and the Model Land Company," 47–75.

9. French, *Semi-Tropical Florida*, 20. French extract also reproduced in Florida Land Improvement Company, *Florida, Its Climate, Soil and Productions*, 7.

10. Davidson, *The Florida of To-Day*, 105.

11. Vaught, *Cultivating California*, 10, Vaught's emphasis.

12. Fite, *The Farmers' Frontier*, 15–34.

13. Postel, *The Populist Vision*, 27.

14. Ibid., 25–59; McMath, *American Populism*.

15. Foner, *Free Soil, Free Labor, Free Men*, xxxvi; Hofstadter, *The Age of Reform*, 28.

16. Trachtenberg, *The Incorporation of America*; Saxton, *The Rise and Fall of the White Republic*, 303–4; Painter, *Standing at Armageddon*, 47–50.

17. Mrs. Judge A. B. Bartlett, "The Connection between Agriculture and Civilization," *Florida Agriculturist* 3, no. 7 (June 30, 1880): 49; J. De Barth Shorb, "Horticultural Fair—Closing Address of President Shorb," *Semi-Tropic California* 2, no. 11 (November 1880): 166–67. For a few of the many references to the two states as "new," see Van Dyke, *Southern California*, 221; and Jacques, *Florida as a Permanent Home*, 7.

18. J. M. Hawks, *The East Coast of Florida: A Descriptive Narrative* (Lynn: Lewis & Winship, 1887), 118, Brochure 157, Florida Ephemera Collection.

19. "Small Farms," *Florida Dispatch* 1, no. 21 (August 14, 1882): 322.

20. "Itinerant," "In the Semi-Tropics," *Los Angeles Times*, March 29, 1885, 4.

21. E. F. Spence, "Los Angeles," *Californian* 1, no. 1 (October 1891): 1.

22. Lindley and Widney, *California of the South*, 49. See also D. Edson Smith, "Ten Acres Enough to Support a Family," in ibid., 369.

23. Lindley and Widney, *California of the South*, 49.

24. Robinson, *Florida: A Pamphlet Descriptive of Its History, Topography, Climate, Soil, Resources, and Natural Advantages*, 165.

25. Varnum, *Florida, Its Climate, Productions and Characteristics*, 46.

26. "State Aid," *Southern California Horticulturist* 1, no. 3 (November 1877): 100.

27. Shannon, *The Farmer's Last Frontier*, 3–25.

28. For debates on the American political economy in the early Republic, see McCoy, *The Elusive Republic*, esp. 76–105.

29. Appleby, *Liberalism and Republicanism in the Historical Imagination*, 253–76.

30. "Semi-Tropical Fruit—Our Market and Possible Production," *Sacramento Daily Union*, May 22, 1875, 1; William H. Mills, "Marketing California Fruits," *Californian* 2, no. 5 (October 1892): 703–7; "Prospectus of the Florida Agriculturist," *Florida Agriculturist* 1, no. 1 (January 3, 1874): 5.

31. Growers in both states obsessed over the potential "overproduction" of semi-tropical fruits because they feared it would reduce their market niche and their agricultural exceptionalism. At the same time, they sought to increase demand for their citrus products in advertisements throughout the North and Midwest that presented them as dietary essentials rather than luxury items. See Sackman, *Orange Empire*.

32. Appleby, *Capitalism and a New Social Order*, ix–x.

33. These are the essential points Carl Schurz stated about tropical countries in "Manifest Destiny," *Harpers* 87, no. 521 (October 1893): 740–42.

34. N. P. Chipman quoted in "The Land of Plenty," *San Francisco Call*, January 28, 1894, 2. See also "Semi-Tropics," *Semi-Tropic California* 3, no. 5 (April 1880): 80.

35. Jacques, *Florida as a Permanent Home*, 5.

36. Smith and Dawson, *The American 1890s*, 388.

37. Turner, *The Significance of the Frontier in American History*, 1–2.

38. See Irsch, *Florida Immigration*, 9.

39. By "Southern Florida," Richmond meant the entire peninsula south of the tourist destinations of the St. Johns River. See Richmond, *Sumter County, Florida*, 10.

40. *Riverside Press and Horticulturist* (August 27, 1887), reprinted in "California," *Florida Dispatch,* September 5, 1887, 747.

41. Trachtenberg, *The Incorporation of America,* 3–7.

42. Irsch, *Florida Immigration,* 10.

43. Chipman, *Report upon the Fruit Industry of California,* 3.

44. Van Dyke, *Southern California,* 172.

45. Truman, *Homes and Happiness in the Golden State of California,* 37.

46. Shorb, "Horticultural Fair," 166–67.

47. "Itinerant," "In the Semi-Tropics," 4.

48. McWilliams, *Factories in the Field;* Stoll, *The Fruits of Natural Advantage;* Walker, *The Conquest of Bread.* See also Street, *Beasts of the Field.*

49. Starr, *Inventing the Dream;* Vaught, *Cultivating California.*

50. Hoag, *California: The Cornucopia of the World* (1883 edition), 45.

51. See Wright, *The Conquest of Bread.*

52. Rolle, *California,* 355; "California Wheat," *Chicago Tribune,* March 4, 1881, 5.

53. "Varied Agriculture," *Sacramento Daily Union,* March 4, 1869, 2.

54. "This crowding of people into immense cities, this aggregation of wealth into large lumps, this marshaling of men into big gangs under the control of the great 'captains of industry,' does not tend to foster personal independence—the basis of all virtues"; Henry George, "What the Railroad Will Bring Us," *Overland Monthly* 1, no. 4 (October 1868): 305. For more on Henry George in San Francisco, see Thomas, *Alternative America,* 173–202. See also Henry George, *Our Land and Land Policy, National and State* (San Francisco: White & Bauer, 1871).

55. George, *Progress and Poverty,* 10.

56. See, for example, "Kearney Coming," *New York Times,* July 11, 1878, 3.

57. B. B. Redding, "Immigration and How to Promote It," *Californian* 5, no. 25 (January 1882): 53.

58. "The Chinese Question," *Los Angeles Herald,* April 3, 1879, 3.

59. Love, *Race over Empire,* 11.

60. Mills, "Marketing California Fruits," 703–7; "Fifty Thousand Acres," *New York Times,* July 27, 1879, 10.

61. Ibid., 707; Sackman, *Orange Empire,* 37–53; Orsi, *Sunset Limited,* 52.

62. Nordhoff, *California for Health, Pleasure, and Residence,* 182–89.

63. Mills, "Marketing California Fruits," 707.

64. C. A. H., "Mistake of His Life," *Semi-Tropic California* 3, no. 5 (April 1880): 67.

65. Charles H. Shinn, "Peculiar Drawbacks of California Farming," *Southern California Horticulturist* 1, no. 6 (March 1878): 185.

66. Trachtenberg, *The Incorporation of America,* 17.

67. Spence, "Los Angeles," 1.

68. Martin, *Supplement to All about California,* 7.

69. *Santa Barbara Index* reproduced in ibid., 14.

70. Brook, *The Land of Sunshine,* 7–8.

71. Lindley and Widney, *California of the South,* 46, Widney's italics.

72. Almaguer, *Racial Fault Lines,* 65–74.

73. Pitt, *Decline of the Californios.*

74. Vischer, *Vischer's Pictorial of California.*

75. Thayer, *Marvels of the New West,* 213.

76. "Los Angeles County," *Pacific Rural Press,* March 29, 1886, 85, California Scrapbook Collec-

tion, volume 12, Los Angeles County—Immigration Association of California, 85, California State Library.

77. Pacific Coast Land Bureau, *Semi-Tropic California: San Diego County*.

78. T. W. Haskins, "Irrigation as a Civilizing Agent," *Land of Sunshine* 1, no. 2 (July 1894): 40.

79. San Pascual Plantation, *Prospectus of the San Pascual Plantation*, n.p.

80. "Letters from the East," 4.

81. Hawley, *The Present Condition, Growth, Progress, and Advantages, of Los Angeles City and County*, 3–54.

82. Ibid., 3.

83. Ibid., 54.

84. "The Colony System," *Los Angeles Herald*, July 18, 1883, 3; Pasadena Transfer and Storage Company, *A Thumb Nail History of Pasadena*.

85. *Crown of the Valley—The Story of Pasadena*, 16.

86. George Bancroft, "First Impressions of Pasadena," in R. W. C. Farnsworth, *A Southern California Paradise* (Pasadena: R.W.C. Farnsworth, 1883), 53.

87. Madden, *California: Its Attractions for the Invalid, Tourist, Capitalist, and Homeseeker*, 7.

88. *California—Self-Supporting Homes!* 9.

89. "Semi-Tropical California," *Semi-Tropic California* (January 1883), 7.

90. *California—Self-Supporting Homes!* 8; "Colonies in Southern California," *Semi-Tropic California* 3, no. 9 (September 1880): 129.

91. Shinn, "Peculiar Drawbacks," 185.

92. Letter by Jac. Humphries in Gulf Coast Land Company, *The Gulf Coast of Florida*, 48–51.

93. Pomona Land and Water Company, *Southern California—Pomona Illustrated and Described*, 40.

94. Van Dyke, *Southern California*, 195.

95. "Proceedings of the Southern California Horticultural Society," *Southern California Horticulturist* 1, no. 1 (September 1877): 3–16; "California Fruit-Growing," *Florida Dispatch* 1, no. 7 (May 8, 1882): 108. See also "Horticulture," *Semi-Tropic California* 4, no. 4 (April 1881): 69.

96. "National Convention of Semi-Tropical Fruit-Growers," *Southern California Horticulturist* 1, no. 1 (September 1877): 27.

97. The California State Board of Trade printed material on the "four citrus belts of the Northern hemisphere": Italy, semi-tropic Florida, southern California, and the Sacramento Valley. See Chipman, *Report upon the Fruit Industry of California*, 3.

98. "New Publication," *Florida Dispatch* 1, no. 3 (April 10, 1882): 5.

99. *Semi-Tropic California* (January 1883). For a review of the periodical's precursor, *Semi-Tropic California and Southern California Horticulturist*, see Los Angeles Herald, December 23, 1879, 2.

100. William Olden, "Good Times," *Semi-Tropic California* 3, no. 2 (February 1880): 11.

101. *Semi-Tropic California* 3, no. 1 (January 1880): 2.

102. *Semi-Tropic California* 3, no. 6 (June 1880): 82.

103. Shorb, "Horticultural Fair," 166–67.

104. *Southern California Advocate* reproduced in *Semi-Tropic California* 3, no. 1 (January 1880): 5.

105. "Homesteads," *Semi-Tropic California* 3, no. 7 (July 1880): 83, emphasis in original.

106. John E. Baur, "A President Visits Los Angeles: Rutherford B. Hayes' Tour of 1880," *Southern California Quarterly* 38 (March 1955): 33–46; *Semi-Tropic California* 3, no. 11 (November 1880): 163; Truman, *Homes and Happiness in the Golden State of California*, 11.

107. "President Hayes and Party," *Los Angeles Herald*, October 24, 1880, 3.

108. Orsi, "Selling the Golden State," 486; Olden, "Good Times," 11.

109. H. M. La Rue, "The Progress of California," *Pacific Rural Press*, September 20, 1879, 180.

110. "California, the Farmer's Paradise," *Sacramento Record Union*, reproduced in *New York Times*, April 3, 1887, 6.

111. Riverside Land and Irrigation Company, *Southern California*, 7–28.

112. Ibid., 27–30; "Letter from Riverside," *Los Angeles Herald*, August 22, 1875, 3.

113. Advertisement by the Riverside Land and Irrigation Company in *Southern California Horticulturist* 1, no. 1 (September 1877): 31.

114. Stoll, *The Fruits of Natural Advantage*, 128. For a discussion of harvesting, see Vaught, *Cultivating California*, 68–94.

115. Edward Brodribb, "Riverside," *Pacific Rural Press*, March 9, 1872, 146.

116. Riverside Land and Irrigation Company, *Southern California*, 15.

117. Van Dyke, *Southern California*, 213, 227.

118. Charles Shinn, "Southern California," *Californian* 3, no. 17 (May 1881): 447.

119. Ibid.

120. Ibid.

121. Hoag, *California: The Cornucopia of the World* (1883 edition), 7.

122. Ibid., 28. Florida promoters made similar comparisons with Midwestern states: see Dennis Eagan, "Sixth Annual Report of the Commissioner of Lands and Immigration," in Eagan, *The Florida Settler*, 5–6.

123. Hoag, *California: The Cornucopia of the World* (1883 edition), 19.

124. Orsi, *Sunset Limited*, 130–65.

125. Chipman, *Report upon the Fruit Industry of California*, 24.

126. Ibid.

127. *California Handbook with State and County Maps*, 113.

128. 'Pioneer,' "A Letter from Ventura," *Daily Alta California*, June 11, 1886, 6.

129. "Interesting Letter from Southern California," *Indiana Farmer*, April 3, 1880, 4 (letter from Calvin Fletcher).

130. "Interesting Letter from California," *Indiana Farmer*, March 18, 1882, 6 (letter from James M. Townsend).

131. *California Handbook with State and County Maps*, 127.

132. "State Board of Trade," *Daily Alta California*, March 18, 1888, 1.

133. "California Triumphant at the World's Fair at New Orleans," Associated Press article reproduced in Hoag, *California: The Cornucopia of the World* [1885 edition], 80.

134. Ibid.

135. Los Angeles Chamber of Commerce, *New Facts and Figures concerning Southern California*, 20.

136. Statement made by C. A. Warner, of Warner Bros., Los Angeles, Folder "Records on Advertising Southern California, 1888," Charles B. Turrill Papers as Manager, San Diego Chamber of Commerce, 1878–1890, California Historical Society.

137. Ibid.

138. Hoag, *California: The Cornucopia of the World* (1883 edition), 27.

139. Southern California was here defined as the six counties of San Diego, Los Angeles, San Bernardino, Riverside, Ventura, and Santa Barbara. See *Report of the Immigration Committee of the California State Board of Trade*, 4.

140. Brook, *The Land of Sunshine*, 6.

141. *Report of the Immigration Committee of the California State Board of Trade*, 4.

142. *Facts and Figures concerning Southern California and Los Angeles City and County*, 5.

143. Dr. A. A. Ward, Del Mar, San Diego County, to Mr. Holabird, Southern California Horticultural Society, 1888, Folder "San Diego Chamber of Commerce, Correspondence, 1888–1900," Charles B. Turrill Papers as Manager, San Diego Chamber of Commerce, 1878–1890, California Historical Society.

144. [Fletcher], "Interesting Letter from Southern California," 4.

145. MacDonald, *Plain Talk about Florida*, 3.

146. Harcourt, *Home Life in Florida*, 56.

147. "Immigration to Florida," *Florida Agriculturist* 1, no. 42 (October 17, 1874): 332.

148. MacDonald, *Plain Talk about Florida*, 4.

149. Carter et al., *Historical Statistics of the United States*, 4: 62–63.

150. Commissioner of Lands and Immigration, State of Florida, *Florida: Its Climate, Soil and Productions*, 4–66.

151. Tebeau, *A History of Florida*, 277–81.

152. Mayo, *Florida, an Advancing State*, 98–99.

153. Commissioner of Lands and Immigration, State of Florida, *Florida: Its Climate, Soil and Productions*, 15. In 1868, T. B. Forbush of the New England Emigrant Aid Company wrote, "We are frequently asked, 'Is it safe for northern people to settle in Florida, away from Jacksonville?'" Forbush, *Florida*, 19.

154. See Foner, *Reconstruction*, 425–59.

155. Eagan, *The Florida Settler*, 6.

156. Ortiz, *Emancipation Betrayed*, 9–32.

157. Commissioner of Lands and Immigration, State of Florida, *Florida: Its Climate, Soil and Productions*, 13.

158. Munroe, *The Florida Annual*, 21.

159. Ibid., 23.

160. Commissioner of Lands and Immigration, State of Florida, *Florida: Its Climate, Soil and Productions*, 42.

161. Ibid., 51.

162. Fry, *Henry S. Sanford*, 87–111.

163. Barbour, *Florida for Tourists, Invalids and Settlers*, 47.

164. S. D. Wilcox, "Prospectus of the Florida Agriculturist," *Florida Agriculturist* 1, no. 1 (January 3, 1874): 5; "The Future of Florida," *Florida Agriculturist* 1, no. 1 (January 3, 1874): 4.

165. "The Future of Florida," 4, italics in original.

166. Advertisement for the *Semi-Tropical* in Jacques, *Florida as a Permanent Home*.

167. J. F. Bartholf, "Dignity of Labor," *Semi-Tropical* 1, no. 2 (October 1875): 94–95.

168. Ibid.

169. "Florida and the Centennial," *Semi-Tropical* 1, no. 1 (September 1875): 63–64.

170. "Florida Items," *Southern California Horticulturist* 1, no. 11 (September 1878): 363; "New Publications—California Fruit Grower's Convention," *Florida Dispatch* 1, no. 2 (April 3, 1882)" 4; "Gathering Lemons," *Florida Dispatch* 1, no. 2 (April 3, 1882): 5 (article reprinted from the *Riverside* [California] *Press*); "California," *Florida Dispatch* 7, no. 22 (May 30, 1887): 464.

171. "Southern Immigration," *New Orleans Times-Democrat*, September 1, 1885, 28, Folder "Papers Relating to the World's Cotton Exposition, New Orleans, 1884–8," Charles Turrill Papers as Manager, Preliminary World's Fair Exhibit, 1892, Bancroft Library, University of California, Berkeley.

172. "Floridiana—Immigration Meeting," *Florida Dispatch* 7, no. 32 (August 8, 1887): 666.

173. "What California Is Doing," *Florida Farmer and Fruit Grower* 1, no. 8 (February 23, 1887): 60.

174. "Report of the Commissioner of Agriculture," *Journal of the Florida House of Representatives of the State of Florida, Third Session, April 7, 1891*, 3. For a comparison of the display trains of the two states that praised California's train over Florida's, see "California vs. Florida—The Exhibits on Wheels of the Two States Compared," *Semi-Tropic Florida*, reprinted in *Sacramento Daily Union*, May 11, 1889, 2.

175. Harrison Reed, "California vs. Florida," *Semi-Tropical* 3, no. 9 (September 1877): 513.

176. Ibid.

177. Ibid., 513–17.

178. Letter by J. F. Richmond printed as "Inducements to Settlers: Good Land to Be Had Cheap," *Florida Dispatch* 7, no. 34 (August 22, 1887): 706.

179. S. Powers, "Florida and California," *Florida Dispatch* 1, no. 14 (April 6, 1887): 108. Land prices varied tremendously in both states, depending on location, access to water, fitness for semi-tropical fruits, and other factors, but a comparison of the range of prices quoted in the following sources from between 1879 and 1892 indicates that Florida acres were generally cheaper than those in California: French, *Semi-Tropical Florida*, 17–19; Harcourt, *Home Life in Florida*, 133; "A Generous Proposition," *Los Angeles Herald*, July 27, 1883, 3; *California Handbook with State and County Maps*, 102.

180. As a consequence of their different harvesting times, Florida and California citrus tended not to compete directly in markets. "California vs. Florida Oranges," *Florida Dispatch* 7, no. 22 (May 30, 1887): 465.

181. A whole book could be written on the competition between citrus growers in California and Florida in these years. For a few examples of the promotional one-upmanship, see Powers, "Florida and California," 465; and Van Dyke, *Southern California*, 192.

182. George D. Watson, "Florida and Southern California Compared," in Ashby, *Alachua, the Garden County of Florida*, 7–10. Watson also contributed his views to the *Ocean Grove Record* of New Jersey in a letter reprinted in the *Los Angeles Times*: "California vs. Florida—What a Visitor Says of Los Angeles," *Los Angeles Times*, April 21, 1885, 2.

183. Watson, "Florida and Southern California Compared," 7–10.

184. Lente, *The Constituents of Climate*, 1.

185. William Olden, "Semi-Tropical California," *Semi-Tropic California* 3, no. 7 (July 1880).

186. "Florida Items," 363.

187. French, *Semi-Tropical Florida*, 36.

188. W. W. Dewhurst, "Letter from Florida," *Indiana Farmer*, October 7, 1876, 6.

189. Ibid.

190. "Settling in Florida," *Baltimore Sun*, reproduced in *New York Times*, August 11, 1878, 10.

191. MacDonald, *Plain Talk about Florida*, 2. See also "Settlers Beware," *Florida Dispatch* 1, no. 5 (May 8, 1876): 1.

192. MacDonald, *Plain Talk about Florida*, 22, 2.

193. Ibid., 22; French, *Semi-Tropical Florida*, 6.

194. *Cincinnati Enquirer* quoted in Reed, "California vs. Florida," 517.

195. For the ongoing debate among historians over the issue of black suffrage during Reconstruction, see Adam Fairclough, "Was the Grant of Black Suffrage a Political Error? Reconsidering the Views of John W. Burgess, William A. Dunning, and Eric Foner of Congressional Reconstruction," *Journal of the Historical Society* 12, no. 2 (2012): 155–88; and Michael W. Fitzgerald, "Reconstruction

Reengineered: Or, Is Doubting Black Suffrage a Mistake?" *Journal of the Historical Society*, 12, no. 3 (2012): 241–47.

196. Barbour, *Florida for Tourists, Invalids and Settlers*, 225; Tyler, *Where to Go in Florida*, 7. See, also, "Northern People in Florida," *New York Times*, February 26, 1883, 1.

197. Commissioner of Lands and Immigration, State of Florida, *Florida: Its Climate, Soil and Productions*, 8; French, *Semi-Tropical Florida*, 53.

198. Davidson, *The Florida of To-Day*, 109–10.

199. Crosby, *Florida Facts Both Bright and Blue*, 123.

200. Robinson, *Florida: A Pamphlet Descriptive of Its History, Topography, Climate, Soil, Resources, and Natural Advantages*, 168; Richmond, *Sumter County, Florida*, 50.

201. Litwack, *Been in the Storm So Long*, 308–9.

202. Ibid.

203. Eagan, *The Florida Settler*, 16.

204. Ibid.

205. Ibid., 17.

206. Rivers and Brown, "African Americans in South Florida."

207. "A Talk with Gov. Drew," *New York Daily Tribune*, May 25, 1877, quoted in Ortiz, *Emancipation Betrayed*, 27.

208. McClure, *The South: Its Industrial, Financial, and Political Condition*, 14.

209. French, *Semi-Tropical Florida*, 20.

210. Grant described Florida—particularly its suitability for tropical fruits and sugar cane—in language reminiscent of his fascination with the Dominican Republic, which he had tried and failed to annex when he was president. See Grant, "Memorandum," in Simon, *The Papers of Ulysses S. Grant*, 20:74–76.

211. Barbour, *Florida for Tourists, Invalids and Settlers*, 162.

212. Grant, extract from the *Philadelphia Ledger*, reproduced in Gulf Coast Land Company, *The Gulf Coast of Florida*, 16–17.

213. Ibid.

214. See Foss, *Florida Facts*, 6; South Publishing Company, *Florida Portrayed*, 8.

215. Florida Land Agency, *Florida: Its Soil, Climate, Health, Production, Resources, and Advantages*, 3.

216. See Gulf Coast Land Company, *The Gulf Coast of Florida*, 16–17.

217. Ibid., 20, italics in original. The Disston drainage scheme and its effects on Florida boosterism are discussed in greater detail in the next chapter.

218. In 1886, when 289 miles were added in the state, *Railway Age* reported that "Florida built more railway track last year than any other state," quoted in Mayo, *Florida, an Advancing State*, 98. See also Varnum, *Florida, Its Climate, Productions, and Characteristics*, 46.

219. Barbour, *Florida for Tourists, Invalids and Settlers*, 3.

220. Ibid., 294.

221. Ibid., 22.

222. Ibid., 294.

223. William H. Martin, "Report," quoted in Florida and Land Improvement Company, *Florida, Its Climate, Soil and Productions*, 31.

224. Ibid., 32, Martin's italics.

225. Ibid., 33.

226. Moore, *Treatise and Handbook of Orange Culture in Florida, Louisiana, and California*, 145, Moore's italics.

227. Jacques, *Florida as a Permanent Home*, 3.

228. Harcourt, *Home Life in Florida*, 16.

229. Crosby, *Florida Facts Both Bright and Blue*, 21.

230. Ibid., 125.

231. The African American writer Zora Neale Hurston grew up in Eatonville. See Hurston, "The Eatonville Chronicles," in O'Sullivan and Lane, *The Florida Reader*, 109–122.

232. Crosby, *Florida Facts Both Bright and Blue*, 111.

233. Davidson, *The Florida of To-Day*, 113–14.

234. Barbour, *Florida for Tourists, Invalids and Settlers*, 238.

235. Harcourt, *Home Life in Florida*, 17, 345.

236. Ibid., 15, 358.

237. Dodd, *Historical Statistics of the States of the United States*, 121, 141.

238. "Tropic and Semi-Tropic Fruits," *Chicago Tribune*, April 3, 1892, 37.

239. Munroe, *The Florida Annual*, 34.

240. Crosby, *Florida Facts Both Bright and Blue*, 23.

241. Hoag, *California: The Cornucopia of the World* (1883 edition), 23–24.

242. Harcourt, *Home Life in Florida*, 17.

243. See I. N. Hoag, "The Basis of the California Fruit Producer's Appeal for Protection," *Pacific Rural Press*, January 30, 1897, 70.

244. Vaught, *Cultivating California*, 46. For Populism in California, see Postel, *The Populist Vision*, 106–15.

245. Charles Shinn, "Social Changes in California," *Popular Science Monthly* (April 1891), Folder "Invoices," Charles H. Shinn Papers, Bancroft Library, University of California, Berkeley.

246. Ibid.

247. MacDonald, *Plain Talk about Florida*, 33.

248. Tebeau, *A History of Florida*, 257.

249. Abbey, "Florida versus the Principles of Populism," 462–75.

250. McMath has noted that "central Florida, though geographically southern, was not part of the cotton south. Its emerging fruit and vegetable farms, made possible by modern transportation and marketing systems, made the Ocala region more like the California valleys than the older staple-crop regions of cotton, tobacco, corn, and wheat, from which the Alliance had arisen"; McMath, *American Populism*, 139.

251. Francis P. Fleming, "Governor's Message," *Journal of the Florida House of Representatives of the State of Florida, Third Session, April 7, 1891*, 35; Proctor, "The National Farmers' Alliance Convention of 1890 and Its 'Ocala Demands,'" 162–63.

252. Myers, *Alachua County*, 2.

253. "That Semi-Tropic Contest," *Daily Alta California*, July 27, 1890, 4.

254. "California and Florida Oranges," *Chicago Tribune*, December 20, 1892, 16; "The Orange in California," *New York Times*, October 19, 1896, 33; "Oranges and Lemons," *Atlanta Constitution*, October 19, 1896, 8.

255. "American Fruit for Americans," *Pacific Rural Press*, July 3, 1897, 6.

Chapter 4. Desert and Swamp

1. Presbrey, *Florida, Cuba, and Jamaica*, 3–4.

2. Fred Pfeiffer, "Drainage vs. Irrigation," *Florida East Coast Homeseeker* 7, no. 2 (February 1905): 8.

3. Nye, *America as Second Creation*, 6.

4 William L. Bragg, "America's Winter Garden," *Florida East Coast Homeseeker* 12, no. 4 (April 1910): 130; "The Oakland Enquirer Says," *Imperial Valley Press*, September 28, 1901, 3.

5. "Distinguished Visitors," *San Francisco Call*, August 13, 1902, 8.

6. Brook, *The Land of Sunshine*, 6; Carter et al., *Historical Statistics of the United States*, 4: 59–60.

7. T. W. Haskins, "Irrigation as a Civilizing Agent," *Land of Sunshine* 1, no. 2 (July 1894): 40; "Florida! Her Statistics and Prosperity," *New Orleans Times-Democrat*, reproduced in *Florida Dispatch* 1, no. 4 (April 17, 1882): 50–51. The latter is an interview with Governor William Bloxham.

8. Los Angeles Chamber of Commerce, *New Facts and Figures concerning Southern California*, 19; Florida Department of Agriculture, *Fifth Census of the State of Florida*, 16–17. At the turn of the twentieth century, the average weight of one box of citrus fruit was seventy-two pounds; see *Imports of Farm and Forest Products, by Countries from Which Consigned*, U.S. Department of Agriculture Bulletin 35 (Washington, DC: U.S. Department of Agriculture, Bureau of Statistics, 1905), 24.

9. "Saving the Swamps," *Los Angeles Herald*, December 15, 1907, 38.

10. Fox, *The American Conservation Movement*.

11. Roosevelt, "Opening Address of the President," 6.

12. Pisani, "Reclamation and Social Engineering in the Progressive Era," 46–63.

13. Hays, *The Response to Industrialism*, 92–119.

14. "Back to the Land," *Florida East Coast Homeseeker* 12, no. 6 (June 1910): 220; Wells, *California for the Settler*, 43.

15. John L. Matthews, "The Rush to the Swamp Lands," reproduced in *Florida East Coast Homeseeker* 12, no. 4 (April 1910): 125.

16. LaFeber, *The New Empire*; Healy, *U.S. Expansionism*, 236.

17. Love, *Race over Empire*.

18. Carl Schurz, "Manifest Destiny," *Harpers* 87, no. 521 (October 1893): 740.

19. William MacLeod Raine, "Where Water Works Wonders," *Sunset* 11, no. 5 (September 1903): 404. See also Nye, *America as Second Creation*, 237.

20. Wells, *Government Irrigation and the Settler*, 7.

21. Gifford, "Southern Florida," 18. Gifford originally wrote this piece for *Forestry and Irrigation* in 1904.

22. Charles Whalen, "Back to the Soil," *San Francisco Call*, June 1, 1912, 4.

23. Newman, "Irrigation—Past and Present," 82.

24. Street, *Beasts of the Field*, xvi–xviii; Hahamovitch, *The Fruits of Their Labor*, 3–7.

25. Stoll, *The Fruits of Natural Advantage*, 125.

26. Street, *Beasts of the Field*, xviii. See also Mitchell, *The Lie of the Land*, 9–28.

27. "From Desert to Garden," *California Homeseeker* 1, no. 3 (April 1902): 256–71.

28. Richard Melrose, "Los Angeles County," *Anaheim Gazette*, February 6, 1879, in Volume 12, Los Angeles County—Immigration Association of California, 10, California Scrapbook Collection, California State Library.

29. Elizabeth Bacon Custer, "Memories of 'Our Italy,'" *Land of Sunshine* 3, no. 2 (July 1895): 51.

30. Pomeroy, *In Search of the Golden West*, 158–62; Charles F. Lummis, "The Southwestern Wonderland," *Land of Sunshine* 4, no. 5 (April 1896): 204–5; James, *The Wonders of the Colorado Desert*; Austin, *The Land of Little Rain*.

31. "Wonders of the Far West," *New York Times*, March 2, 1907, 121.

32. Lummis, "The Southwestern Wonderland," 204.

33. Keeler, *Southern California*, 11.

34. Robert Gregg, "The Climatic Advantages of San Diego," *San Diego Union*, October 20, 1883, in Volume 21, San Diego County California Pamphlets—Immigration Association of California, 22, California Scrapbook Collection, California State Library.

35. Vail, *"Both Sides Told," or Southern California as It Is*, 16–17.

36. Lummis, "The Southwestern Wonderland," 204.

37. Weigle, "From Desert to Disney World"; "El Camino Real," *Sunset* 1, no. 6 (October 1898): 88.

38. Lummis, "The Artist's Paradise," *Land of Sunshine* 6, no. 6 (May 1897): 233–39.

39. Alice Rhoades Pickrel, "The Desert Maiden," *Land of Sunshine* 13, no. 4 (September/October 1900): 229.

40. Nutting, *To the Pacific Coast via the Sunset Route of the Southern Pacific Company*, 10.

41. Charles Shinn, "Southern California," *Californian* 3, no. 17 (May 1881): 446.

42. Wells, *California for the Settler*, 43.

43. "Irrigation in Semi-Tropical Countries," *Daily Alta California*, May 8, 1872, 2.

44. Pisani, *From Family Farm to Agribusiness*, 284.

45. Hoag, *California: The Cornucopia of the World* (1883 edition), 25.

46. Sackman, *Orange Empire*.

47. Pisani, *From Family Farm to Agribusiness*, 283.

48. *California Handbook with State and County Maps*, 113; *Report of the Immigration Committee of the California State Board of Trade*, 6.

49. Brook, *Irrigation in Southern California*, 16–19.

50. Ibid., 19.

51. Pacific Coast Land Bureau, *Semi-Tropic California: San Diego County*, 5.

52. See Lee, "William Ellsworthe Smythe and the Irrigation Movement," 289–311.

53. William E. Smythe, "The Conquest of Arid America," *Century* 50, no. 1 (May 1895): 94–95.

54. Ibid.

55. Ibid., 95.

56. Ibid.

57. Robert Gregg, "The Climatic Advantages of San Diego," *San Diego Union*, October 20, 1883.

58. R. R. Newman, "Irrigation—Past and Present," *Sunset* 1, no. 5 (September 1898): 82.

59. "Redlands," *Sunset* 4, no. 2 (December 1899): 73.

60. "Two States Compared," *San Francisco Call*, February 23, 1896, 20.

61. "Los Angeles Temperature," *Los Angeles Herald*, September 3, 1905, 1.

62. Lionel A. Sheldon, "Southern California: Conditions Conducive to Progress of Civilization," *Californian* 5, no. 2 (January 1894): 208.

63. Alla Aldrich Clarke, "In Orange Land—Riverside," *Sunset* 8, no. 3 (January 1902): 113.

64. Ibid., 113–15.

65. Brook, *Irrigation in Southern California*, 16.

66. Stern, *Eugenic Nation*, 19; see also Sackman, *Orange Empire*, 61–63.

67. Keeler, *Southern California*, 72.

68. Stern, *Eugenic Nation*, 20.

69. David Starr Jordan, "Helping the Indians," *Sunset* 22, no. 1 (January 1909): 57; C. W. Barton, "Riverside's New Indian School," *Sunset* 7, no. 6 (October 1901).

70. Quotation in Sackman, *Orange Empire*, 20.

71. Clarke, "In Orange Land," 117–18.

72. Barton, "Riverside's New Indian School."

73. *Rural Californian* (January 1883). The quotation was reproduced in Pomona Land and Water Company, *Southern California—Pomona Illustrated and Described*, 37.

74. Owen Capelle, "A Famous Festival," *Land of Sunshine* 2, no. 4 (March 1895): 73.

75. Brook, *The Land of Sunshine*, 15.

76. Ibid.

77. "A Thrifty and Progressive Settlement," *Rural Californian* (November 1886).

78. "Southern California Immigration Association," *Los Angeles Times*, January 1886.

79. Brook, *The Land of Sunshine*, 15–18.

80. "Vigorous Growth of California," *Imperial Valley Press*, January 4, 1902, 2.

81. J. P. Baumgartner, "Riverside," *Sunset* 4, no. 2 (December 1899): 75.

82. In the 1880s, some boosters recognized the semi-tropical potential of these interior deserts. Walter Lindley and J. P. Widney wrote that the valley system at the bottom of the Colorado River "may be irrigated and made productive" and that "for sugar-cane and other semi-tropic agricultural products, [it] has probably no equal in North America": Lindley and Widney, *California of the South*, 27.

83. Brook, *The Land of Sunshine*, 6.

84. William E. Smythe, "Our Great Pacific Commonwealth," *Century* 53, no. 2 (December 1896): 300–307.

85. "Irrigation in California," *Sunset* 13, no. 4 (August 1904): 382.

86. Orsi, *Sunset Limited*, 226–27.

87. McWilliams, *California: The Great Exception*, 301–3.

88. Ibid., 301.

89. William E. Smythe, "An International Wedding," *Sunset* 5, no. 6 (October 1900): 299.

90. Ibid., 286–300.

91. "What the Tourist Will See," *Imperial Valley Press*, February 22, 1902, 8.

92. Ibid.

93. Advertisement for the town of Silsbee, *Imperial Valley Press*, May 10, 1902, 4.

94. "A Magnificent Avenue," *Imperial Valley Press*, February 22, 1902, 8.

95. Wells, *Government Irrigation and the Settler*, 9; Smythe, "An International Wedding," 299.

96. "From Desert to Garden," 256.

97. "Southern California's Program for Development," *Imperial Valley Press*, May 10, 1902, 1.

98. McWilliams, *California: The Great Exception*, 302.

99. "Salton Sea Blame," *Washington Post*, January 13, 1907, 1.

100. Orsi, *Sunset Limited*, 226–37.

101. Shepard, *Semi-Tropic California*, 11.

102. Ibid., 11–22.

103. "Highest Tide of Colonists," *Imperial Valley Press*, November 9, 1907, 2.

104. H. J. Whitley of the California-Mexico Company even traveled to Egypt to gather "information concerning methods of irrigation and agriculture," which he planned to apply to Imperial Valley. "Letters from Egypt," *Imperial Valley Press*, April 4, 1908, 10.

105. "Irrigation Possibilities of the Colorado River," *Imperial Valley Press*, January 24, 1903, 8.

106. Harry Webster, "Making a Garden out of a Desert," *Los Angeles Herald Sunday Magazine*, February 20, 1910, 16.

107. Wells, *California for the Settler*, 43.

108. "Imperial Valley Boosters," *Imperial Valley Press*, July 24, 1909, 8.

109. E. F. Howe, "Creating a Humid Strip through the Southwest," *Imperial Valley Press*, May 10, 1902, 5.

110. William Ellsworth Smythe quoted in International Irrigation Congress, *Official Report of the International Congress Held at Los Angeles*, 107.

111. Tout, *Imperial Valley*, 5.

112. Charles S. Aiken, "The Surprise of the Desert," *Sunset* 21, no. 5 (September 1908): 3.

113. Webster, "Making a Garden out of a Desert," 16.

114. Tout, *Imperial Valley*, 5–11.

115. "Southern Pacific Sells Big Tract," *New York Times*, January 18, 1914, 25.

116. See Stoll, *The Fruits of Natural Advantage*, 124–154.

117. Gonzales, *Labor and Community*, 25.

118. Wells, *Government Irrigation and the Settler*, 12.

119. Smythe, "An International Wedding," 299; A. J. Wells, "Helping the Indian," *Sunset* 19, no. 1 (May 1907): 89–90.

120. Sam G. Austin, "True Appreciation of 'American Nile Valley,'" *Los Angeles Times*, April 24, 1910, 7.

121. "California's Opportunity in Cotton Growing," *Pacific Rural Press*, January 12, 1918, 34, 50.

122. Wilbur Jay Hall, "Just Like Dixie Land," *Sunset* 24, no. 2 (February 1910): 173–75.

123. Ibid., 175.

124. "Cotton Pickers Coming," *Imperial Valley Press*, September 3, 1910, 2.

125. "Woman Cotton Grower," *Boston Globe*, April 13, 1913, 10.

126. McWilliams, *California: The Great Exception*, 302.

127. "Cotton on Pacific Coast," *New York Times*, June 26, 1914, 17.

128. "Can Furnish Laborers," *Imperial Valley Press*, August 6, 1910, 5.

129. "Cotton on Pacific Coast," 17.

130. "Imperial Valley, Land of Promise," *Imperial Valley Press*, March 12, 1910, 9.

131. Ibid., 10.

132. Imperial Valley—The Egypt of America, advertisement in *Sunset* (September 1908): 12.

133. Advertisement for Imperial Valley, *Imperial Valley Press*, March 12, 1910, 11.

134. Wells, *California for the Settler*, 47.

135. Austin, "True Appreciation of 'American Nile Valley,'" 7.

136. "Imperial County, Land of Promise Fulfilled," *Los Angeles Times*, January 1, 1916, 17; Bourdon Wilson, "Imperial Valley the Ideal," *Sunset* 25, no. 6 (December 1910): 710–11; Walter V. Woehlke, "The Land of Before-and-After: The Miracle-Story of Imperial Valley, California," *Sunset* 28, no. 4 (April 1912): 391–98; "Imperial Valley, Land of Promise," *Imperial Valley Press*, March 12, 1910, 9.

137. "Boosters for the Valley," *Imperial Valley Press*, April 16, 1910, 8.

138. Florida Land Agency, *Florida: Its Soil, Climate, Health, Production, Resources, and Advantages*, 2.

139. Dennis Eagan, "Report of the Commissioner of Lands and Immigration," in *Journal of the Proceedings of the Assembly of the State of Florida, Seventh Session, January 6, 1874*, 139.

140. "Hark from the Swamps a Doleful Sound," *Los Angeles Times*, January 24, 1894, 4.

141. George D. Watson, "Florida and Southern California Compared," reproduced in Ashby, *Alachua, the Garden County of Florida*, 8–10.

142. Ibid., 8.

143. S. Powers, "Florida and California," *Florida Farmer and Fruit Grower* 1, no. 14 (April 6, 1887): 108.

144. Rose, *The Swamp and Overflow Lands of Florida*, 1.

145. Florida Department of Agriculture, *Fifth Census of the State of Florida*, 16.

146. Fruit Grower, *Fruit and Vegetable Growing in Manatee County*, 5; MacCauley, *The Seminole Indians of Florida*, 530.

147. Davis, "The Disston Land Purchase," 201–11.

148. Tebeau, *A History of Florida*, 278.

149. Grunward, *The Swamp*, 90–94.

150. Davidson, *The Florida of To-Day*, 68.

151. Foss, *Florida Facts*, 3.

152. Orange, Polk, Hernando, Hillsborough, and Sumter were the five counties referred to specifically by Disston's Florida Land and Improvement Company in Florida Land and Improvement Company, *Florida, Its Climate, Soil and Productions*, 2. See also Florida Department of Agriculture, *Fifth Census of the State of Florida*, 16–17.

153. Mayo, *Florida, an Advancing State*, 99.

154. "Colony Excursions," *Farm, Field and Fireside*, March 14, 1896, 2.

155. McLin, *Florida: A Pamphlet Descriptive of Its History, Topography, Climate, Soil, Resources, and Natural Advantages, in General and by Counties*, 14.

156. William D. Bloxham, "Governor's Message," in *Journal of the Proceedings of the Assembly of the State of Florida, Twelfth Session, January 2, 1883*, 12–39; McClure, *The South: Its Industrial, Financial, and Political Condition*, 18.

157. Munroe, *The Florida Annual*, 38.

158. "Everglades Drainage," *Christian Science Daily Monitor*, reproduced in *Everglade Magazine* 2, no. 2 (June 1911): 6.

159. South Publishing Company, *Florida Portrayed*, 34; Grunwald, *The Swamp*, 9–80.

160. Marchman, "The Ingraham Everglades Exploring Expedition," 3–43.

161. James E. Ingraham, "One Man's Work," unpublished manuscript, 1909, 3, Box 1: "Correspondence 1854–1919—Misc.—Railroads," James Edmundson Ingraham Papers, George A. Smathers Libraries, University of Florida. For a biographical sketch of Ingraham, see Poleo, "James Edmundson Ingraham," 93–118.

162. "The Story of the Everglades," *Florida East Coast Homeseeker* 12, no. 4 (April 1910): 122.

163. "Progress of Florida," *Florida Agriculturist* 30, no. 44 (1903): 687.

164. *The Nation's Garden Spot* (Wilmington: Atlantic Coast Line Railroad, 1913), 17, Brochure 113, Florida Ephemera Collection.

165. Dupuy, "Cooperatives in Citrus Marketing," 275–301.

166. "Florida and California," *Los Angeles Times*, January 7, 1898, 6.

167. Ibid.

168. "Southern California and Florida," *Los Angeles Times*, January 30, 1897, 6.

169. See Proctor, *Napoleon Bonaparte Broward*.

170. W. M. Walker, "Napoleon B. Broward—Father of Everglades Drainage," *Suniland* 1, no. 6 (March 1925), 26. On anti–Southern Pacific feeling in the West, see Orsi, *Sunset Limited*.

171. Broward, *Open Letter of Governor N. B. Broward*, 1.

172. Broward, "The Call of the Everglades," *Florida East Coast Homeseeker* 12, no. 4 (April 1910): 126.

173. Tebeau, *A History of Florida*, 330.

174. Broward, *Open Letter of Governor N. B. Broward*, 1.

175. Grunwald, *The Swamp*, 130-135.

176. Broward, *Open Letter of Governor N. B. Broward*, 1.

177. Gifford, "The Everglades of Florida and the Landes of France," 10.

178. "The Year 1905—the Prosperous East Coast," *Florida East Coast Homeseeker* 8, no. 1 (January 1906): 3.

179. Brown and Hudson, "Henry Flagler and the Model Land Company."

180. "Mr. Walter Waldin's Display," *Florida East Coast Homeseeker* 9, no. 4 (April 1907): 119–20.

181. Ibid., 119.

182. Walter Waldin in *Miami Metropolis* (August 13, 1907), reproduced in "No Other Country Like Florida," *Florida East Coast Homeseeker* 9, no. 9 (September 1907): 291.

183. Waldin, *Truck Farming in the Everglades*, 5. In part a response to industrialism and urbanization, the back-to-the-land movement of the early twentieth century sought a return to farming, although it often described it as a new and scientific form of agriculture that decreased the isolation of traditional country life. For obvious reasons, the back-to-the-land movement was intimately connected to state efforts to irrigate deserts and drain swamps, thereby creating new frontiers for agricultural settlement. See, for example, "Back to the Land Bureau: The Florida Everglades," *Chicago Tribune*, October 13, 1912, 6.

184. "Saving the Swamps," *Los Angeles Herald*, December 15, 1907, 38.

185. Broward, "The Call of the Everglades," 126.

186. Pfeiffer, "Drainage vs. Irrigation," 8; "Climatic Comparisons from Government Bulletin," *Everglade Magazine* 2, no. 2 (June 1911): 11. See also "Everglades Drainage," *Christian Science Daily Monitor*, reproduced in *Everglade Magazine* 2, no. 2 (June 1911): 6.

187. "Reclaiming the Everglades," *Atlanta Constitution*, April 29, 1912, 4.

188. Former governor William Jennings quoted in "The Story of the Everglades," *Florida East Coast Homeseeker* 12, no. 4 (April 1910): 122–23. His 1902 trip to California was remarked on by California newspapers, which reported that "the Governor of Florida is here, representing California's only companion in the Union in the production of tropical and semi-tropical fruits": "Distinguished Visitors," *San Francisco Call*, August 13, 1902, 8.

189. R. E. Rose in *Miami Metropolis*, reproduced in "Value of Florida Muck Lands After Thoroughly Drained," *Florida East Coast Homeseeker* 12, no. 2 (February 1910): 54.

190. A New Everglade Book, advertisement, *Everglade Magazine* 1, no. 10 (February 1911): 13.

191. Gifford, "The Everglades of Florida," 102.

192. Rose, *The Swamp and Overflow Lands of Florida*, 18.

193. Rhodes and Dumont, *Guide to Florida for Tourists, Sportsmen and Settlers*, 217.

194. "Ralph D. Paine Says," *Florida East Coast Homeseeker* 12, no. 4 (April 1910), 129.

195. Bertha Comstock, "Reclaimed Muck Lands," *Tropic* 1, no. 4 (July 1914): 21.

196. *Everglade Magazine* 1, no. 10 (February 1911): 2. The quote is from the masthead of the magazine.

197. "Professor Wiley on Sugar," *Florida East Coast Homeseeker* 12, no. 4 (April 1910): 135; Gifford, "The Everglades of Florida and the Landes of France," 7.

198. DeCroix, *Historical, Industrial, and Commercial Data of Miami and Fort Lauderdale*, 167, 175.

199. Everglades Land Sales Company, advertisement, *Everglade Magazine* 2, no. 2 (June 1911): 13.

200. Gifford, "Trees as an Aid to Drainage," 23. Gifford originally wrote this piece for *La Hacienda* in 1911.

201. "Boosting the Renewed South," *Florida East Coast Homeseeker* 14, no. 1 (January 1912): 20.

202. Gifford, "Southern Florida," 13.

203. Gifford, "Fruit Quality in Tropical Florida," *Miami News*, September 28, 1909, 30.

204. See, for example, "This Hot Weather Menu," *Washington Post*, July 29, 1906, 8.

205. Gifford, "Fruit Quality in Tropical Florida," 30.

206. See Willoughby, *Across the Everglades*.

207. Jordan, *The East Coast of Florida*, 48.

208. Edmonds, "The Glowing Destiny of Florida," 27.

209. Tebeau, *A History of Florida*, 287.

210. *Florida Tourist and Southern Investor's Guide*, 11.

211. Florida East Coast Hotel Company, *East Coast of Florida*, 68.

212. For a typical example of the earlier, fearful depictions of the Seminoles as a "mongrel race . . . all blood-hungry and revengeful," see Davidson, *The Florida of To-Day*, 20.

213. Ibid., 19–20.

214. Willard L. Bragg, "The Picturesque Seminoles," *Florida East Coast Homeseeker* 12, no. 4 (April 1910): 147.

215. Florida East Coast Hotel Company, *East Coast of Florida*, 68–69.

216. For two important interpretations of the "marketing" of the Seminoles in the twentieth century, see Mechling, "Florida Seminoles and the Marketing of the Last Frontier"; and West, *The Enduring Seminoles*.

217. Justin G. Jarvis, "Florida's Seminoles—Savages of Southern Sunshine," *Suniland* 1, no. 6 (March 1925): 25.

218. Ibid., 22.

219. Lee Chandler Persons, "Trees, Shrubs, and Blossoms of Florida," *Florida Review* 4 (1910): 395.

220. Gifford, "The Everglades of Florida and the Landes of France," 11.

221. Rhodes and Dumont, *Guide to Florida for Tourists, Sportsmen and Settlers*, 216.

222. Ibid., 212–13.

223. DeCroix, *Historical, Industrial, and Commercial Data of Miami and Fort Lauderdale*, 170–71.

224. Meindl, Alderman, and Waylen, "On the Importance of Environmental Claims-Making," 689.

225. Rose, *The Swamp and Overflow Lands of Florida*, 15–17.

226. For an excellent study of both the significance and the flaws of the Wright report on the Everglades, see Meindl, Alderman, and Waylen, "On the Importance of Environmental Claims-Making," 682–701.

227. Tebeau, *A History of Florida*, 349.

228. "Florida Land Probe Starts," *Atlanta Constitution* (February 10, 1912), 7; "Tell The Truth about Florida," *Florida East Coast Homeseeker* 13, no. 12 (December 1911).

229. "The Florida Everglades," *Boston Globe*, February 9, 1912, 10.

230. Dovell, "Thomas Elmer Will, Twentieth Century Pioneer."

231. "Californian Will Raise Cane," *Florida East Coast Homeseeker* 13, no. 7 (July 1911): 262–63.

232. "First Farm in the Everglades," *Florida East Coast Homeseeker* 12, no. 4 (April 1910): 122–23.

233. Clase D. Vallette, "Preparation," *Everglade Magazine* 2, no. 2 (June 1911), 2.

234. *Investigation of the Everglades.*

235. Earl E. Moore, Editor, *Plaindealer* of Cleveland, Ohio, to William M. Larkin, Chicago, Illinois, April 25, 1912, in *Investigation of the Everglades*, 8.

236. Day Allen Willey, Baltimore, Maryland, to William M. Larkin, Chicago, Illinois, May 6, 1912, in *Investigation of the Everglades*, 12; W. J. Etten, Managing Editor, *Grand Rapids News*, to William M. Larkin, Chicago, Illinois, May 7, 1912, in *Investigation of the Everglades*, 6.

237. Advertisement by Everglade Land Sales Company, *Florida East Coast Homeseeker* 12, no. 4 (April 1910): 120.

238. "The Story of the Everglades," 124.

239. Waldin, *Truck Farming in the Everglades*, 6.

240. Waldin, "No Other Country Like Florida," *Florida East Coast Homeseeker* 9, no. 9 (September 1907), 291.

241. "Progress of Florida," 687.

242. For example, see Gifford, "Looking Ahead. Views on Everglades Topics," *Tropic* 1, no. 4 (July 1914): 6. African American field workers were similarly featured in an advertisement by the Florida East Coast Railway Company, Model Land Company, and other Florida land companies in *Florida East Coast Homeseeker* 12, no. 4 (April 1910): 113.

243. Advertisement for Okeechobee Park by Florida Land Development Company, *Florida East Coast Homeseeker* 12, no. 4 (April 1910): 115.

244. Ibid.

245. Clase D. Vallette, "Cooperation the Watchword," *Everglade Magazine* 1, no. 10 (February 1911): 2.

246. "Great Imperial Valley, Theme of W. H. Holabird," *Los Angeles Times*, October 2, 1912, 5; "Land of Promise for Rich and Poor," *Imperial Valley Press*, February 15, 1908, 11; Reynolds, *Standard Guide to Florida*, 79.

247. Nye, *America as Second Creation*, 228.

248. Pisani, *From Family Farm to Agribusiness*, xi.

249. "Two Hundred Thousand Acres of Cotton," *Los Angeles Times*, January 1, 1925, 13.

250. See, for example, "Can Furnish Laborers," *Imperial Valley Press*, August 6, 1910, 5; "Cotton Pickers Coming," *Imperial Valley Press*, September 3, 1910, 1.

251. See, for example, "Cheap Labor," *Los Angeles Herald*, June 12, 1908, 4.

252. "Arguments on Mexican Labor Bill Listened To," *San Jose News*, February 24, 1928, 43.

253. Cletus Daniel, *Bitter Harvest*, reproduced in Chan and Olin, *Major Problems in California History*, 280.

254. "Everglades Waters Flood Florida Towns," *Atlanta Constitution*, October 5, 1922, 12.

255. "Irrigation Possibilities of the Colorado River," 8; "The Prosperity of Egypt," *Florida East Coast Homeseeker* 12, no. 4 (April 1910): 140; The Amazing Tale of Tamiami Trail, advertisement in *Miami Metropolis*, July 5, 1921, 10.

256. "Send Florida to the Deserts," *Miami News*, February 4, 1916, 4.

257. Excerpt from James E. Ingraham, "Keep Your Head above the Financial Water and Bet on the Growth of the Country," *Manufacturer's Record*, January 26, 1922, "Correspondence 1854–1919—Misc.—Railroads," James Edmundson Ingraham Papers, Box 1, George A. Smathers Libraries, University of Florida.

258. Meindl, Alderman, and Waylen, "On the Importance of Environmental Claims-Making," 696–97.

259. Fox, *The Truth about Florida*, 98.

260. Hahamovitch, *The Fruits of Their Labor*, 116–21.

261. Mayo, *Florida, an Advancing State*, 262.

262. Stockbridge and Perry, *Florida in the Making*, 231.

263. Whitfield, "Florida's Fudged Identity," 29.

264. John Gifford, "Fruit Quality in Tropical Florida: What It Is and How to Make It," *Miami News*, September 28, 1909, 30.

Chapter 5. "New Edens of the Saxon Home-Seeker"

1. Smith, *Virgin Land*, 142.

2. *Semi-Tropic California* 3, no. 5 (April 1880): 71; Chapin, *Florida, 1513–1913*, 141.

3. For typical California and Florida promotional critiques of urbanization in the Northeast, see, for example, E. F. Spence, "Los Angeles," *Californian* 1, no. 1 (October 1891): 3; Harcourt, *Home Life in Florida*, 15.

4. On the myth of a benign environment in Los Angeles, see Davis, *Ecology of Fear*.

5. Deverell, Hise, and Sloane, "Orange Empires: Comparing Miami and Los Angeles," 145–52.

6. Ibid. Gregory Bush's article, although primarily interested in the 1920s, dealt briefly with the promotional links between Miami and Los Angeles in the 1910s: Bush, "'Playground of the U.S.A.,'" 153–72.

7. Charles Dudley Warner, "Race and Climate," *Land of Sunshine* 4, no. 3 (February 1896), 106.

8. Schlesinger, *The Rise of the City, 1878–1898*.

9. See the chapter on urbanization in Hays, *The Response to Industrialism, 1885–1914*, 47–68.

10. Cronon, *Nature's Metropolis*; Schlesinger, *The Rise of the City*, 68.

11. Noble, *The Progressive Mind, 1890–1917*, 1–22; Boyer, *Urban Masses and Moral Order in America, 1820–1920*, vii.

12. Josiah Strong, "The Problem of the Twentieth Century City," *North American Review* 165, no. 490 (September 1897), 343; Higham, *Strangers in the Land*; Riis, *How the Other Half Lives*; "The Strain of City Life," *Manufacturer and Builder* 18, no. 9 (September 1886), 211.

13. Wilson, *The City Beautiful Movement*.

14. Spence, "Los Angeles," 8.

15. DeCroix, *Historical, Industrial, and Commercial Data of Miami and Fort Lauderdale*, 215.

16. Pictorial American, *Greater Los Angeles, Illustrated*, 74.

17. Charles F. Lummis, "In the Lion's Den," *Land of Sunshine* 4, no. 3 (February 1896): 141.

18. Charles F. Lummis, "In the Lion's Den," *Land of Sunshine* 3, no. 3 (August 1895): 135.

19. "Stroller Takes Observations in Miami and Tells of Things Which He Sees," *Miami Metropolis*, January 9, 1912, 7.

20. Ibid.

21. George, "Colored Town," 436; DeCroix, *Historical, Industrial, and Commercial Data of Miami and Fort Lauderdale*, 24, 34.

22. "Los Angeles, an Ideal City of Ideal Homes," *Los Angeles Herald*, September 3, 1905, 38.

23. Wade, "Urbanization," 187–205.

24. Starr, *Inventing the Dream*, 130.

25. Walter V. Woehlke, "Los Angeles—Homeland," *Sunset* 26, no. 1 (January 1911): 3.

26. Fogelson, *The Fragmented Metropolis*, 78–82.

27. "Semi-Tropic America," *Los Angeles Times*, August 13, 1882, 3. See also Stanonis, "Through a Purple (Green and Gold) Haze," 109–31.

28. "Semi-Tropic America," 3.

29. Ibid.

30. "Los Angeles Temperature," *Los Angeles Herald*, September 3, 1905, 1. Benjamin Truman made a similar comparison but with Nice, France, instead of New Orleans: "With the bare exception of Nice—where the climate is semi-tropical, of course, yet often bleak and humid, there is no city on the globe to be at all compared with Los Angeles, whose attractions cannot be adequately enumerated"; Truman, *Southern California*.

31. "Semi-Tropic America," 3.

32. Los Angeles Chamber of Commerce, *New Facts and Figures concerning Southern California*, 19–20.

33. Ibid.

34. Art Illustrating Association, *Attractive Los Angeles*, n.p.

35. "The Los Angeles Chamber of Commerce," *Pacific Rural Press*, January 30, 1898, 65.

36. "Tourists Flock to Big Hotels," *Los Angeles Herald*, June 25, 1906, 2; Southern Pacific, *California South of Tehachapi*, 9–12.

37. "Los Angeles—A City of Gardens," *Los Angeles Bulletin*, October 26, 1885, California Scrapbook Collection, vol. 12, Los Angeles County—Immigration Association of California, California State Library.

38. Brook, *Los Angeles, California—The City and Country*, 31.

39. "City Life," *Los Angeles Times*, August 15, 1895, 16.

40. Bokovoy, "Inventing Agriculture in Southern California," 77–78.

41. Advertisement by Western Avenue Land and Water Company, Los Angeles, in *California Homeseeker* 1, no. 4 (May 1902): 275.

42. Charles F. Lummis, "Los Angeles, the Metropolis of the Southwest," *Land of Sunshine* 3, no. 1 (June 1895): 48.

43. "Los Angeles Socially," *Los Angeles Times*, January 1, 1886, California Scrapbook Collection, vol. 12, Los Angeles County—Immigration Association of California, 53, California State Library.

44. Charles F. Lummis, "In the Lion's Den," *Land of Sunshine* 3, no. 1 (June 1895): 39.

45. "Eastern Libraries," *Land of Sunshine* 1, no. 3 (August 1894): 58; Charles F. Lummis, "In the Lion's Den," *Land of Sunshine* 3, no. 1 (June 1895): 39; Charles F. Lummis, "In the Lion's Den," *Land of Sunshine* 3, no. 3 (August 1895): 133.

46. Charles F. Lummis, "My Real Brownies," *Land of Sunshine* 7, no. 1 (June 1897): 5–9.

47. *Land of Sunshine* 2, no. 2 (January 1895): 35.

48. On the link between California citrus and the eugenics movement, see Sackman, *Orange Empire*, 61–63.

49. *Land of Sunshine* 2, no. 2 (January 1895): 35.

50. "The Right Kind of People," *Land of Sunshine* 2, no. 1 (December 1894): 30.

51. Lummis, "Los Angeles, the Metropolis of the Southwest," 46.

52. "Not Long To Wait," *Los Angeles Herald*, April 15, 1901, 6.

53. "Editorial," *Land of Sunshine* 2, no. 2 (January 1895): 34–35.

54. Ibid., 34.

55. "The Right Kind of People," 30.

56. *Land of Sunshine* 2, no. 5 (April 1895): 91.

57. Lummis, "Los Angeles, the Metropolis of the Southwest," 47.

58. Fogelson, *The Fragmented Metropolis*, 1.

59. Jackson, *Crabgrass Frontier*, 113–15.

60. Ibid., 122.

61. See "Good Roads Bureau," *Los Angeles Herald*, April 20, 1895, 21; "The Good Roads Convention," *Los Angeles Herald*, October 27, 1900, 6.

62. "Los Angeles Way," *Los Angeles Herald*, March 21, 1910, 4.

63. Lummis, "Los Angeles, the Metropolis of the Southwest," 48.

64. Jackson, *Crabgrass Frontier*, 139–40.

65. Pictorial American, *Greater Los Angeles, Illustrated*, 74.

66. See *California Souvenir Views*; and *Southern California, the Land of Heart's Desire*.

67. Fogelson, *The Fragmented Metropolis*, 70–72.

68. See Culver, *The Frontier of Leisure*.

69. Lummis, "Los Angeles, the Metropolis of the Southwest," 48.

70. "La Fiesta de Los Angeles," *Land of Sunshine* 4, no. 6 (May 1896): 261.

71. Charles Frederick Holder, "Home Life in Southern California," *Land of Sunshine* 7, no. 6 (November 1897): 260.

72. "The Superior Northerner," *Land of Sunshine* 3, no. 5 (October 1895): 209–11.

73. Charles Frederick Holder, "Home Life in Southern California," *Land of Sunshine* 7, no. 6 (November 1897): 260.

74. Warner, "Race and Climate," *Land of Sunshine* 4, no. 3 (February 1896): 103.

75. Warner and Twain, *The Gilded Age*; Charles F. Lummis, "In the Lion's Den," *Land of Sunshine* 4, no. 2 (January 1896): 87.

76. Warner, "Race and Climate," 103.

77. Ibid., 103–4.

78. Ibid., 104.

79. Ibid.

80. Ibid. Warner's vision of semi-tropical California had staying power: the article was reprinted in full in *Out West* 1, no. 45 (February 1917): 38.

81. Higham, *Strangers in the Land*, 7–110.

82. "Los Angeles, an Ideal City of Ideal Homes," *Los Angeles Herald*, September 3, 1905, 38.

83. Fogelson, *Fragmented Metropolis*, 80-81.

84. Brook, *Los Angeles: The Chicago of the Southwest*.

85. Ibid.

86. See, for example, "Contractors' Ultimatum," *Los Angeles Herald*, September 13, 1906, 4.

87. Kazin, "The Great Exception Revisited," 393.

88. Ibid.

89. Brook, *Los Angeles: The Chicago of the Southwest*.

90. Otis, "Los Angeles: The Ardent Hebe of the Sensuous South," 87.

91. Ibid.

92. David Starr Jordan, "The Japanese Problem in California," *Land of Sunshine* 25, no. 4 (March 1907): 225–29.

93. In 1930, Mexicans were the largest minority group in Los Angeles; 97,000 lived there. The figure for Los Angeles County was 167,000. See Fogelson, *The Fragmented Metropolis*, 77.

94. Kazin, "The Great Exception Revisited," 390.

95. Quotation in Deverell, *Whitewashed Adobe*, 38.

96. Ibid., 61.

97. "Week of Gay Carnival," *Washington Post*, February 9, 1896, 21.

98. "La Fiesta de Los Angeles," *Washington Post*, May 1, 1894, 8.

99. Lummis, "La Fiesta de Los Angeles," *Land of Sunshine* 4, no. 6 (May 1896): 271.

100. Southern Pacific, *California, South of Tehachapi*, 5.

101. Ibid, 9–11.

102. Sanchez, *Becoming Mexican American*, 63–86.

103. Spence, "Los Angeles," 1.

104. Sanchez, *Becoming Mexican American*, 72–77.

105. Lummis, *Land of Sunshine* 3, no. 3 (August 1895), 135.

106. Southern Pacific, *California South of Tehachapi*, 11.

107. Charles F. Lummis, "In the Lion's Den," *Land of Sunshine* 7, no. 2 (July 1897): 69.

108. "Editorial," *Land of Sunshine*, 34.

109. *Los Angeles Times* quoted in "No Sectionalism," *San Francisco Call*, March 18, 1905, 8.

110. "The Way to Be Fair," *Los Angeles Herald*, January 24, 1906, 4; "Spirit of the South Is Not Californian," *Los Angeles Herald*, September 15, 1909, 6.

111. "Time for Division Not Now," *Los Angeles Herald*, June 9, 1906, 6; "City Club Will Hear State Division Debate," *Los Angeles Herald*, March 16, 1907, 4.

112. "Hope for Action at This Session," *Los Angeles Herald*, March 2, 1907, 5.

113. Jackson, *Crabgrass Frontier*, 139.

114. Los Angeles Chamber of Commerce, *Los Angeles County, California*.

115. Hampton, *Los Angeles: A Miracle City*, 20.

116. Woehlke, "Los Angeles—Homeland," 16.

117. *California Development Board Monthly Bulletin*, Folder "California History Pamphlets, Vol. 2," 6th Series, San Francisco Public Library Special Collection.

118. *The Mentor: Southern California, the Land of Sunshine* 4, no. 21 (December 1916): 4.

119. Interestingly, in the 1920s, the Bureau of the Census changed the ethnic status of Mexicans living in United States from "white" to "nonwhite," a contributing factor to the reason Los Angeles's non-white population rose from 5.2 percent in 1920 to 14.2 percent in 1930. Fogelson, *Fragmented Metropolis*, 82.

120. Benton, *Semi-Tropic California*, 42.

121. Ibid.

122. "Los Angeles, the Paradise of the World," *Los Angeles Herald*, September 3, 1905, 39.

123. Mayo, *Florida, an Advancing State*, 316.

124. Miami's population in 1930 was roughly equivalent to that of Los Angeles in 1900. Similarly, in 1930 Florida had reached the percentage of urban residents that California had had in 1900. Susan B. Carter, et al., *Historical Statistics of the United States: Millennial Edition*, 1:192, 213.

125. Florida Department of Agriculture, *Fifth Census of the State of Florida*, 16–17.

126. Winter, *Florida: The Land of Enchantment*, 157–272.

127. "The Year 1905—The Prosperous East Coast," *Florida East Coast Homeseeker* 8, no. 1 (January 1906): 7.

128. Florida East Coast Hotel Company, *East Coast of Florida*, 60.

129. Jordan, *The East Coast of Florida*, 1–48.

130. Frederic J. Haskins in *Kansas City Journal*, reproduced in *The Story of the Reclaimed Everglades: Southern Florida*, 1.

131. Emerson, "E. V. Blackman," 96–97.

132. Blackman, *Miami and Dade County, Florida*, 91–92.

133. Ibid., 18.

134. "The Year 1905—The Prosperous East Coast," 7.

135. Wilson, "Miami: From Frontier to Metropolis," 34. See also Wilson, "We Choose the Sub-Tropics," 19–45.

136. Charles F. Lummis, "In the Lion's Den," *Land of Sunshine* 3, no. 2 (July 1895): 82.

137. Florida East Coast Hotel Company, *East Coast of Florida*, 60; Florida East Coast Railway, *The Story of a Pioneer*, 27.

138. Ward, *The Lure of the Southland*, 11.

139. Mohl, "Shadows in the Sunshine," 63–81.

140. Shutts, *Florida, "The East Coast,"* 79.

141. "Directing Attention to Miami," *Miami Herald*, January 3, 1912, 2.

142. On constructions of female beauty in the South, see Roberts, "Pretty Women: Female Beauty in the Jim Crow South."

143. "The Baby Show," *Florida East Coast Homeseeker* 9, no. 4 (April 1907): 119.

144. DeCroix, *Historical, Industrial, and Commercial Data of Miami and Fort Lauderdale*, 181.

145. Florida East Coast Hotel Company, *East Coast of Florida*, 66–67.

146. Ibid., 7.

147. M. S. Burbank, "The Florida Citrus Exchange," *Everglade Magazine* 2, no. 2 (June 1911): 8. Into the 1920s boosters of Florida agriculture continued to look to California for methods of improving the growing and marketing of the state's crops. See Stockbridge and Perry, *Florida in the Making*, 75–89.

148. Brother Powell in *St. Petersburg Times*, reprinted in "Powell Is Anxious to Know," *Florida East Coast Homeseeker* 9, no. 9 (September 1907): 290. See also "Why Advertising Pays," *Florida East Coast Homeseeker* 12, no. 10 (November 1910): 426.

149. The California Promotion Committee, "Business Methods of Building Up the State: The Importance of Making Cities Attractive," circular, July 1905, and The California Promotion Committee, "Monthly Bulletin of Progress," July 28, 1905, both in Printed Ephemera Collection, Portfolio 2, Folder 23, Library of Congress.

150. "Business Methods of Building Up the State."

151. "Powell Is Anxious to Know," 290.

152. "Miami Destined to Become Los Angeles of Eastern U.S.," *Miami Metropolis*, February 10, 1910, 8; "Miami's Future Brighter than Los Angeles," *Miami Metropolis*, March 27, 1914, 1. See also "Miami—A Los Angeles," *Miami Metropolis*, December 13, 1912, 4; and "Miami, the Los Angeles of the East," *Miami Metropolis*, January 6, 1920, 10.

153. "Miami—A Los Angeles," 4.

154. "More Building, Fewer Deaths Here Than on Pacific Coast," *Miami Metropolis*, September 18, 1915, 1.

155. "500,000 in Few Years for Miami—New Resident of this City Compares South Florida Metropolis with Los Angeles, California," *Miami Metropolis*, November 15, 1912, 6.

156. Isidor Cohen quoted in "Brings Good Advice from Section of Big Boosters," *Miami Metropolis*, June 14, 1912, 3.

157. Ibid.

158. William Jennings Bryan quoted in "Prominent Educators Forecast Miami Future," *Miami Metropolis*, February 24, 1916, 4; Adams, "Some Pre-Boom Developers of Dade County," 37.

159. "Miami's Resources Unparalleled" *Miami Metropolis*, June 25, 1915, 6; Ward, *The Lure of the Southland*, 7.

160. Sessa, "Miami on the Eve of the Boom: 1923," 6.

161. George, "Traffic Control in Early Miami," 3.

162. "Miami's Resources Unparalleled," 6.

163. "Miami Prosperous When Hit By Storm," *New York Times*, September 21, 1926, 3.

164. "President W. F. Blackman's Address," *Florida East Coast Homeseeker* 5, no. 5 (May 1903): 5.

165. Ibid.

166. Bank of Bay Biscayne, Miami, *The First Thirty Years of Miami and the Bank of Bay Biscayne*, 24.

167. E. A. Waddell, "Miami City and County," *Florida East Coast Homeseeker* 12, no. 4 (April 1910): 138.

168. Stockbridge and Perry, *Florida in the Making*, 149–52.

169. Ibid., 151.

170. Blackman, *Miami and Dade County, Florida*, 22–23.

171. Chapin, *Florida, 1513–1913*, 501.

172. Ibid.

173. Ward, *The Lure of the Southland*, 35.

174. Wilson, "Miami: From Frontier to Metropolis," 26.

175. Nelson, "Palm Trees, Public Relations, and Promoters," 383–402.

176. *Miami by the Sea: The Land of Palms and Sunshine* (1917).

177. Perman, *Struggle for Mastery*, 258–59.

178. McLin, *Florida: A Pamphlet Descriptive of Its History, Topography, Climate, Soil, Resources, and Natural Advantages, in General and by Counties*, 277.

179. Kharif, "Black Reaction to Segregation and Discrimination in Post-Reconstruction Florida," 169–70.

180. Fields, "Tracing Overtown's Vernacular Architecture," 322–34.

181. Kharif, "Black Reaction to Segregation and Discrimination in Post-Reconstruction Florida," 170–71.

182. DeCroix, *Historical, Industrial, and Commercial Data of Miami and Fort Lauderdale*, 18.

183. Ibid., 30.

184. Ibid., 24.

185. Blackman, *Miami and Dade County, Florida*.

186. Mohl, "Shadows in the Sunshine," 66–67.

187. Ibid., 67.

188. For the selling of segregation by southern boosters, see Hale, *Making Whiteness*, 138–51.

189. Shutts, *Florida, "The East Coast,"* 8.

190. "Emigration to the South," *Chicago Times-Herald*, reproduced in *Florida Agriculturist* 30, no. 17 (April 22, 1903): 254.

191. A. R. Moore, "The Peerless One," *Florida Review* 1, no. 2 (February 1909): 78.

192. Ortiz, *Emancipation Betrayed*, 205–28.

193. Ira Reid quoted in Mohl, "Shadows in the Sunshine," 68.

194. DeCroix, *Historical, Industrial, and Commercial Data of Miami and Fort Lauderdale*, 20.

195. Rainbolt, *The Town that Climate Built*, 35; Nelson, "Palm Trees, Public Relations, and Promoters," 384; *Miami by the Sea: The Land of Palms and Sunshine* (1917 and 1919).

196. George E. Merrick, "The Heir of Tropic Spring," in Merrick, *Songs of the Wind on a Southern Shore, and Other Poems of Florida*, 64.

197. See *Miami by the Sea: The Land of Palms and Sunshine* (1917 and 1919).

198. Herbert N. Casson, "The New Florida," *Florida East Coast Homeseeker* 12, no. 3 (March 1910): 80.

199. Dumont, *Miami*.

200. Ibid.

201. "Florida and Miami as Others See Them," *Miami Metropolis*, July 28, 1920, 4.

202. Simpson, *Where to Go in California*, 26, Simpson's italics.

203. *Miami, Florida, "The Magic City,"* 1.

204. *Miami by the Sea: The Land of Palms and Sunshine* (1917).

205. Zimmerman, "Paradise Promoted," 24–26; Fox, *The Truth about Florida*.

206. Fox, *The Truth about Florida*, 7–8.

207. Bush, "Playground of the U.S.A.," 153–72; Shutts, *Florida, "The East Coast,"* 15.

208. Shutts, *Florida, "The East Coast,"* 105.

209. Edmonds, "The Glowing Destiny of Florida," 23–24.

210. Merrick, *Coral Gables Homes, Miami, Florida*, 19.

211. "Millions of Capital Drawn to Miami," *New York Times*, March 15, 1925, 1.

212. Fogelson, *The Fragmented Metropolis*, 74.

213. Eberle and Riggleman's Economic Service, *Weekly Letter*, September 7, 1925, quoted in Deverell, Hise, and Sloane, "Orange Empires: Comparing Miami and Los Angeles," 147–48.

214. William Jennings Bryan, "The Sunshine State," in Shutts, *Florida, "The East Coast,"* 17.

215. G. D. Brossier, "Here's Why I Would Bet My Last Dollar on Miami," *Miami News*, January 27, 1921, 13.

216. Ibid.

217. Anne O'Hare McCormick, "Miracle Men on Florida's Gold Coast," *New York Times*, March 8, 1925, 3.

218. Mackle, "Two Way Stretch," 17–29.

219. Stockbridge and Perry, *Florida in the Making*, 286.

220. "Florida Boom Matched Here," *Los Angeles Times*, February 14, 1926, 16.

221. Shutts, *Florida, "The East Coast,"* 16.

222. Reynolds, *Standard Guide to Florida*, 63.

223. Corse, *Florida, Empire of the Sun*, 33.

224. "Miami Busy Again but Avoiding Boom," *New York Times*, February 17, 1929, 53.

225. Rainbolt, *The Town that Climate Built; Miami the Beautiful*.

226. Hampton, *Los Angeles: A Miracle City*, 20.

227. Arthur Brisbane quoted in Mayo, *Florida's Resources and Inducements*, 61.

Conclusion

1. Letter from B. F. Shubert, "Peculiar Dream Comes True," *Florida Agriculturist* (April 22, 1903), 253.

2. Florida was also a major cattle producer.

3. J. P. Widney, "The Division of the State," *Californian* 3, no. 14 (February 1881): 125.

4. "East Now Seeks California Apples," *San Francisco Call*, August 30, 1908, 46.

5. Gregory, "The Shaping of California History," 20.

6. Florida East Coast Railway, *East Coast of Florida* (1923), 1.

7. *Orange County, Florida*, 3.

8. Los Angeles Chamber of Commerce, *Los Angeles County, California*.

9. Vance, "California and the Search for the Ideal," 202.

10. For more on the effect of the Great Depression on California, see Davis, *City of Quartz*.

11. "Links Number 200," *New York Times*, December 18, 1923, 24; O. O. McIntyre, "New York Day by Day," *New York Times*, July 17, 1937, 4.

12. *Los Angeles and Vicinity*; Mayo, "Florida—Yesterday, Today, and Tomorrow," in McRae, *Why I Like Florida*, 101.

13. See Derr, *Some Kind of Paradise*; Steinberg, *Down to Earth*, 176–83.

14. De Waal, *The Caucasus*, 82–83.

15. All quotes in ibid. See also Ilf and Petrov, *Little Golden America*.

16. De Waal, *The Caucasus*, 82–83.

17. Love, *Race over Empire*.

18. See, for example, White, *Our New Possessions*, 16–17; and Halstead, *The History of American Expansion*, 8, 25.

19. John L. Stevens to Secretary of State John Foster, quoted in Love, "White Is the Color of Empire," 81.

20. White, *Our New Possessions*, 16–17.

21. Halstead, *The History of American Expansion*, 8–9.

22. White, *Our New Possessions*, 16–17.

23. Musick, *Hawaii: Our New Possessions*, 8.

24. Ibid., 30, my italics. See also King, *The Southern States of America*, 405.

25. Halstead, *The History of American Expansion*, 8–9, 25.

26. Quotation from "The American Anti-Imperialist League Denounces U.S. Policy, 1899," in Hoffman and Gjerde, *Major Problems in American History*, 2:92; Roosevelt, *The Strenuous Life*, in ibid., 90–91.

27. Halstead, *The History of American Expansion*, 24, 8.

28. E. J. Wickson, "Distinctive Features of California Horticulture," in California, State Board of Trade, *California, Early History*, 53.

29. White, *Our New Possessions*, 492.

30. Chipman, *California . . . Its Resources and Advantages*, 44.

31. The scholarship on U.S. overseas expansion in the 1890s is vast and rich with debate. For a useful discussion, see LaFeber, *The New Empire*, 1–61.

32. See "Shall We Annex Hawaii?" *Los Angeles Herald*, June 27, 1897, 15.

33. Charles F. Lummis, "In the Lion's Den," *Land of Sunshine* 4, no. 5 (April 1896): 237.

34. Charles F. Lummis, "In the Lion's Den," *Land of Sunshine* 12, no. 3 (February 1900): 192–93.

35. Ibid.

36. Lummis, "They Mistake Their Audience," *Land of Sunshine* 13, no. 4 (September–October 1900): 295.

37. Los Angeles Chamber of Commerce quoted in Atchison and Eshelman (Historians, Etc.), *Los Angeles, Then and Now*, 52.

38. Winter, *Florida: The Land of Enchantment*, v.

39. Pike, *The United States and Latin America*, 166.

40. Harry Ellington Brook, "In Tropic America," *Land of Sunshine* 15, no. 6 (December 1901): 507.

41. Ibid., 508–11.

42. David Starr Jordan, "Mexico—A New Nation in an Old Country," *Sunset* 2, no. 5 (March 1899): 83–87.

43. Gifford, "Southern Florida," 20.

44. "Somewhat Tropical Suggestions," *Pacific Rural Press*, July 23, 1898, 50.

45. "Directing Attention to Miami," *Miami Herald*, January 3, 1912, 2.

46. Herbert N. Casson, "The New Florida," *Florida East Coast Homeseeker* 12, no. 3 (March 1910): 89.

47. "Canal to Work Great Changes," *Atlanta Constitution*, February 13, 1910, 6.

48. "Professor to Lecture on Value of Canal," *San Francisco Call*, July 5, 1911, 19; Phelan, "Commerce and Commercial Relations of California," 152.

49. Benton, *Semi-Tropic California*, 17, 52.

50. Charles F. Lummis, "In the Lion's Den," *Land of Sunshine* 3, no. 3 (August 1895): 135.

Bibliography

Archives and Libraries

Bancroft Library, University of California, Berkeley, Berkeley, California

Charles Howard Shinn Papers, 1890–1923
Charles B. Turrill Papers as Manager, Preliminary World's Fair Exhibit, 1892

California Historical Society, San Francisco, California

Charles Turrill Papers as Manager, San Diego Chamber of Commerce, 1878–1890

California State Library, Sacramento, California

California Scrapbooks Collection, volume 12, Los Angeles County—Immigration Association
of California, ca. 1883–1896
San Diego County—California Pamphlets

Library of Congress, Washington, D.C.

Printed Ephemera Collection

George A. Smathers Libraries, University of Florida, Gainesville, Florida

James Edmundson Ingraham Papers
Florida Ephemera Collection

Newspapers and Periodicals

Atlantic Monthly
Atlanta Constitution
California Homeseeker
Californian
Daily Alta California
Everglade Magazine
Florida Agriculturist
Florida Dispatch
Florida East Coast Homeseeker

Florida Farmer and Fruit Grower
Imperial Valley Press
Indiana Farmer
Los Angeles Herald
Lost Angeles Times
Miami Metropolis
Miami Herald
The Mentor: Southern California, the Land of Sunshine
Monthly Bulletin—Florida Bureau of Immigration
New York Times
Pacific Rural Press
Rural Californian
San Francisco Call
Semi-Tropic California
Semi-Tropical
Southern California Horticulturist
Sunset
Tropic

Other Published Primary Sources

Art Illustrating Association. *Attractive Los Angeles*. Chicago: Art Illustrating Association, 1899.

Ashby, John W. *Alachua, the Garden County of Florida. Its Resources and Advantages*. Gainesville: Alachua County Immigration Association, 1888.

Atchison and Eshelman (Historians, Etc.). *Los Angeles, Then and Now*. Los Angeles: Geo. Rice & Sons, 1897.

Atlantic and Gulf Railroad General Passenger Department. *Guide to Southern Georgia and Florida*. Savannah: Morning News Steam Printing House, 1879.

Austin, Mary. *The Land of Little Rain*. Boston: Houghton Mifflin Company, 1903.

Bank of Bay Biscayne, Miami. *The First Thirty Years of Miami and the Bank of Bay Biscayne, 1896–1926*. Miami: Bank of Bay Biscayne, 1926.

Barbour, George. *Florida for Tourists, Invalids and Settlers: Containing Practical Information regarding Climate, Soil and Productions*. New York: D. Appleton & Company, 1882.

Beauties of the Ocklawaha and Tampa. Philadelphia: J. Murray Jordan, 1890.

Belmore Florida Land Company. *Florida, the Land of Sunshine, Oranges, and Health*. Chicago: Belmore Florida Land Company, 1885.

Benton, F. Weber. *Semi-Tropic California: The Garden of the World*. Los Angeles: Benton, 1914.

"Bethesda": A Traveller's Criticism on Our Health Resorts, Their Scenery, Climatic Peculiarities, and Curative Influence. Boston: Billings, Clapp & Co. 1885.

Blackman, E. V. *Miami and Dade County, Florida: Its Settlement, Progress and Achievement*. Washington, D.C.: Victor Rainbolt, 1921.

Brinton, Daniel G. *A Guide-Book of Florida and the South, for Tourists, Invalids, and Emigrants*. Philadelphia: Geo. Macle, 1869.

———. *Races and Peoples: Lectures on the Science of Ethnography*. Philadelphia: D. McKay, 1901.

Brook, Harry Ellington. *The County and City of Los Angeles in Southern California*. Los Angeles: Times-Mirror Company, 1893.

———. *Irrigation in Southern California*. Los Angeles: Los Angeles Printing Company, 1893.

———. *The Land of Sunshine: Southern California*. Los Angeles: Southern California Bureau of Information, 1893.

———. *Los Angeles: The Chicago of the Southwest*. Los Angeles: Los Angeles Chamber of Commerce, 1904.

———. *Los Angeles, California—The City and Country*. 23rd ed. Los Angeles: Los Angeles Chamber of Commerce, 1910.

Broward, Napoleon B. *Open Letter of Governor N. B. Broward to the People of Florida* N.p.: n.p., 1906.

Byrne, Baynard. *Florida and Texas: A Series of Letters Comparing the Soil, Climate, and Productions of These States*. Ocala: East Florida Banner Office, 1866.

California. State Board of Trade. *California: Early History, Commercial Position, Climate, Scenery, Forests, General Resources . . . 1897–98*. San Francisco: California State Board of Trade, 1898.

California Development Board Monthly Bulletin. San Francisco: California Development Board, June 1915.

California Handbook with State and County Maps. San Francisco: California State Board of Trade, 1892.

California Souvenir Views: A Collection of 64 Views of California and Arizona. Los Angeles: B. R., 1902.

California—Self-Supporting Homes! San Francisco: Southern Pacific Company, 1889.

Carter, Charles F. *The Missions of Nueva California: An Historical Sketch*. San Francisco: Whitaker & Ray, 1900.

———. *Some By-Ways of California*. San Francisco: Whitaker & Ray, 1902.

Carter, Susan B., Scott Sigmund Gartner, Michael R. Haines, Alan L. Olmstead, Richard Sutch, and Gavin Wright, eds. *Historical Statistics of the United States: Millennial Edition*. Vol. 1, *Population*. Cambridge: Cambridge University Press, 2006.

———. *Historical Statistics of the United States. Millennial Edition*. Vol. 4, *Economic Sectors*. Cambridge: Cambridge University Press, 2006.

Chapin, George M. *Florida, 1513–1913, Past and Future: Four Hundred Years of Wars and Peace and Industrial Development*. Chicago: S. J. Clarke, 1914.

Chipman, N. P. *California . . . Its Resources and Advantages: Tenth Annual Report*. San Francisco: California State Board of Trade, 1900.

———. *Report upon the Fruit Industry of California—Its Growth and Development and Present and Future Importance*. San Francisco: California State Board of Trade, 1889.

Clyde Steamship Company. *Beautiful St. John's River through the Heart of Tropical Florida*. N.p.: Clyde Steamship Company, 1896.

Commissioner of Lands and Immigration, State of Florida. *Florida: Its Climate, Soil and Productions*. New York: Fisher & Field, 1870.

Corse, Carita Doggett. *Florida, Empire of the Sun: A Description of the Living Advantages of Florida*. Tallahassee: Florida State Hotel Commission, 1930.

Crosby, Oliver Martin. *Florida Facts Both Bright and Blue: A Guide Book to Intending Settlers, Tourists, and Investors, from a Northerner's Standpoint*. New York: South Publishing Co., 1887.

Crown of the Valley: The Story of Pasadena. Pasadena: Publicity Department, Pasadena & Maryland Branches, Security Trust & Savings Bank, 1924.

Daniells, T. G., ed. *California: Its Products, Resources, Industries and Attractions: What It Offers the Immigrant, Homeseeker, Investor and Tourist.* Sacramento: California Louisiana Purchase Exposition Committee, 1904.

Davidson, James Wood. *The Florida of To-Day: A Guide for Tourists and Settlers.* New York: D. Appleton & Co., 1889.

DeCroix, F. W. *Historical, Industrial, and Commercial Data of Miami and Fort Lauderdale, Dade County, Florida.* St. Augustine: The Record Co., 1911.

Dennett, Daniel. *Louisiana as It Is: Its Topography and Material Resources.* New Orleans: Eureka Press, 1876.

Dodd, Donald B. *Historical Statistics of the States of the United States.* Westport: Greenwood Press, 1993.

Dodge Art Publishing Company. *Illustrated Florida.* Buffalo: Dodge Art Publishing Co., 1882.

Dumont, Earl Royce. *Miami.* Miami: Montray Corporation, 1921.

Dupuy, William Atherton. "Cooperatives in Citrus Marketing." In Nathan Mayo, *Florida, an Advancing State, 1907-1917-1927: An Industrial Survey,* 275–301. Tallahassee: Florida State Legislature, 1928.

Eagen, Dennis. *The Florida Settler, or Immigrants' Guide.* Tallahassee: C. H. Walton, 1874.

Edmonds, Richard H. "The Glowing Destiny of Florida." In Nathan Mayo, *Florida's Resources and Inducements. Eighteenth Biennial Report.* Part 1, 1923–24. Tallahassee: T. J. Appleyard, 1924.

Emerson, Charles S. "E. V. Blackman." In E. V. Blackman, *Miami and Dade County, Florida: Its Settlement, Progress and Achievement,* 96–98. Washington, D.C.: Victor Rainbolt, 1921.

Facts and Figures Concerning Southern California and Los Angeles City and County. Los Angeles: Los Angeles Chamber of Commerce, 1888.

Farnham, T. J. *Life, Adventures, and Travels in California.* New York: Nafis & Cornish, 1855.

Farnsworth, R.W.C. *A Southern California Paradise.* Pasadena: R.W.C. Farnsworth, 1883.

Florida Department of Agriculture. *Fifth Census of the State of Florida, Taken in the Year 1925.* Tallahassee: T. J. Appleyard, 1926.

Florida East Coast Hotel Company. *East Coast of Florida.* St. Augustine: J. D. Rahner, 1901–2.

Florida East Coast Railway. *East Coast of Florida.* St. Augustine: Florida East Coast Railway, 1901.

———. *East Coast of Florida.* St. Augustine: Florida East Coast Railway, 1923.

———. *Florida: A Trip from Jacksonville to—Havana.* St. Augustine, Fla.: C. F. Hopkins, 1900.

———. *Florida East Coast: The East Coast of Florida Is Paradise Regained.* Jacksonville: Florida East Coast Railway Company, 1904.

———. *The Story of a Pioneer: A Brief History of the Florida East Coast Railway and Associated Enterprises, Flagler System, 1885–86 . . . 1935–36.* St. Augustine: The Record Company, 1936.

Florida East Coast Railway and Florida East Coast Hotel Company. *Florida East Coast Railway and Hotels: "America's Tropical Kingdom."* Jacksonville: J. P. Beckwith for the Florida East Coast R'y Co. and the Florida East Coast Hotel Co., 1901.

Florida Land Agency. *Florida: Its Soil, Climate, Health, Productions, Resources, and Advantages.* Jacksonville: Florida Land Agency, 1875.

Florida Land and Improvement Company. *Florida, Its Climate, Soil, and Productions.* New York: Florida Land and Improvement Company, 1881.

Florida, Sub-Tropical Exposition: Jacksonville, Fla., January to May 1888. Jacksonville: Sub-Tropical Exposition, 1888.

Florida Tourist and Southern Investor's Guide. Cedar Rapids, Iowa: C. F. Bates & Co., 1898.

Forbush, T. B. *Florida: The Advantages and Inducements which It Offers to Immigrants*. Boston: New England Emigrant Aid Company, 1868.

Foss, James H. *Florida Facts, Found after a Four Years' Search*. Boston: Rand Avery Company Printers, 1886.

Fox, Charles D. *The Truth about Florida*. New York: Charles Renard Corporation, 1925.

French, Seth. *Semi-Tropical Florida: Its Climate, Soil, and Productions*. Chicago: Rand, McNally & Co. 1879.

Fruit Grower. *Fruit and Vegetable Growing in Manatee County, Florida*. Norfolk: General Industrial Department, Seaboard Air Line Railway, 1910.

Falfurrias, "the Land of Heart's Delight," in Semi-Tropical South Texas. Falfurrias: Falfurrias Immigration Company, n.d.

George, Henry. *Our Land and Land Policy, National and State*. San Francisco: White & Bauer, 1871.

George, Henry. *Progress and Poverty*. New York: Modern Library, 1879.

Gifford, John. "The Banana and the Papaw." In Gifford, *The Everglades and Other Essays*, 38–41. Kansas City: Everglades Land Sales Co., 1911.

———. "The Everglades of Florida." In Gifford, *The Everglades and Other Essays*, 95–103. Kansas City: Everglades Land Sales Co., 1911.

———. "The Everglades of Florida and the Landes of France." In Gifford, *The Everglades and Other Essays*, 1–12. Kansas City: Everglades Land Sales Co., 1911.

———. "Southern Florida—Notes on the Forest Conditions of the Southernmost Part of This Remarkable Peninsula." In Gifford, *The Everglades and Other Essays*, 13–20. Kansas City: Everglades Land Sales Co., 1911.

———. "Trees as an Aid to Drainage." In Gifford, *The Everglades and Other Essays*, 21–26. Kansas City: Everglades Land Sales Co., 1911.

Halstead, Murat. *The History of American Expansion, and the Story of Our New Possessions*. New York: The United Subscription Book Publishers of America, 1899.

———. *Pictorial History of America's New Possessions*. Chicago: The Dominion Company, 1902.

Gulf Coast Land Company. *The Gulf Coast of Florida: The Gulf Coast Reserve . . . Just Opened to Travel by Railway and Steamboat*. Chicago: Gulf Coast Land Company, 1885.

Hampton, Edgar Lloyd. *Los Angeles: A Miracle City*. Los Angeles: Los Angeles Chamber of Commerce, 1928.

Harcourt, Helen. *Home Life in Florida*. Louisville, Ken.: John P. Morton & Co., 1889.

Hardy, Lady Duffus. *Down South*. London: Chapman and Hill Limited, 1883.

Hawley, A. T. *The Present Condition, Growth, Progress, and Advantages, of Los Angeles City and County, Southern California*. Los Angeles: Los Angeles Chamber of Commerce, 1876.

Henshall, James. *Camping and Cruising in Florida*. Cincinnati: Robert Clarke & Co., 1884.

Hoag, Isaac N. *California: The Cornucopia of the World: Room for Millions of Immigrants*. Chicago: Rand McNally, 1883.

———. *California: The Cornucopia of the World: Room for Millions of Immigrants*. Chicago: Rand McNally, 1885.

Hopkins, Caspar. *Common Sense Applied to the Immigrant Question*. San Francisco: California Immigrant Union, 1869.

Ilf, Ilya, and Eugene Petrov. *Little Golden America: Two Famous Soviet Humorists Survey These United States*. New York: Farrar & Rinehart, 1937.

Ingram, H. K. *Florida: Beauties of the East Coast.* Jacksonville: Jacksonville, St. Augustine & Indian River Railway, 1892.

International Irrigation Congress. *Official Report of the International Congress Held at Los Angeles.* Los Angeles: International Irrigation Congress, 1893.

Investigation of the Everglades: As Seen by the Brightest Minds of Today. Kansas City: Chambers Land Co., 1912.

Irsch, Francis. *Florida Immigration: An Address to the County Commissioners, Corporations, Land Owners, and Citizens of Florida.* Jacksonville: DaCosta Printing & Publishing House, 1891.

Jackson, Helen Hunt, *Glimpses of Three Coasts.* Boston: Roberts Brothers, 1892.

———. *Ramona: A Story.* 1884; repr., New York: Signet Classic, 1988.

Jacques, D. H. *Florida as a Permanent Home: Embracing a Description of the Climate, Soil, and Productions of the State.* Jacksonville: Chas. W. Blew, 1877.

James, George Wharton. *The Wonders of the Colorado Desert.* New York: Little, Brown & Company, 1906.

James, Henry. *The American Scene.* 1907; repr., New York: Scribner's, 1946.

Johnstone, E. McD. *"By Semi-Tropic Seas": Santa Barbara and Surroundings.* Buffalo: Matthews, Northrup & Co., 1888.

Jordan, J. Murray. *The East Coast of Florida.* Philadelphia: J. Murray Jordan, 1901.

Journal of the Proceedings of the Assembly of the State of Florida, Seventh Session, January 6, 1874. Tallahassee: Florida House of Representatives, 1874.

Journal of the Proceedings of the Assembly of the State of Florida, Twelfth Session, January 2, 1883. Tallahassee: Florida House of Representatives, 1883.

Journal of the Florida House of Representatives of the State of Florida, Third Session, April 7, 1891. Tallahassee: Florida House of Representatives, 1891.

Keeler, Charles A. *Southern California.* Los Angeles: Passenger Department, Santa Fe Railroad, 1899.

Kenworthy, Charles J. *Climatology of Florida.* Savannah: Morning New Steam Printing House, 1880.

Kidd, Benjamin. *The Control of the Tropics.* London: MacMillan & Co. Ltd, 1898.

King, Edward. *The Southern States of America.* London: Blackie & Son, 1875.

Lands of the Semi-Tropic Land and Water Company, San Bernardino County, California. Map. San Francisco: Britton & Rey, 1890.

Lanier, Sidney. *Florida: Its Scenery, Climate and History.* Philadelphia: J. P. Lippincott & Co., 1876.

Lee, Henry. *The Tourist's Guide of Florida: Illustrated with Wood-Cut Scenes of Florida, Etc.* New York: Leve & Alden Printing Co., 1885.

Lente, Frederick D. *The Constituents of Climate: With Special Reference to the Climate of Florida.* Louisville: Richmond & Louisville Medical Journal Book and Steam Job Print, 1878.

Lindley, Walter, and Joseph P. Widney. *California of the South: Its Physical Geography, Climate, Resources, Routes of Travel, and Health-Resorts.* New York: D. Appleton & Co., 1888.

Long, Ellen Call. *Florida Breezes.* Jacksonville: Ashmead Bros. Printers, 1882.

Los Angeles and Vicinity, California. San Francisco: Cardinell-Vincent Company, 1915.

Los Angeles Chamber of Commerce. *Los Angeles County, California: What To See & How To See It.* Los Angeles: Los Angeles Chamber of Commerce, 1924.

———. *New Facts and Figures concerning Southern California: Including the Actual Experience of Individual Producers.* Los Angeles: Los Angeles Chamber of Commerce, 1891.

MacCauley, Clay. *The Seminole Indians of Florida*. Washington: Smithsonian Institution, 1887.

MacCurdy, Rahno Mabel. *The History of the California Fruit Growers Exchange*. Los Angeles: G. Rice & Sons, 1925.

MacDonald, John. *Plain Talk about Florida: For Homes and Investments, Part One*. Eustis: MacDonald, 1883.

Madden, Jerome. *California: Its Attractions for the Invalid, Tourist, Capitalist, and Homeseeker*. San Francisco: H. S. Crocker & Co., 1890.

Martin, William H. *Supplement to All about California and the Inducements to Settle There*. San Francisco: California Immigrant Union, 1876.

Mayo, Nathan. *Florida: The March of Progress*. Tallahassee: Florida Department of Agriculture, n.d. [ca. 1939].

———. *Florida, an Advancing State, 1907-1917-1927: An Industrial Survey*. Tallahassee: Florida State Legislature, 1928.

———. *Florida's Resources and Inducements. Eighteenth Biennial Report*. Part 1, 1923–24. Tallahassee: T. J. Appleyard, 1924.

McClure, A. K. *The South: Its Industrial, Financial, and Political Condition*. Philadelphia: J. B. Lippincott Co., 1886.

McLin, B. E. *Florida: A Pamphlet Descriptive of Its History, Topography, Climate, Soil, Resources, and Natural Advantages, in General and by Counties—Prepared in the Interest of Immigration*. Tallahassee: T. B. Hilson, 1904.

McRae, W. A., *Why I Like Florida: A Compilation of Letters and Gems of Thought from Men and Women of Renown who have Visited Florida or Become Citizens of the State* (St. Augustine: The Record Company, 1923).

Miami, Florida, "The Magic City." Miami: N.p., 1920.

Miami the Beautiful. Miami: N.p., n.d. [ca. 1920s].

Merrick, George. *Coral Gables Homes, Miami, Florida*. Miami: George Merrick, n.d. [ca. 1920s].

Merrick, George E. "The Heir of Tropic Spring." In Merrick, *Songs of the Wind on a Southern Shore, and Other Poems of Florida*. Boston: The Four Seas Company, 1920.

Miami by the Sea: The Land of Palms and Sunshine. Miami: Miami Chamber of Commerce, 1917.

Miami by the Sea: The Land of Palms and Sunshine. Miami: Miami Chamber of Commerce, 1919.

Moore, T. W. *Treatise and Handbook of Orange Culture in Florida, Louisiana, and California*. New York: E. R. Pelton & Co., 1886.

Munroe, C. K., ed. *The Florida Annual—Impartial and Unsectional, 1885* (New York, 1885.

Musick, John R. *Hawaii: Our New Possessions*. New York: Funk & Wagnalls Company, 1898.

Myers, O. A. *Alachua County: Her Attractive Features and Public Improvements*. Gainesville: Cannon and McCreary, 1892.

Nordhoff, Charles. *California for Health, Pleasure, and Residence: A Book for Travelers and Settlers*. New York: Harper & Bros., 1872.

Nutting, L. H. *To the Pacific Coast via the Sunset Route of the Southern Pacific Company, from New Orleans to Los Angeles and San Francisco*. New York: New York General Agency, 1885.

Orange County, Florida. St. Augustine, Fla.: The Record Company, 1926.

Otis, Harrison Gray. "Los Angeles: The Ardent Hebe of the Sensuous South." In J. E. Scott, *Los Angeles, the Old and the New*, 81–93. Los Angeles: Times-Mirror House, 1911.

Pacific Coast Land Bureau. *Semi-Tropic California: San Diego County*. San Francisco: Pacific Coast Land Bureau, 1891.

Pasadena Transfer and Storage Company. *A Thumb Nail History of Pasadena.* Pasadena: Pasadena Transfer and Storage Company, n.d.

Phelan, James D. "Commerce and Commercial Relations of California." In *California—Its Products, Resources, Industries and Attractions—What It Offers the Immigrant, Homeseeker, Investor and Tourist,* edited by T. G. Daniells, 146–53. Sacramento: California Louisiana Purchase Exposition Committee, 1904.

Pictorial American. *Greater Los Angeles, Illustrated: The Most Progressive Metropolis of the Twentieth Century.* Los Angeles: The Pictorial American, 1907.

Pomona Land and Water Company. *Southern California—Pomona Illustrated and Described.* Pomona: Pomona Land and Water Company, 1885.

Presbrey, Frank. *Florida, Cuba, and Jamaica.* New York: Plant System, 1900.

Rae, W. F. *Westward by Rail.* London: Longmans Green & Co., 1870.

Rainbolt, Victor. *The Town that Climate Built: The Story of the Rise of a City in the American Tropics.* Miami: Parker Art Printing Association, n.d.

Report of the Immigration Committee of the California State Board of Trade. San Francisco: California State Board of Trade, 1895.

Reynolds, Charles B. *Standard Guide to Florida.* New York: Foster & Reynolds, Co., 1921.

Rhodes, Harrison, and Mary Wolfe Dumont. *Guide to Florida for Tourists, Sportsmen and Settlers.* New York: Dodd, Mead and Company, 1912.

Richardson, Joseph. *Florida: The East Coast and Keys.* St. Augustine: Florida East Coast Railway Company, 1895.

Richmond, John F. *Sumter County, Florida: Its Situation, Climate, Soil, Productions, People, Transportation, Lines, Lakes, Rivers.* Philadelphia: McCalla & Stavely, 1882.

Riis, Jacob. *How the Other Half Lives: Studies among the Tenements of New York.* 1890; repr., New York: Hill & Wang, 1967.

Riverside Land and Irrigation Company. *Southern California.* San Francisco: Bacon and Company, 1879.

Robinson, A. A. *Florida: A Pamphlet Descriptive of Its History, Topography, Climate, Soil, Resources, and Natural Advantages.* Tallahassee: Florida Bureau of Immigration, 1882.

Rogers, Lewis. *Climate in Pulmonary Consumption: and, California as a Health Resort.* Louisville: John P. Morton & Co., 1874.

Roosevelt, Theodore. "Opening Address of the President." In *Proceedings of a Conference of Governors in the White House, Washington, D.C., May 13–15, 1908,* edited by Newton C. Blanchard, John Franklin Fort, James O. Davidson, John C. Cutler, and Martin F. Ansel, 3–13. Washington, D.C.: Government Printing Office, 1909.

Rose, R. E. *The Swamp and Overflow Lands of Florida—The Disston Drainage Company and the Disston Purchase: A Reminiscence.* Tallahassee: Rose, 1916.

San Pascual Plantation. *Prospectus of the San Pascual Plantation, Incorporated March 31st, 1870 for the Cultivation of Semi-Tropical Fruit & Other Productions in a Tract of 1750 Acres Near Los Angeles.* San Francisco: Cubery & Co. 1870.

Semi-Tropic California—Citrus Fruit Area of the State. San Francisco: California State Board of Trade, 1902.

Shaw, Abram Marvin. *California as a Health Resort.* Boston: J. S. Adams, 1885.

Shepard, A. D. *Semi-Tropic California.* San Francisco: Southern Pacific Company, 1898.

Shutts, Frank B. *Florida, "The East Coast": Its Builders, Resources, Industries, Town and City Developments.* Miami: Miami Herald, 1926.

Simon, John Y. *The Papers of Ulysses S. Grant.* Vol. 20, *Nov. 1, 1869–October 31, 1870.* Carbondale: Southern Illinois University Press, 1995.

Simpson, W. H. *Where to Go in California.* Chicago: Rand McNally, 1899.

Southern Pacific Company. *California South of Tehachapi: From Notes by the Agents.* San Francisco: Southern Pacific Passenger Department, 1908.

Stockbridge, Frank Parker, and John Holliday Perry. *Florida in the Making.* New York: The de Bower Publishing Co., 1926.

Stowe, Harriett Beecher. *Palmetto Leaves.* Boston: James R. Osgood & Co., 1873.

Strong, Josiah. *The New Era; or, the Coming Kingdom.* New York: Baker and Taylor, 1893.

The Story of the Reclaimed Everglades: Southern Florida. Kansas City: Florida Fruit Lands Company, 1912.

South Publishing Company. *Florida Portrayed: Its Sections, Climate, Productions, Resources, Etc.* London: South Publishing Company, 1884.

Southern California, the Land of Heart's Desire: Its People, Homes, and Pleasures, Art and Architecture. Los Angeles: Los Angeles Morning Herald, 1912.

Thayer, William M. *Marvels of the New West.* Norwich, Conn.: Henry Bill Publishing Company, 1890.

Tolderness, T. W. *Peoples and Problems of India.* London: Thornton Butterworth Limited, 1912.

Tout, Otis B. *Imperial Valley, California.* San Francisco: Sunset Magazine Homeseekers' Bureau, 1907.

Truman, Benjamin C. *Homes and Happiness in the Golden State of California.* San Francisco: H. S. Crocker & Co., 1884.

———. *Semi-Tropical California: Its Climate, Healthfulness, Productiveness, and Scenery.* San Francisco: A. L. Bancroft & Company, 1874.

———. *Southern California.* Los Angeles: M. Rieder, 1903.

Turner, Frederick Jackson. *The Significance of the Frontier in American History.* 1893; repr., New York: Ungar, 1963.

Tyler, Daniel G. *Where to Go in Florida.* New York: W. M. Clarke, 1881.

Upham, Samuel. *Notes from Sunland, on the Manatee River, Gulf Coast of South Florida, Its Climate, Soil and Productions.* Philadelphia: E. Claxton & Co., 1881.

Vail, Mary. *"Both Sides Told," or Southern California as It Is.* Pasadena: West Coast Publishing Company, 1888.

Weinberg, Albert. *Manifest Destiny: A Study of Nationalist Expansionism in American History.* Chicago: Quadrangle Books, 1935.

Van Dyke, Theodore. *The Rifle, Rod, and Gun in California.* New York: Fords, Howard & Hulbert, 1881.

———. *Southern California.* New York: Fords, Howard & Hulbert, 1886.

———. *The Still Hunter.* New York: Fords, Howard & Hulbert, 1883.

Varnum, John P. *Florida, Its Climate, Productions and Characteristics: A Hand Book of Important and Reliable Information for the Use of the Tourist, Settler and Investor.* New York: South Publishing Co., 1885.

Views of Florida. Portland, Me.: Chisholm Bros., 1890.

Vischer, Edward. *Vischer's Pictorial of California*. San Francisco: Joseph Winterbur & Company, 1870.

Waldin, Walter, *Truck Farming in the Everglades*. [Miami]: Walter Waldin, 1910.

Ward, C. H. *The Lure of the Southland: Miami and Miami Beach, Florida*. Miami: C. H. Ward, 1915.

Warner Bros. *Southern California: A Semi-Tropic Paradise*. Los Angeles: Times-Mirror Co., 1887.

Warner, Charles Dudley, and Mark Twain. *The Gilded Age: A Tale of Today*. Hartford: American Publishing Co., 1873.

Wells, A. J. *California for the Settler: The Natural Advantages of the Golden State for the Present Day Farmer*. San Francisco: Southern Pacific Company, 1914.

———. *Government Irrigation and the Settler. California, Oregon, Nevada and Arizona, including a Description of the Imperial Valley Project*. San Francisco: Southern Pacific Passenger Department, 1910.

White, J. W. *Jacksonville, Florida, and Surrounding Towns*. Jacksonville: J. W. White, 1890.

White, Trumbull. *Our New Possessions: A Graphic Account, Descriptive and Historical, of the Tropic Islands of the Sea which Have Fallen under Our Sway*. Philadelphia: Elliot, 1898.

Whitney, J. H. *Florida Everglades Review*. Chicago: Florida Everglades Land Company, 1910.

Willis, Nathaniel P. *Health Trip to the Tropics*. New York: C. Scribner, 1853.

Willoughby, Hugh. *Across the Everglades: A Canoe Journey of Exploration*. Philadelphia: J. P. Lippincott Co., 1898.

Winter, Nevin O. *Florida: The Land of Enchantment*. Boston: The Page Company, 1918.

Secondary Sources

Abbey, Kathryn T. "Florida versus the Principles of Populism, 1896–1911." *Journal of Southern History* 4, no. 4 (1938): 462–75.

Adams, Adam G. "Some Pre-Boom Developers of Dade County." *Tequesta* 17 (1957): 31–46.

Albion, Michele Wehrwein. *The Florida Life of Thomas Edison*. Gainesville: University Press of Florida, 2008.

Almaguer, Tomas. *Racial Fault Lines: The Historical Origins of White Supremacy in California*. Berkeley: University of California Press, 1994.

Angermann, Erich. "Challenges of Ambiguity: Doing Comparative History." In Erich Angermann, Carl Degler, and John A. Garraty, *Challenges of Ambiguity: Doing Comparative History*, 1–20. New York: Berg, 1991.

Appleby, Joyce. *Capitalism and a New Social Order: The Republican Vision of the 1790s*. New York: New York University Press, 1984.

———. *Liberalism and Republicanism in the Historical Imagination*. Cambridge: Harvard University Press, 1992.

Arnold, David. *The Problem of Nature: Environment, Culture, and European Expansion*. Maiden: Blackwell, 1996.

———. "'Illusory Riches': Representations of the Tropical World, 1840–1950." *Singapore Journal of Tropical Geography* 21 (January 2000): 6–18.

Aron, Cindy. *Working At Play: A History of Vacations in the United States*. Oxford: Oxford University Press, 1999.

Baptist, Edward E. *Creating an Old South: Middle Florida's Plantation Frontier before the Civil War.* Chapel Hill: University of North Carolina Press, 2002.

Barron, Stephanie, Sheri Bernstein, and Ilene Susan Fort. *Made in California: Art, Image, and Identity, 1900–2000.* Los Angeles: University of California Press, 2000.

Baur, John E. *The Health Seekers of Southern California, 1870–1900.* San Marino, Calif.: The Huntington Library, 1959.

———. "A President Visits Los Angeles: Rutherford B. Hayes' Tour of 1880." *Southern California Quarterly* 38 (March 1955): 33–46.

Bean, Walter. *California: An Interpretive History.* New York: McGraw-Hill, 1978.

Beard, George M. *American Nervousness—Its Causes and Consequences.* New York: Putnam & Sons, 1881.

Bird, S. Elizabeth, ed. *Dressing in Feathers: The Construction of the Indian in American Popular Culture.* Boulder, Colo.: Westview Press, 1996.

Bokovoy, Matthew. "Inventing Agriculture in Southern California." *Journal of San Diego History* 45, no. 2 (1999): 71–80.

Boyd, Mark F. "The Seminole War: Its Background and Onset." *Florida Historical Quarterly* 30, no. 1 (1951): 3–115.

Boyer, Paul. *Urban Masses and Moral Order in America, 1820–1920.* Cambridge: Harvard University Press, 1978.

Braden, Susan R. *The Architecture of Leisure: The Florida Resort Hotels of Henry Flagler and Henry Plant.* Gainesville: University Press of Florida, 2002.

Bramson, Seth. "A Tale of Three Henrys." *Journal of Decorative and Propaganda Arts* 23 (1998): 112–43.

Brown, William E., Jr., and Karen Hudson. "Henry Flagler and the Model Land Company." *Tequesta* 46 (1996): 47–75.

Bush, Gregory. "'Playground of the U.S.A.: Miami and the Promotion of Spectacle." *Pacific Historical Review* 68, no. 2 (1999): 153–72.

Camarillo, Albert. *Chicanos in a Changing Society: From Mexican Pueblos to American Barrios in Santa Barbara and Southern California, 1848–1930.* Cambridge: Harvard University Press, 1979.

Chan, Sucheng. *This Bitter-Sweet Soil: The Chinese in California Agriculture, 1860–1910.* Berkeley: University of California Press, 1989.

Covington, James C. *The Seminoles of Florida.* Gainesville: University Press of Florida, 1993.

Cox, Karen L. *Dreaming of Dixie: How the South Was Created in American Popular Culture.* Chapel Hill: University of North Carolina Press, 2011.

Cronon, William. *Nature's Metropolis: Chicago and the Great West.* New York: W. W. Norton & Co., 1992.

Culver, Lawrence. *The Frontier of Leisure: Southern California and the Shaping of Modern America.* Oxford: Oxford University Press, 2010.

Daniels, Roger T. *Coming to America: A History of Immigration and Ethnicity in American Life.* New York: HarperPerennial, 1990.

Davis, Mike. *City of Quartz: Excavating the Future in Los Angeles.* London: Pimlico, 1998.

———. *Ecology of Fear: Los Angeles and the Imagination of Disaster.* New York: Metropolitan Books, 1998.

Davis, T. Frederick. "The Disston Land Purchase." *Florida Historical Quarterly* 17, no. 3 (1939): 201–11.

Degler, Carl N. "In Making Historical Comparisons Focus on Common National Issues." In Erich Angermann, Carl Degler, and John A. Garraty, *Challenges of Ambiguity: Doing Comparative History*, 21–30. New York: Berg, 1991.

Derr, Mark. *Some Kind of Paradise: A Chronicle of Man and the Land in Florida*. Gainesville: University Press of Florida, 1998.

Deverell, William, Greg Hise, and David C. Sloane. "Orange Empires: Comparing Miami and Los Angeles." *Pacific Historical Review* 68, no. 2 (1999): 145–52.

Deverell, William. *Whitewashed Adobe: The Rise of Los Angeles and The Remaking of Its Mexican Past*. Berkeley: University of California Press, 2004.

De Waal, Thomas. *The Caucasus: An Introduction*. Oxford: Oxford University Press, 2010.

Dovell, J. E. "Thomas Elmer Will, Twentieth Century Pioneer." *Tequesta* 8 (1948): 21–55.

Dumke, Glenn. *The Boom of the Eighties in Southern California*. San Marino: Huntington, 1944.

Eacker, Susan A. "Gender in Paradise: Harriet Beecher Stowe and Postbellum Prose on Florida." *Journal of Southern History* 64, no. 3 (1998): 495–512.

Fairclough, Adam, "Was the Grant of Black Suffrage a Political Error? Reconsidering the Views of John W. Burgess, William A. Dunning, and Eric Foner of Congressional Reconstruction." *Journal of the Historical Society* 12, no. 2 (2012): 155–188.

Fields, Dorothy Jenkins, "Tracing Overtown's Vernacular Architecture." *Journal of Decorative and Propaganda Arts* 23 (1998): 323–32.

Fite, Gilbert C. *The Farmers' Frontier, 1865–1900*. New York: Holt, Rinehart & Winston, 1966.

Fitzgerald, Michael W., "Reconstruction Reengineered: Or, Is Doubting Black Suffrage a Mistake?" *Journal of the Historical Society* 12, no. 3 (2012): 241–247.

Fogelson, Robert. *The Fragmented Metropolis: Los Angeles, 1850–1930*. Berkeley: University of California Press, 1993.

Foner, Eric. *Free Soil, Free Labor, Free Men: The Ideology of the Republican Party before the Civil War*. Oxford: Oxford University Press, 1995.

———. *Reconstruction: America's Unfinished Revolution, 1863–1877*. New York: Harper & Row, 1988.

Foote, Stephanie. *Regional Fictions: Culture and Identity in Nineteenth-Century American Literature*. Madison: University of Wisconsin Press, 2001.

Foster, John T., Jr., and Sarah Whitmer Foster. *Beechers, Stowes, and Yankee Strangers: The Transformation of Florida*. Gainesville: University Press of Florida, 1999.

Fox, Stephen. *The American Conservation Movement: John Muir and His Legacy*. Madison: University of Wisconsin, 1985.

Fry, Joseph A. *Henry S. Sanford: Diplomacy and Business in Nineteenth-Century America*. Reno: University of Nevada Press, 1982.

George, Paul S. "Colored Town: Miami's Black Community, 1896–1930." *Florida Historical Quarterly* 56, no. 4 (1978): 432–47.

———. "Traffic Control in Early Miami." *Tequesta* 37 (1977): 3–18.

Gerson, Noel B. *Harriet Beecher Stowe: A Biography*. New York: Praeger, 1976.

Giltner, Scott. *Hunting and Fishing in the New South: Black Labor and White Leisure after the Civil War*. Baltimore. Md.: John Hopkins University Press, 2008.

Gonzales, Gilbert. *Labor and Community: Mexican Citrus Worker Villages in a Southern California County, 1900–1950*. Chicago: University of Illinois Press, 1994.

Gregory, James. "The Shaping of California History." In *Major Problems in California History*, edited by Sucheng Chan and Spencer Olin, 17–22. Boston: Houghton Mifflin Company, 1997.

Griffin-Pierce, Trudy. *Native Americans: Enduring Cultures and Traditions*. New York: Metro-Books, 1996.

Grunwald, Michael. *The Swamp: The Everglades, Florida, and the Politics of Paradise*. New York: Simon & Schuster, 2006.

Gutierrez, David G. "Significant to Whom?: Mexican Americans and the History of the American West." *Western Historical Quarterly* 24, no. 4 (1993): 519–39.

Hahamovitch, Cindy. *The Fruits of Their Labor: Atlantic Coast Farmworkers and the Making of Migrant Poverty, 1870–1945*. Chapel Hill: University of North Carolina Press, 1997.

Hale, Grace Elizabeth. *Making Whiteness: The Culture of Segregation in the South, 1890–1940*. New York: Random House, 1999.

Hays, Samuel P. *The Response to Industrialism*. Chicago: University of Chicago Press, 1995.

Healy, David. *U.S. Expansionism: The Imperialist Urge in the 1890s*. Madison: University of Wisconsin Press, 1970.

Hedrick, Joan D. *Harriet Beecher Stowe: A Life*. Oxford: Oxford University Press, 1994.

Higham, John. *Strangers in the Land: Patterns of American Nativism, 1860–1925*. New Brunswick, N.J.: Rutgers University Press, 1988.

Hillyer, Reiko. "Designing Dixie: Landscape, Tourism, and Memory in the New South, 1870–1917." Ph.D. diss., Columbia University, 2007.

Hoffman, Elizabeth Cobbs, and Jon Gjerde, eds. *Major Problems in American History*. Vol. 2, *Since 1865*. Boston: Houghton Mifflin Co., 2007.

Hoffman, Joel M. "From Augustine to Tangerine: Florida at the U.S. World's Fair." *Journal of Decorative and Propaganda Arts* 23 (1998): 48–85.

Hofstadter, Richard. *The Age of Reform*. New York: Random House, 1955.

Hughes, Robert. *American Visions: The Epic History of Art in America*. London: Harvill Press, 1997.

Hyde, Anne. *An American Vision: Far Western Landscape and National Culture, 1820–1920*. New York: New York University Press, 1990.

Jackson, Kenneth T. *Crabgrass Frontier: The Suburbanization of the United States*. Oxford: Oxford University Press, 1985.

Jacobson, Matthew Frye. *Barbarian Virtues: The United States Encounters Foreign Peoples at Home and Abroad, 1876–1917*. New York: Hill and Wang, 2000.

Kaplan, Amy, and Donald E. Pease, eds. *Cultures of United States Imperialism*. Durham, N.C.: Duke University Press, 1993.

Kasson, John. *Civilizing the Machine: Technology and Republican Values in America, 1776–1900*. New York: Penguin, 1976.

Kazin, Michael. "The Great Exception Revisited: Organized Labor and Politics in San Francisco and Los Angeles, 1870–1940." *Pacific Historical Review* 55, no. 3 (1986): 371–402.

Kenny, Judith T. "Climate, Race, and Imperial Authority: The Symbolic Landscape of the British Hill Station in India." *Annals of the Association of American Geographers* 85, no. 4 (1995): 694–714.

Kerber, Stephen. "Florida and the World's Columbian Exposition of 1893." *Florida Historical Quarterly* 66, no. 1 (1987): 25–49.

Kharif, Wali R. "Black Reaction to Segregation and Discrimination in Post-Reconstruction Florida." *Florida Historical Quarterly* 64, no. 2 (1985): 161–73.

Kropp, Phoebe. "'All Our Yesterdays': The Spanish Fantasy Past and the Politics of Public Memory in Southern California, 1884–1939." Ph.D. diss., University of California, San Diego, 1999.

Kurutz, Gary. *Benjamin C. Truman: California Booster & Bon Vivant.* San Francisco: The Book Club of California, 1984.

Kurutz, K. D., and Gary Kurutz, *California Calls You: The Art of Promoting the Golden State, 1870–1940.* Sausalito: Windgate Press, 2000.

LaFeber, Walter. *The New Empire: An Interpretation of American Expansion, 1860–1898.* Ithaca, N.Y.: Cornell University Press, 1963.

Lears, T. J. Jackson. *No Place of Grace: Antimodernism and the Transformation of American Culture, 1880–1920.* Chicago: University of Chicago Press, 1981.

Lee, Lawrence B. "William Ellsworthe Smythe and the Irrigation Movement: A Reconsideration." *Journal of Southern History* 41, no. 3 (1972): 289–311.

Litwack, Leon. *Been in the Storm So Long: The Aftermath of Slavery.* New York: Knopf, 1979.

Love, Eric T. *Race over Empire: Racism & U.S. Imperialism, 1865–1900.* Chapel Hill: University of North Carolina Press, 2004.

———. "White Is the Color of Empire: The Annexation of Hawaii in 1898." In *Race, Nation, & Empire in American History,* edited by James T. Campbell, Matthew Pratt Guterl, and Robert G. Lee, 175–211. Chapel Hill: University of North Carolina Press, 2007.

Mackle, Elliott. "The Eden of the South: Florida's Image in American Travel Literature and Painting, 1865–1900." Ph.D. diss., Emory University, 1977.

———. "Two Way Stretch: Some Dichotomies in the Advertising of Florida as the Boom Collapsed." *Tequesta* 33 (1973): 17–29.

Marchand, Roland. *Advertising the American Dream: Making Way for Modernity, 1920–1940.* Berkeley: University of California Press, 1986.

Marchman, Watt P., ed. "The Ingraham Everglades Exploring Expedition, 1892." *Tequesta* 7 (1947): 3–43.

Mathes, Valerie Sherer. *Helen Hunt Jackson and Her Indian Reform Legacy.* Norman: University of Oklahoma Press, 1997.

May, Robert E. *Manifest Destiny's Underworld: Filibustering in Antebellum America.* Chapel Hill: University of North Carolina Press, 2002.

McCoy, Drew R. *The Elusive Republic: Political Economy in Jeffersonian America.* Chapel Hill: University of North Carolina Press, 1980.

McMath, Robert C. *American Populism: A Social History, 1877–1898.* New York: Hill & Wang, 1993.

McWilliams, Carey. *California: The Great Exception.* Berkeley: University of California Press, 1949.

———. *Factories in the Field: The Story of Migratory Farm Labor in California.* 1935; repr., Berkeley: University of California Press, 1999.

———. *Southern California Country: An Island of the Land.* New York: Ayer, 1949.

Mechling, Jay. "Florida Seminoles and the Marketing of the Last Frontier." In *Dressing in Feath-*

ers: *The Construction of the Indian in American Popular Culture*, edited by S. Elizabeth Bird, 149–166. Boulder, Colo.: Westview Press, 1996.

Meindl, Christoper F., Derek H. Alderman, and Peter Waylen. "On the Importance of Environmental Claims-Making: The Role of James O. Wright in Promoting the Drainage of Florida's Everglades in the Early Twentieth Century." *Annals of the Association of American Geographers* 92, no. 4 (2002): 682–701.

Merk, Frederick. "Imperialism Was the Antithesis of Manifest Destiny." In *American Imperialism in 1898: The Quest for National Fulfillment*, edited by Richard H. Miller, 21–36. New York: John Wiley & Sons, 1970.

Mitchell, Don. *The Lie of the Land: Migrant Workers and the California Landscape*. Minneapolis: University of Minnesota Press, 1996.

Mohl, Raymond. "Shadows in the Sunshine: Race and Ethnicity in Miami." *Tequesta* 49 (1989): 63–80.

Monroy, Douglas, *Thrown Among Strangers: The Making of Mexican Culture in Frontier California*. Berkeley: University of California Press, 1990.

Mormino, Gary, and Raymond Arsenault. "Introduction." In Susan R. Braden, *The Architecture of Leisure: The Florida Resort Hotels of Henry Flagler and Henry Plant*. Gainesville: University Press of Florida, 2002.

Nelson, Richard Alan. "Palm Trees, Public Relations, and Promoters." *Florida Historical Quarterly* 61, no. 4 (1983): 383–402.

Noble, David W. *The Progressive Mind, 1890–1917*. Minneapolis: Burgess, 1981.

Nye, David E. *America as Second Creation: Technology and Narratives of New Beginnings*. Cambridge, Mass.: MIT Press, 2003.

———. *Narratives and Spaces: Technology and the Construction of American Culture*. Exeter: University of Exeter Press, 1997.

O'Connor, Kaori, ed. *Nordhoff's West Coast: California, Oregon and Hawaii*. New York: KPI, 1987.

Orsi, Richard. "Selling the Golden State: A Study of Boosterism in Nineteenth Century California." Ph.D. diss., University of Wisconsin-Madison, 1973.

———. *Sunset Limited: The Southern Pacific Railroad and the Development of the American West, 1850–1930*. Berkeley: University of California Press, 2005.

Ortiz, Paul. *Emancipation Betrayed: The Hidden History of Black Organizing and White Violence in Florida from Reconstruction to the Bloody Election of 1920*. Berkeley: University of California Press, 2005.

O'Sullivan, Maurice, and Jack C. Lane, eds. *The Florida Reader: Visions of Paradise from 1530 to the Present*. Saratoga: Pineapple Press, Inc., 1991.

Painter, Nell Irvin. *Standing at Armageddon: The United States, 1877–1919*. New York: W. W. Norton, 1987.

Patterson, Gordon. *The Mosquito Crusades: A History of the American Anti-Mosquito Movement from the Reed Commission to the First Earth Day*. Piscataway, N.J.: Rutgers University Press, 2009.

Perman, Michael. *Struggle for Mastery: Disfranchisement in the South, 1888–1908*. Chapel Hill: University of North Carolina Press, 2001.

Pike, Fredrick B. *The United States and Latin America: Myths and Stereotypes of Civilization and Nature*. Austin: University of Texas Press, 1992.

Pisani, Donald J. *From Family Farm to Agribusiness: The Irrigation Crusade in California and the West, 1850–1931*. Berkeley: University of California Press, 1984.

———. "Reclamation and Social Engineering in the Progressive Era." *Agricultural History* 57, no. 1 (1983): 46–63.

Pitt, Leonard. *Decline of the Californios: A Social History of the Spanish-Speaking Californias, 1846–1890*. Berkeley: University of California Press, 1966.

Plaag, Eric W. "'There Is an Abundance of Those Which are Genuine': Northern Travelers and Souvenirs of the Antebellum South." In *Dixie Emporium: Tourism, Foodways, and Consumer Culture in the American South*, edited by in Anthony J. Stanonis, 24–49. Athens: University of Georgia Press, 2008.

Poleo, Barbara A. "James Edmundson Ingraham: Florida, Flagler, and St. Augustine." *El Escribano: St. Augustine Journal of History* 40 (2003): 93–118.

Pomeroy, Earl. *In Search of the Golden West: The Tourist in Western America*. Lincoln: University of Nebraska Press, 1990.

Postel, Charles. *The Populist Vision*. Oxford: Oxford University Press, 2007.

Pozzetta, George E. "Foreigners in Florida: A Study of Immigration Promotion, 1865–1910." *Florida Historical Quarterly* 53, no. 2 (1974): 164–80.

Proctor, Samuel. *Napoleon Bonaparte Broward: Florida's Fighting Democrat*. Gainesville: University Press of Florida, 1957.

———. "The National Farmers' Alliance Convention of 1890 and Its 'Ocala Demands,'" *Florida Historical Quarterly* 28, no. 3 (1950): 161–81.

Rabinowitz, Howard. *The First New South, 1865–1920*. Arlington Heights, Ill.: Harlan Davidson, Inc., 1992.

Richardson, Heather Cox. *The Death of Reconstruction: Race, Labor, and Politics in the Post–Civil War North, 1865–1901*. Cambridge: Harvard University Press, 2001.

Rifkin, Mark. *Manifesting America: The Imperial Construction of U.S. National Space*. Oxford: Oxford University Press, 2009.

Rivers, Larry E. and Canter Brown Jr. "African Americans in South Florida: A Home and a Haven for Reconstruction-Era Leaders." *Tequesta* 56 (1996): 5–23.

Roberts, Kathleen. "Pretty Women: Female Beauty in the Jim Crow South." Ph.D. diss., University of North Carolina at Chapel Hill, 2005.

Rogin, Michael Paul. *Fathers and Children: Andrew Jackson and the Subjugation of the American Indian*. New Brunswick: Transaction, 1991.

Rolle, Andrew. *California: A History*. New York: Thomas Y. Crowell Co. 1969.

Rosaldo, Renato. "Imperialist Nostalgia." *Representations* 26 (Spring 1989): 107–22.

Rowe, Anne E. *The Idea of Florida in the American Literary Imagination*. Gainesville: University Press of Florida, 1992.

Sackman, Douglas C. *Orange Empire: California and the Fruits of Eden*. Berkeley: University of California Press, 2005.

Said, Edward. *Culture and Imperialism*. London: Vintage, 1994.

Sanchez, George J. *Becoming Mexican American: Ethnicity, Culture, and Identity in Chicano Los Angeles, 1900–1945*. Oxford: Oxford University Press, 1995.

Saxton, Alexander. *The Indispensable Enemy: Labor and the Anti-Chinese Movement in California*. Berkeley: University of California Press, 1971.

———. *The Rise and Fall of the White Republic: Class Politics and Mass Culture in Nineteenth-Century America*. London: Verso, 1990.

Schlesinger, Arthur M. *The Rise of the City, 1878–1898*. Chicago: Quadrangle, 1933.

Sessa, Frank B. "Miami on the Eve of the Boom: 1923." *Tequesta* 11 (1951): 3–25.

Shalhope, Robert E. "Toward a Republican Synthesis: The Emergence of an Understanding of Republicanism in American Historiography." *William and Mary Quarterly* 29, no. 1 (January 1972): 49–80.

Shannon, Fred. *The Farmer's Last Frontier: Agriculture, 1860–1897*. New York: Holt, Rinehart and Winston, 1961.

Shofner, Jerrell. *Nor Is It Over Yet: Florida in the Era of Reconstruction, 1863–1877*. Gainesville: University Press of Florida, 1974.

Silber, Nina. *The Romance of Reunion: Northerners and the South, 1865–1900*. Chapel Hill: University of North Carolina Press, 1993.

Simon, Bryant. *Boardwalk of Dreams: Atlantic City and the Fate of Urban America*. Oxford: Oxford University Press, 2004.

Slotkin, Richard. *Regeneration through Violence: The Mythology of the American Frontier, 1600–1860*. Middletown, Conn.: Wesleyan University Press, 1973.

Smiley, David L. "The Quest for the Central Theme in Southern History." *South Atlantic Quarterly* 71, no. 3 (1972): 303–15.

Smith, Henry Nash. *Virgin Land: The American West as Symbol and Myth*. New York: Knopf, 1957.

Smith, Henry Nash, ed. *Popular Culture and Industrialism, 1865–1890*. New York: New York University Press, 1967.

Smith, Susan Harris, and Melanie Dawson, eds. *The American 1890s: A Cultural Reader*. Durham, N.C.: Duke University Press, 2000.

Spickard, Paul. *Almost All Aliens: Immigration, Race, and Colonialism in American History and Identity*. New York: Routledge, 2007.

Spivack, John. "Paradise Awaits: A Sampling and Brief Analysis of Late Nineteenth Century Promotional Pamphlets on Florida." *Southern Studies* 21 (Winter 1982): 429–38.

Stanonis, Anthony. "Through a Purple (Green and Gold) Haze: New Orleans Mardi Gras in the American Imagination." *Southern Cultures* 14, no. 2 (2008): 109–31.

Starr, Kevin. *Americans and the California Dream, 1850–1915*. Oxford: Oxford University Press, 1973.

———. *Inventing the Dream: California through the Progressive Era*. Oxford: Oxford University Press, 1985.

Steinberg, Ted. *Down to Earth: Nature's Role in American History* (Oxford: Oxford University Press, 2002.

Stern, Alexandra Minna. *Eugenic Nation: Faults and Frontiers of Better Breeding in Modern America*. Berkeley: University of California, 2005.

Stoll, Steven. *The Fruits of Natural Advantage: Making the Industrial Countryside in California*. Berkeley: University of California Press, 1998.

Street, Richard Steven. *Beasts of the Field: A Narrative History of California Farm Workers*. Stanford, Calif.: Stanford University Press, 2004.

Tebeau, Charlton W. *A History of Florida*. Coral Gables: University of Miami Press, 1971.

Thomas, John L. *Alternative America: Henry George, Edward Bellamy, Henry Demarest Lloyd and the Adversary Tradition.* New York: Belknap, 1983.

Thompson, Tommy R. "Florida in American Popular Magazines, 1870–1970." *Florida Historical Quarterly* 82 (2003): 1–15.

Trachtenberg, Alan. *The Incorporation of America: Culture and Society in the Gilded Age.* New York: Hill & Wang, 1982.

Vance, James E. "California and the Search for the Ideal." In *Regions of the United States* edited by John Fraser Hart, 185–210. New York: Harper & Row, 1972.

Vaught, David. *Cultivating California: Growers, Specialty Crops, and Labor, 1875–1920.* Baltimore, Md.: John Hopkins University Press, 1999.

Wade, Richard C. "Urbanization." In *The Comparative Approach to American History*, edited by C. Vann Woodward, 187–205. Oxford: Oxford University Press, 1997.

Walker, Richard. *The Conquest of Bread: 150 Years of Agribusiness in California.* New York: New Press, 2004.

Weigle, Marta. "From Desert to Disney World: The Santa Fe Railway and the Fred Harvey Company Display the Indian Southwest." *Journal of Anthropological Research* 45 (Spring 1989): 115–37.

West, Patsy. *The Enduring Seminoles: From Alligator Wrestling to Ecotourism.* Gainesville: University Press of Florida, 1998.

Whitfield, Stephen. "Florida's Fudged Identity." *Florida Historical Quarterly* 71 (April 1993): 7–29.

Wiebe, Robert H. *The Search for Order, 1877–1920.* New York: Hill and Wang, 1967.

Williamson, Edward C. *Florida Politics in the Gilded Age, 1877–1893.* Gainesville: University Press of Florida, 1876.

Wills, Jocelyn. *Boosters, Hustlers, and Speculators: Entrepreneurial Culture and the Rise of Minneapolis and St. Paul, 1849–1883.* St. Paul: Minnesota Historical Society Press, 2004.

Wilson, William H. *The City Beautiful Movement.* Baltimore, Md.: John Hopkins University Press, 1994.

Wood, Gordon. *The Creation of the American Republic, 1776–1787.* Chapel Hill: University of North Carolina Press, 1969.

———. *Empire of Liberty: A History of the Early Republic, 1789–1815.* Oxford: Oxford University Press, 2009.

Woodward, C. Vann. *Origins of the New South, 1877–1913.* Baton Rouge: Louisiana State University Press, 1977.

Woodward, C. Vann, ed. *The Comparative Approach to American History.* Oxford: Oxford University Press, 1997.

Worster, Donald. *Rivers of Empire: Water, Aridity, and the Growth of the American West.* New York: Pantheon Books, 1985.

Wrobel, David. *Promised Lands: Promotion, Memory and the Creation of the American West.* Lawrence: University Press of Kansas, 2011.

———. *The End of American Exceptionalism: Frontier Anxiety from the Old West to the New Deal.* Lawrence: University of Kansas Press, 1993.

Youngs, Larry R. "The Sporting Set Winters in Florida: Fertile Ground for the Leisure Revolution, 1870–1930." *Florida Historical Quarterly* 84 (Summer 2005): 57–78.

Zimmerman, Tom. "Paradise Promoted: Boosterism and the Los Angeles Chamber of Commerce." *California History* 64 (Winter 1985): 22–33.

Index

The letter *i* following a page number denotes an illustration.

San Bernardino (CA), 29
San Bernardino County (CA), 30, 123, 128
Sanborn, Kate, 53
San Diego (CA), 97, 159; Chamber of Commerce,
    47, 54, 61, 137; Panama-California Exposition in,
    2, 172, 197; suburbanization, 161–62
San Diego & Eastern Railroad, 130
San Diego County (CA), 30, 123–24; Immigration
    Association, 90
Sanford (FL), 72, 102
Sanford, Henry, 72, 102
San Francisco (CA), 2, 20, 28, 95; Chinatown
    in, 30; growth of, 159; as market for fruits, 92;
    rivalry with Los Angeles, 171; and unions, 169;
    Panama-Pacific Exposition in, 197; violence of
    1850s in, 24; Workingmen's Party in, 88
San Gabriel Valley (CA), 30
San Joaquin Valley (CA), 28–29, 30, 135
San Luis Obispo County (CA), 30, 123
San Pedro harbor (CA), 164
Santa Ana (CA), 58
Santa Barbara (CA), 52, 57
Santa Barbara County (CA), 30
Santa Fe Railroad, 47, 51, 58; and Grand Canyon,
    122; Passenger Department, 122; and promotion,
    122, 126; shipping fruits, 98
Santa Monica (CA), 56
Schurz, Carl, 13, 120, 212n33
Scribner's, 41
Sebring, General, 103
Segregation. See Jim Crow
Seminole (Indians): booster representations of, 138,
    145–48; and the Everglades, 145–47; mixed-race
    history of, 34, 146–47; population, 138; tourist
    camps, 147; wars, 2, 18, 21, 33–34, 138
Semi-Tropical, 7, 102–3. See also Reed, Harrison
Semi-tropical, definition of, 1–2, 8–10, 13–14,
    110–11. See also Agriculture
Semi-Tropical California (Truman), 30–32. See also
    Truman, Benjamin
Semi-Tropical Exposition, 2, 115, 219n250. See also
    Ocala
Semi-Tropical Florida (French), 108, 109i. See also
    French, Seth
Semi-tropical fruits, 1, 28, 81–116, 119–29, 140, 189–
    90, 207n46, 212n31, 217n180, 217n181, 232n147
Semi-Tropic California, 93–94
Semi-Tropic California (Benton), 2, 197
Semi-Tropic California (Shepard), 133

Semi-Tropic Land and Water Company, 128i
Seward, William Henry, 22
Sewell, Everest George, 174–75, 182, 183
Sharecropping, 101
Sheldon, Lionel, 125
Sherman Institute, 127
Shinn, Charles, 6, 95–96; on desert, 123; on market-
    ing fruits, 92; on small farms, 89; on Spanish
    fantasy past, 49, 57
Shorb, J. De Barth, 86
Silsbee (CA), 131
Silver Springs (FL), 66
Slavery, 8, 18, 19, 32–35; and cotton, 101
Slotkin, Richard, 70
Smythe, William E., 9, 124–25, 152; on Colorado
    Desert, 130
South Carolina, 38
Southern California: A Semi-Tropic Paradise (War-
    ner Bros.), 54–55i. See also Warner Bros.
Southern California Bureau of Information, 62, 64i
Southern California Fruit Exchange, 115, 127–28.
    See also California Fruit Growers' Exchange
Southern California Horticultural Society, 86, 93;
    formed, 92
Southern California Immigration Association, 92,
    93, 103
Southern California Paradise, A (Bancroft), 92
Southern Literary Messenger, 36
Southern Pacific Railroad, 7, 26, 30, 51–52, 159;
    and California Immigration Commission, 96;
    Colton station, 94; and Grand Canyon, 122;
    and Imperial Valley, 131–34; land ownership
    in California, 22–23; lines in California, 28, 51,
    91; Passenger Company, 133, 170; as promoter
    of settlement, 82, 92; and rates, 133; seen as
    "octopus," 141; shipping fruits, 98; and Sunset,
    127; Sunset Route, 73
Southern States of America, The (King), 41–43. See
    also King, Edward
South Florida Railroad, 108, 110, 140
Soviet Sub-Tropics, 191
Soviet Union compared to semi-tropical America,
    191–92
Spain, 9–10, 54; colonies lost to the United States
    in Spanish-American War, 193; former owner-
    ship of California and Florida, 20–21
Spaniards, 10, 49, 125, 194; and Fountain of Youth,
    66; in Key West, 67; in Los Angeles, 160
Spanish-American War, 192–93

HENRY KNIGHT is lecturer of American Studies at Northumbria University.

The University Press of Florida is the scholarly publishing agency for the State University System of Florida, comprising Florida A&M University, Florida Atlantic University, Florida Gulf Coast University, Florida International University, Florida State University, New College of Florida, University of Central Florida, University of Florida, University of North Florida, University of South Florida, and University of West Florida.